Building the "Goodly Fellowship of Faith"

Building the "Goodly Fellowship of Faith"

A History of the Episcopal Church in Utah, 1867–1996

Frederick Quinn

Utah State University Press
Logan, Utah

Utah State University Press
Logan, Utah 84322-7800

Manufactured in the United States of America
Printed on acid-free paper

Library of Congress Cataloging-in-Publication Data

Quinn, Frederick.
Building the "goodly fellowship of faith" : a history of the Episcopal Church in Utah, 1867–1996 / by Frederick Quinn.
p. cm.
Includes bibliographical references and index.
ISBN 0-87421-593-5 (cloth : alk. paper)
1. Episcopal Church--Utah--History. 2. Utah--Church history. I. Title.
BX5917.U8Q85 2004
283'.792--dc22

2004019244

To the women of the
Episcopal Church in Utah,
1867 to the present,

In the heavenly kingdom,
the blessèd have their dwelling place
and their rest for ever and ever.
—refrain from the Magnificat, feast of any saint

Contents

Introduction

> The past does not repeat itself, but sometimes it rhymes.
> —Mark Twain

The past draws us to it like a magnet, and a question many new church members soon ask is, "What is the history of the Episcopal Church in this place?" The obvious first response in Utah is to read the *Reminiscences of a Missionary Bishop* by Daniel S. Tuttle, the territory's first missionary bishop, who arrived by stagecoach in July 1867. The Tuttle work is remarkable; the quality of its travel writing belongs with the best products of the nineteenth century, but the book is over a century old, and only parts of it are about Utah. Tuttle had a vast missionary district including Montana and Idaho, and in 1886 left Utah to become bishop of Missouri and, through seniority, presiding bishop of the Protestant Episcopal Church in the United States from 1903 until his death in 1923. Abiel Leonard, Tuttle's successor as bishop from 1888 to 1903, was a less colorful figure who worked hard and consolidated the gains of Tuttle's time, and advanced them as means would allow.

Then came another commanding presence and gifted writer, Franklin Spencer Spalding, bishop from 1904 until his tragic death in September 1914. He was killed by a speeding motorist while crossing a Salt Lake City street at night. Spalding's short book on Mormonism and extensive writings on Christian socialism made him a national figure. Spalding was also opposed to American participation in World War I. His successor, Paul Jones, 1914–1918, was added to the Calendar of the Episcopal Church for his witness to peace during World War I.

Jones was a socialist and pacifist whom the leadership of St. Mark's Cathedral parish and St. Paul's parish sought to remove, with the support of Tuttle, by then head of the Episcopal Church in America. Jones resigned on December 20, 1917, effective April 11, 1918, but the question is—what would the church have done had he not resigned? Jones steadfastly held to a defensible Christian position, had strong support among the non-Salt Lake City clergy and laity, and was a gifted pastor and administrator. A bishop could be tried for heresy or immorality, but Jones was never formally charged with *anything*.

The 1920s and 1930s especially were a hard time for the church. Bishop Arthur W. Moulton, 1920–1946, struggled to keep church doors open and salaries paid. A World War I veteran, Moulton was also an advocate for peace with the Soviet Union, and to his surprise and everybody in Utah's, was one of the first recipients of the Stalin Peace Prize in 1951. Three peace activist bishops in a row for Utah.

Bishop Stephen C. Clark, 1946–1950, had impressive postwar plans for the church in a growing state. His annual convocation reports were filled with vision and energy, but he died after a few years in office. His successor, Richard S. Watson, 1951–1971, a sometime actor and former attorney, was the last of the missionary bishops. Watson was a highly popular figure who drew on Clark's planning and built several new churches with limited resources during the state's expansive postwar growth period. In 1971 the national church abolished missionary districts in favor of independent dioceses, and the Utah church was cut loose to function on its own.

In the juvenescence of the newly independent Diocese's life in 1971 came a new bishop, Otis Charles, heralded by trumpets, balloons and firecrackers at his consecration. It was the 1970s. There was never a dull moment in his time, one in which the new Utah diocese successfully confronted most issues facing the modern church, including the introduction of the new prayer book and hymnal, the ordination of clergy for limited local ministries, the place of women clergy in the ordained ministry, and the church as a moral voice on issues from capital punishment to the Vietnam War. Charles accepted a prestigious appointment as dean of the Episcopal Divinity School, Cambridge, Massachusetts, in 1986, "came out" as a gay man, and on retiring divorced his wife of many years and later took a male partner at a church ceremony in San Francisco.

The autocratic George E. Bates followed as second bishop of the independent diocese, 1986–1996, and represented a difference in style and substance from his predecessor. Shortly after his arrival Bates sold St. Mark's Hospital on December 31, 1987, for nearly 100 million dollars (the exact sum was always at issue) and the diocese went from poverty to affluence overnight. Bates hired a staff of twenty-four persons for a diocese of twenty-one churches. Visions of shared mission and examples of sustained local stewardship in the small, struggling diocese gave way to a dependence on seeking monies from the bishop.

This story ends with the consecration of a Utah native and one of the Episcopal Church's first women bishops, Carolyn Tanner Irish, on May 31, 1996, as bishop coadjutor (assistant bishop with the right of succession). On June 29, 1996, with Bates's retirement, she became the diocese's tenth bishop. Born into a prominent LDS family of educators, studies at Stanford, Michigan, and Oxford universities led Irish to the Episcopal Church, and to work with the Shalem Institute and several parishes in Michigan and the Washington, D. C., area, including Washington National Cathedral. Since I am married to Bishop Irish, this history of the diocese's first 130 years concludes at the time of her consecration.

Boundaries of the large diocese shifted during its history and only in the twentieth century were state and missionary district coterminous. The original Missionary District of Montana, Idaho, and Utah existed from 1867 to 1880. Next it was the Missionary District of Idaho and Utah, 1880–1886, followed by the Missionary District of Nevada and Utah, 1886–1898. The Missionary District of Salt Lake, 1898–1907, became the Missionary District of Utah from 1907 to 1971, when Utah became an independent diocese. The state's southeast corner was ceded to a separate Navajoland Area Mission in 1977.

* * *

What does the historian of a church write about? At first, I resisted building this work around the tenure of Utah's bishops. The arguments can be anticipated; it would call undue attention to them, the church is more than bishops, etc. But the problem is that the small, isolated church in Utah *was* centered on its bishops. They were its public figures, policy makers, and fundraisers; they had the power given them by virtue of their office in an episcopal, not a congregational church, and left the most extensive records of the church in their time.

This is a work of analysis by an independent scholar and historian, and not an official or commissioned institutional history. There is a tendency in older "official" church histories to write as if the participants were all saints, or at least Sunday school merit badge winners, but anyone who has read or written other forms of history knows that human motives range from altruistic to self-serving. I have described the times, events, and personalities as written sources and, in later times, written sources and oral interviews would allow. In such a process the historian both searches and evaluates at every level, determining which documents to use, what information to extract from them, what to say about an issue, person, or institution. This does not mean being bland and indecisive; human motives are complex and issues, especially the kinds churches deal with, are notoriously untidy. At the same time, it is the historian's task to assemble a full spread of facts about participants while painting a picture of them that is fair, if not always flattering.

Also, the historical narrative emerges out of the materials available to the historian, and not from what the historian wishes they would say. It is not a question of bringing a predetermined point of view to the subject, then finding facts to support it. Instead, the challenge is to take the source materials—archival records, newspaper accounts, and the testimony of oral witnesses for later periods—and ask the question, "What do they tell us?" Several people told me that Bishop Arthur W. Moulton was the only highly placed Utah church leader to condemn the lynching of an itinerant African American coal miner, Robert Marshall, who was killed in Price, Utah, on June 18, 1925. It would have been like Moulton to speak out on such an issue, consistent with the outspokenness of the Episcopal Church on racial injustice, and a tribute to his civic courage, which he frequently demonstrated elsewhere.

The only problem was there was no written evidence that Moulton said anything at all about the Marshall lynching. I read and reread his convocation addresses of the period, consulted other historians, and worked the University of Utah's aging microfilm viewing machines while pouring over photographed reels of old newspapers of the time. All I found was a letter from Moulton to the governor's office asking what he should tell the national church if they asked about the state's position on Marshall's lynching.

Those who look for a history of every parish, clergy member, and building improvement should return this book immediately to its shelf. Not every parish or priest was included, due often to a lack of documentation and space.[1] Many laity and clergy's lives contributed to the larger picture of the church, but only traces of their stories remain. I wish I could have found Harriet Tuttle's letters to her traveling husband, or the letters of Katherine Murray, who ministered in adverse, isolated conditions in Whiterocks in the early twentieth century, or the papers of William F. Bulkley, who spent over fifty years in Provo and Salt Lake City, and went everywhere by rickety auto, keeping small congregations together in the 1920s, '30s, and '40s. The history of the Episcopal Church in Utah would have gained another valuable source document, Arthur S. Moulton's autobiography, if a relative had not burned it.

Utah is a young diocese, independent for only three decades at this writing. Archives were not extensive for many parish churches. Outside of

Salt Lake City, documentary sources were plentiful in Ogden and Logan, less so elsewhere. Information on construction or improvements to buildings was more readily available than details about what clergy preached or taught. But it is a boring book that begins, "This church was built in 1905, the stained glass window was added in 1910, and the roof repaired three years later."

Tuttle and Spalding were the two coordinates around which future episcopates coalesced. Both were high energy, strong personalities, outspoken, in Tuttle's case, as a missionary bishop literally building a church from nothing, and in the instance of Spalding, as the moral conscience of the wider church on social issues. Yet the tendency of the Utah church was to want a pastoral, less publicly visible bishop to follow an activist one. Thus Leonard came after Tuttle, the affable Moulton followed Jones, and Bates, who rarely spoke out on issues, succeeded the outspoken Charles.

In Utah, the church encountered an unusual range of local, national, and international issues: potentially tense relations with the Latter-day Saints, encounters with the state's dwindling Native American populations, World War I, socialism and pacifism, Prohibition, the Great Depression, World War II, responses to population growth, ministry to first Japanese then Hispanic communities, political issues with moral implications like the Vietnam War, and wider questions close to home like nuclear testing, dumping nuclear waste in the Utah desert, and the planned deployment of the MX missile defense system within the state. In short, Utah was a microcosm, responding to or reflecting most topics facing the larger church. Surprisingly absent were any voiced concerns about the environment, despite the state being both a major mining center and a source of unsurpassed natural beauty and ecological complexity.

While I originally wondered if material was adequate to write a history of the Episcopal Church in Utah, an abundance of topics and sources emerged. When the Vernal opera house owner of an earlier era said Episcopalians could use his premises any time because "the Episcopals were ladies and gentlemen and didn't spit all over the floor," he uttered a truth about that denomination. Episcopalians are a highly literate church population that leave a significant paper trail, but are rarely demonstrative. God's chosen frozen, we have been called. Months were spent with nearly sixty boxes of diocesan archives in the Special Collections of the J. Willard Marriott Library of the University of Utah and the more than fifty boxes at the Utah State University Library Special Collections and Archives in Logan. This gave me a solid base from which to begin writing. The tiny scrawl of the former diocesan historiographer, Professor Harold Dalgliesh, not only pointed me to many valuable documents, but his carefully organized work made it easy for a later generation of researchers to find what they need quickly. A. J. Simmonds, his successor, was also skilled in finding and commenting on documents. Gradually the picture took shape.

Serendipitously, sources emerged from unexpected places. John Dixon Stewart shared his choice library of historic Utah original editions with me. David Jones, son of Bishop Paul Jones, and his wife, Pat, arrived in Utah with a car full of documents on Paul Jones. They were retracing the journey of David's famous father, and had collected material in Scranton, Pennsylvania; New Haven, Connecticut; Antioch, Ohio; and other cities where Utah's fourth bishop had worked. Jane Moulton Stahl asked what she could do with her collection of papers from her grandfather, Bishop Arthur W. Moulton, including a copy of his FBI file. Thelma Ellis lent me her pale blue 1950s traveling case filled with original documents and photographs carefully collected over more than seventy years at Good Shepherd, Ogden. Francis L. Winder gave me over a hundred early black and white photos carefully mounted on display board by his predecessor as archdeacon, William F. Bulkley, who lived in Utah for fifty-eight years and carefully depicted the story of the church and its times for use in lectures. I wanted to share my findings with parishes, and did so at "History Days" in places like St. John's, Logan, and St. Michael's, Brigham City, where carefully preserved material from earlier times emerged from trunks and attics, and the memories of participants.

I wish I could meet graduate students seeking a thesis topic or colleagues looking for a next book to write. One ready topic is *The Life and Writings of Daniel S. Tuttle.* Tuttle was a giant of the church in nineteenth-century America, and his *Reminiscences* only scratch the surface. A person of spiritual depth and thoughtfulness, he deserves a modern biography. He belongs with such other formative figures in the early life of the Episcopal Church in America as James Lloyd Breck, "The Apostle of the Wilderness," which is how Minnesota and Wisconsin were once known, Jackson Kemper, who worked extensively in the mid- and southwest and established missions among Native Americans in Missouri, and John Henry Hobart, whose work in upstate New York in the first half of the nineteenth century paralleled Tuttle's in Utah in the century's second half. Breck, Kemper, and Hobart have found places in the Episcopal Church's calendar of exemplary figures; a case can be made as well for including Tuttle in their numbers.

Another subject is the *Life of Franklin Spencer Spalding, Bishop and Socialist.* Spalding was every bit as richly textured and memorable as Tuttle, but belongs to a different era. A third study might be *Paul Jones, Pacifist and Pastor.* Jones merits a more extended study than he has received to date. Generally known for his conflict with church leadership over World War I, he was also a tireless visitor to small missions and commentator on the larger issues facing the church.

H. Baxter Liebler was a quirky character with a long, colorful ministry among the Navajo. He was likewise a pioneer in reversing the extant church policy toward Native Americans, and his writings were extensive. More modern subjects might include a biography of Otis Charles, whose episcopate contended with most of the structural, political, liturgical, and sexual issues facing the church. Another topic is the sale of St. Mark's Hospital and its financial consequences, and how that changed the character of the diocese. In short, the Utah Diocese contained an unusually high number of interesting bishops and issues. Jones made it to the Episcopal Church's Calendar, listing historic and more modern people who led exemplary lives of witness to their beliefs. But many would argue that, in addition to the obviously qualified Tuttle, Spalding and Liebler were equally deserving of commemoration for their sustained witness in their own times.

Other, broader topics emerge. Men wrote most of the documents about the church and occupied the ecclesial offices until recent times, but it was often women who held the church together. They raised the money, a dime here and a dollar there, to build churches, buy organs, and furnish rectories. They read Morning Prayer in vacant parishes, taught generations of Sunday school students the basics of the faith, visited the sick, comforted the dying, cooked the parish meals that were the basis of fellowship, and adorned simple country altars with flowers and fair linen cloths. Some, like Sara Napper in Salt Lake City and Lucy Carter and Katherine Murray on the Ute reservations, worked long years in demanding or isolated settings at half the salary their male counterparts received. It is to them that I dedicate this book.

Another study could be the Native American work of the Episcopal Church in Utah. There was Liebler in the south among the Navajo in the 1940s and 1950s and Milton Hersey earlier to the east among the Utes, but that is by no means the whole story. Liebler was an accommodationist, an ultra-high-churchman coexisting in the same hogan with traditional Navajo healers, while Hersey, with utter sincerity, tried to dismantle major local rites like the Sun Dance, not realizing their importance to Native American society. It is a sad and difficult history to write, a story of Native Americans's lands being seized, people being subjugated and betrayed through broken treaties, and their own religion misunderstood and culture denigrated. In this the Episcopal Church was the willing or thoughtless co-agent with the government, "elevating the Red Man" on the one hand while on the other suppressing traditional structures that had provided social and cultural cohesion.

* * *

Writing a history of the Episcopal Church in Utah was a different challenge for a historian whose earlier books were about religion, law, and history in other contexts. As I assembled a time line of people, institutions, and issues on the Church in Utah, oral interviews led to additional information. Such interviews were structured around dates, such as events in the life of a particular parish, or a subject, like the introduction of locally ordained clergy into the ministry of the church. They also provided an opportunity for significant and insightful participants to recall past eras in the life of the church.

This project became a race against the clock when one valuable source, Robert Gordon, the close associate of Bishops Charles and Bates, died before I could interview him, and another, Thelma Ellis, the living memory of Church of the Good Shepherd, Ogden, was stricken ill on the eve of our planned encounter. Still other persons moved away, became ill, or no longer remembered events in which they had participated. In some sessions I asked an elderly person to give an even approximate date of an event, but memories had faded with age. A line from the hymn "O God, Our Help in Ages Past" suggests the transitory nature of the historian's enterprise: "Time like an ever rolling stream bears all our years away: they fly, forgotten, as a dream dies at the opening day."[2]

Western history, Utah history in particular, was a new subject for me. Except for brief exposure to the "frontier thesis" arguments of a bygone era, I knew little of such history, and less about Utah, which I imagined to be the history of Latter-day Saints arriving by covered wagon and the subsequent battles over theocracy and polygamy. Regional history has undergone the evolution all historical research and writing has experienced in recent decades, including greater use of anthropological source materials, exploration of minority and gender issues, the integration of cultural activities into the study of history, and the balancing of individual biography and institutional life in historical narratives. Numerous accounts on Latter-day Saints history have been written that have little bearing on the history of the Episcopal Church in Utah. Less well known but no less important is the work of a recent generation of Utah social historians writing on non-Mormon populations and issues. Many such persons gave generously of their time and insights in the completion of this project, and I acknowledge their contributions.

Religious history, finally, is the history of the encounter of a people with the living God. That is the narrative theme of the Bible. Church history is thus far more than history about buildings, budgets, positions taken on controversial issues, and membership numbers, although it is also that. What people prayed about and what was preached about in churches is included when available. The powerful description of Bishop Tuttle regarding the ministry of Emily Pearsall (pp. 27–28) and Bishop Jones describing the winter burial of a Native American child on the Ute reservation (pp. 87–88) are two such examples. So is the satisfaction of Sara Napper over a church pageant well done in a small, struggling parish (p. 69), H. Baxter Liebler's baptism of a Navajo baby (pp. 144–45), and the statement of Bishop Watson, old and tired now, about seeing a new vision of the emerging church under a new generation's leadership. But the subjects of most people's intense prayers are infrequently and imperfectly committed to paper. Moments of deep religious encounters are difficult to describe, and are rarely articulated in source documents; when found, they are a pearl of great price.

The joy for most historians comes in shaping their material, deciding how and why things happened as they did, then molding the result into presentable narrative form and sculpting its conclusions. It is also the excitement of a moment of discovery, as in rereading Bishop Tuttle's description of his encounter with Brigham Young and seeing a meaning in it quite different than that which previous commentators had taken for granted. Or coming upon a letter where Bishop Watson summarized exactly how he saw his delicate relationship with Father Liebler and the Navajo mission. Historical research is also detective work; the researcher sifts patiently through box after box of material for clues, abandons false leads, is satisfied when new material confirms already reached conclusions, and is pleased when new insights are forthcoming that might advance a fuller interpretation. Beyond that I see no grand themes to history; so much of what it is possible to write depends on the materials that are available. Instructive for those who read and write history, or wonder about its real life applicability, is the advice of American historian and one-time Librarian of Congress, Daniel J. Boorstin, "Planning your future without looking at your past is like putting cut flowers into the ground and expecting them to grow."

This book was written at a time when each day's news brought accounts of the sexual misadventures of Roman Catholic clergy. Was that a theme in the life of the Episcopal Church in Utah? Since the Archives did not contain individual clergy personnel files, there was little evidence on the subject, except for information about the church trial of the cathedral's dean on child molestation charges early in the twentieth century, and the Church Army worker on a Ute reservation who was sent to federal prison for child molestation in the 1950s. All Saints', Salt Lake City, dismissed an associate clergy member for improper sexual activity in the late 1960s, and the parish became divided over how the matter was handled.

More common were cases of poorly paid clergy leaving a string of debts, but, again, few of these made the archives. There were also a fair number of clergy–congregation fallings out, probably no more so than in other places. Clergy–bishop stresses bubbled to the surface at various points, and cathedral–bishop relations were a source of periodic tension as well. Tuttle tried to solve the problem, Leonard alluded to it, Spalding and Jones encountered it, both Moulton and Watson encountered it. And, when the cathedral's leaders wanted to remove Charles as its rector in the 1970s, the bishop threatened to move his cathedra, or official seat, to St. Stephen's, West Valley City, a new mission quartered in a temporary cinder block building.

One day in late spring, sitting with piles of documents around me, I happened on the Easter Vigil reading in Ezekiel 37:1–15 about the dry bones coming together in a great rattling noise. That seemed an apt metaphor for the historian's work, to give the bones of Utah Episcopal Church history a trace of the life they once had, providing such depth as the sources would allow, recreating their life and purpose in a new context. As it happened, on Easter Eve 2004 I visited Thelma Ellis, historian of Good Shepherd Church, Ogden. The sun was setting over the Great Salt Lake; the Christmas poinsettia we had brought her earlier gave way to an Easter lily. Thelma's treasures surrounded her in the assisted living center high above the town: an early photograph of the church where she had spent her life, her collection of church historical records, a document she was working on in her frail handwriting. "The tumors are spreading, I can't wear a dress any more," she said, pointing to the widening stomach of a tiny, frail woman. I asked about some of the church personalities she had known and observed over seventy years. Most of all, I was trying to keep our three-year conversation going. So was Thelma; she gave me a copy of a document, as she did each time we visited. "I may not be here next time you come," she said matter-of-factly. That night's Great Vigil of Easter at Good Shepherd began with a collect about hearing "the record of God's saving deeds in history." I was asked to read the Dry Bones lesson, that momentous and poetic passage, with a tiny flashlight that cast a faltering blue illumination on perhaps four lines at a time. "Mortal, can these bones live?" Ezekiel is asked. The dry bones in the desert valley rattled and came together, flesh and breath were added, graves opened, and Israel returned to its land. If this work of history helps future readers to find their place in the land, and to give the times, issues, and personalities a momentary breath of life, its purpose will have been amply achieved.

Acknowledgments

The Special Collections staff of the J. Willard Marriott Library of the University of Utah have been extraordinarily helpful, especially Gregory Thompson, director; Walter Jones, assistant head of Special Collections; and Stanley Larsen, archivist. Equally valuable were the Utah State University Library Special Collections and Archives in Logan. My thanks go to Stephen Sturgeon, manuscript curator, and Daniel Davis, photograph librarian, for the high professionalism experienced in working in their respective collections. The library of the General Theological Seminary of New York City was a treasure trove with its complete run of *The Spirit of Missions*, the Episcopal Church's monthly magazine on mission activities from 1836 to 1939, when it was replaced by *Forth*, from 1940 to 1959, which contained only minimal material about Utah. General also houses the Howard Chandler Robbins Collection of Bishops' Papers, containing material from bishops Tuttle, Spalding, and Moulton, all General graduates. Although there were 255 items in the Tuttle collection, most were after he had moved from Utah to Missouri, and the smaller Spalding (23 items) and Moulton (22 items) collections were largely about travel plans or polite acknowledgments of receipt of funds or books.

The Utah Historical Society Archives, stored in a historic building of an earlier era, the Rio Grande Railroad Depot, was a similar source of rich materials. Both the Church Archives and Church History Library of The Church of Jesus Christ of the Latter-day Saints, Salt Lake City, were efficient in tracking down early LDS-related church history publications.

The Pierpont Morgan Library in New York City is a major depository for nineteenth century Episcopal bishops's papers, which include over thirty Tuttle letters and some by Leonard as well, in the Autographs and Manuscripts of the Bishops of the Protestant Episcopal Church in the U. S. A. Collection.

The Archives of the Episcopal Church, Austin, Texas, contains wide holdings on the early Missionary Church, including extensive letters from Tuttle, Leonard, Spalding, Moulton, and some of the early women missionaries. Mark. J. Duffy, archivist, and Jennifer Peters, archivist for research and public service, offered skilled and hospitable service during my visit there, as did the library of the Episcopal Theological Seminary of the Southwest.

Jay Gitlin and Elizabeth Sherrod of Yale University's Howard R. Lamar Center for the Study of Frontiers and Borders assisted my research in New Haven, as did George Miles and the staffs of the Beinecke Rare Book & Manuscript Library, the Sterling Memorial Library, and the Mudd Library. The Bodleian Library of Oxford University and the Bancroft Library of the University of California, Berkeley, and the Library of the Graduate Theological Union, of which the Church Divinity School of the Pacific is a part, were helpful as well. The late Jean Ann McMurrin, interlibrary loan librarian of the Salt Lake City Library, time and again came up with difficult-to-locate sources, cheerfully and efficiently. The staff of St. Mark's Cathedral, especially Dean F. Q. (Rick) Lawson, Alan Phillips, and Bonnie Lambourne, parish administrator, helped me search that institution's historical documents collection. The Episcopal Diocese of Utah staff patiently answered my numerous queries. I am grateful to David Bailey, Kathy Bryden, Stephen F. Hutchinson, Daniel J. Webster, Mary Kay Williams, and Bonnie Jean Winder for their help.

Rustin Kimsey, retired bishop of Eastern Oregon, and his wife Gretchen, deserve special thanks for their hospitality and wisdom. Dirk Rinehardt Pidcock provided recollections of his eight years spent in team ministry with Bishop George E. Bates in Pendleton, Oregon.

SueAnn Martell, director, the Western Mining & Railroad Museum, Helper, Utah, provided valuable information on the Episcopal Church's early twentieth century work among the mining and railroad communities of Carbon County.

Many scholars and participants in Utah church history gave generously of their time and counsel to me, in addition to the benefit of their writings or filming, including: Mary Sudman Donovan, April Chabries Haws, Anita Jones, Brigham Madsen, the late Dean L. May, Marjorie S. May, John S. McCormick, Robert S. McPherson, Philip F. Notarianni, Floyd O'Neil, Kent Powell, John R. Sillito, and Douglas Warren.

Marilyn Hersey Brown provided extensive information about her grandfather, Milton J. Hersey and his work with the Utes. Jane Burdick introduced me to the Utah State Historical Society's well-organized archives. Richard Kuhns lent me a carefully compiled scrapbook of newspaper clippings, photos, and letters on the growth of the church in Carbon County. Cindy Kurowski showed me the well-organized St. Paul's Archives, and Jody Smith of St. Paul's was invariably helpful. Marjorie S. May shared the results of her research on H. Baxter Liebler with me. Cheryl P. Moore and Dan

Andrus suggested several leads on Utah history. Debora Jennings shared with me the records of St. Jude's, Cedar City, which the parish thought had been destroyed in a 1988 fire. Stephen Keplinger gave me copies of some of the extensive records kept by St. David's, Page, Arizona. David Jones, son of Bishop Paul Jones, and his wife, Patricia, a journalist, shared with me memories of the bishop's Utah and Antioch, Ohio, days.

Sue Rehkopf, archivist of the Episcopal Diocese of Missouri, found hard-to-locate material on Bishop Tuttle's time in Missouri. Jeanne Simmonds, widow of one of the diocesan historiographers, A. J. Simmonds, lent me a cache of documents assembled and meticulously annotated by her late husband, whose family had lived for six generations in the Cache Valley. Jane Moulton Stahl, granddaughter of Bishop Moulton, provided both reminiscences of her grandfather and records of his time in Utah, including his FBI file. Julie A. Barrett and Susan Koles of Rowland Hall–St. Mark's School introduced me to the impressive contribution of Utah's Episcopal church-sponsored schools. Sue and Jim Duffield at Whiterocks, Brian and Cheri Winter in Brigham City, and Ruth Eller in Logan all shared with me the results of History Days conducted at their parishes. Edwin (Mac) Baldwin, Anne S. Peper, and Rev. Leonard D. (Len) Evens showed me the carefully collected archives of St. Mary's, Provo. Dr. C. William Springer shared with me the early archives of All Saints', Salt Lake City. Coi Drummand-Gehrig of the Denver Public Library, Western History Collection, found important but difficult-to-locate material on Franklin Spencer Spalding. Judy Hanley and Beckie Raemer led me through the records of St. Luke's, Park City. Robert I. Woodward, archivist, St. John's Cathedral, Denver, Colorado, provided material on Bishop Spalding's early years there.

Alan F. Blanchard, president, and Dr. Matthew J. Price, director of Analytical Research, the Church Pension Fund, New York City, helped me understand Utah's finances in a wider church context.

President Kermit Hall of Utah State University, Logan, and Professor Norman Jones and the USU History Department do much to make that institution a lively center for cross-disciplinary inquiry, from which I have profited, along with countless others.

Jane Shaw, dean of Divinity, New College, Oxford University, read sections of the manuscript. John Alley, history editor of Utah State University Press, was both a meticulous editor and a wise counselor.

Oral interviews were conducted with Dorothy Alley, Robert M. Anderson, James W. Beless, Jr., Linda and Jack Besselievre, Alan F. Blanchard, Anne and Hall Blankenship, Elvira Charles, Otis Charles, Virginia Cochrane, J. A. Frazier Crocker, Jr., Betty Dalgliesh, Bill Dalgliesh, Elizabeth Dalaba, Stanley Daniels, Clifford Duncan, James S. Eckels, Thelma Ellis, C.

Matthew Gilmour, William J. Hannifin, Dovie Hutchinson, Stephen F. Hutchinson, Lisa M. Jones, Quentin F. Kolb, Tony Larimer, F. Q. (Rick) Lawson, Joan Liebler, Barbara Losse, William F. Maxwell, Madaleene D. Martinez, Kathryn Miller, Jerry Oldroyd, Paula Patterson, Dona Pedersen, Nancy Pawwinnee, Wayne Pontious, Jack Potter, Pablo Ramos, W. Lee Shaw, John Dixon Stewart, Julie Fabre Stewart, Reed Stock, Alan L. Sullivan, Alan C. Tull, Lincoln Ure, III, Bonnie Jean Winder, Francis L. Winder, and Bradley S. Wirth.

Photos and illustrations contained in this book are in the public domain, or are used with the permission of the Utah State Historical Society, the Western Mining & Railroad Museum, Helper, Utah, and the Utah State University Special Collections.

The cover drawing of Church of the Good Shepherd, Ogden, is by the Rev. Kenneth W. Green, a former commercial artist and rector of St. John's, Logan, from 1984 to 1994. I am grateful to Rev. Adam S. Linton, rector of Good Shepherd parish, for calling my attention to it.

Prayers

For the Diocese

O God, by your grace you have called us in this Diocese to a goodly fellowship of faith. Bless our Bishop(s) *N.* [and *N.*], and other clergy, and all our people. Grant that your Word may be truly preached and truly heard, your Sacraments faithfully administered and faithfully received. By your Spirit, fashion our lives according to the example of your Son, and grant that we may show the power of your love to all among whom we live; through Jesus Christ our Lord. *Amen.*

—from *The Book of Common Prayer,* 1982

1

Daniel S. Tuttle

The Pioneer Bishop

(1867–1886)

> Out from the training in church schools may emerge in most wholesome manner and degree, faith that is not afraid to reason and reason that is not ashamed to adore.
>
> —Bishop Tuttle, 1906

> We are in a foreign country.
>
> —Bishop Tuttle, 1876

Daniel S. Tuttle, who arrived by stagecoach in Utah in the summer of 1867, was the first permanent Protestant missionary to settle in Salt Lake City. Two decades earlier the Latter-day Saints had settled there and Brigham Young, their leader, had declared, "This is the place." A small number of Protestants also came to Utah, drawn by new industries like mining, banking, overland transportation, and the military. And the Episcopal Church, a century old now and established in the East, turned its eyes westward.

Daniel Sylvester Tuttle, son of an upper New York state Methodist blacksmith–farmer, was born on January 26, 1837, in Windham, New York. He became an Episcopalian as a young man through the influence of the Rev. Thomas S. Judd, rector of the rural church in Windham, later Ashland, where Tuttle grew up. (The Episcopal church, Trinity Church, was situated in town; the Methodist church was two miles away.) Judd, whom Tuttle called "a second father," tutored the ten-year-old in Latin and Greek, and arranged for his admission to a nearby school, the Delaware Academy at Delhi. Tuttle paid for his room and board by milking cows and doing farm chores. He entered college as a second-year student and graduated from

Columbia College in 1857, second in his class. He had worked his way through college by tutoring students in classics and mathematics. Although Tuttle originally hoped to be a teacher, he also had a deep interest in the church. After graduating from the General Theological Seminary in 1862, he became assistant to the rector of Zion Church, in Morris, two hundred and thirty miles northwest of New York City. A classmate at General, George W. Foote, soon to be Tuttle's brother in law, had invited him to visit Zion, where Foote's father, the rector, was ill. An active parish of more than 200 communicants, it combined farmers and merchants, old families and new. Tuttle was elected assistant minister on August 23, 1862, and named rector after Foote's death in November 1863 at a salary of $800 a year. Seven calls came quickly from other parishes, some almost doubling his salary, but Tuttle stayed in Morris five years. On September 12, 1864, he married his mentor's eldest child, Harriet, four years younger than himself.

"Morris made me strong physically," he later wrote. Under the church's horse-shed he assembled a set of parallel bars and each summer afternoon swam in a nearby millpond. Then, and later as a traveling missionary bishop, Tuttle seemed indefatigable; in twenty-seven years of ministry he missed only two Sunday services because of illness.[1] Life in upstate New York was not demanding and Tuttle was free much of the week to work on his Sunday sermon. On Saturdays he swam to a small island in the middle of a nearby stream and "between two trees, almost joined together at the root, I set up a rude pulpit board, and there . . . I spread out my sermon for the next day, and preached it, loud and full, with the birds for listeners. The exercise helped my voice. Emphasis took to itself right inflections. Eye and hand and bodily posture familiarized themselves with their duties and adjusted themselves to the ways of most efficient work."[2]

Tuttle's time with Foote was formative. Although the older man had been stricken by a stroke and soon would die, he freely shared the experiences of his long, productive ministry with an eager young assistant and during these months Tuttle's outlook on the church and ministry were formed. In this sentence Tuttle summarizes his view of the pastor's role: "If children love him, and women respect him, and men have confidence in him; if the happy are happier to welcome him among them, and the sorrowful lighter in heart, more hopeful of the future, and stronger for duty, by his coming, if he is a prophet among them in the true sense of the word, that is, one speaking for God and the realities of the world invisible, then it seems to me, the daily life and pastoral conserve of such a man of God with his flock will contribute far more to their spiritual advancement than any special efforts he can make as priest of the Church or preacher of the Word."[3]

The tranquil life of the upstate New York rural parson changed abruptly. On October 5, 1866, a year short of the required age of thirty, Tuttle was named a missionary bishop, the youngest person ever selected as a bishop in the Episcopal Church in America.[4] His vast territory included Montana, Utah, and Idaho. Previously there was only a huge missionary district of the "Northwest," with features as vague as in an early explorer's map. It included Nebraska, Wyoming, Colorado, Utah, Nevada, the Dakotas, Montana, and Idaho. Only one Episcopal church existed, in Boise, Idaho, but it had no resident clergy.[5]

The Episcopal Church did not establish missionary districts until 1835. Until then, each diocese covered a state. Such bishoprics were not sought after. Another person had turned down the Montana–Utah–Idaho offer before it came to Tuttle, as would be the case with his successors Leonard, Spalding, and Moulton. Isolation was real, travel was burdensome, funding almost nonexistent, and living conditions were often unhealthy and dangerous. Missionary bishops were nominated by the House of Bishops and confirmed by the House of Deputies. The Domestic and Foreign Missionary Society was created at this time as the church's agency to carry out missionary work.

The House of Bishops was small, less than thirty members in 1860. Probably, when the western position was decided on, colleagues asked New York's Bishop Horatio Potter to recommend a strong, self-reliant younger candidate, and Potter suggested Tuttle, who had tutored his sons and spent summer vacations with the Potter family, and who was doing excellent work in a sizable rural parish.[6]

Tuttle was consecrated bishop on May 1, 1867, in Trinity Chapel, New York City, with Bishop Potter presiding, commencing what would become a nearly fifty-six year episcopate, the first nineteen years in the West, followed by thirty-seven years in Missouri. It included almost two decades as presiding bishop, which came to him through seniority. After leaving Utah, he returned several times for brief interims between bishops, and participated in the consecration of four of his successors and the removal of one. When he died on April 17, 1923, he had been a bishop for fifty-five years, eleven months, and seventeen days, one of the longest such tenures in the history of the Anglican Communion.

A church publication remarked in 1867, "Bishop Tuttle goes forth as the fifth missionary bishop west of the Mississippi. . . . Full of youthful vigor and elasticity, and thoroughly wonted to country life, he will bear fatigue, exposure, and peril as the natural incidents of his career."[7] It was an apt description of what lay ahead.

The new bishop needed clergy to go west with him and called in his chips. His friend and brother-in-law, George W. Foote, left for Salt Lake

City on April 5, 1867, "after detentions and perils from floods and snows," and arrived in early May. The Rev. G. D. B. Miller, rector of a nearby church, married now to Mary T. Foote, Tuttle's sister-in-law, left next for Boise City, Idaho, and the Rev. E. N. Goodard, who had a nearby parish in the Catskills, agreed to go west as well with his new wife. Thomas W. Haskins, a recent seminary graduate and friend of Foote's, joined the party.

The Trip West as Missionary Bishop of Montana, Utah, and Idaho

Leaving his wife and small son in New York for the next eighteen months, Tuttle headed west on May 23 from Albany, New York, following the Union Pacific Railroad to its terminus at North Platte, Nebraska. Not all of the clergy Tuttle eventually recruited completed the arduous journey. On the night of February 6, 1871, a train carrying the Rev. Morelle Fowler, his wife, and three children, from Batavia, New York, apparently collided with a coal oil train on a bridge near Hamburgh in western New York state. The Fowler family and many passengers died by drowning or burning.[8] The Fowlers were remembered by a stained glass window in St. Mark's Cathedral, Salt Lake City, until the window was destroyed in a 1935 fire.

While sections of Tuttle's *Reminiscences* belong with the leading travel writing of their period, his strong religious convictions are evident throughout the work. In this description, written in Omaha, Nebraska, on June 2, Tuttle ministered to the family of a clergy colleague:

> I have come home to a very sad house. Little Norah Woolworth, two years and a half old, and one of the brightest of children, is dying, probably of brain fever, or congestion. She has been very precocious, and has been probably doomed to this, to speak humanly, by her active brain. The mother has not left her bedside for three days and nights, and will not leave her. Last night I prevailed on Mr. W. to take some sleep, and I myself sat up till 2 A.M. I have had prayers with the parents and for the child and the tears flow freely from the eyes of us all. I sympathize with them deeply.[9]

Tuttle's train arrived three hundred miles out in the Nebraska plains on Tuesday, June 4. Further departure was delayed by reports of hostile Native Americans. The bishop bought a rifle in Denver and wrote his last will and testament. Reports of an ambushed stagecoach, the death of its driver, and the escape of another Episcopal clergyman heading toward Denver sobered him. The fleeing priest survived by discarding his clothes and swimming to an island in the middle of a river where he was later rescued by U. S. Army troops searching for deserters. "We stayed five days in the crowded, hastily constructed, high-priced hotel in North Platte," Tuttle wrote.

> We could get only one bedroom appropriated to us, so the two clergymen slept on their blankets on the office floor. Each night after the ladies had retired I lay down on the floor in their room with a blanket and a pillow, my revolver under the latter. The novelty of sleeping on the floor or on the ground wore off in later years, for hundreds and hundreds of my night rests have been taken that way.[10]

On June 26 the party left Denver by stagecoach, and arrived in Salt Lake City on July 2. Tuttle's first dispatch from his new destination described the trip:

> We rode day and night until Friday noon, having for more than a hundred and fifty miles through the hostile country an escort of three cavalrymen. It seemed very strange to look out of the coach on moonlight nights and see the horses and armed riders galloping by our side. In less dangerous countries our escort consisted of only one rifle-armed man sitting beside the driver. Every night at dusk I felt very nervous, for dusk and daybreak are the favorite times to attack. But thanks to our merciful and loving heavenly Father we have been watched over throughout, and have not seen a hostile Indian from Denver to here.[11]

The last twenty-five miles were "the grandest and strangest" as the party descended the Wasatch Range. It was July but mountaintops were still covered with snow. The stagecoach heading for Salt Lake City met hundreds of loggers moving toward the mountains for wood.[12] He described his entrance into Salt Lake City:

> [Haskins] was quite taken aback at sight of my cartridge pouch in front, my pistol behind, my trousers in my boots, and my dark features. He declares that he thought the driver had a brother of the reins and whip beside him, and did not recognize me at all. . . . First, we went to Clawson's bathrooms for a delicious bathe, which cost us seventy-five cents each. Then we came here to the Revere House for tea. Welcome was the sight of our meal, and Miller's mouth watered when a full pint of luscious strawberries was placed in front of each of us. O how good were the new potatoes, and green peas, and string beans, and fresh turnips we

> had for dinner today. After dinner we all went up to George's and got our letters.[13]

Three days after arriving, on July 5, 1867, Tuttle wrote his wife, describing a city with "streets straight and wide, rills of irrigating water running along the sides to refresh the growing shade trees . . . yards and gardens filled with peach, apple and apricot trees, of grapes, and all vegetables." Almost every family had a cow, he wrote, adding, "a herd-man or herd-boy drives them all over the river every morning, and watches them and brings them back at night. For this he charges three cents a day per head. This morning as I arose, the herd-boy, dinner pail in hand, was driving more than two hundred cows along in front of the Revere House to cross the Jordan."[14]

Tuttle looked the part of a rugged missionary bishop. Period photographs show him with an athlete's build, a strong, squarish face, firm jaw, and deep-set eyes, attentive to those around him, a portrait that could easily fit into a gallery of "Westward Ho!" explorers, soldiers, miners, and settlers, but it would stand above most for its owner's commanding presence. He was in robust health, and undue introspection and melancholy were not features of his personality. Still, despite his stolid exterior, Tuttle acknowledged, a decade into his episcopacy, "anxiety possesses our hearts, and care chisels some lines on our faces, in planning and working to keep our obligations met and things vigorously moving on."[15]

The bishop's activist manner was demonstrated in numerous examples throughout his long ministry, including an instance in a stagecoach when "a so-called doctor . . . by manner and act was insulting to a colored woman in the coach. . . . I reproved him, and when he repeated the offense, I shook him soundly. At the next station, he got out and slunk entirely away from our sight."[16]

The territory assigned to the thirty-year-old "Bishop of Montana, having jurisdiction also in Utah and Idaho" represented 340,000 square miles of land, of which nearly 85,000 belonged to Utah. Possibly there were 155,000 inhabitants, not including Native Americans. During the next nineteen years, Tuttle estimated traveling over 40,000 miles by horse, stagecoach, or railroad, crossing empty plains, burning deserts, rocky roads, and snow-filled passes. He held services in nineteen Utah towns, fifty-two in Montana, and fifty in Idaho. After fourteen years Montana was withdrawn from his responsibilities, but demands for his time in the north were substantial and Tuttle never made it south of Salt Lake City until 1873, and then only for a brief visit to Beaver, where a preaching station was established from 1873 to 1885. Later, in 1880, he visited Silver Reef, where a church existed from 1880 to 1893.

The missionary bishop spent several months each year traveling by coach, or by train when it became available in the 1870s, and stagecoach drivers recognized him as a regular passenger. The main stagecoach route was between Salt Lake City and Colliston, Utah; there it divided into roads leading to Boise, Idaho, and Helena, Montana. Twice Tuttle crawled from overturned coaches and once he was chased by a grizzly bear. (Even a bishop should avoid a mother and cubs.) On a stagecoach north from Salt Lake City, Tuttle encountered "a squad of half naked Indians, who were resting under the shade of a high cliff. I was startled, but observed that the driver did not even deign to look at them, and that they too scarcely looked at us, and made not the slightest movement toward molesting us."[17] That night was a "night of peril and suffering." The peril came from a night crossing of the swollen, swiftly coursing Snake River; the suffering came from an attack of mosquitoes. "My hands and arms grew tired, my face and neck swollen and sore, my whole nervous frame was diseased," Tuttle wrote, leaping from the fully moving stagecoach for relief.[18]

Tuttle's reports are consistent throughout these years, marked by a similarity of message. First came a statement of hope and a specific enumeration of needs, such as the cost of buildings, salaries, or scholarships. Next, he thanked his donors, the Dioceses of New York, $1,412.43, Pennsylvania $176, Massachusetts $28. Total funds raised in 1868, Tuttle's first year as bishop, were $10,809. The sums and donors changed little through the years. "My needs are, much money for our Salt Lake work; considerable money for the general work; good men to help us to preach the blessed Gospel."[19] Groups like the New York Bible and Common Prayer Book Society, the Protestant Episcopal Tract Society, and the Evangelical Knowledge Society sent their publications westward after Tuttle visited them. The files of missionary bishops like Tuttle contain many letters that begin, "Thank you for your generous contribution of" $1, $3 or $5.

The western bishop made periodic trips back East to raise funds, a crucial part of the work of any such missionary leader. Other missionaries and missionary bishops were making similar rounds, often to the same audiences. In 1884 Tuttle spent seven months—and in 1885 four months—visiting eastern parishes, giving talks, and meeting with potential donors. (He was also on the road each year to Montana and Idaho, including a nine-week visitation to Montana in 1874, a three-month tour in 1876, and six months worth of visitations in 1880.) It was a pattern his successors followed, and often they, as he did, reported donations coming in far below needs. "I was received most kindly and welcomed most cordially everywhere, and generous aid was ministered to our wants. Not to the degree, I must honestly say, adequate to those wants. But, it may be as honestly said, perhaps to the degree that may be best and most wholesome for us." He cautioned the struggling church "as one who has seen the givers of the east and knows their views, their habits, and their wishes. . . . It is not wise in us to act upon the expectation that eastern gifts will come to us."[20]

Eastern churches looked on the western mission field much as they would on China or South America, inviting missionary speakers to tell their stories, and supporting missions with money, supplies, and personnel. Such personal relationships continued for over a century and were a lifeline of support for the church in Utah. Tuttle maintained lasting ties with St. Paul's Chapel, a historic lower Manhattan church, part of Trinity Parish, Wall Street, which he had attended while in New York. Years later, he carried a cross on his watch chain carved from a pew in St. Paul's where George Washington worshipped following his swearing in as President of the United States. When St. Paul's remodeled, the wooden cross over its altar was transported to St. Paul's, Virginia City, Montana. A Sunday school teacher, Jane Mount, who has worked with Tuttle, was memorialized by her sisters, Maria, Charlotte, and Susan, who sent Tuttle $25,000 to found St. Paul's Chapel, Salt Lake City, and later provided St. Paul's and Church of the Good Shepherd, Ogden, with rectories.

The Utah into which Daniel Tuttle arrived had recently become a territory of the United States. Brigham Young and the Latter-day Saints had settled there in 1847, when Utah was still part of Mexico. In 1880 it became an American territory following the Treaty of Guadeloupe Hidalgo. The industrious Mormons organized a shadow "State of Deseret" with a constitution and government and petitioned Congress for admission to the Union, something they would be denied for almost forty years because of polygamy and the theocratic Mormon government. The 1860s were not the 1960s and the civil tolerance of a later era was not a feature of the early decades of Mormon history. A persecuted minority, driven westward by hostile local and federal governments, the LDS Church was reviled in the press and public square. And just as the new Zion was being built under their autocratic control, a steady stream of outsiders arrived as settlers, wanting to hold public office, convert the heathen Mormons, and establish businesses, a formula for continual friction and, at times, violence.

Great Salt Lake City was a town of twelve to fifteen thousand inhabitants in the late 1860s, Provo had three to four thousand residents, and other cities like Ogden and Logan claimed a thousand each. Ogden became a major western railroad center in 1869 with the coming of the transcontinental railroad. The region's non-Mormon population, whom the Latter-day Saints called "Gentiles," was estimated at a thousand persons; about two hundred worked for the stage company, others were miners, traders, and government officials.[21] Such non-LDS populations were the base from which the Episcopal missionary district drew its core membership, although ex-LDS members joined as well, especially some former Church of England members converted by LDS missionaries in the United Kingdom to come to Utah.

Members of Tuttle's party were not the first Episcopalians to set foot in Utah, but the first to stay. An English clergyman, on his way across the country, had been invited to speak in the Tabernacle and another Episcopal missionary bishop, J. C. Talbot, had passed through Salt Lake City during the Civil War, but was not allowed to preach in the open air, nor would anyone rent him a house in which to hold services. Bishop Talbot, on his stage coach journey to Nevada, "had eaten a few meals in Utah and that was all," Tuttle wrote.[22]

The first episcopal residence was an adobe house at the corner of Main Street and 300 South, rented for sixty dollars a month. Later, when the cathedral was built, the Tuttles found a residence at 454 East First South, which they initially shared with other clergy familes. Of the original residence Tuttle said, "It was originally built, I feel sure, for a polygamist for there were three front doors," Tuttle noted.[23] The residence was not far from a Mormon meetinghouse. One day, during an LDS church conference, a person appeared at the door and asked, "'Is the bishop in?' 'No,' came the answer. 'Is the bishop's wife in?' 'No.' 'Is any one of his other wives in?'"[24]

A Congregational church chaplain attached to Camp Douglas, a military post on the strategic bench above Salt Lake City, had led Protestant church services in 1865 and 1866. Camp (later Fort) Douglas was built in 1862 to control the Native Americans, watch the Latter-day Saints, and protect the overland mail. The minister, Norman McLeod, a vocal anti-LDS cleric, preached periodically at Independence Hall, a non-LDS auditorium in the midblock of Third South. McLeod left Utah soon after his Sunday school superintendent, a land speculator and physician, was lured from his house and assassinated. The assailant was never found.[25] Thus when the advance party of Foote and Haskins arrived in May 1867, they found a functioning Sunday school of fifty to sixty persons and three women communicants, Mrs. Hamilton, Mrs. Durant, and Mrs. Tracy. For the next three years, the Episcopalians held the only regular Protestant services in Utah. Tuttle described one of the early Salt Lake City services in a letter to his wife dated July 7, 1867. He had just returned from a morning service at Independence Hall.

> There was a congregation, I should think, of about a hundred. Mrs. Hamilton played the Mason & Hamlin that the church people have purchased, and we have all the chants but the Te Deum. Mr. Goddard

> took the first part of the service, Mr. Haskins the latter. I read the ante-communion, and George [Foote] the epistle, and Mr. Miller preached a capitally good sermon from: "That My joy may be in you, and that your joy may be full." The offertory alms amounted to $15.75. George gave notice of confirmation and communion for next Sunday.[26]

Elsewhere he reflected on the place of the Prayer Book in the missionary district:

> In many places in the mountains I was shown by one or another miner, or lawyer, or business man, a copy of the Prayer Book with the information that they had used it in reading the burial service in the days before any minister had come among them. Not a little one among the blessings bestowed by the Prayer Book is this of affording simple and fit guidance and help to a frontier people in reverently and religiously laying by the sacred bodies of the dead.[27]

By October 8, 1867, Tuttle, with Foote and Haskins, launched a printed appeal to eastern donors that began, "A strange community we are living among; a strange social atmosphere environs us. . . . Increasing thousands of children are growing up in this Territory, who have never heard of any other religion than the Mormon; who know nothing of any other social system than Polygamy."[28] The church's great need was $15,000 to purchase an acre and a quarter of land on which to build a school. For Tuttle, "the great feature of the work is the teaching and training of the children."

The initial results of the church's activity set the tone for a pattern of slow, steady growth. Church work had begun on May 1, 1867. In its first sixteen months in Utah there were 73 baptisms, 31 confirmations, 44 registered communicants, 5 marriages, 11 burials, 150 young people in Sunday schools, 13 teachers, 100 students in a grammar school of 6 teachers, and local contributions of $3,970.[29] By September 1869 Tuttle had settled in Salt Lake City with his family, and he stayed there until 1886; in 1883 he was able to report that, "St. Mark's Rectory, which is my own residence, has been improved by the addition of a bathroom, and by the building of a much needed barn."[30]

Meeting Brigham Young: "My Policy Will Be to Have as Little as Possible to Do with Him"

Only one encounter between the Episcopal bishop and the LDS leader took place, a perfunctory exchange a week after Tuttle's arrival. Because Tuttle made some kind observations about Young following their meeting, later observers might believe that the civil relations of a later century between Latter-day Saints and Episcopalians were the norm in the 1860s, but that was not the case. Tuttle was critical of Mormonism in national church publications and as a speaker on his fundraising tours, although his manner was conciliatory while in Utah. Young was battling the federal government at this time and his relations with Protestant groups were sharp-edged, as recounted by a westward-voyaging Presbyterian minister, Jotham Goodell, in his 1852 letters, *A Winter with the Mormons.*[31]

On July 9, 1867, Tuttle called on Brigham Young, in the company of George Foote and Warren Hussey, a recently arrived business entrepreneur and Episcopal lay leader. Earlier Hussey said Young was tired of the abuse heaped on the Latter-day Saints, and welcomed Episcopalians who "are men of education and better sense; they are gentlemen and any gentleman is welcome here, no matter what his creed."[32] Foote and Haskins had earlier asked Young for a place to open a school. Young promised to help, Foote said, but "his promises of assistance were hollow and hypocritical."[33]

The "Lion of the Lord", as Young was called, was leaving his office as the bishop arrived. Tuttle wrote, "As we neared the gate he was coming out, comfortably dressed in white coat and vest and linen trousers . . . good watch-chain, umbrella under his arm, light gaiters on his feet. He has a pleasant face and voice, is somewhat corpulent in person, is of medium height, and has gray eyes, sandy whiskers, and light brown hair." Had there been a mix up about the time of the visit? If Young had been expecting Tuttle, he would not be leaving his office, and if the encounter was a casual drop in, it would suggest a less than substantive meeting was planned between the two church leaders.

Young returned to his office, which reminded Tuttle of a lawyer's chambers, filled with iron safes, tables, and hundreds of pigeonholes stuffed with documents.[34] After exchanging pleasantries about where they were born in the East, Foote remarked positively on the recent Fourth of July celebration, which reminded him that Utah was part of the United States. In those years, the Latter-day Saints sometimes flew the American flag at half-mast on the Fourth of July as a sign of protest of the federal government. "Perhaps so," Young replied, "but they rather seem to me to be the Disunited States, for I see by the morning telegrams that the most rigorous military despotism is to be enforced in the south." It was an informed remark by Young. A sizable contingent of the United States Army had moved to Utah and Young had been waging an active guerilla war against federal forces. The territory's petitions for statehood had been denied, and the Prophet was locked in a prolonged struggle with the national government over plural marriages and theocratic government, front-burner issues for many years.[35]

Most of the recorded conversation was between Young and Foote, with Tuttle as an observer. Then Young showed Tuttle a sample of Green River gold, and remarked to Foote in such a way as to indicate that he was aware of town gossip, "I am told that you have heard it said that I have taken the property of Amasa Lyman," an apostle who was feuding with Young. "Is it so?" Foote denied being the source of such gossip. Young persisted, "Two ladies told me that this report was made and that you were present and heard it." "No," Foote replied, "I have heard no such report, perhaps Mr. Haskins may have been the man, but it was not I." Young ended the conversation, "Mr. Foote, I just want to say to you what I said to the Catholic priest when he came here; if you hear rumors flying about touching me or this people, come right here with them and I will always set things right. That's the best way."[36] Possibly the LDS leader was setting the record straight, possibly he was warning Foote.

So went the one encounter between Tuttle and Young. Tuttle put the best face on it. "We were most civilly and courteously treated in this call, but I was not asked to call again. In voice and conversation and manner Mr. Young seemed pleasant and courteous and far less course [*sic*] than when he is speaking in public. I did not detect any violation of grammar or of good sense or of good taste on his part during our call."[37]

Tuttle was more graphic in expressing his opinion of the LDS leader in a letter to his absent wife. "He is so powerful a man in everything here, and so unscrupulous a man, I fear, in most things, that my policy will be to have as little as possible to do with him. With his keen sightedness he must know, that if not in will yet in reality, by our services and our school, we are putting our clutches to his very throat."[38] Elsewhere the bishop called Young "shrewd, practical, industrious, energetic, temperate to the degree of abstemiousness," adding, "he was conscious of fitness to rule, and others unhesitatingly accorded him leadership."[39] Young never asked to see Tuttle again, and there is no record of his impressions of the meeting.

If only the brief passage on the meeting of the two leaders in *Reminiscences* is read, Tuttle appears more conciliatory than in his other writings. "Doubtless the question will be asked, What think you of Mormonism?" Tuttle wrote in his first report as a missionary bishop in 1867 in *The Spirit of Missions,* the national church's missionary monthly magazine. He repeated the answer he gave then word-for-word nineteen years later on leaving Utah. "I needed not to have come to Utah, to think and know that Mormonism, so far as it has any fixed theology about it, is a wild heresy; in its practical operation, a deluder of ignorant people; in its allowed system of polygamy, illegal, immoral, cruel, and infamous."[40] Although he acknowledged the validity of LDS baptism, "we cannot admit them to our altar," Tuttle said, because "they admit so much pernicious error into their doctrine that it would not be fit for an evangelical Church to affiliate with them."[41]

It was an age where religious differences were sharply stated from the pulpit and in the press, and Tuttle and some of his successors could strike a responsive chord with potential funding sources by portraying the severity of the Mormon challenge. The early Episcopal bishops, Tuttle and Spalding, were the most vocal in their public criticism of the Latter-day Saints, with Jones not far behind. Later bishops confined their comments to the issue of accepting or not accepting LDS baptisms.

Of the LDS Church's secretive hierarchy, the bishop said, it "must be acknowledged to be a power with tremendous and terrible possibilities enwrapped in it." He added, "Mormon priestly domination is un-American and anti-American. By all Americans it should be firmly opposed. But let the instruments and weapons of opposition be reason, argument, education, enlightenment, influence, persuasive truth. In my years of contention with the Mormons I did not feel at liberty to use any other weapons."[42] He spoke of the "monstrous Mormon delusion" in several articles in *The Spirit of Missions* and in his annual reports, adding, "May the Lord speed its downfall, despotic, treason-breeding, woman-debasing, soul-destroying thing that it is!"[43]

Tuttle called LDS religious buildings "strange, bare, hideous barns." "There is no specimen of descent ecclesiastical architecture here," he observed. "There is no bell to summon worshippers together; not one, in this town of more than twenty Mormon meeting houses."[44]

The bishop cautioned against expecting the Latter-day Saints to convert easily. In 1873 he estimated the Episcopal church had baptized 244 persons, of whom 144 were Latter-day Saints or children of Latter-day Saints.[45] "We are in a foreign country," he said of Utah in 1876. Brigham Young was ill and Tuttle, like his successor Abiel Leonard, erroneously predicted the LDS Church would collapse with the Prophet's death.[46] "It is not so arrogant as it once was," he said of the Latter-day Saints in 1885, adding, "A wholesome dread pervades the breasts of the guilty ones that the American government firmly intends to prosecute its present enforcement of the penalties against polygamy." John Taylor, Brigham Young's successor, and George Q. Cannon, his first counselor, were in hiding. "There is much joy with us that the government is causing the majesty of the law to be respected," the bishop concluded.[47] In a lengthy article on "Mormons" in an 1891 *Religious Encyclopedia*, however, he said, "It is a mistake to count the Mormons a mere horde of sensualized barbarians. . . . There were large numbers of

God-fearing people among them, the exodus from Nauvoo had served as a winnowing van. Temperate, heroic, striving individuals emerged but the strong demand for obedience to the priesthood changes fair-minded and kindhearted men into unjust and unfeeling agents of a despotic system."[48]

For their part, the Latter-day Saints regarded Tuttle as a fair opponent; compared to the strident polemicists of other denominations he was a voice of reason. He acknowledged their opposition, "yet their anger worked itself off in newspaper tirades against us. These we never answered or noticed, and so, thank God, our property rights and our personal safety and comfort have never been interfered with." (Killings of Gentiles and property confiscation were the stuff of rumors, if not actualities, in the hostile Utah climate of the 1870s.) "The Mormons have treated us outwardly with civility and courteous respect, forced from them, I hope and trust, by our evident honesty and our daily manifestation of kind but firm conscientiousness."[49]

Tuttle's opposition to polygamy was widely known locally. A non-LDS paper commented after one of his sermons, "It would have done the believers in the pretended revelation of celestial marriage great good to have heard this Christian minister disapprove the divinity of the practice among the people of Utah."[50] The bishop believed plural marriages were flourishing. He wrote his wife, "I think it is now a desperately, hideously, growingly strong institution. . . . In numbers, by immigration and polygamy, the Mormons are multiplying astonishingly. They hold all the soil. Their children are carefully trained and see and know nothing else, as to religion and social life, but Mormonism and polygamy."[51]

Women in plural marriages supported the system out of religious conviction, he concluded, even if they personally suffered from it. "To their nature it was a calamity and hateful. To their spirit it was religious duty and a call for self-sacrifice. Therefore they were loyal to it, determined to live it, and if need be, to die for it."[52] Only strong external intervention would end plural marriages. Tuttle wrote following Young's death, "I am beginning to conclude that nothing human, but the strong determination of the United States government, expressing itself by the rigid execution, if needful, of military law will put a stop to this curse."[53]

Strategy on Schools

Education was the linchpin of Tuttle's strategy for church growth. He was originally a teacher, and saw the church expanding not by confronting the Latter-day Saints, but by building schools in several growing cities to educate a generation of newcomers to Utah, and where Utah children might be exposed to a wider world than they had previously known. Also, some of the former Church of England members who had converted to the LDS faith and come to America now had second thoughts. Some returned to their original church, and sent their children to its schools. Other students came from the growing number of Protestants moving into Utah with the expansion of the mining industry, railroads, and other businesses. The bishop said, "Out from the training in church schools may emerge in most wholesome manner and degree, faith that is not afraid to reason and reason that is not ashamed to adore."[54]

With his focus on education, the bishop was responding to an obvious need in Utah life. Originally Young favored only a rudimentary education for young Mormons, limited to basic literacy, to which was added animal husbandry, commerce, and bookkeeping. Utah's public education system was a scattering of elementary schools run from LDS wards. Young did not want Gentiles teaching his young people. A vote on a public school system was defeated four to one in 1874, and it was not until 1890 that the Collett bill was passed, creating a public school system. Once Utah became a state in 1896, its public education system was exemplary for many years.[55]

Tuttle kept his eye on the prize. Start with parish day schools. When funding allowed it, a seminary, college, and university would follow—but that never happened.[56] Thus Tuttle encouraged mission schools in Salt Lake City in 1867; Logan in 1873; and Ogden, Plain City, and Layton in 1886. The schools grew in numbers but not financially. When Utah's public school system began in 1890, church policy was to support public education and only the Salt Lake City private church schools remained.

The linchpins of his program were St. Mark's Grammar School, a day school for boys and girls, founded on July 1, 1867, and St. Mark's School for girls, another day school, which opened for business on August 29, 1881, and later became Rowland Hall. The $5,000 to start the school was given as a memorial by the wife and daughter of Benjamin Rowland, a wealthy Philadelphia industrialist. The Rev. R. M. Kirby, school chaplain and St. Mark's Cathedral pastor for nearly eleven years, had married Rowland's daughter, Virginia, who had died shortly before Kirby came to Utah in 1871. The school's beginnings could not have been more inauspicious. Three old dry good stores and a half-ruined adobe bowling ally were found on Main Street between 200 and 300 South, a place "gutted by the Mormons under the pretense that it was an immoral resort."[57] Two single unpainted board partitions created two classrooms, and "a few plain pine desks, such as were used a hundred years ago, were ordered."[58] The schools moved about frequently in their early years. Independence Hall was once a school site, as was Groesbeck's store on Main Street, and a location opposite City Hall. St. Mark's girls' school once occupied the basement of St. Mark's Cathedral, and was known for several years as the "Basement School."[59] Meanwhile, the numbers of miners, ranchers, and business people from out of state grew in Utah, as did demand for quality private education. The church school sought to be "a home away from home" for young ladies from remote ranches and mining camps, a place where they could both receive a sound college preparatory education and thoughtful religious instruction. By 1873 St. Mark's Grammar School was able to move into its own building at 141 East 100 South, and by 1876 it had enrolled 463 students. Meanwhile, the "School on the Hill," as Rowland Hall was known, had moved to a lot on A Street and First Avenue, and in 1882 enrolled seventeen boarding and thirty day students.

Tuition costs were a problem for many students. Tuttle launched a series of forty-dollar scholarships, the sum that would cover annual tuitions, and promoted them as a staple of his appeals in the East, as did his successors.[60] The church raised five hundred such scholarships in twenty years. They "are the rain and the dew to refresh and invigorate us. . . . Our bills are met, our hearts are cheered, and scores and scores of children, otherwise neglected, are being trained to the useful, the true and the pure," he wrote.[61] By 1885 there were 700 pupils in Episcopal church schools in Utah, 500 of them from LDS families.[62]

Elsewhere the pioneer bishop said of education for young women, "Many a girl . . . is getting fitted, by God's blessing, to be a wife and mother of a far different sort from the poor creatures around us here."[63] Reflecting on his educational policies years after he had left Utah, Tuttle observed, "Our schools are to be reckoned, I am quite sure, among the redeeming, regenerating, and disenthralling influences which have changed the fanatical, oligarchic community of 1867 into the American Utah of today [1900]."[64]

Years later, the relationship between bishop and school was humorously described in the Rowland Hall yearbook, the *Crimson Rambler*:

> The grounds, up to a few feet from the entrance, were covered with a fine healthy growth of alfalfa which furnished nourishment for the bishop's and chaplain's cows and for various stray animals of the neighborhood. Instead of tennis and basketball the girls used to take their exercise in chasing away the alien herd, so that the bishop's cow might not lack its daily rations.[65]

St. Mark's Cathedral, "A Bishop's Church"

The other pillars of Tuttle's ministry in Utah were St. Mark's Cathedral, the first non-LDS permanent church structure in Salt Lake City, and St. Mark's

Hospital, which soon became a major institution in the Intermountain West. "St. Mark's" was originally selected as a name because one of the original Utah clergy, George W. Foote, once served at St. Mark's Church-in-the-Bowery, New York City (1799),[66] the oldest incorporated Episcopal Church in the United States.

Richard Upjohn (1802–1878), a leading British-American architect, designed the cathedral. The building was expensive and $45,000 was needed to complete it. Hussey, who soon went bankrupt, provided a loan. While in New York, the bishop secured the loan with an old friend, Cortlandt De Peyster Field, who contacted friends and raised an additional $2,000 for the cathedral. The bishop laid the cathedral's cornerstone on July 30, 1870, and on May 21, 1871, services were moved from Independence Hall, their site for the last four years, to the cathedral basement at 231 East 100 South. Tuttle said, "A congregation of two hundred was present, and more than fifty went away for want of room. Our church proper, when completed, will seat about four hundred. It is a most substantial church; the walls, and bell tower, and cross, of honest, massive stone, with a dry, light and well ventilated basement for our Sunday school of two hundred and twenty scholars."[67]

Foote returned to Salt Lake City with $15,000 in May 1870, after a six-month successful fundraising campaign in the East. He expected to be named rector of St. Mark's. But at the parish's organizing meeting on November 18, 1870, the vestry elected the bishop as rector instead and passed a resolution saying the bishop would always be ex officio rector of the cathedral parish. Tuttle accepted, providing he could nominate the assistant clergy as a way of avoiding factions.[68] Foote resigned the next day, effective January 1, 1871. Tuttle faced a classic church fight at the parish's organizational meeting. He tried to avoid it by having Foote nominate him as rector; in turn he would appoint Foote as his assistant. Foote opted instead to run against Tuttle and lost five to two. The conflict's backlash affected Tuttle, who wrote, "I am sorry to lose George and must take the church building matter entirely upon myself until the vestry can get into shape to assume care."[69] In a rare note of loss he wrote to E. N. Goodard, now resident in Montana, "Dear friend, were it the Lord's will, how much happier would I be at Morris."[70]

On Ascension Day, May 14, 1874, the missionary district's seven clergy and several missionary bishops gathered for the cathedral's consecration. Tuttle called it "a bishop's church, strong, plain, but beautiful, and complete in its appointments." At day's end he said, "I for one went to bed all tired out, but happy as a boy who had been on the winning side in a match at baseball, and full of humble thanksgiving to the good Lord who has sent reward to the poor sort of labor of my last seven years."[71]

What is a cathedral in an American context? The word comes from the Middle English "cathedra," meaning "chair," or the seat of a bishop, one of the visible signs of a bishop's authority and the unity of the missionary district or diocese. "An American cathedral must be, I take it, a bishop's church; a church in which the bishop is immediate as well as ultimate controller and rector," Tuttle stated. "We cannot import any ready-made article for our service. Even the noble foundations of our mother Church of England must be object lessons for us to study, rather than patterns for us to imitate. . . . I count it an error, therefore, to copy with painstaking carefulness the nomenclature, method of organization, mode of worship, and rules of management of English cathedrals."[72] Tuttle's handcarved walnut episcopal chair, with its heavy wooden canopy large enough to shield an Austrian village cross, was given in memory of a Morris, New York, friend of the bishop's, I. W. Moss, transported eighteen thousand miles by ship around the Cape of Good Hope to San Francisco, and then overland by ox cart to Salt Lake City.[73]

Was the cathedral an independent parish church where the bishop appeared twice a year at Christmas and Easter, or was it the chief parish of the scattered missionary district? Tuttle knew bishop–dean relations could be fraught with potential tension. "Troubles thick as blackberries are likely to interfere," he wrote, adding that a cathedral risks becoming "a very storm-center of disunity and disharmony."[74] Rectors, vestries, and wealthy parishioners comfortable in their ways may be jealous. The contrasting cries will be "The bishop belongs to us all equally" and "What right has he to establish his cathedral church in our midst and lure away and appropriate for it our parishioners?"[75]

The bishop foresaw the sources of conflict and established his own position before the Salt Lake City cathedral was ever a reality.

> There seem to be reasons why it is well for a bishop to have his own cathedral. Some of them are these: (1) He does not wish that the pastor element of his nature should be left to perish or atrophy. True he is *pastor pastorum* [pastor of the pastors] but that oversight is found to have really more of the administrative and executive than the pastoral to it. He has been a pastor before he was a bishop, close to the hearts and lives and souls and love of people; it is a joy to him that in the cathedral congregation there is room enough for him to have gracious exercise of this longing of his heart.[76]

The second reason for a bishop to lead the cathedral congregation is that "it is not seemly that he and his family should be merely parishioners in some parish church, in which church his right and authority are no greater than in any church of his diocese, and where, if he wish to preach, or to confer orders, or to celebrate the Holy Communion, it is necessary for him to ask permission of the rector."[77] A bishop in the cathedral, he argued, could train younger clergy and set broad norms for liturgical worship. He realized that "the bishop cannot be a martinet . . . he cannot insist that the services shall be minutely and exactly as he prefers they should be." But cathedral services "can stand forth, not by a hard and fast law, but by way of steady example, as the norm for the diocese."[78]

Potential friction in dean–bishop relations was real and Tuttle quickly spotted it, primarily over the dean's role. "He must have a dean [who would be] the real pastor. The bishop cannot stay at home enough and cannot find enough time to be pastor . . . . The bishop's dream of a church of his own, therefore, becomes much modified in actual experience." The exercise will only work if all parties exercise "prudent self-restraint and [the] constant exercise of considerate courtesy."[79] Tuttle thus carved out the foundation of a workable relationship between bishop and dean, but in future decades the cathedral–diocesan relationship was marked by periodic tension.

Why did Tuttle not intervene more decisively on Foote's behalf? "Ah! American bishops need take care how they use the emphatic *must.* As a general thing not much good comes from that sort of thing," he said.[80] Years later, Tuttle reflected on the cathedral, "Prayers and tears and hopes and fears and sacred memories, as well as altar and walls and gifts and memorials, were consecrated in that noble building in the mountains, to which my heart turns even now in the deepest tenderness."[81]

St. Mark's Hospital

In May 1872, the Church opened St. Mark's Hospital in a rented adobe house at 500 East 400 South, funded largely from dollar-a-month dues paid by individual miners, and from contributions from the local business community. Local industrial growth had resulted in a demand for medical care; silicosis, called "miner's Consumption," was widespread and lead poisoning at times accounted for more than half the hospital's patients; safety conditions were poor and accidents frequent. Amputations were a common surgical procedure, with physicians employing skills learned on the job in the Civil War. The damaged limb was removed with a saw, and the wound cauterized. Nitrous oxide (laughing gas) provided an anesthesia of sorts.[82] Several Salt Lake City citizens subscribed to the hospital's support and four eastern donors sent $630. A parishioner from Grace Church, Brooklyn, New York, provided a year's supply of medicines and a local physician, Dr. John Hamilton, a former army surgeon, gave his services. Hamilton and Major

Edmund Wilkes, a mine superintendent, were both members of St. Mark's and had presented the hospital idea to Tuttle. In 1875 Tuttle noted that five hundred patients had been cared for and that all but $589 of the hospital's $9,500 budget was raised locally.[83] The hospital moved a block north in 1876 and could house a dozen patients at a time. When Tuttle left Utah in 1886, he estimated that 4,776 patients had received care at the hospital since its opening.[84]

Ogden, Logan, Corrine, and St. Paul's Chapel, Salt Lake City

James and Lydia Lucelia Webster Gillogly were a distinctive presence in the early Utah church. The ministerial couple almost single-handedly built the Church of the Good Shepherd in Ogden into a thriving church in an alien setting. On the day of their marriage, June 30, 1870, the couple left Wetherfield Springs in western New York for Ogden, Utah, a growing town of 5000 persons, and an important east–west railroad juncture for the Union Pacific, Central Pacific, and Utah Central railroads. Earlier that year T. W. Haskins had come from Salt Lake City to hold the first Episcopal church services in the recently built Union Pacific Railway passenger room, and Tuttle led two worship services there, as well, in April 1870. On July 18 the Gilloglys arrived in Ogden, the only Protestant missionary couple in a Mormon town. On Sunday Gillogly held both morning and evening services in the passenger room. "There were fourteen persons present in the morning and about twenty-five in the evening. They were all railroad people," Mrs. Gillogly wrote in 1900 when she was asked to contribute a history of the Gillogly's ten-and-a-half years together in Utah.[85]

When trains were late, services waited. Sunday school met in a corner of the waiting room while the fruit stand did an active business in another. Trains passed during the service; talking, singing, and swearing were plainly heard from the platform, as was the conversation of card players in an adjoining room. Gillogly said, "That is what I call discouraging, but God Willing I shall not give up yet."[86]

The expanding railroad community wanted a school for its children. The Church rented a former saloon for six dollars a month. A local carpenter made desks and chairs and a sheet was hung in a corner to make a vestry-room. Rough local lumber was used and during winter boards were nailed over cracks to keep out the cold. "In this place the School of the Good Shepherd was started with thirteen scholars, October 1, 1870."[87]

The first year in Ogden was a difficult one for the young couple. Hordes of grasshoppers devastated crops and gardens, 135 cases of smallpox were reported that summer, and many persons died from a lack of proper sewage.

In the winter, trains were sometimes snowed in for several days. At one point the town was thirty days without mail. The newly-married couple lived in a railroad freight car for several months. A curtain divided their car into a bedroom and sitting room. Next they rented three rooms in an LDS home where they stayed for two years until the church could provide them with a residence. A polygamous widow of a Mormon bishop offered to rent a two-room log house for thirty dollars a month, "but we objected to such extortion. Of course the Mormons did everything in their power to keep us from getting a foothold. . . . Mud and stones were thrown at our place of meeting and jeering noises were made round about. Any whom we approached were warned to have nothing to do with us on pain of expulsion from their church or boycotting in business. The children were taught that we were terrors come to work them great harm, and I have seen them run at our approach as if we were lions from the jungle."

No LDS member would sell or rent land to the Church at a reasonable price, but Henry Lawrence, a member of the principal non-Mormon political party, the Liberal Party, offered the church a corner lot with a tannery on it. "That Prince of Givers, John D. Wolfe of New York City," contributed $1,500, and Tuttle found additional funds from eastern friends to refurbish a tannery as a school. The first church services were held there on April 16, 1871, and soon the busy day school was launched. In 1874 John W. Hamersley, a New York City lawyer, whose children Tuttle had tutored, gave $9,500 for a church as a memorial to his daughter, Catherine L. Livingston, who had died in childbirth at age twenty-two. An attractive Gothic Revival building was designed by the prominent Canadian–English architect Gordon W. Lloyd, whose Detroit, Michigan, office produced many leading midwestern church buildings. The Church of the Good Shepherd was consecrated on February 6, 1875. Thirty-two persons took communion and a plate offering of forty gollars was received. And the school continued to grow. Gillogly said he would raise half the needed funds if Tuttle would provide the rest. Gillogly's net worth was only $3,500, but he gave liberally, and soon a new school was built. Later he mortgaged his house to raise funds for the church.

In the summer of 1876 several English residents of nearby Plain City, who had come to America as LDS members, wished to return to their native church. They asked Gillogly to start services in Plain City, which he did in the town's public school house on September 3, 1876. On Sundays he made the ten-mile trip in each direction by horse between Ogden services.[88] By April 1877 a total of $2,295 had been raised to buy land and erect a small church and schoolhouse attended by sixty Sunday school and forty-five day students. Plain City was launched, and continued a tenuous existence for many years. The building was sold in 1956, since the church had not been used for services for several years, and the structure became a community center.

Gillogly never lacked plans. He would have liked to start a church hospital in Ogden, a reading room, and an aid society to help the poor. The activist pastor also found himself a party to a libel suit. In January 1880 the sheriff called at a cabin next door to reclaim a door and two windows allegedly stolen by a poor woman from the deserted property of a wealthy LDS railroad agent. Gillogly intervened on behalf of the charwoman and her three children and sent the sheriff away. He also discovered that the woman had removed the door and windows from the abandoned property before the railroad agent purchased it and wrote an article, "A Mean Man," for the Liberal paper, *The Dispatch.* John Reeves, the property owner, responded with a fifty-dollar libel suit. The trial was postponed several times during 1880 and 1881, and ended with Gillogly's death in 1881.

In late 1880 Gillogly's health failed; he died at home on February 14, 1881, age thirty-seven, bedridden for three weeks with a stomach ailment. His wife was pregnant with their fifth child.[89] The vicar was the first person buried in the cemetery he had purchased for the Church of the Good Shepherd. A large marble column was erected in his memory, but vandals destroyed it in January 1883. The church and the city council, composed of LDS members, offered a reward, but the culprits were never found.

In the decade the Gilloglys were in Ogden, the number of families attending church increased from 4 to 63 and the number of Sunday school children rose from 8 to 140. It was a time of creative growth on all fronts. "The people worked in remarkable harmony," Mrs. Gillogly recalled. "The long established Ladies Aid Society was ever active in raising money to help in church work. They gave many entertainments, socials, suppers, etc., to induce people to give money in exchange for innocent pleasures. The choir was noted for being free from quarrels, and many gave their musical talents to enhance the pleasures of the worship of the people."[90]

Tuttle remained solicitous of the Gillogly family all his life. On March 7, 1881, he wrote Mrs. Gillogly, saying she would receive the full $250 payable that quarter for her husband's salary. The bishop added an additional $50 and $16.65 came from another source.[91] Mrs. Gillogly stayed on in Ogden for seven years, teaching music and leading the Band of Willing Workers, a group of young women, who gave her a golden thimble at her departure. Older church members presented her a silver tea set. When he became bishop of Missouri, Tuttle obtained a position for her daughter at St. James Military Academy, Macon, Missouri, and Mrs. Gillogly lived there from 1891 until moving to Alameda, California, several years later. Her memories of a decade in Ogden, written for the parish many years later, provides one of the few narratives of early Utah Episcopal Church life from a perspective outside of Salt Lake City.

Tuttle came north to Logan, a frontier town of 2000 inhabitants. He arrived on the first train operated by the Utah and Northern Railroad on January 31, 1873, along with William H. Stoy, soon to be missionary-in-charge of the new congregation of St. John's. "It is stony ground," the bishop said. A contemporary account reported, "Through the hostility of the Mormon heresy toward the Church, the missionary was unable to rent a suitable building in which to hold Divine worship; he was therefore obliged to rent a small adobe building known as the 'Bakery.'. . . Here the first Christian services ever held in Northern Utah [i.e., north of Ogden, sixty miles distant] were celebrated."[92]

St. John's congregation also opened a school that year. As in Ogden, the non-LDS community did not want to enroll their children in the crowded and poorly run LDS schools. The school remained open until 1896; by then public education was improved and the missionary district closed most of its hard-to-run and expensive-to-maintain schools. Possibly a thousand students attended the church schools in Logan, Ogden, and Plain City during this period; in Logan most of the students were of Mormon birth and one of the charges against a local Mormon in 1874 was that he felt "justified in sending his children to the Gentile School."[93]

Stoy first rented the bakery, then moved to larger quarters holding 100 students. In 1876 the church purchased two lots at the corner of Center Street and 300 West, and in 1888 a frame building was constructed and called St. John's House. Stoy was supported by a lay person, Joseph Richardson, a New York entrepreneur who had come west to invest in railroads and who built the railroad from Ogden to Soda Springs at the request of Brigham Young. Stoy stayed five years at St. John's, after which Logan had difficulty attracting a permanent clergy person until 1906 with the arrival of a remarkable pair of clergy, Paul Jones and Donald K. Johnson.

The transcontinental railroad was completed on May 10, 1869, near Corrine, on the west bank of Bear River not far from Brigham City. Corrine was promoted as a growing non-LDS commercial center to rival Salt Lake City. The key to its success was monopolizing the profitable transportation industry to Montana's mines. But this lasted only eight years, until 1878, by which time traffic had shifted to the recently completed Utah and Northern Railroad. Corrine was bypassed through a direct link between the mines and

Salt Lake City. Thus ended "Corrine the Fair, the Gentile Capital of Utah." Briefly a town of fifteen hundred persons, it was the site of banks, stores, and newspapers, one quartered in a tent, and a center of vocal anti-LDS activity as well. Good Samaritan Episcopal Church was the first Protestant church to hold services in Corrine in 1869, a year before the cathedral's cornerstone was laid in Salt Lake City. The church's early days could have sprung from the pages of a Bret Harte short story. Church members competed with a foot race at the opening service. A local newspaper described the event:

> The rector of St. Mark's Church, Salt Lake City, paid us a visit and held service in the City Hall, early in June, 1869, the congregation consisting of six devout citizens, and during service a crowd of two hundred gathered in front of the building and organized a foot race, which so disgusted the reverend gentleman that it was months before he could be induced to return to Corrine.[94]

A small adobe chapel was soon constructed, without windows or doors, A local paper described it as "a beggarly array of empty benches" with "here and there a worshiper." The lectern was an empty dry goods box, the seats were made of scrap wood. Money from the East, local subscriptions, and entertainments, such as an old folks' concert, allowed for modest improvements, including an organ with eight stops.[95]

Finding qualified clergy for the western mission churches was a constant problem, and for nearly six years Tuttle or other clergy visited the struggling Corrine congregation monthly. A resident minister was hired in 1871, but lasted only six months. The Rev. Ballard S. Dunn had a checkered past and a shaky present. Booted out of an Oakland, California, parish, he had previously been a Confederate supporter in Texas and backed an unsuccessful plan to help Southerners emigrate to Brazil. Church attendance was negligible during Dunn's tenure, allowing him time to prospect for gold. "On one occasion only Nat Stein, the local poet, showed up for church, so the Reverend Dunn and Stein retired to the parsonage to pound quartz in a mortar and to test it for gold."[96] The church's statistical report for 1878 listed twelve communicants, one marriage, and offerings of $113. Corrine was becoming a ghost town and the church closed a few years later.[97]

Tuttle was not content to leave St. Mark's as Salt Lake City's only parish. By January 1879 he held Sunday school services in a room of a house on the town's edge. Within a few weeks the numbers stabilized at about forty persons and talk began of building a new church. Land was purchased for

$2,750, and in April 1880, ground was broken for St. Paul's Chapel at the corner of Main Street and 400 South. The church remained there until deconsecrated on Easter Day, March 31, 1918. By then the congregation had moved to a new location on the northeast corner of 300 South and 900 East in the city's expanding suburbs.

The original St. Paul's cornerstone was laid on May 3, 1880, as more than two hundred members of Utah's Masonic lodges gathered in full regalia, preceded by the Camp Douglas regimental band. The Masonic lodges had close connections with the Episcopal and other Protestant churches, and were a source of fellowship for the isolated Gentiles. Most early Episcopal bishops were Masons. Judge Frank Tilford, the Grand Master, delivered an oration and in the cornerstone placed a sealed box containing church and Masonic documents, newspapers, a collection of coins, and a 1879 view of Salt Lake City. A newspaper account said the procession "was decidedly the most imposing and best composed that ever filed through our streets" and the address was "pregnant with thought and abounding in historical facts."[98]

By October 31, 1880, the building that would comfortably seat 230 persons was ready for occupancy. A newspaper account described the striking new "semi-Gothic" building, with its elaborate tower and one-ton bell. California redwood, Cache Valley sandstone, ironwork from Cincinnati and Detroit, and stained glass windows "of the latest modern patterns" from Chicago were among its features. Two stoves, one at each end of the church, would soon be replaced by steam heat. The pulpit, communion table, and chancel chairs were of carved black walnut.

St. Paul's first rector, Samuel Unsworth, was a local resident who had attended St. Mark's School, St. Stephen's College, Annandale, New York, and General Theological Seminary. For the last two years he had worked out of St. Mark's parish, holding Sunday evening services in the Seventh Ward, until St. Paul's was built. The non-LDS *Salt Lake Tribune* writer said Gentiles could take pride in the permanent new church building established "in the heart of a people following the behests of a faith founded in iniquity and contained in corruption," concluding, "The mountains which envision us on all sides, and out of whose bowels the enduring stone was quarried to rear up these emblems of civilization, can echo back the pealing toll of the bells as they summon the worshippers to their devotions."[99]

Tuttle was also responsible for securing a burial place for Protestants. He called the LDS cemeteries "the most forlorn of all forlorn places. . . . The one in Salt Lake was so forbidding a place, without trees or grass, or care, that we all shrank from burying our dead therein."[100] In 1877 George E. Whitney, St. Mark's junior warden and a lawyer, lobbied Congress to grant twenty acres of the Camp Douglas military reservation as a "Gentile" cemetery, to be called Mount Olivet. "Our example shamed the Mormons into taking better care of their own grounds," Tuttle wrote.[101] A second Episcopal cemetery was laid out in Ogden where Gillogly obtained land from the city.

Women in the Early Church in Utah

Women provided much of the church's organizing activity in Utah, although Tuttle gives his name to its founding era, and the sacramental and preaching line was passed on through male priests exclusively until the 1970s. Notwithstanding, almost all the male clergy brought with them wives active as teachers and church organizers in the frontier setting. The women raised money for new buildings, taught Sunday school, prepared the church's altars, visited the sick, and cooked meals for parish gatherings. Meanwhile, a steady stream of female mission teachers, and later deaconesses, came from the East to teach in Utah church schools. Women were the core workers at the new St. Mark's Hospital. Their evangelism was no less real because it was at a hospital bed or in a classroom rather than from a pulpit. From the earliest days, women's names and activities find their places in the reports, often in the "Women's Auxiliary" entries. Beyond the names, numbers, and activity descriptions, we search for accounts that will add flesh to the dry bones of some of the personalities met briefly in such published accounts.

Mrs. William Hamilton presided over music programs at St. Mark's for twenty-six years, and the women of St. Mark's raised money for both a church organ and a rectory, formed several guilds for mutual support, service, and friendship, and in 1883 raised one thousand dollars for the poor. Sometimes their activity reached out of the state; in 1884 Tuttle reported a local branch of the Women's Auxiliary had sent a set of altar linens to a church in Hailey, Idaho, and mailed a box of mission supplies to a new church in North Carolina. Tuttle said, "the women of the church, through its agency, may be cheered in feeling that they are . . . members of one strong body of willing and active workers as extensive as the nation itself."[102]

The isolated Utah women were not alone; a small but effective national office supported them as its means allowed. It was run in New York by two energetic sisters, Julia Emery, who spent twenty-five years there, and Mary Abbot Emery, later Twing, who worked for forty years, cheerfully answering letters, seeking funds, counseling isolated missionaries, and gratefully responding to donors.

Tuttle's reports contain numerous letters expressing thanks to eastern women's groups for Prayer Books, Christmas gifts, and boxes and barrels of educational and medical supplies. A $500 endowment from a woman in Cleveland provided scholarship money for St. Mark's School, and a "lady from Philadelphia and her friends" paid for the episcopal residence in Salt Lake City.[103] Mrs. J. McGraw Fiske of Ithaca, New York, left $10,000, which went to the new Rowland Hall for young women. "The women of the land are particularly interested in this work," Tuttle wrote of the Utah church schools, adding, "A lady gave me $5,000 to begin with. Two other ladies, one in Philadelphia, and one in Boston have sent me each $1,000 for it."[104] And the Mount sisters of New York City generously supported Tuttle's work in Utah.[105]

The historian Mary Donovan has identified seven women workers who played key roles in the Episcopal Church's growth in Utah in 1899, including the principal of Rowland Hall school, the superintendent of St. Mark's Hospital Training School for Nurses, a missionary worker at Whiterocks, the Secretary of the Girls Friendly Society and registrar of the missionary district, and a Salt Lake City missions visitor. A deaconess had spent a summer with the mission, and another was about to start a hospital internship before returning to Utah.[106]

Emily Pearsall Remembered

One of the most active ministries was that of Emily Pearsall, cousin of a junior warden when Tuttle was at Morris, New York. She arrived in Salt Lake City in 1870 and undertook an active pastoral ministry for two years, until her death from cancer on November 5, 1872, at age thirty-eight. What Tuttle wrote of her could have described other women workers as well.[107]

> She came to us in April, 1870. . . . She taught singing and sewing in our St. Mark's school. She had a Bible class for girls one afternoon in the week. She took charge of the host of little ones in the infant class of the Sunday school. Sunday afternoons she went into neglected neighborhoods on the outskirts of the city and held cottage meetings. She was overseer of the homes of the "pensioners" of our Charity Fund. She was the judicious distributor of the contents of our "Clothing-Room," provided from the boxes and barrels kindly sent us from the East. She was a constant visitor among the poor and the families on her carefully-prepared list numbered hundreds. She became known for good over the entire city, and not a few of the sad polygamous women came to her for sympathy and counsel. Sometimes her gentle heart sank for sorrow; often it burned with hot

> indignation over what she heard and saw and knew. Her discreet sense and her untiring patience, however, always kept the way open for her to go whither she would in all the city, among Mormons and Gentiles, on her errands of good. . . . The work of the last month of her life she gave up to our St. Mark's Hospital, as temporary Matron.
>
> For six months a growing tumor had been sapping her life. Night by night, as she expressed it, she was lying down by the side of death. Yet her remarkable cheerfulness never forsook her; and work; and work for others she would busy herself with, if she could lift her finger. She most dreaded the coming of a time when she would be unable to work, and would become a care and burden to others. God saved her from that one dread. He gave her the happiness of dying almost in the midst of working. Not four days from the time that she came from her month's service at the Hospital, He took her unto Himself.
>
> Her home was in my house. Here she died. She suffered excruciating pain at the last, and could not say much to us. But she joined in our prayers for her; and we were kneeling at her bedside, in the Service of the Holy Communion, when she peacefully breathed her last.
>
> Near the time of a glorious sunset of a clear afternoon, we buried her on the hillside of St. Mark's Cemetery. The children, the poor, the sad, the friendless, followed her in large numbers to the grave, and ere we came away we sang the "Gloria in Excelsis," fittest funeral hymn for her.[108]

Pearsall was buried in Mt. Olivet Cemetery. The city's poor contributed pennies for an $80 gravestone and a Pearsall memorial window was installed in St. Mark's Cathedral in 1900, probably made by the renowned Bavarian firm, Franz Mayer of Munich.

We can draw some conclusions about the place of his wife, Harriet, in Tuttle's life and work as well. His letters to her in the original eighteen months they were separated are among his most vivid commentaries, discussing travel, personalities encountered, religious issues faced, and decisions made. Her replies, if they exist, have not been located, but at various places in his *Reminiscences* Tuttle records his close relationship with his wife, who played the organ, led the singing, visited the sick, extended hospitality to visitors, handled her husband's correspondence and business dealings, and was his closest advisor. "If the duties laid upon me have been at all successfully discharged, it has been her wise judgment and rare efficiency and unwearied activity that have made the success due. Justice, at the expense of delicacy, demands this rendering of honor to whom honor is due."[109]

Harriet E. Tuttle headed the Women's Auxiliary in both Utah and later Missouri, wrote for its publications, attended its national meetings, and, through decades of work, knew its national and local leaders. She was president of the Ladies Literary Club of Salt Lake City from 1881 to 1882.[110] She was also the mother of their seven children; a son, Asom Herbert, died in 1917; a daughter, Christine, died in 1922. Two sons outlived their parents, Dr. George Tuttle, who lived in St. Louis, Missouri, and Arthur, a mining engineer, who worked in Mexico. Twins, Katharine and Howard, were born on January 26, 1873, but died within a few months. A daughter, Harriett, was born on March 8, 1872 in Salt Lake City. Tuttle was traveling by train through Wyoming on August 19, 1899, when he received a telegram informing him of his wife's death at age fifty-eight after a short illness. His diary contained a poignant entry:

> My precious, faithful, loving wife. The Holy Spirit helps me. Goodbye till the great Easter Day. May I lose myself in others till I rest by her side. God be merciful to me a sinner. God's sunshine kindly lights up the sand hills as I ride by. I can see them through the tears, and have faith in and recognize his loving mercy. Goodbye! Along these very plains she rode in the stage with me *thirty-one* years ago. God be thanked for her! God mercifully bring me HOME with her by and by.[111]

1886—Departure for Missouri

Once before, on June 1, 1868, shortly after his arrival in Utah, the Diocese of Missouri had elected Tuttle its bishop, but he declined, having just begun his mission in the West. When the second call came on May 26, 1886, Tuttle accepted and left for Missouri in August, satisfied he had done his best in the vast district committed to his care. The numbers had grown gradually during his episcopate and signaled the place the Episcopal Church would have in Utah during the next century, a small, struggling minority of a few thousand persons whose material resources would be minimal as well.[112]

The balance sheet on the Tuttle years was one of steady, incremental growth in a difficult setting, concentrated on parishes in Salt Lake City and key northern towns, plus the cathedral, schools, and hospital. In his final report as missionary bishop, he said that during his nineteen years local churches in the missionary district raised $440,063 for their support and, "through my own hand gifts from the east," an additional $368,102, were raised. By 1886 there were six churches and six clergy. St. Mark's, Salt Lake City, with 265 communicants was the largest parish. St. Paul's Chapel had 59; Good Shepherd, Ogden, 95; St. John's, Logan, 38; St. Paul's, Plain City, 25. Good Samaritan, Corinne, had shrunk to two communicants. In Utah that year there were 100 infant baptisms, 23 adult baptisms, 47 confirmations, 51 marriages, and 60 burials. More than 688 young people attended Sunday schools with 51, while 749 persons attended parish schools, with 29 teachers.[113]

The LDS-owned *Daily Evening News* on August 26, 1886, said of the departing bishop,

> Kind, courteous and urbane, yet dignified and firm in his demeanor, he has made friends among people of various shades of opinion. . . .
>
> Although very pronounced in his opposition to the Mormon faith, he has not acted as an enemy to the Mormon people. So far as we are aware he has not, like many of his cloth, used his ecclesiastical influence towards the oppression and spoliation of the Latter-day Saints, but has on many occasions borne testimony to their good qualities, in public and in private. We respect a consistent antagonist.[114]

It was not a final goodbye; from 1886, when he left for Missouri, until his death on April 17, 1923, Tuttle also served as presiding bishop from 1903 to 1923, a tenure exceeded only by William White, the Episcopal Church's first presiding bishop. Tuttle was a bishop for almost fifty-six years, one of the longest tenures in the history of the Anglican Communion. He was called on several times as temporary administrator of the Missionary District of Utah during episcopal vacancies, or to delegate that role to others. He helped determine the selection of the second bishop, buried the third, worked for the removal of the fourth, and presided over the consecration of the fifth. Daniel S. Tuttle cast a long shadow.

2

Abiel Leonard

The Bishop as Builder

(1888–1903)

> If you succeed in building and maintaining a church here we think you can succeed anywhere.
>
> —resident of Vernal, Utah, to Bishop Leonard

> If you do not receive a reply to your letter within thirty days, you may know that I am absent on a visitation. Always address me at Salt Lake City.
>
> —from Bishop Leonard's letterhead

The nearly sixteen-year, cautious but competent episcopate of Abiel Leonard is bracketed by the more highly visible terms of Daniel S. Tuttle and Franklin Spencer Spalding, two giants of the national church. His role was like appearing in the batting order between Lou Gherig and Babe Ruth. As in the case of Tuttle, another candidate had turned down the missionary bishop's post before it was offered to Leonard, who "was finally prevailed upon to accept the post."[1] Leonard was a hard worker who built nineteen missions and raised $300,000, a substantial feat, for he had neither Tuttle's contacts nor his charisma.

Leonard was born on June 26, 1848, and grew up in Fayette, Missouri, where his father was a state Supreme Court judge, land speculator, and slave owner.[2] A distant relative and namesake served as a chaplain to George Washington in the American Revolution. On his mother's side, Leonard was descended from Connecticut Congregationalists. From Fayette days he developed a lifelong friendship with Ethelbert Talbot, later missionary bishop of Wyoming and Idaho, bishop of Central Pennsylvania for thirty years, and, briefly, presiding bishop after Tuttle's death. Mrs. Leonard and Mrs. Talbot were friends, "and many a time the two little babies were rocked by the same old black mammy in the same cradle," the *Salt Lake Utah Herald* reported at Leonard's death.[3]

The future bishop graduated from Dartmouth College in 1870 and from General Theological Seminary in 1873. After eight years in the Diocese of Missouri as rector of Calvary Church, Sedalia, and Trinity Church, Hannibal, he moved to Atchison, Kansas, as rector of Trinity Church, where he stayed for seven years. His wife, Flora Terry, came from Sedalia, and the couple had five children. An unsuccessful candidate in the election for bishop of Missouri (he lost to Tuttle), he was named a missionary bishop at age thirty-nine, most likely with the support of Tuttle. Consecrated bishop in St. Louis, Missouri, on January 25, 1888, by Tuttle and several other bishops, Leonard's vast missionary district was realigned in 1895, making him bishop of Nevada, Utah, and Western Colorado. Realigned once more in October 1898 and now called the Missionary District of Salt Lake, it still included slices of Nevada, Colorado, and Wyoming. Leonard in 1900 described his territory as "one of the most extensive and difficult in the American church."[4]

The bishop was often on the move, sometimes by train, but mostly by stagecoach. Once while visiting the mining town of Eureka, Nevada, he held a service on the second floor of a saloon when a bullet whizzed through the floor not far from his feet. His letterhead contained a printed reminder, "If you do not receive a reply to your letter within thirty days, you may know that I am absent on a visitation. Always address me at Salt Lake City." In his 1902 report he wrote,

> Last year I traveled 20,000 miles of which 12,000 were traveled in the district, and 1000 of those miles were made by stage, and this means a great consumption of time. As a result I am away from Salt Lake three-fourths of the time, and it is not unusual to be away three or four weeks at a time. A man with young children would need to become acquainted with his children after each of such trips. One of my own children, when very young, wanted to know after I returned from a long trip, "Whether I would remain to lunch."[5]

Three types of communities existed in late-nineteenth-century Utah, Leonard believed: mining towns, with a ready clientele for the church and money to support it; railroad towns, which were unstable because the work force moved frequently; and agricultural communities, filled with poor farmers trying to establish themselves in new places. The scattered farm communities would be attracted to the church, but rural churches had few prospects of self-sufficiency. He avoided work in large LDS-dominated communities, focusing instead on mixed urban centers like Salt Lake City and Ogden, and on the church's schools and hospital, which he continued to enlarge.

Elsewhere Leonard wrote in *The Spirit of Missions,* the church's monthly missionary magazine, "We are far away in these mountains, far from the great centers of wealth, influence, and learning. The people who have come hither are those who have come to regain their health in this invigorating climate; poor people, having no capital, who have come where they fancy that opportunities are more numerous; or young people first setting out in life. There are few conventionalities, and the moral tone is not so high as in more settled communities. Mining is, of course, the great industry."[6]

Leonard was far more cautious than Tuttle and had fewer resources and contacts. "My own policy has always been to be exceedingly careful about going into any of these towns to do missionary work," he wrote. Sometimes opportunities were lost because "we did not know in which way to turn to secure the proper missionary, or to find some needed money with which to support him."[7] The adjective "sober" fits Leonard's character. He was exacting on clergy and parishes. Stingy giving by parishes and the lack of motivation by clergy, he said, makes "us all hang our heads with shame," adding, "Let us remember that our first duty is to the great church; that to her we owe our highest allegiance, and that when we have discharged this duty we may rightly consider lesser claims."[8]

His comments on public issues were rare, though in 1903 he did send a letter to Rabbi Louis G. Reynolds of Salt Lake City. Leonard was unable to attend a meeting where Russian persecution of Jews was discussed, but remarked, "I should certainly desire to be counted at all times as on the side of fair and righteous dealings, and if any word of mine could be helpful in such a cause, I should be glad to speak it."[9]

Leonard was temperate in his infrequent remarks on the Latter-day Saints. Several anti-LDS organizations, such as the New Movement for the Redemption of Utah and the Overthrow of Mormonism, tried to enlist the bishop's support, but he dodged them. In a state of 275,000 persons, 200,000 of whom were Latter-day Saints, he told a colleague, "It has never been our custom to antagonize the Mormons. . . . I do not see how we could accomplish any good results by so doing. I think they respect us as much, if not more, than any other religious body. Of course, they do not love us any too much and would prefer our room to our company, but as long as there must be other people here, I think they look kindly upon us."[10]

Utah wrestled with several acute political issues with moral implications in the 1890s. A public school system for Salt Lake City had been voted down in 1874; the LDS Church issued a decree renouncing plural marriages on September 28, 1890, and on January 4, 1896, statehood came to Utah. But harsh memories lingered on of the federal government's restrictive policies toward the former territory. The presence of large concentrations of military troops was a powerful reminder of the government's force, as were the numerous anti-Mormon and anti-polygamy bills passed by Congress, and threats of voter disenfranchisement, property confiscation, and prison sentences were real.[11]

New Churches, Problems with Clergy, Leonard as Administrator

Twelve Utah parishes existed at the beginning of the twentieth century, but only the four longest-established ones had full-time clergy, only one of whom had been in Utah more than three years. The 1902 annual report listed 375 communicants at St. Mark's Cathedral and 275 at St. Paul's Chapel, Salt Lake City, and 137 at Good Shepherd, Ogden. The total number of Utah communicants was 916 persons.[12] Leonard also had responsibility for seventeen other parishes in Nevada, Wyoming, and Colorado, which took up much of his time.

Money was tight in Utah, and in 1901 the church's missionary budget was $100,000 short of its national goal. Notwithstanding the severe financial situation, the bishop edged ahead. Properties were secured in Provo, where services had probably been held in a store building on Center Street since 1892, and Springville, as was a site for a new mission in the southern part of Salt Lake City. Congregations were formed in Layton and Eureka, a growing mining town. The Rev. O. E. Ostenson in 1901 began work in Vernal, a town of six hundred persons in northeastern Utah. Services were initially held in Jake Workman's Opera House, where the proprietor was pleased to lend his premise to the new church because "Episcopals were ladies and gentlemen and didn't spit all over the floor."[13] A local person had told the bishop, "If you succeed in building and maintaining a church here we think you can succeed anywhere."[14]

A new congregation, St. Luke's, was organized in the wide-open mining town of Park City in 1888. A women's guild and a Brotherhood of St. Andrew's chapter did much of the preparatory work, and in 1889 a small wooden church was constructed on Park Avenue. An 1889 article in *Church Notes* stated,

> About nine days ago a poor man was found dead on the mountains near here, having committed suicide while insane it is supposed. The

> members of St. Andrew's Society raised money enough to bury him and took charge of the funeral. The church service was read at Lawrence's Hall, and the young men accompanied the body to the grave. An ice cream and strawberry festival, held last week under the auspices of the St. Andrew's Society and the Guild of Willing Hands, cleared $106 for the widow and children of the poor lunatic.[15]

The Park City church led a tenuous existence until destroyed in a June 1898 fire that burned down much of the town. Determined church members met in the City Hall, began rebuilding, and replaced the structure in 1901. A pot-bellied stove by the pulpit provided heat.

Two other small Salt Lake City churches were built in Leonard's time. St. Peter's Chapel was constructed in 1891 on the grounds of St. Mark's hospital as a chapel for hospital patients and staff, and as a neighborhood church. St. John's Chapel was opened in 1890 at 900 East and Logan Avenue. Previously, the congregation had met in a nearby barn, but a plain wooden building was constructed, followed by a chapel that could comfortably seat forty persons. Both churches never grew; St. John's was closed in the early 1940s and St. Peter's a decade later.

His voluminous correspondence shows Utah's second bishop to be a patient, detail-oriented administrator. Leonard worked hard, reflecting in 1900, "I have not been away from my work for two years, with the exception of a few weeks last Fall when I was well nigh broken down. I expect therefore to spend two months in the East this winter."[16] Frustration pervades his reports; money problems were endemic, progress slow, and clergy and some laity were only partially responsive to the bishop. Many of his letters thank a donor for a dollar, or move small sums of money about to pay for a church property or a building improvement. As other bishops would, he urged clergy to pay their personal debts, about which he sometimes received letters from creditors. Leonard also reminded the clergy that collections taken during his visitations should be added to the bishop's discretionary fund.

> Let the people be taught to feel that they have a distinct and definite interest in the bishop as an individual, and in the personal work which he may be called to do. . . . We feel very sure that if this thought were presented to the people, and commented upon from time to time, a decided interest in the matter would be awakened.[17]

The extensive Leonard correspondence provides insights into clergy personnel conditions in the huge new missionary district, reflecting difficulties missionary bishops faced. It was hard to recruit and retain qualified clergy for the poorly paying, isolated churches, and attending to those in need of financial or medical attention was a reoccurring problem. The rector of St. Paul's Chapel, Salt Lake City, Ellis Bishop, had resigned because "he could not stand the strain upon his nervous system made by the high altitude of this intermountain region" and another clergy left to "go for the winter to a warmer climate in Texas."[18] Once Leonard wrote, "Our western work has suffered greatly in the past from untrained and tactless men. So far as I am concerned, I am disposed to cover a few places well with good men, rather than spend time, money and strength with men who are utterly unfit to cope with our Western work."[19]

Leonard was solicitous of his more able clergy. When he heard that O. E. Ostenson, who had built up the church in Vernal, was traveling to Salt Lake City, he wrote, "I would suggest that if the train is late you had better stay all night at Price and come down on the morning train. Even when the train is on time it is almost midnight when it gets here. Telegraph me from Price when to expect you, and if I am not at the train, come right up to the house. If you have time in Price call on Judge [William H.] Frye who, although not a churchman is interested in our services. Mr. McDonald the Station Agent is a Knight Templar."[20]

While most of his letters were guarded, sometimes Leonard's enthusiasm for a prospective hire crept through. He told one candidate, "I want you because I feel that you would be such a strength to the work, not only at St. Paul's but throughout the jurisdiction. I want all the strong men that I can find to lean upon. One thing it seems to me which should commend this work is that it is not finished, but just in that condition where a good, earnest and industrious man can make a wonderful impression."[21] Some placements did not work out, as in this letter from Leonard to another bishop:

> The writer is not of course a first-class man. If he were I should not be disposed to let him go. He is as men go an average sort of a person, a man I should judge of about fifty years of age. He is inoffensive, does not make any trouble, and gets along well with people. He is in no sense attractive, but if you have some quiet country work where people do not demand too much, he will get along very well. To succeed in this part of the world, one must be very active, and have some ability as a preacher as well as an organizer. . . . I should be very glad if you could give him something, and I do not want you to feel that I am trying to push off on you a man who is utterly worthless. That is not by any means the case.[22]

At the same time, he wrote directly to the minister in Provo about problems with his performance:

> I am in a good deal of a quandary about you. I must speak very frankly to you and say the people do not want you to return to Springville and Provo. They say that your voice is weak and that they can't hear what you have to say. They also criticize your untidy appearance in dress. You know that I told you a year ago I could only pay you a stipend of five hundred dollars and that the balance of the support must come from the people. I am satisfied that you would get nothing there. Then as a further complication you have applied to Bishop Hare for work saying that you do not like Utah, and that you want to go East, and so on and so forth. Under all these circumstances it seems useless for you to go back to Springville and Provo and stay there a little while, and then when I cannot get anyone else to pull up stakes and go away.[23]

Not all of his clergy encounters went smoothly. In 1902 he noted relations between bishop and rector in Ogden had cooled, and ties between "the bishop and his clergy and the several congregations ought to be of the most affectionate and loyal character. I am not aware that I have done anything to cause these relations to be otherwise. To be perfectly frank, I have felt that there has not been entire frankness displayed with me in the conduct of the work." [24] Relations were no better at the cathedral. "Bishop Leonard's work was always handicapped by the trouble he had with the Rector of St. Mark's," George C. Hunting, superintendent of St. Mark's Hospital observed.[25]

In another situation, Leonard demonstrated touching pastoral care for one of two alcoholic clergy. Seeking help from the bishop of Pennsylvania, he wrote,

> I have a young clergyman who has a terrible inheritance. His mother and grandfather I am told died of delirium tremens. . . . The young man of whom I speak seems to have inherited this terrible tendency. I need hardly say that he has made a sad fall. He seems penitent enough and willing to make amends. . . . What to do is the thing which perplexes me. He has no money nor have I. He should be in a sanitarium under constant restraint for several months. I do not like to let go of him for this means the destruction of a human soul. It is not a time for me to lecture him because he is not in a physical condition to appreciate what I might say. I think I have said enough to show you what a sad case this is. Now to the point. Is there any church institution in or about Philadelphia where such a man could be treated?[26]

Neither Tuttle's lucidity nor Spalding's intellectual flare were in Leonard's makeup. The bishop was a steady, consistent person of uncomplicated faith, always using capital letters when typing GOD, and rarely showing any emotion except profound sadness once at the death of his son, and frustration when he temporarily lost the use of an eye. He was an almost Dickensian accountant in the keeping of records, and it frustrated him that clergy did not do likewise, so he could compile accurate church statistics. "I cannot speak in too strong terms about this matter. It puts your bishop in an uncomfortable position—he appears to be derelict in his own duty, when in reality the fault lies with those who have been so careless in the preparation of their own reports."[27]

A typical entry (September 22, 1899) describes the financial problems he faced. "I as bishop of Salt Lake am borrowing $1,000 from the Utah National Bank. . . . On October 15 I shall probably be compelled to borrow $3,000 and pay up everything. I shall consolidate all I borrowed and give a note for six months. My plan is to give the bank a check on deposit for $4,000 my wife and I have in the Deseret Savings Bank . . . and then I shall have to [word unintelligible] this amount from church people and pay it off little by little. What a shame that a bishop should be compelled to do this by carrying on work which other religious people do so cheerfully. I pray GOD to send new friends to help carry [this] important work."[28]

Elsewhere, Leonard sought such economies as he could find. "I told Mr. Kinney [in Eureka] the other day the Baptists might use our building on any occasion which did not conflict with our own plans for holding services, and that they might pay for the use of it of $1.25 for each and every occasion, payment to be made to you. It was further agreed between us that if by reason of the increased number of services the electric light bill should be increased, they would have to stand the additional expenses."[29]

Each year the bishop was given a complimentary railroad pass, which he had to apply for in person. He wrote a Wall Street banker whom he knew, "I want to get a pass over both the Union Pacific and the Southern Pacific from Ogden to San Francisco, as I have for a good many years. I should very much prefer to get them in New York if possible, than to approach the local people here in the West. My duty as bishop takes me over both roads; I have been able to make some traffic for the roads as I have built up congregations along the way. If you happen to know Mr. E. H. Harriman I should be very glad if you can help me in these two directions."[30]

On June 21, 1898, in response to the state's newly enacted civil code, Leonard filed an Articles of Incorporation of the Corporation of the Episcopal Church in Utah. The seven-member Corporation was headed by the bishop and was allowed purchase and sell property. At least three members must be laity. Trustees held three-year terms and were bonded for $500 each.[31]

Few comments about liturgical matters were touched on in his writings. Once he noted that recent Prayer Book revisions allowed for Morning Prayer, the Litany, and Holy Communion to be distinct and separate services, but that some parishes were neglecting one or another of the services, and not properly observing a rubric in the communion rite where "there are distinct directions as to when the Commandments may be omitted and how often the long exhortation of the communion office shall be read."[32]

"I do not myself object to a somewhat ornate service," he wrote a perspective applicant for St. Paul's, Salt Lake City. "We have nothing advanced in this whole jurisdiction." The cathedral had a mixed choir of men, women, and boys, communion at an early Sunday service, and on holy days and Friday mornings at eleven o'clock. "There are two eucharistic lights, wafer bread made here in the city, and a mixed chalice, although there is no ceremony attending to any of these things. St. Paul's has substantially the same things. The people there, however, do not care anything for the lights and I have thought myself that I would remove them before the next rector came."[33] Elsewhere, Leonard advised a publisher of church books to prepare a compact prayer book and hymnal for mission use, one lightweight enough for a bishop to carry a hundred copies by stagecoach.[34] Rubrics could be avoided, a single short canticle should suffice after each lesson, and "the service of baptism for infants is more important than the burial of the dead." Episcopalians could never agree on a list of hymns, and Leonard weighed in, stating "not more than 16 of the 53 hymns which you have are such that people whom we ordinarily meet can sing. I have pinned in the book a list of the hymns which it seems to me are more suitable for mission purposes."

The cornerstone for a new St. Mark's Hospital at 200 West and 800 North was laid on July 31, 1892, and the building was completed in July 1893, where it stayed until 1978. The location's advantage was its closeness to the Wasatch Hot Springs in an era when hydrotherapy was widely used. Mrs. Leonard lent $10,000 for construction costs of the three-story Victorian structure. By 1893 it had treated 6,251 cases, including 2,900 of lead poisoning, 667 various injuries, 344 cases of inflammatory rheumatism, 152 of typhoid, 128 of syphilis, 63 of alcoholism, 58 of pneumonia, 52 of tuberculosis, and 35 of gunshot wounds.[35]

St. Mark's 30 to 35 beds soon proved too small, and additional wings were added in 1896 and 1903, giving the hospital a 125-bed capacity, making it equal to its rival, Holy Cross Roman Catholic Hospital. An isolation ward was added, as was a laboratory and a steam sterilizer, plus a microscope and an x-ray machine, both representing new technologies. Once the rope-operated elevator to the third floor operating room broke, dropping a patient to the basement, so for several years patients were carried to and from the operating room by stretcher, tilted awkwardly to a near-vertical position. In 1894 a two-year training school for nurses was launched. The original female nursing students were also a source of cheap domestic labor, doing much of the hospital's janitorial work, while living in the crowded hospital basement. By 1907 a new home housing thirty-five nurses was opened, named for Bishop Leonard.[36]

St. Mark's School was closed in 1894, two years before Utah achieved statehood, but Rowland Hall remained open, offering one of the few possibilities in the region for young women to achieve an education. "A typewriting machine [has been moved into the Hall], and eight of the young ladies are learning the beautiful and accuracy-teaching art," a 1888 school publication stated. Elsewhere, it said "the angular hand seems to have come to stay, and is taught in all female schools of reputation. No lady of the present day can afford to write in the old-fashioned round hand." Science laboratories, a gymnasium, and a chapel were added to the school. Both music and French were taught, and the building consisted of a large house set on spacious grounds with a drawing room, library, two classrooms, dining room, kitchen, and upstairs bedrooms. By 1901 the school housed 50 boarders and nearly 150 day students; a gift of $30,000 from Pittsburgh industrialist Felix R. Brunot allowed the building of additional classroom space.[37]

Women, 1889—The Three-Woman Delegation from St. John's, Logan Is Denied Seating at Convocation

Several women were active in paid institutional ministry positions in Utah during Leonard's time: as teachers, nurses, city missionaries, and missionaries to Native Americans. Sarah J. Elliott, a deaconess, worked at Rowland Hall. In his 1899 report, Leonard noted that her earlier missionary work in Moab included gathering, at her own expense, a Sunday school of eighty pupils.[38] Fannie D. Lees of St. Paul's chapel had just graduated from the deaconess training school in Philadelphia and was now in a hospital training program before returning to St. Mark's Hospital, where she would assume a leadership role. Her sister, Nellie Lees, worked for the church for a year, claiming the salary eventually destined for Fannie on her return. Lucy Nelson Carter had completed six months with a hospital in Virginia before resuming work with the Utes at Whiterocks, where she stayed for many years. Grace D. Wetherbee of New York City had spent a summer working with Carter and the Native Americans, and Ellen Lees had been busy as a city missioner in Salt Lake City, dividing her time between the cathedral, St. Paul's chapel, and St. Peter's mission, which St. Paul's supported from 1890–1989.[39]

In 1889, three women delegates were elected to the missionary district's convocation from St. John's, Logan, but were denied seating. Their presence was not dealt with directly. A motion was made that the Report of the Committee on Credentials be referred back to that group with instructions that the name of the Logan delegates be stricken from the roll on account of ineligibility.[40] Women did the work of the church, but it would take almost a century for them to be given formal status as convocation delegates, then as lay readers and chalicists, and eventually as priests and bishops.

Native American Policy: "To Elevate the Red Man"

Native American hunters and gatherers roamed the state and beyond in the early nineteenth century, but newly arrived Mormon settlers steadily pushed them away from more desirable lands, especially in the state's fertile plains and valleys. Indigenous peoples fought back or made treaties, which were systematically broken by settlers and the U. S. Government. Agents appointed to protect Native American interests were mostly low-level politicians who used their positions to acquire choice land for themselves. Hiring relatives as teachers, padding pay rolls, and favoring the white business community were their stock in trade. Most were powerless or little inclined to defend the Native Americans in land disputes or other conflicts, such as when LDS farmers strung up wire fences to keep Native American herds from encroaching on newly claimed farms.

On the eastern Utah reservations the Utes constituted three bands, the White Rivers, the Uintahs, and the Uncompahgres. The Utes, who had once ranged widely through the eastern Great Basin, the Colorado Plateau, and the Rocky Mountains in search of food and trade, were mobile, and their flexible social system could adapt to both times of deprivation and plenty. A family might hunt with other bands in the summer in the mountains, descend to the forests and plateau valleys to gather nuts and seeds in the fall, spend the winter in less harsh lands, and resume fishing in streams or lakes during the spring. Utes thus traversed wide territories, without rigid boundaries, while living in close symbiosis with the land, its seasons, and resources.[41] At times Utes formed larger groups for warfare, hunting, or, in spring, for social and ritual interaction. Ute society was versatile and unencumbered. The dead were quickly buried in rock crevices, their possessions buried with them, given away, or burned. Skin teepees or bush dwellings were burned as well as a way to avoid ghost sickness.

Indigenous populations were declining precipitously. The intrusion of white settlers worked swift consequences on Native Americans. Population estimates are difficult to come by, but in 1859 the number of Utah Utes may have been forty-five hundred; by 1877 it was estimated at eight hundred.[42] A Colorado Ute described the situation, most likely in the 1860s:

> Longtime ago, Utes always had plenty. On the prairie, antelope and buffalo, so many Ouray can't count. In the mountains, deer and bear, everywhere. In the streams, trout, duck, beaver, everything. Good Manitou gave all to Red Man; Utes happy all year. White man came, and now Utes go hungry a heap. Game much go every year—hard to shoot now. Old man often weak for want of food. Squaw and papoose cry. Only strong brave live. White man grow a heap; Red man no grow—soon die all.[43]

It was in such a setting that Tuttle, who rarely commented on Native American affairs, in 1877 recommended that the Indian Bureau be turned over the War Department, where the Office of Indian Affairs had been before 1849, and which attracted higher-quality officers. Tuttle wrote from Montana, "the Indians are cheated, maltreated, and exasperated, and the settlers and soldiers pay the penalty with their lives. Deeper and deeper is my conviction that, for this far western region, the best practical reform is to turn over the Indian Bureau to the War Department. . . . The Indians [would] be treated with fairness now to them unknown and the missionaries, coworking with the military, would greatly reduce the provocations to warfare."[44]

The forced removal of the Uncompahgre Utes from western Colorado to eastern Utah took place in 1882. The Bureau of Indian Affairs opened a school at Randlett, four miles south of Fort Duchesne, but it was never used, as there was no water supply near the school site, which was then moved to Whiterocks. Colonel J. F. Randlett, post commandant and acting Indian agent, was an active Episcopalian, and in 1894 invited Archdeacon Frederick W. Crook to hold the first service at Fort Duchesne. Crook wrote,

> On Sunday, a most unique service was held in one of the large rooms. To the left sat a group of colored United States soldiers; in the center were the children of the Indian school, surrounded by bucks and squaws, with little papooses done up in those odd baby spoons, or baskets, clad in every variety, from buckskin to the vari-colored and thin calico, such as contractors only know how to sell. Around the priest were the white employees, with only a few people from the Mormon settlement, present at the agency on trade, and attracted by the novelty. Six nationalities were represented.[45]

Government and missionary policy was to "civilize" Native Americans by forcing hunters and gatherers to become farmers. Its immediate goal was "to get the Indians out of the blanket and into trousers—and trousers with a pocket in them and with a <u>pocket that aches to be filled with dollars</u>" [underlining in the original]. Forcing mobile hunters to become settled farmers had devastating effects on Native American life and culture.[46] White settlers and missionaries equated hunting—as a way of life—with savagery. They believed the only successful future for Native Americans would come from ownership of small individual plots of land. Standard 160-acre farm allotments thus became the basic Native American settlement, allowing the government to open the remaining reservation lands for exploitation in 1905. Yet, of all employment possibilities, the least successful option to offer Native Americans as a ticket into a new world was the struggling isolated farm. The land was poor and the distance required to transport crops to railroads was an insurmountable barrier. A special agent described the Uintah reservation's small farms. They were "blending so quietly with nature itself, that the line of separation seems really blurred and lost." A farm was a "few acres fenced, right in the open meadow, closely surrounded and hemmed in by a rich green sward—the whole family at work or play in the corn, potatoes, peas, and beans, children, babies and all. . . . Their greatest happiness is in the complete domestic circle that is their greatest comfort—often the only one."[47]

The subsequent story of Native American–white relations is one of continued mistrust, sharply decreasing indigenous numbers, and further loss of land. Gilsonite, used in the manufacture of paints, gypsum, and asphalt, was discovered in the southern part of the reservation in 1885, and in 1887 Congress passed the General Allotment Act, which broke up reservations and gave miners and ranchers access to Native American lands.[48] In the mid-1880s the reservations encompassed about four million acres, but by 1909 they were reduced to about 360,000 acres, of which the Utes' allotments totaled about 250,000 acres.[49] Native Americans received small annual payments of money and food in exchange for land, but to collect payment had to register with non–Native American names recognizable to agency clerks. Thus Native Americans were given names like Evangeline, Charles Dickens, Uriah Heep, and David Copperfield when the agents's ideas ran low.[50] Annuities were quickly spent, often on cheap liquor, and alcoholism was added to the reservation's medical problems.

Episcopal Church work among Native Americans began in Leonard's time. Despite Tuttle's labors as a builder of the church in the West, he never commenced work among Native Americans and they are rarely spoken of in his extensive writings. It would be far easier to find clergy and money to build churches and schools in growing frontier towns than to engage in a ministry among the even more isolated indigenous peoples. In his *Quarterly Message,* a printed local church publication, of September 1893, Leonard noted that a government Indian school had been opened and an active church member was employed by it. Two planned government boarding schools would house seventy-five and forty children, respectively. Native Americans were not admitted to white schools in that era. In 1894 he wrote, "There are probably 5,000 Indians in the Missionary Jurisdiction of Nevada and Utah. I have never sought an opportunity to do any missionary work among them for the very excellent reason that I have had neither the man nor the means to carry out the work. . . . Will you not help us to elevate the Red Man?" he asked, in a fundraising appeal for $3,000 to build a chapel and mission house.[51] A parcel of land was assigned by Randlett, and in 1895 Leonard raised $2,500 to build the Church of the Holy Spirit and a mission house. Native Americans initially feared the schools as sources of diseases for which they had no natural immunity. A 1901 measles epidemic at Whiterocks killed seventeen out of sixty-five students; other outbreaks were less severe, but equally frightening to the local people.[52]

Congress decreed that different reservations should select different churches for religious and educational work. The Utes on the Uintah reservation picked the Episcopal Church, most likely on the advice of Colonel Randlett. From 1896 to 1898 George S. Vest, the first Episcopal minister to the Utes, was stationed at Holy Spirit Mission, Leland, on the reservation. Then, in 1899, he established St. Elizabeth's Mission at Whiterocks, where a church was built in 1904.[53] In 1901 Leonard asked Bishop Henry Y. Satterlee of Washington, D. C., to contact the Commissioner of Indian Affairs and request that an out-of-state, non-Mormon, non-polygamous Indian Agent be appointed in Utah. Leonard knew such political appointments were usually local payoffs, and said "the Indians do not fare any too well because of this constant meddling with the Indian Department on the part of local people."[54] Leonard would not publicly criticize policies or employees of the Bureau of Indian Affairs. When Lucy N. Carter wrote him from the reservation about a local dispute with the Bureau, he said he did not "think it is wise for our missionaries to interfere with government business. . . . If you missionaries incur the ill-will of the government employees on the Reservation they can make life a burden for you and our work a drag."[55] On the same day he wrote an episcopal colleague, complaining that too often the government employees were unfit for work, but regretting the disposition of missionaries to criticize them. "My advice to our workers is, to keep to themselves as much as possible and in all things to keep their own counsel, and under no circumstances to antagonize any of them. In a difficulty between these employees to be entirely neutral. To make them feel we are trying to cooperate with them in doing all that the government requires."[56]

In 1901 the bishop appealed to eastern contributors. "Will you not all feel a disposition to right, in some measure, some of the wrongs which we have done to the Red Man in the past by giving him a place in your interest and affections for the future?" At the same time, he wrote the commandant at Whiterocks: "We are simply trying to supplement the work of the government and doing only such things as the government is not able to do."[57] He told the commanding general of the U. S. Army, "I am cooperating with the Indian Department in every way that I can in the effort to civilize the Indians." Then he asked for commissary privileges for the newly arrived resident missionary, M. J. Hersey, since "the nearest general supply store is six or seven miles away, and it is inadequately supplied with goods for family use."[58]

Milton J. Hersey became the lead missionary to the Utes in 1898. A grocer from Washington State and a self-educated lay preacher, Hersey spent two years as a lay missionary in Arizona before coming to Utah. Ordained a deacon in 1901 following a study course with Bishop Leonard, he was made a priest in 1909 by Bishop Spalding. Hersey (1866–1948) and his wife Ruby (1869–1916), until her death of cancer, were tireless workers in northeastern Utah, where Hersey was elected in 1908 as president of the Colorado Park Irrigation Company. He actively supported public health improvements, as well. The missionary worked equally among the white and Native American communities. For the whites he was a circuit rider, making the long trek from Vernal to Whiterocks, Fort Duchesne, and Randlett. Eventually the dirt roads were paved, and finally in 1916 a "machine," as automobiles were called, replaced Hersey's horse and buggy. By 1919 the "Victory Highway," later Route 40, was built, reducing distances further.

Hersey worked hard. If someone was ill or dying, Hersey and his wife were among the first to arrive with food. One visitor to the mission in 1907 wrote, "It may be that a squaw is dying of old age and she is beyond any aid of medical science. Whose business is it? Mr. Hersey's, of course. Carry her to the hospital where she is washed, clothed, fed and cared for by Mr. and Mrs. Hersey, as a matter of course. If she dies, Mr. Hersey with his own hands makes her coffin, places her in it, and buries her with the rites of the church in consecrated ground."[59]

Money for reservation work was hard to come by, and life was difficult for missionaries. Mrs. Hersey was pleased to be finally living in an actual wooden house, "How delightful it is to sleep in the pleasant, airy room with two windows and a transom." The furnishings included a large dry goods box turned into a sideboard and another box which became a bookcase, covered with red cotton flannel and decorated with local artifacts.

A valuable contributor to mission work was Lucy Nelson Carter, who had come to Whiterocks from Virginia in 1896, and who spent thirty-four years working with Native Americans. Shortly after arriving at the reservation at age thirty-one, Carter bought a pony and began visiting nearby camps, teaching a few words of English to women and children, and urging them to wash their faces and braid their hair. Katherine Murray, a Boston teacher and nurse, joined Carter and began a Bible class for children.[60] In 1903, Carter wrote, construction would soon begin on a small house-infirmary. To save money, the bathroom and running water had been removed from the plans, and the women found "carrying water into the house a very severe task, and what we shall do when there are several more babies and patients to take care of I don't know," wrote Carter.[61]

The plan was to build St. Elizabeth's Mission House and Hospital, and Carter, who had no special training in mission work, returned to her native Virginia for a six-month course in nursing. Once back on the reservation she shoveled rubbish from a room in an old building, evicted rats, and stayed there until the new St. Elizabeth's was finished in August 1903. Soon she was called "Mother to the Ute babies" for caring for abandoned Native American infants. Carter recalled taking a sick child whose mother had died into the mission house. "This baby lived long enough—eight months—to take such a place in my heart that there was no more room for loneliness, and to leave such a void when she died, that I was tempted to give the work up and go somewhere else. But afterward I felt that I did the right thing in staying."[62]

The new facility contained three bedrooms for the missionaries and six beds in a ward for the sick, plus an operating room. Carter remarked, "The first night I slept in my pleasant, airy room, a *real* room, not a stuffy cubby-hole, it seemed so delightful; and when the first storm with pouring rain beat upon the windows, we sat and looked at it with so much satisfaction, knowing that it would not come in, either under the door or through the roof."[63]

In 1903, Carter wrote an article in *The Spirit of Missions* about East Wind and Red Moon, two orphans whom the missionaries informally adopted. She claimed that, when a local mother died, the baby was often buried alive, and that the indigenous belief was the mother's spirit would not be happy until the baby's spirit joined it.[64] Several such abandoned infants were left with the missionaries.

Katherine Murray, who spent 1903–1905 at the mission, had been a teacher and a nurse in the Boston slums for seven years, and later attended the Boston City Hospital Training School. Her reports chronicle a patient struggle to overcome hardships, including isolation and below-zero temperatures for much of the winter. She poignantly described carrying water from a distant brook in winter, and breaking pond ice with an axe. Ill children stayed with her, as did women beaten by drunken husbands, and she and Lucy Carter brought food to the sick, dressed wounds, and attended to numerous young males who had fallen from horses and broken or fractured bones. In 1904 she wrote,

> The Bible class is in a more promising state now than it has been. It has seemed to be in a dying condition. Some evenings I have had only a single listener. It is now so flourishing that I am thankful God gave me courage to hold to my purpose. We have the beginning of a chapel, the lumber, and some money. I long to see it rise and hope someday a good missionary will stand at its altar and make a fight against the terrible gambling and drinking which goes on in this place. The Indians cannot be helped until the white men are stopped.[65]

Religious education was segregated at the mission station: Native Americans met with Carter in the morning, and children of the reservation and fort employees with Murray in the afternoon. Mothers met each week for Bible study and sewing; seventeen children gathered for a Missionary Society, and the community gradually raised $20 for the mission nursery. Both women often visited nearby camps on horseback.[66] Rosa Camfield, an Englishwoman, followed Katherine Murray and worked in various locations—Whiterocks, Randlett, or Vernal—until her death in 1935.[67] In 1907 she described the mission's western plains Gothic church that could seat fifty people, with its twelve clear glass windows, and packing box altar covered by a white cloth. She and Carter were busy at Christmas preparing both white and Native American children to sing and appear in plays.[68]

If information on women missionaries is hard to come by, more scarce is information about women Indian leaders. Once such figure was Chipeta, wife of the Uncompahgre Chief Ouray at Leland. She was reputed to be the only woman allowed to attend tribal meetings, supported the mission, knew the bishop, and was buried in an Episcopal funeral at her death in 1924.

Dead at Age Fifty-Six

On December 3, 1903, Bishop Leonard died from typhoid fever after an illness of three weeks. Before the funeral, clergy in full vestments stood watch around the clock by the open casket in the cathedral, changing every three hours. Local newspapers enjoyed writing about Episcopal ceremonies, which were more colorful than LDS rituals. A newspaper included in its account: "White plumes and dark sashes of Knights Templar, with Masonic aprons, white and purple or white and black surplices of the clergy, choir boys clad in white and black, nurses in their uniforms and caps, banks of wondrous flowers, candles on the altar, a sorrowing multitude that packed St. Mark's Cathedral, a huge purple casket with a palm laid upon it. . . . The whole front of the church was banked with flowers. . . . The bishop's chair, at the left of the altar, was covered with purple velvet, palms, and violets."[69] The value of Leonard's estate at probate was $3,000 left to his wife, and a dollar to each of his five children.

Bishop Tuttle returned from St. Louis to bury his successor, but the train was late, so he headed by streetcar through the snow to Mt. Olivet Cemetery to read the committal service instead.[70] Both Masonic and Episcopal services were held at the grave site, and the three Utah clergy pallbearers present were all master masons.[71]

What is the balance sheet on Leonard's almost sixteen years in Utah? When the bishop arrived, there were four resident clergy in the state and four in Nevada. He started and maintained nineteen missions during his years in the West, and raised over $300,000. Leonard baptized over 3,500 persons and confirmed over 1,800. Both Rowland Hall and St. Mark's Hospital were expanded during his tenure. More than $25,000 was expended on new buildings for the school, and a new hospital was built, accommodating 125 patients. St. Mark's Cathedral was enlarged.[72] Working within the parameters of his time, Leonard did his best with Native American work. Having few resources at his disposal, he aligned himself with the government, hoping that better-quality administrators and teachers would be sent to the reservations. He did not take a public stand in defense of Native Americans; that would have been inconsistent with his temperament and out of character with the Episcopal Church in that age. A newspaper editorial called Leonard "kind and charitable to all" and "an efficient worker and a highly revered friend," adding, "We cannot recall any of his public utterances which would distinguish him as a profound thinker, great scholar, or fluent speaker."[73] Still, Leonard left a library of two thousand volumes to the missionary district. It was a record of solid achievement.

3

Franklin Spencer Spalding

The Socialist Bishop

(1904–1914)

> Indeed I am a socialist. Why not, aren't you? I am a Marxian Socialist, and I'm a socialist in every sense of the word.
> —Bishop Spalding to a reporter

> Do not despair the day of small things.
> —Zechariah 4:10, Spalding's suggested motto for the Missionary District of Utah

For fourteen years, from 1904 to 1918, two socialist bishops with national reputations for their outspokenness led the Utah missionary district. The assumption might be that they were somehow otherwise deficient as church leaders, but both Franklin Spencer Spalding and Paul Jones were tireless visitors to isolated communities, skilled pastors, and able administrators when a balance sheet is drawn on the whole of their controversial episcopates.

Socialism held a respected, albeit a minority position, in American political life in the early twentieth century, attracting a broad spectrum of workers, farmers, intellectuals, reformers, and small business people. During that time the Social Gospel made a deep impact on American religious life, its basic arguments being that Christ preached justice and equity for all people, and that the church should not be primarily the church of the rich, but should contend with economic powers and principalities on behalf of the poor and voiceless. Women's suffrage and better educational and health care possibilities for children were all parts of the package. Socialism was a force in Utah politics as well. More than a hundred Socialists were elected to public office in nineteen different communities between 1900 and the party's demise in the 1930s. Socialist support was widespread in the growing mining centers, and from 1911 to 1913, the Utah State Federation of Labor backed the Socialist Party's political platform and ticket. Contrary to popular myths, most Utah Socialists were native-born. Thus Bishops Spalding and Jones were not Don Quixotes tilting at windmills, but articulate reformers well-positioned within an established strain of American political thought.[1]

Franklin Spencer Spalding was born in Erie, Pennsylvania, on March 13, 1865, the first of five children of the Episcopal rector there. Eight years later his father, John F. Spalding, became missionary bishop of Colorado, Wyoming, and New Mexico, and the family moved west, although Franklin returned to Princeton University and General Theological Seminary for his education. Little of Spalding's deep commitment to the plight of workers was evident in his Princeton–General years. Princeton was a school priding itself in turning out "young Christian gentlemen." Rote memorization was the preferred way of learning, but Franklin was an avid debater with an analytical, inquiring mind. He was also an amateur athlete, third baseman on his class team, and won nearly thirty medals, most of them in track and field events. Later, when he joined his father in Colorado, the tall, thin, bespectacled Spalding, his penetrating eyes framed by large glasses, played fullback on the Denver Athletic Club's football team.

At General Seminary Spalding joined the "Western Missionary Club," a group of students dedicated to the Episcopal Church's westward expansion, much as other mission groups supported overseas church work in China or South America.[2] In 1891 Spalding was among seven General graduates to serve in Colorado as missionaries. Ordained a deacon by his father on June 3, 1891, his first parish was All Saints', in a North Denver suburb. On June 1, 1892, he was ordained a priest and became headmaster of Jarvis Hall, the church's school for boys. He stayed there until Easter 1897, when his father's old parish, St. Paul's in Erie, called him as rector. In 1898 Spalding spent his vacation in Wyoming climbing the Grand Teton, a treacherous 13,770-foot peak surrounded by glaciers, deep chasms, and snowfields. Crawling their way along a slippery ledge with the possibility of a 3,000-foot drop a few inches to their side, the three climbers pulled themselves along a narrow ledge, sometimes hanging over open space. Spalding said, "We had been climbing for eleven hours. It was a grand sight, one of the grandest on earth."[3] A route to the top and a waterfall were later named after Spalding.

Erie was an industrial town, and it was there that the thirty-two-year-old rector developed a lasting interest in social issues. Once, some workers asked their minister if new industrial machines really helped the working class, as management claimed. Spalding concluded the new machinery did not reduce prices, nor did the workers gain better salaries and working conditions. In fact, many lost jobs when replaced by machines.[4] "I was forced to realize," he wrote later in *The Christian Socialist*, "that thousands who had as good a right to the fullness of life as I had, did not have a ghost of a chance."[5]

A galvanic event for the young rector was the 1898 visit to Erie of Eugene Debs, the Socialist presidential candidate. Spalding was asked to introduce Debs, but declined, saying this was "out of his sphere." That fall, Spalding was named the city's Labor Day speaker.[6] While expressing sympathy for the plight of workers, he also criticized unions for allowing women and children to work in factories, not to supply the necessities of life, but to "increase their luxuries."[7] The trade unionists responded by urging women not to return to work. This in turn produced friction in the parish, since one of the factories belonged to a vestry member, who resigned in protest. By then Spalding's political loyalties had changed from Republican, to Democrat, to Socialist, although he never joined the Socialist Party, as did his successor, Paul Jones.

Meanwhile, an old family friend, Bishop Boyd Vincent of the Diocese of Southern Ohio, had advanced Spalding's name for the vacant Utah opening. On October 19, 1904, Spalding wrote his mother (his father had died in 1902), "It is just what I didn't want as you know, for it is hard being a bishop, so thankless, and Utah is the hardest of them all." Spalding's main concern was that he would have to spend much time fundraising, a task for which he had little appetite.[8] He was consecrated bishop at St. Paul's, Erie, on December 4, 1904, at age thirty-nine. Daniel Tuttle, now presiding bishop as well as bishop of Missouri, was chief consecrator.

Spalding's Socialism: "Read Karl Marx"

Spalding backed into socialist and communist theory from his own life experience, not from any special interest in political thought. He was a Christian first and a Socialist second. Spalding's socialism was grounded in the New Testament. His political theory was derived from biblical teachings, such as the Sermon on the Mount. Moses was the first biblical revolutionary, Spalding believed, followed by an infinitely greater revolutionary, Christ. This was not idle theory, but a call to action. "Ye cannot serve God and Mammon." There was no turning back.[9]

"Indeed I am a socialist," Spalding once told a reporter. "Why not, aren't you? I am a Marxian Socialist, and I'm a socialist in every sense of the word. . . . Under the present individualistic system of government we reach the wealthy and refined and take care of them but socialism reaches the masses."[10] Returning to General Seminary on a recruitment trip, he told students "read Karl Marx" and *The Communist Manifesto,* but traditional Marxists or Communists would find his brand of socialism maddeningly deviant.[11]

Spalding, in a 1905 commencement address, said rhetoric about "masses and classes" was limited and limiting. He pleaded for "a higher appeal than the appeal to self-interest or to class interest; there are nobler rewards than the rewards of material prosperity."[12] In a 1908 consecration sermon for the bishop of Western Colorado, he charged the prelate to "go forth as the Bishop of Socialism and Trade Unionism, of Communism and Prohibition, of Ethical Culture and New Thought, of truth held by all men, at all times and in all places, and truth which was only discovered yesterday." Spalding was not asking his friend and classmate, Bishop Edward J. Knight, to be a Communist or Ethical Culturalist, but to challenge conventional society and its beliefs. His point was, "we are Apostles of Christ, not private chaplains to rich parishioners, not earnest men hampered with small and confining surroundings, not privates required to obey the orders of others whom we are not sure of, but leaders, with no superior save Christ, the King."[13]

Could he be both a bishop of the church and an advocate for a controversial political system? Yes, Spalding reasoned.[14] Careful to separate his sermons from his lectures to workers, he was first of all a pastor, then a preacher, a fundraiser, rural evangelist, and a chief administrator of a demanding missionary district. Spalding held these roles in balance, and his steady record of achievement makes him one of the most remarkable figures in the American church of his era.

Opposition in Salt Lake City, Confrontation in Garfield

His socialism drew increasing opposition in Salt Lake City, although rural clergy, especially those who worked with the miners, were supportive of it. Much of the lay leadership of the small Episcopal churches in Utah's capital fell to a handful of business entrepreneurs, bankers, and lawyers, self-made successful persons with limited horizons. In Europe, the Pope had condemned socialism, and the Roman Catholic Church in America quickly followed suit. The Latter-day Saints, once proponents for the utopian State of Deseret, by 1914 had become super-patriots. "He has told the rest of the world some things it did not know about socialism," an editorial in the *Inter Mountain Republican* stated. "By the fact of this telling—he being a much respected man—the community has a better opinion of it. . . . It hasn't won the public, but people are not so hostile as they were, for they have been told the truth about it in temperate language, by a temperate man."[15]

When the bishop visited the Oregon Shortline office in Salt Lake in 1911 to receive his annual free pass, the manager said his favoring workers over the company meant he would receive no free transportation that year. The bishop calmly replied he could not surrender his right to free speech for a railroad pass.[16] Although he could have confronted the lower-level management figures who took issue with him, Spalding never did so. Many were trying to be Christians, he reasoned, and were themselves but cogs in a machine.

Things came to a head in the mining town of Garfield in 1910. The Utah Copper, Boston Consolidated, and American Smelter companies had large mining operations spread for six miles along the Great Salt Lake. Many workers lived in small shacks on company land. For such a setting Spalding had found an ideal missionary, Maxwell W. Rice, a youth worker, graduate of Williams College and Cambridge Seminary, and a skilled amateur boxer. Although he lived in the bunkhouse and ate with the workers, Rice played tennis with the management staff and circulated easily in both worlds. Working with the laborers until his hands were blistered in the hot sun, he helped them build a small church, roofed with corrugated tin. Soon a Sunday school for fifty children opened, a kindergarten was formed, social clubs for men and women sprang up, and religious services were held on Sundays and Wednesdays. The only problem was the church was built on company land.

The flash point came when some Scotch and Welsh miners asked if they could meet on Wednesday evenings to discuss social issues. Rice readily agreed and management learned that Socialists were meeting on company property. The resident manager said the church could not use the building for such purposes and the workers should be fired. Spalding and Rice met with the local manager who was caught in the middle, carrying out orders from above. Six years later, the manager reflected, "I wouldn't tell Rice this, but perhaps we had, in our efforts to pay dividends, overlooked the men."[17] The manager called Spalding "a great man who always did what he thought was right."[18]

It was 1910, and the missionary bishop looked ahead. "If God gives me strength quietly to live and work and teach the absolute need of Social Revolution, nothing less, ten years from today I'll have done more good in Utah than if I could stir up a strike at Garfield or bankrupt the Utah Copper Co." But time was short; Spalding had only four more years to complete his work.[19]

In August 1913, the Episcopal Church met in General Convention at the Cathedral of St. John the Divine in New York. Spalding was a featured speaker. This was his most important national audience, and his topic was "The Church and Democracy." War clouds loomed, and by now the church and capitalism issue was nearly as contentious as the Civil War, civil rights or any of the great issues with which the church historically wrestled.

Spalding opened by describing the manager who told him to stay away from social issues in his church, and of the railway official who would not renew his annual pass because he spoke to striking workers. The bishop did not condemn these people, but expressed admiration for them. They were merely doing their jobs, he said. But there was another audience for the church, the working people, and their needs were no less important to organized religion, he concluded. "Surely there can be no doubt on which side the church of Jesus Christ ought to stand, where the issue is between dollars and men. . . . She must take her place on the side of the worker, giving him, from her Master, self-control and courage and hope and faith, so that he may fight his battle and win his victory, which is not his victory alone, but the victory of society; the victory of cooperation, of love over selfishness." The Church, to be a real power in society, "must cease to be merely the almoner of the rich and become the champion of the poor.[20] The heart of Spalding's address was

> we worship in a great church like this, and it makes us forget the slums just over the way; we wear our holy vestments, and we forget the millions who have only rags to wear; we debate our canons and names, and we forget the toiling workers who are pleading for a living wage; we discuss hymns and prayers, and we forget that there are ten-thousands of thousands whose hearts are too heavy to sing and whose faith is too weak to pray.[21]

Reaction was swift, much of it critical. "Why shouldn't I accept money from the mill owners?" a southern bishop asked. "Never have that man in our parish again," another listener told her rector. Two wealthy New Yorkers who may have misheard Spalding when he criticized Joseph Smith as a medium and psychic told him, "Bishop, we do not think that we can support you, for we understand that you are a spiritualist."[22] Others pleaded with Spalding to stop preaching about economic issues, and church leaders, enraged by his position, withheld substantial donations to missions. Friends said his reputation was suffering.[23] A month later he wrote, "I sometimes wonder whether the Protestant Episcopal Church and social service can live together. I did get jumped on so hard for the speech I made at the General Convention from the great lights of the Church, both male and female." In a letter to his mother he asked "whether the time will ever come when it will be my duty to resign from the Church for the sake of the Church, for I cannot quite see how I can stop speaking out what I think God's spirit shows me as the truth."[24]

Work among the Utes

Shortly before Spalding's arrival, the Episcopal Church had begun a ministry to the Ute peoples in the state's northeast. Bishop Abiel Leonard had supported efforts to "elevate the Red Man" whose land had been taken and who was now placed on restricted farm lands with undesirable soil. Shock waves from the resultant swift change of lifestyles reverberate over a century and a half later. Well-intentioned, prayerful missionaries came to work in Utah, but few spoke the Ute language in more than rudimentary phrases. The Native Americans were considered "pagan" or "uncivilized" and their traditional beliefs were viewed with curiosity at best and as barbarian at worst. Thus the Episcopal Church of that time, like other denominations and the federal government, contributed generously to helping people on one hand while dismantling their culture on the other. The church worked closely with the government. Neither side knew much about Native American work, but the government had more money to spend than the church. Sometimes the Indian agents were principled, competent people, but many represented the dregs of the job seekers of that era. In 1905 the Ute lands were again opened for white settlement, and 6,400 plots of 160 acres each were given to non–Native American applicants.

The gulf between Native American belief and Christian thought was wide. Spalding recalled a lantern show his predecessor, Bishop Leonard, had given on the crucifixion. The Native American response to it was "white man he kill God, we no want his church." Of his audience, Spalding said, "they are a stolid lot and one can't tell whether they understand or not."[25]

The bishop believed the American military were poor models for the Native Americans. Many of the troops were lazy, often were drunk, and had ready access to Fort Duchesne's brothels.[26] In 1908 he wrote that the work at Whiterocks was seriously handicapped by the inefficiency of the local government school. Two plans were advanced, one to turn the school over to the church, which was rejected on the grounds of separation of church and state. The second was for the church to organize and staff the school, after which the government would assume responsibility for it.[27] "It is a very critical time for the Utes," Spalding wrote in 1911. "Whether they like it or not, they are being forced to adopt the customs of white men." A trader had told him that during the past year he had sold more white man's clothing and fewer blankets than ever before, and that laws against liquor sales were making an impact. "Trade and civil law are thus lifting them out of their savagery."[28]

Spalding was enthusiastic about the Whiterocks Native American work, and made the arduous journey there twice a year. His 275-mile trip by road and railroads crossed into Colorado as well. The last train stop was in Dragon, fifty-seven miles through the "bad lands" to Ouray. Spalding used the Dragon schoolhouse for a church service in 1908. His was the third public meeting that day. The first, a Republican rally, drew fourteen persons, the second, a Democratic gathering, drew twenty-four members, and "at our service there were fifty!"[29]

The Indian agent told Spalding the local inhabitants would receive their annual payments the following day, and "I want you to tell them how wrong and foolish it is to get drunk." Spalding recalled his sermon, speaking slowly, allowing Charley Mack, the interpreter, to adapt the message for local use. Spalding spoke of four kinds of houses, the Native American log house or *wickiup.* Next came the "Washington House," where the agent lives and enforces the decrees of the "Great White Father" in Washington. Then there was the schoolhouse, and lastly God's house, where "we learn what the Great Spirit, our Father in Heaven, wishes us to do," especially through the "ten great laws." Spalding then focused on the Seventh Commandment, with special emphasis on keeping "our bodies in temperance, soberness and chastity." When the government payment money was distributed, "not a single full-blooded Ute Indian was found drunk. . . . The guardhouse was quite empty, except for one poor, foolish half-breed. I wonder whether white people pay any better attention to sermons than that."[30]

The Bear Dance and Sun Dance

Episcopalians and other missionaries and secular workers among Native Americans believed the Bear Dance and Sun Dance, the dominant ritual manifestations of Ute culture, were grossly pagan, and set about dismantling such practices. Missionaries of that era, like others dealing with Native American affairs, did not realize such ritual events helped hold indigenous societies together in times of stress.

"This heathen dance and custom which create such widespread interest and attract such crowds, the Church is rightfully trying to break up," Hersey stated.[31] The Bear Dance, named for the swaying movement of a bear and carrying the symbolism of a bear emerging from winter hibernation, was an annual spring event among the Utes. It took place just before the spring camps moved out to begin the long hunting season. Ancestors were appeased by the dance, protection was asked against illness and attacks, favor was invoked for the coming hunt, and courtships as well as divorces took place after a long, cold winter.[32] Hersey wanted to have marriages solemnized in the church. "for even though they have an old love, a more congenial mate they will choose, these children of nature, without a thought involved in the breaking of family ties."[33] "One can understand and sympathize, too, with this unhappy minority who long for the wild, roaming freedom of other days, the exciting hunt and the chase for buffalo and deer and game, their clashing bloody encounters with other wandering tribes," he reflected, adding, "Those days can only be lived again in memory, for the Indian must be civilized and Christianized."[34]

Hersey's substitute for the Bear Dance took place on the first Wednesday after Easter. The local Ute population, possibly 250 people, was invited to a barbeque where "dozens and dozens of eggs are hard boiled and oven after oven of bread is baked," and coffee and pie were served. Potato, sack, and pie races replaced the traditional ceremonies designed to affirm tribal solidarity and recall the Native Americans's past. "The pie races are most amusing, since they must eat their pie with their hands tied behind them. The winners receive prizes of something useful," Hersey noted.[35] Then he told the Resurrection story and urged the Utes to solemnize their weddings through lasting church unions. Someone from the Indian Bureau urged them to establish permanent birth, marriage and death records, and have deeds to their lands.

The Sun Dance, the central rite of the local people, grew out of the social and cultural stresses Utes encountered in the late nineteenth century, when they were driven from their territory, defeated, and forced to switch from being hunters and gatherers to becoming farmers on poor lands. The dance was both an affirmation of traditional culture and values and a distinctively anti-white statement, providing "power to the powerless," as the title of an anthropological study described it.[36] The Sun Dance was a three-day ceremony, held in July, and included socializing, healing rites, horse racing, card playing, construction of a sweat lodge for a purification ceremony, and extensive gift-giving, closing with an elaborate meal. Shamans, singers, musicians, dancers, and participants all had a role in this complex event. The event was called a Sun Dance, because each morning the dancers prayed with the rising of the sun for health and power.[37] They did not pray to the sun.

The sun symbol represented binary forces; its rays were both hot and cold, and dry and wet forces competed as well. The dance took place around a wooden center pole, a young green tree. As it died, its powers (*puwa*) were channeled to participants. The rite's content was not easy to categorize, with additions and deletions depending on locale and practitioners. Sometimes a Cross and other Christian symbols were added, but as cultural symbols rather than as statements of Christian belief.[38]

When the Bureau of Indian Affairs outlawed the dance in 1913, the resourceful Utes reintroduced it as a "Thanksgiving Dance" or "Harvest Dance," to the satisfaction of their overseers.[39]

Bishop Spalding on the Road

The bishop was often on the road three weeks at a time. Within three months of arriving in the missionary district in 1905, Spalding visited scattered missions, including those in Colorado and Nevada. A period photo shows a downtown signboard in front of an Ogden shop announcing, "Admission Free, Bishop Spalding at the Episcopal Church, Every Night at 7:30 P.M. This Week and Sunday. Come! Come! Come!"[40] His letters to his mother and others came from places like the Gore-View Hotel, Kremmling, Colorado, "New and Nicely Furnished. . . . Table always supplied with the best" or the Oxford Hotel, Hayden, Colorado, "A hot favorite with commercial men . . . a new hotel newly furnished and kept strictly up to date."

The National Church had designated $1,500 for Utah work; Spalding had to raise the rest. St. Mark's Hospital was $35,000 in debt for needed improvements, and Rowland Hall required money for scholarships and salaries. Spalding was a hands-on leader; when he arrived in Vernal and saw the resident missionary filling his icehouse, Spalding joined him in lifting blocks of ice. The bishop was first of all a pastor throughout his ten-year episcopate. He was there to meet the train when clergy arrived in town and was solicitous of them and their families, remembering birthdays and anniversaries with generous letters. He delegated work easily, and often told clergy "We must plan together" or "You're the bishop here." He constantly rallied his small band of clergy and laity, saying, "We must not stop to argue about our fitness. Trying is our business. Success is in God's hands."[41]

The missionary district had been realigned again to encompass Utah and parts of Wyoming, Nevada, and Colorado. It was not until 1907 that Utah was established as a separate missionary district. Roads were few, and travel was by stagecoach, train, and automobile, which gradually replaced the horse as the preferred mode of transportation. Sometimes progress was torturously slow. On one rural visit east of Salt Lake, spring floods had washed out the road and one night the bishop's wagon overturned in a stream. Spalding was soaked, waded across four knee-deep streams, and walked to the nearest town of Bonanza. After drying out, next day he rode on to White River and Dragon. "I arranged for services and had a fine crowd out at 8 P.M. and the next morning came on to Salt Lake feeling absolutely none the worse in any way."[42] In another place, he wrote during winter, "the worst thing about traveling this time of year is the difficulty of keeping clean, for you can't take a bath in a lard pail of water and that is about as much as you can keep melted."[43]

Spalding was busy. A bishop's visit would include calls at the homes or offices of church members, meetings with church bodies, and evening services. If no resident clergy were present, the bishop would baptize as well as confirm, and if it was a town with no church or preaching station, he went from door to door inviting persons to attend services. Sometimes he borrowed a community hall or another denomination's church.[44] In a letter to his mother, written atop a suitcase while waiting for a train to Park City, Spalding said he had called on twenty-five people that day, held a service and baptisms in a church that had not been visited in a long time, and had not received his salary from the Board of Missions for several months.[45]

The bishop kept his sense of humor throughout. When one mission announced "Bishop Spalding will continue to talk until next Sunday night," he wrote, "I do seem to keep pretty steady at it."[46] Later he jokingly said of his fellow socialists, "they are a great deal fonder of hearing anybody else listen than of hearing anybody else talk," and "it means they are dead in earnest and absolutely sure of their faith, but it also means that a socialist paper is a very doubtful financial venture."[47]

College ministries were of special interest to Spalding. At Princeton, religious discussion centers had been formative for him, and in two college towns, Logan and Salt Lake City, he pioneered an intellectual Christian presence by building the sort of young men's center–religious installation common in many eastern universities. Logan was the site of the State Agricultural College and Brigham Young College, an increasingly prosperous commercial town with prospects for reviving an active Episcopal Church. "I'm hoping for great things for Logan," he wrote in 1906. He raised about $15,000, a substantial sum for that time, to build a church and rectory, and, during one of his trips East, recruited Donald K. Johnson and Paul Jones, recent Yale University and Episcopal Theological School graduates. An attractive new building was erected across from the northeast corner of Tabernacle Square and was consecrated in January 15, 1909. Between 1,500 and 2,000 persons visited St. John's House each month during its heyday. Johnson accepted a call to a Pennsylvania church in 1911, and Jones moved to Salt Lake City in 1913. After that, activity at the Episcopal church in Logan dwindled and was not fully revived until the 1940s.

At one point Spalding asked a young cleric, Henry Knox Sherrill, later presiding bishop of the Episcopal Church (1947–1957), to take over the Logan mission. Although Sherrill declined, he vividly recalled meeting Spalding. "There was something about him which aroused my sympathy, stimulated my mind, and stirred my conscience." Spalding was "tall and spare, with a penetrating mind, skeptical of conventional ways and phrases, and a remarkable combination of personal fearlessness and humility." The bishop described work in Utah: "This is a small but difficult field. I drove a number of miles last Sunday to hold services in a shack. I was there before anyone else, lighted the fire in the stove, swept out the place. A little group came who thought I ought to thank them for the privilege of speaking to them. I spoke on one's duty to one's neighbor. A drunken woman interrupted and said that one should look out for oneself. As I tried to straighten her out, I recalled that two months before I had preached the same sermon in Grace Church in New York, where everything was beautiful. All I can say is God calls some of us to do this work. As for myself, I love it and would not be anywhere else."[48]

The bishop hoped to duplicate the Logan college mission at the University of Utah and in Provo. When Mrs. Thomas J. Emery of Cincinnati gave him $25,000 in 1913 as a memorial to her son who had died during his second year at Harvard College, Emery Memorial House at the University of Utah became a reality. A resident home for twenty men representing several denominations (few Episcopalians actually lived there), it contained a library, small chapel, meeting rooms, basement swimming pool, tennis court, gymnasium, and dining hall, plus two Japanese servants, allowing residents to discuss Tennyson's poems unhindered by distracting chores. But as fraternities multiplied and college social life grew, Emery House floundered. During the Depression it became a municipal boy's club, and in 1948 was sold to the Roman Catholic Church for a Newman Center.

The Provo center never got off the ground, lacking both funds and clergy with the skills to launch it, but an active church was built in Provo. They had purchased a lot for five hundred dollars and St. Mary's, Provo, was consecrated by Bishop Spalding on September 12, 1907. Spalding called the church "a little box of a place, an old dwelling fixed nicely inside." At one Sunday service he drew twenty-nine persons in the morning, and the same number at night. Meanwhile, "throngs were coming out of the Mormon tabernacle," a large building that could hold two thousand persons. Organizing the small church was difficult, he acknowledged. "I tried to encourage the vestry committee but only two came to church and they were hopeless."

The Rev. George Townsend, a colorful Irish priest and Oxford University graduate, became the first resident Episcopal cleric in Provo, 1904–1909. Townsend had come west with his sister for his health. The congregation at that time was eleven persons, and the Women's Guild served lunches to raise funds for a new church while Townsend entertained audiences with poetry recitals in his thick Irish brogue. He reportedly drove each Friday afternoon with his horse and wagon to a brickyard where he gathered rejected bricks, which he and church members then laid in the walls of the new building. Townsend also helped found small Episcopal congregations in nearby Springville and Eureka, voiced support for a public library in Provo, and helped Brigham Young University organize a track team. Spalding called Townsend "a shy, timid Irishman" who told the bishop, who arrived for tea and crackers at 5:30 P.M. and stayed until 7:30, "Really, I must tell you if you don't go to the hotel you won't get any supper." Townsend left for Tennessee in 1909, and eventually returned to Ireland. Three clergy served Provo during the next five years, and church membership grew to twenty-nine.[49]

Spalding's episcopacy coincided with the mining industry's expansion in Utah and neighboring states. Self-sufficient, resilient clergy were needed to minister in such a setting. "A poor, puny ritualist would not be much better than the graduates of the Moody Bible School" in a setting of salons, dance halls, and cheap theatres, he concluded.[50] Spalding wanted the church to provide a place of healthful recreation and, "if the men have a chance and real inducements are given, they will come to worship, or to hear a lecture, or to listen to good music any night of the week."[51] Since miners worked in shifts, he spoke both during days or nights. Spalding had a basic "Christian Socialism" lecture, and another on "Spiritualism" in which he exposed "mediums and psychics like J. Smith," the Latter-day Saints founder whom he believed realized some of his visions from epileptic seizures.[52]

In a 1905 diocesan address, Spalding candidly laid out the problems he faced in recruiting clergy. His goal was to have all clergy salaries a minimum of a thousand dollars a year, and to find self-reliant, intellectually able clerics. Spalding told his listeners, "We want the best men we can get and when we get them we want to keep them. It takes a better man to succeed in a small western town than in an eastern cathedral. This is not because the people make so many demands upon him, but because they make so few. . . . I have heard more poor preaching in the west than in the east. I fear there are quite as many mental sluggards out here as there are in many parts of the country, and yet if the preacher is to make himself felt in this western country he must study and read and think with all his might."[53]

"There is not enough in any Utah community for a strictly technical priest to do," Spalding told the clergy in 1909. "If I were to choose a motto for the District of Utah I think I should choose the words, 'Do not despise the day of small things.' [Zechariah 4:10] We have few clergy, we have few mission stations, we have few church buildings, we have few confirmations, and we can expect only a very slow growth. There is the temptation to discouragement, and what is still worse, contentment with small effort. . . . We may not breathe a very intellectual atmosphere in the towns in which we live, and yet there is all the more responsibility resting upon us to be constant readers and faithful students."[54]

The district was large and the clergy few—thirteen priests, including the bishop in 1910, serving 3 parishes, 22 missions, 1,200 communicants, and 975 Sunday school pupils.[55] All but two of the clergy had come within the last five years, which would suggest that ordained persons were hard to come by for Utah, and hard to retain. Salary money was always scarce. Representative figures in 1912 included M. J. Hersey, $1,200 for Native American work, W. W. Rice in Garfield, $500, Paul Jones in Logan, $900, and William F. Bulkley in Provo, $850. Spalding's salary was $3,000. Sometimes the bishop could supplement these figures with money raised on trips or funds from the Board of Missions, and parishioners contributed goods and some money, but Utah's clergy were poorly paid, and turnover was high.[56]

The bishop had once complained that the Episcopal residence, a large downtown house, was "so empty and big and ugly." He never married, he wrote his mother, because "I would be a most unsatisfactory kind of husband for any woman to have, for if I am to do this work well, I shall have to be away so much that to ask a woman to marry me is to ask her to be very lonely."[57] His life was one of constant movement. In 1911, Spalding took part in 262 church services and attended 195 meetings, preached 120 times and delivered 148 other addresses. The numbers did not vary much in other years.[58]

Spalding was a strong personality and, like his successor Arthur W. Moulton, had some sharp exchanges with the national Board of Missions. Why should he be forced to take risks and borrow money for clergy salaries? Why couldn't the national church do this instead? He was responsible for a vast missionary district, which, like Tuttle, he often compared to a foreign country, yet the national church wanted him to make periodic long fundraising trips to the East. Some of his strongest language was directed at Bishop Arthur S. Lloyd, president of the Board of Missions. "No, my dear friend, your plan does not appeal to me. It lacks definiteness. . . . It asks me to have all the faith and it does not, I frankly confess, show the Board of Missions to be brave enough or wise enough to justify my having faith in it."[59]

Spalding had little patience for quibbles over church structure and politics. Shortly before his death in 1914, he wrote,

> The Church must become Christian, and, therefore, missionary in its real essence. It must realize it can only know the Doctrine by doing the work. The Church's history, its form of government, its liturgical services offer constant temptation to waste time and thought and dissipate energy. Just as truly as the individual must forget himself in the cause to which he is devoted, if he is to advance the interests of that cause, so the Church must forget herself, her boastings about her Catholic heritage, her efforts to perfect her liturgical forms, her fussing over already too complicated national, Provincial, and Diocesan organization and make it her one and only duty to keep her members to be like Jesus Christ, who lived and died to save men from sin and all the misery which sin creates. She must realize that the only reason there is a Church is that collective action is more efficient than individual action. We in Utah are a feeble folk and we have little or no influence over the Church at large—but we can do our duty in the little sphere of service to which Christ has called us.[60]

The Cathedral Dean Is Deposed for Molesting Choir Boys, 1905–1908

Spalding had been bishop for only a year and was on an eastern fundraising mission when, shortly before Christmas 1905, James. B. Eddie, dean of St. Mark's Cathedral, wrote the bishop of his immediate resignation, adding, "I ought to have done so a year ago or more when the doctor advised me to leave. I have apparently a nervous collapse. When you return matters will be explained to you."[61] Eddie, his wife, and four children had come from Carson City, Nevada, to St. Mark's Cathedral in 1900, and were now en route to California, where Eddie found a temporary job as a reporter with the Pasadena *Raven.* The "matters" the cathedral dean alluded to were multiple accusations of sexual exploitation of young male choir members over several years. This led to a church inquiry, trial, and to Eddie's deposition from the ministry on January 8, 1908.

At first the cathedral tried to keep the resignation quiet. On December 14, a cathedral vestry member wrote Spalding, "do not show this letter or give the matter any more publicity than you can help or communicate with anyone here asking for details or explanations. We will explain everything by word of mouth."[62] On January 29, 1906, Graham F. Putnam, of the cathedral vestry, wrote Spalding again, asking him to return urgently from New York. "Dean Eddie went away on our advice because a serious charge was made against him. This charge he denies." The bishop was asked to find a new dean. "There is no disposition on the part of the vestry to call any one until we have had an opportunity to consult with you in the matter. Under the agreement between the bishop and the vestry made in 1895 by which the office of Dean was created, the vestry's choice must be confirmed by the bishop."[63]

Meanwhile, George C. Hunting, superintendent of St. Mark's Hospital, wrote Spalding on January 30, 1906. When the accusations surfaced, he said, a delegation of vestry members called on the dean, who "did not deny the accusations but instead said, 'I have a shadow of a recollection that these things are true.' He asked our advice and we advised his resignation. Mr. Brown told him he ought to get out of town within forty-eight hours. He went in twenty-four and Mrs. Eddie went with him. She later returned and told several people her side of the story and I do not think to this day she knows all the filthy details."[64] The resignation was accepted, and the vestry agreed to pay Eddie's salary until that Easter.

Spalding had two choices: to return home immediately, or complete his fundraising tour, which was helping eradicate the hospital's debt. He had raised $15,000 to build a separate nurses's building, and nearly $19,000 toward reducing the hospital debt. "Please tell Mrs. Eddie and Dean Eddie that when I know the facts I will try to judge wisely and lovingly. Tell them that I will not come to any hasty conclusion but that when the eastern duties are done I will—by God's help—see that the right prevails."[65]

The story broke in the local press on March 7, 1906. The *Utah State Journal*, Ogden, wrote the cathedral dean was accused of "gross depravity with numerous boys" from well-known families. "He affirms the charges are all unfounded. Local papers have been asked to suppress the story."[66] "Dean Eddie in Public Disgrace," the *Deseret Evening News* headlined a May 16, 1906, account announcing the findings of a three-member Commission of Inquiry Spalding had appointed to examine the allegations. The Commission's report recommended Eddie resign or face trial. "The exact nature of the charges cannot be printed, but as near as can be stated for publication, they involved the gravest charges of immorality against the dean and covered a long period."[67] The charges were sexual abuse through the genital manipulation of four young men, either at the cathedral or at a church camp over a period of several years.

It took almost a year to complete arrangements for the trial. Church attorneys had to be found, depositions taken, and three out-of-state clerical judges appointed. The trial was held at St. Mark's Cathedral in December 1906, and on January 25, 1907, the Ecclesiastical Court returned a verdict of guilty against Eddie on five counts of immorality, four specific charges and one general charge covering "several and different occasions within five years last." It recommended the bishop depose Eddie under canon law.[68] Eddie appealed, but a Church Appeals Court sustained the verdict on October 7, 1907.

Spalding then deposed the former cathedral dean from the ministry on January 8, 1908, in a public church court session in the cathedral undercroft. A newspaper headline read "Salt Lake Minister is Deposed by Bishop, Women Weep and Men of Congregation Hiss When Severe Sentence is Read." After the sentence was read, Eddie sprang to his feet and said, "Thank you, Bishop, this is in harmony with your injustice of the past." Eddie attacked the bishop frontally, and thus avoided discussing the trial issues of sexual abuse of the young men. The bishop had appointed the judges, the deposed dean argued, so naturally they would favor his position. (The three judges actually came from Colorado and Nevada.) The trial violated legal norms, Eddie continued, because the testimony of the four boys could not be corroborated by other sources. Besides, "the charges were months and years old and all were stale."[69]

Finally, the deposed dean compared his trial to that of Archbishop Thomas Cranmer, who was burned at the stake in the sixteenth century.[70] Eddie's statement repeated those of his counsel, principally that he was denied a public trial. Church attorneys replied the judges could keep the proceeding private to protect the four young men. Eddie was invited to have six representatives present at all times, but had refused.[71] "They ought to be called 'victims' rather than accomplices," the church attorneys stated, noting that the Dean had previously admitted having sexual relations with the boys.[72]

Tuttle, as presiding bishop, was apprised of the case by Spalding. "If I were you," he wrote Spalding on January 16, 1908, "I would write a kindly letter to Mr. Eddie quietly claiming that the canons and your duty to the church have obliged you to act, disclaiming any personal feeling against him, commending him to God's guidance and help—and if you can afford it [underlining in the original] enclosing a check for $25 to help him along in the terrible days . . . that must now face him in caring for his little family."[73] Throughout the three-year period, Spalding's letters to Eddie remained pastoral while stressing his desire to see a fair investigation and trial.

"Dear Brother," Spalding wrote Eddie on January 24, 1908, shortly after Eddie had been deposed,

> I want you to feel that you have my most profound sympathy. . . . I have tried to put myself in your place and think what I would have done. Of this I am sure, that your temptation must have been a mysterious and powerful one which I cannot understand but which God only can estimate and that you must, for years, have put up a fight which makes the moral struggles of a mortal man seem petty. . . . I feel sure that you did not want the church to suffer and that the fear that it might be harmed made your course the harder. Perhaps that is why you made your defense as personal as you did. Please for the sake of Mrs. Eddie,

> who need not know where it comes from, let me help you to this little extent, for I know you must need aid in the struggle for those you love more than anything else in the universe. Do not think you must answer this letter.[74]

Eddie returned Spalding's check three days later in an impassioned letter, and told the bishop he and his wife "could not accept anything at your hands, even were our children starving." He accused Spalding of being both prosecutor and judge, and of trampling on "every principle of justice, every instinct of right to secure my condemnation."[75]

Sexual matters were not discussed in public forums in the early twentieth century, still less in the church, and once the former dean was deposed, a curtain of silence descended on the cathedral and community, and the case was rarely discussed, or alluded to.

Spalding on Mormons

Three basic strategies were employed by churches in dealing with the Latter-day Saints. First, the frontal attack some Protestant groups employed. Second, the studied indifference of the Roman Catholic Church. Third, Bishop Tuttle's approach was to preach the Gospel, state his differences with the dominant religion, but avoid direct confrontations and concentrate instead on building up mission schools.

Spalding tried a different approach. He sought a religious dialogue with the Latter-day Saints, and would raise differences in a non-threatening way, and hope to thus speed the evolution of the LDS along. Shortly after arriving in Utah, he wrote his mother, "I am patiently reading the Book of Mormon. It is terrible rot, but I suppose I ought to know it if I am to represent the district adequately."[76]

The heart of Spalding's approach to the Latter-day Saints was a carefully reasoned pamphlet widely distributed across the state. It took Spalding four years to write *Joseph Smith, Jr., as a Translator* (1912). Its basic argument was simple—all the texts from which the *Book of Mormon* had been translated by Joseph Smith, Jr., were unavailable; an angel had kept them. But Smith had translated and published another ancient book in 1842, *The Book of Abraham*, from an original Egyptian manuscript. How accurate was Smith as a translator? If the *Book of Abraham* was a faithful translation, most likely the *Book of Mormon* would be as well. If the *Book of Abraham* was spurious, then other basic LDS texts were questionable as well.

To settle the matter, Spalding sought the opinions of twelve leading world Egyptologists. "If," he wrote, "in the judgment of competent scholars, this translation is correct, then the probabilities are all in favor of the correctness of the *Book of Mormon.* If, however, the translation of the Book of Abraham is incorrect, then no thoughtful man can be asked to accept the *Book of Mormon,* but on the other hand honesty will require him, with whatever personal regret, to repudiate it and the whole body of belief which has been built upon it."[77]

From Oxford, London, Munich, Chicago, Berlin, New York, and Philadelphia came the replies, and the results were devastating. The verdict: the text was a widely-used burial document commonly placed in ancient Egyptian tombs and no *Book of Abraham* at all. "The *Book of Abraham,*" wrote Dr. Arthur C. Mace of the Department of Egyptian Art of the Metropolitan Museum of New York, "is pure fabrication. Five minutes' study in an Egyptian gallery of any museum should be enough to convince any educated man of the clumsiness of the imposture." He called Joseph Smith's interpretation of some of the illustrations in the document "a farrago of nonsense from beginning to end."[78] Other responses were similar in content.

"This pamphlet was not published to tell the Gentiles about the Mormons, but rather to tell Mormons about themselves," Spalding wrote when *Joseph Smith, Jr.,* was issued. Though it became hotly controversial in the Mormon press, Spalding never sought to provoke the controversy, just open a thoughtful debate. He sent copies to high school and college teachers throughout Utah, newspaper editors, presidents of Stakes, and the LDS Church leadership. The Mormon's Deseret Book Store sold two hundred copies.

Latter-day Saints' reaction to Spalding's publication was swift. The *Deseret Evening News* devoted several full pages to it. Thirty answers from LDS apologists were printed in the church press and reprinted in the *Improvement Era.* Responses were essentially "there's nothing new here, these objections have been raised before," and "the basic issue is one of faith, not the content of documents." Brigham Young's daughter, Susan Young Gates, a leading LDS journalist–novelist, combined both positions in a letter to the editor. " I know by the spirit of revelation that the *Book of Abraham* is true, and that its contents from cover to cover, are revelations. . . . Build up your own church, Dr. Spalding; we shall applaud all your efforts along that line; but keep your hands off the Church of Christ."[79]

"On the whole, I think the venture was worthwhile," Spalding later recalled. "The Mormon controversialists have acknowledged the fairness of the spirit in which the pamphlet was written, although they all seem to be writing for their co-religionists rather than for the larger world of scientific discussion."[80] "Historical development of Christianity has no interest to the

Mormon," he concluded, adding, "Surely many members of the Church of the Latter-day Saints must feel uncomfortable as they use the confident final tone of certainty involved in the claim they possess the only religion which is not an abomination to God."[81] Spalding added his own view: "A God who has still many more things to reveal to His People did not keep silent for hundreds of years and does not now limit Himself in inspiring prophets for His children to the hierarchy residing in Salt Lake City."

A Wider Awareness of Women

The district's annual report listed nine women missionaries in 1909: six of them at work among the Utes; plus Deaconess Frances Knepper in Provo, where she stayed for two years.[82] One of the most remarkable early twentieth century Utah women missionaries was Sara Napper, who worked for many years in the bishop's office in Salt Lake City, and was a diocesan registrar and social worker in several parishes. Born in London in 1845, Napper had come to Utah in 1892, and had been both a schoolteacher and a missionary.[83] Since the bishop was absent for several weeks at a time, she kept the diocesan office running and answered correspondence on her own. Her salary in 1904 was $250 a year, a quarter of that of most male clergy. Her stipend met only half her expenses, and Spalding worked to raise it. A 1908 quarterly check for $100 from Church Mission House noted, "Those receiving stipends from the Society are expected to take offerings for its works and to aid in the circulation of its Stated Publications."[84] Salary checks were not sent from New York until reports were received from missionaries in the field. "The Treasurer will await this report at the close of the quarter before sending stipend," the form stated.

Hospitalized at one point as a result of a streetcar accident, Napper sent her sister, Emily, to take her place at meetings. Napper's reports reflect the quality of her interaction with others; a typical entry, "I was particularly touched by the request of four girls in one family that they might be allowed to keep their mite boxes a week or two longer, as their father had but little work and they had not been able to put anything in. The following Sunday they brought with them a quarter of a dollar in each, and said father had some work this week and he said he was so glad to help the work of the Sunday school."[85]

In 1905 she was busy as the layperson in charge of St. Peter's Chapel, a mission in the city's northwest on St. Mark's Hospital grounds founded in 1891. In her organizational efforts at St. Peter's, she made more than three hundred calls between September and November 1902. Napper prepared a confirmation class, and organized a guild that sewed weekly for St. Mark's

Hospital. "Very busy happy times we had," she concluded.[86] In 1910 she moved to St. John's, a Salt Lake City mission chapel at 900 East and Logan Avenue, founded in 1890 at a cost of one hundred dollars for a frame building that seated forty persons, where she continued the same busy activities. The Utah United Thank Offering, which she organized, sent money to a church hospital in China, collected funds for Armenia and Near East Relief, and prepared an "Alaskan box" for a mission there. One of her most enthusiastic activities was organizing children's pageants. Of one, *The Builders of the City,* she wrote,

> I know our dresses and properties did not reach a high ideal, but the children's delivery of the words, the way in which they entered into the spirit of the thing, was deeply interesting and when the "Child" asked in earnest, pleading tones, "What can I do?" tears came into many eyes, and I am sure we all determined to help more faithfully in the building.[87]

During her spare time, Napper also assembled a history of the missionary district, drawn largely from convocation addresses and similar documents. Moulton later remembered Napper as a "little lady walking spiritedly down the street with her books and her papers as if she might have stepped out of one of Charles Dickens's novels."[88] Napper did not retire until 1927, at age eighty-two, and died four years later.

In 1909 Spalding wrote, "Our women workers have helped so greatly that we look forward eagerly to others who are coming." "[They] have not had an easy year," he noted, "and yet they have done such good work that in spite of difficulties the Indian children have made unusual progress, and they have all decided to carry on the work another year at least."[89] He welcomed several additional women workers—including Cornelia L. Edwards, a trained nurse, stenographer, Sunday school superintendent, and Girls' Friendly Branch Secretary—to join the Herseys at Vernal. Emma L. Gale took on the demanding work of Parish Visitor in Salt Lake City four days a week, then traveled to the mining community of East Garfield to organize a Sunday school and mothers's group.[90]

Women raised much of the money for the missionary district. In 1910 Spalding needed $10,450 to pay his staff of missionaries. The national church provided $3,969, and the second highest contribution came from the diocesan Women's Auxiliary, $1,900, while combined parishes raised a similar sum.[91] By 1910 there were ten women workers and ten active male clergy. Dr. Mary C. James, a Bryn Mawr College graduate and medical doctor, spent two years working among the Utes,[92] where tuberculosis was rampant, trachoma widespread, and the filth triggered diseases of the skin and eyes.[93]

In his 1914 annual address to the church, Spalding noted, "These are days in which women are demanding for themselves a larger share in the world's work and we are glad that we have in Utah so many women who find that larger sphere of influence and service in the work of Christ and His Church."[94] The presence of such women is recorded in annual reports, sometimes with the same names for several years. But only with their death or departures is more learned about them, usually a brief obituary in a local paper or mention in an annual report. Yet they held the church together, and the historian's hope is that somewhere the letters Lucy Clark wrote from the reservation or those Frances Knepper or Sara Napper sent to relatives will appear, allowing a fuller description of their activity.

Mission Priorities, Moving beyond Salt Lake City

Spalding was determined to expand missionary activities beyond the Utah state capitol. The bishop knew many smaller communities well from his travels. He described one trip to Cedar City, then 242 miles by train to Lund, a small town on the route to Los Angeles, and then by auto or stage forty miles to his destination. Motor vehicles were new to Utah in 1910. This time Spalding made the last segment by stage, with the strong wind whining steadily for at least six hours. "But the wind went down with the sun. The moon and the stars came out with a brilliance known only to the desert, and the still evening air was fragrant with the perfume of fruit blossoms and lilacs."[95]

In Cedar City to deliver a commencement address, Spalding was invited by the local LDS bishop to speak in the tabernacle, whose chief visual adornment was an engraving of Joseph Smith, Jr. dressed in a general's uniform. Communion of bread and water was distributed, and Spalding spoke in the morning on how to raise children, then in the afternoon on the difference between true religion and superstition, probably excerpted from one of his talks on Joseph Smith, Jr. After the service, he encountered the town's eighty-four-year-old patriarch, who had come from Wales many years earlier and converted to Mormonism. "I haven't heard those prayers for many a long year," he said, recalling his Anglican upbringing. "Then you still belong to my flock, and I will have to look after you," Spalding said. "Yes, I guess they've never disfellowshipped me," was the reply.[96] On the following day, the bishop visited his counterpart in the Mormon bishop's flourmill, where the latter read from the Book of Nephi about the coming of Jesus Christ to America. Spalding and his LDS counterpart disagreed about ways of dating the earth's evolution and about plural marriages.[97]

Spalding was also an early advocate of inter-faith cooperation, as shown by his comments on the foreign missionaries's presentation at the 1908 Pan-Anglican Congress in London.

> The religions of India, China and Japan have contributions even to Christendom which we must not despise. The watchword of the missionary today must be "Christ came not to destroy but to fulfill." If it be true that the truth only can bind men together, then in every religious system held by multitudes, there must be truth, and if the men who held the partial truth are ever to be brought to fuller light, it will be by the recognition of the truth they already hold, not by emphasizing their errors.[98]

While at General Seminary, Spalding developed a lifelong aversion to church ritual, a staple in the curriculum of that school, which had been deeply influenced by the Oxford Movement a generation earlier.[99] When he was named a bishop in 1904, Spalding said, "The chief thing about being a bishop seems to be getting a ring and a pectoral cross. Of course they are all kind but somehow the thing seems so small and petty when you take in all those frills. . . . I positively declined to accept the pectoral cross. The whole thing is rapidly making me sick."[100] Later, while in London for a Lambeth Conference of all Anglican bishops, Spalding was asked to preach at All Saints', Margaret Street, among the highest of the high churches in its liturgical practice. An acolyte in red slippers greeted him and ushered Spalding into an antechamber that looked like it contained "a bier with heavily embroidered coverlets spread over it." Spalding was told he should wear these articles and "pontificate." "I looked at them aghast," the bishop recalled. "All my Puritan blood rose up in me. Though the service was about to begin I said, 'I can't wear these things.'" A compromise was reached; Spalding remained outside the chancel until the sermon, then entered the pulpit to preach.[101]

The bishop also held strong views on church music. "There are certain hymns in the hymnal to this day I intensely dislike, simply because I had to sing them under a careless Sunday school superintendent Sunday after Sunday until I was heartily sick of them," he recalled. Spalding urged a year's embargo on "Onward, Christian Soldiers," "Stand Up, Stand Up for Jesus," "Work, for the Night is Coming," "Golden Harps are Sounding," "and that singularly lugubrious hymn, 'There is a Friend for Little Children,' which suggests that all the good children are dead."[102]

Spalding wrote different words for several of the church's more militant hymns, for example:

Onward, Christian workers,
Laboring for peace,
By the love of Jesus
Making strife to cease.
Christ, the lowly toiler,
Tells us what to seek,
Wretched are the mighty,
Blessed are the meek.

Chorus
Onward, Christian workers,
Marching on to peace,
By the love of Jesus
Making strife to cease.[103]

For the hymn, "Go Forward, Christian soldier," another of the church's "fight songs," he wrote:

"Go forward, Christ's explorer,
Seek honest men and strong
Who love the ways of honor
And hate the deeds of wrong;
Make them the valiant leaders,
Support them in their search
For every hidden weakness
In Nation and in Church."[104]

Fundraising for St. Mark's Hospital, Rowland Hall

Fundraising was a major part of a missionary bishop's responsibilities. The church was poor, most missions were relatively new, and there was no assured income beyond a meager subsidy from the national church. Additionally, Utah had a cathedral to support, its schools, and St. Mark's Hospital, which was always requiring modern equipment. A new wing had been added in 1903, with a much-needed operating room and kitchen.[105] The hospital increased its daily room charge to $1.50 in 1907. Much of the money came from mining and steel companies that had contracts with the hospital to treat injured employees. The hospital administrator, T. S. Pendergrass, said the hospital should both increase its fees and expand its base so that new physicians arriving in Salt Lake City would refer patients to St. Mark's.[106] Spalding raised the $53,000 to pay the hospital's debt and build a nursing school named for Bishop Leonard. It featured a living room and single rooms for older nurses, while probationers were assigned two or three to a room.[107] By September 1914, the hospital had cared for 2,853 patients that year, and revenues were $84,000. The medical staff was thirty-two full- or part-time physicians, and almost fifty nurses.[108] During one month, the patients included Americans, Irish, Greeks, Finns, Austrians, Swedes, Japanese, Italians, Scots, and Germans.[109]

Rowland Hall School was also an interest of Spalding's. He insisted that the flagship school not become an elitist institution whose main purpose was sending students to eastern colleges and universities, but educate young women to live in Utah's smaller communities. He resisted raising tuition to $500 in 1905, because many of the most deserving girls could not afford it. The sort of student Spalding had in mind was the "girl who in all probability would, after graduation, go back to her home and become influential, either as a teacher in the school or as mother of a family. The students usually became churchwomen before graduation, and thus through them the high standards of Christian womanhood were carried into the valleys and mountains."[110]

In 1909, Spalding told local Episcopalians it was necessary for him to leave on an extended fundraising mission. The numbers were bleak, and the Board of Missions provided only a small portion of the missionary district's budget. There were 1,233 communicants, a hundred more than in the previous year. Some of the diocesan assessments were $350 for St. Mark's Cathedral, $100 for Ogden, $30 for Logan, $15 for Vernal, $5 for Eureka, and $2.50 for the Theodore mission.[111] Dances, rummage sales, and bridge–whist parties, Spalding cautioned church members, were a poor substitute for planned giving.[112]

Although until now the Utah bishops had sought their funds in the East, in 1909 Spalding journeyed to California, Washington, and Oregon, visiting potential donors and giving talks there. The hard work of Bishop Tuttle brought three parishes to self-sufficiency, Spalding reflected, adding, "The churchmen in St. Mark's Cathedral, St. Paul's Parish, the Church of the Good Shepherd, hold their property under false pretenses if they do not exhibit missionary enthusiasm and render earnest missionary service."[113]

Bishop Spalding and the New Vicar in Park City

Spalding had difficulty finding a clergy person for the small, struggling mission in Park City. Somehow Frederick A. Jefferd, a rolling stone English cleric who rarely stayed in a parish more than two years, appeared as a candidate for an opening there. Jefferd arrived on June 12, 1912, and was gone by winter. Park City was a rough silver and lead mining town at that time, filled with bars and brothels. The Spalding–Jefferd exchange was pathetic yet funny in places. Jefferd was hired for $900, but immediately after arriving wanted the sum raised to $1,500 plus a house. Spalding replied that $900 was on the high end of missionary district salaries.

Days after the new vicar arrived he wrote the bishop, complaining about his quarters, a single room in the rear of the church. "The neighbor's water closet, over a hole in the ground, is but three yards off the bed in this room, and moreover there is a running stream but a foot off the back of the house, so that the ground underneath this room is saturated with sewerage, and over this of course the clergy have been sleeping." Spalding replied, "I did not ask you to go to Park City and send me a report on the conditions of the Church and the inadequacy of the salary and other matters you write of. I know conditions in Park City better than you could possibly learn them in less than one week. . . . If you think the room in the rear of the Church unsanitary and inconvenient there is no compulsion for you to live there."

Jefferd struck back, "It appears of little use to me writing you, as your mind seems to be made up, therefore wait till you come here, and we will enlighten you, that is if you are teachable on that point. . . . You yourself [underlining in the original] live in a nice house and have all you wish. Why am I to be denied even necessary things? I intend having a social meeting next week. Please let me know what date (for certain) you are coming and I will call the friends together to meet you. We can have a nice social evening together."

Meanwhile, Jefferd planned an outdoor rally, and sent Spalding the bills. He hired three large (400 candle-power each) electric lights, hung two from poles in the road, and another over the bandstand for effect. "Of course you understand nothing like this has ever been attempted here," he reminded the bishop. The central attraction was a lantern slide show on "The Prodigal Son," projected onto a cloth sheet hung on one side of the road. Jefferd asked Spalding to find the lantern and slides and pay for them, adding, "If you care to come, of course you must go out with us in your robes."

Later, when Spalding arrived in Park City on July 17 for an agreed-upon meeting, Jefferd had left town, leaving no word of his whereabouts. Spalding left a note: "Of course I am greatly disappointed not to see you. I confess I cannot understand your failing to remain in town when I wrote that I would come today."

Back in town the next day, Jefferd fired off a response that he had been too busy to open his incoming mail and, "Don't forget that if you come only twenty or thirty miles and received a disappointment, that I came 3,000 miles and then only to get a far worse [underlining in the original] one on arrival here. Your suggestion for me to go to Salt Lake City to see you on Saturday was made in ignorance of how the trains run. Judging from the tone of your letter I'd not think any useful purpose will be served by my seeing you."

Meanwhile, church attendance in the growing town of 4,000 persons declined. A member wrote Spalding that Jefferd was in Salt Lake City every week, and expressed surprise he did not visit the bishop, adding, "Our congregation decreases every Sunday. There were six in the morning and twelve in the evening last Sunday. It seems too bad to keep a minister here, there are so few."[114]

On November 20, 1912, Spalding wrote a final pastoral missive to the sulking English cleric. "It is indeed sadly humiliating for a man who has entire confidence in himself and his ability to do a large and important work and receive fuller compensation, to find himself unappreciated and in a small and limited field. I know you will not care for sympathy and I will not irritate you by offering it. . . . In the western part of the United States, especially in the Intermountain region, there are other clergymen, able and cultured, who are struggling with the same handicap of uncongenial surroundings and unresponsive fellow citizens. Perhaps they get comfort in trying to realize that Nazareth was much the same sort of a town as that in which they live."[115]

Jefferd soon left. He returned to England and the Diocese of Canterbury in 1913 as a licensed preacher, a nonparochial position, and within a year disappeared from church rolls. In one of his letters to his mother, Spalding described the situation in Park City. "Mr. X, the clergyman here, is the oddest man I have ever known. When I first wrote him that I was coming up he replied that it was a free country and that if I wanted to come I could, but that since he didn't care to see me he should certainly leave the town. . . . He thinks he is capable of being Archbishop of Canterbury and he isn't captivating Park City! But it was funny to hear him urge on the people in his sermon on the grace of humility!"[116] In August 1913, H. E. Henriques, active as a priest in Utah and Nevada from 1907 to 1953, came to Park City to revive work there on a part-time basis. He journeyed weekly to Salt Lake City as chaplain at St. Mark's Hospital and at Emery House, and in 1915 became vicar of St. John's Chapel, Salt Lake City.

Death Comes to the Bishop

A voluminous letter writer, Spalding often worked at his desk at home in the evening. On September 25, 1914, he finished some letters that would be his last. "I'm on my way to Eureka and Provo," he wrote, "to see how the Rices were getting on at Eureka," and then to check on a mining cave-in where four of the dead men belonged to the church. Of the person who would soon be his successor, he wrote, "Jones is certainly taking hold splendidly in Salt Lake."[117]

It was about 9 P.M. when the bishop left his house at 444 East First South Street, headed for the mailbox at the corner of South Temple and E Street. There was not much traffic at night in Salt Lake City, but as he stepped into the street an automobile sped down South Temple, a wide avenue with a downward grade. Spalding saw the two-and-one-half ton Lozier touring car coming and moved aside, expecting it to pass him, but the driver, Adrienne King, the seventeen-year-old daughter of a local judge, turned the vehicle toward him instead. Spalding "was thrown to the pavement with terrific force, was dragged fully fifty feet, and died within five minutes of the accident, without regaining consciousness," a newspaper account reported, adding the vehicle "dashed with terrific impact against a steel tower used as a support for the electric and trolley wires. . . . So heavy was this impact that the uprights of this steel tower were bent, and one was snapped."[118] The next day an editorial asked for "something to prevent huge machines, with their throbbing engines driving them on as agents of death."[119] No charges were ever brought against the judge's daughter, whose ribs were bruised and front teeth knocked out. In a public statement delivered the day after Spalding's death, the judge expressed regrets but said his daughter was within the fifteen-mile-an-hour speed limit. This is difficult to believe considering the long distance Spalding was dragged, the impact of the car on the steel pole, and the bruises and other injuries sustained by the driver in the crash.

Two days later, St. Mark's Cathedral was filled for a memorial service, after which the coffin was carried to the railway station by an honor guard of Sons of the American Revolution, to which Spalding belonged. The railroad officials who once denied Spalding a courtesy pass made a private car available to carry his remains to Denver. At the railroad terminal, "employees in overalls, officials in broadcloth, runners in red uniforms, and yardmen on duty near the scene" stood with bared heads as the cortege passed.[120] After a service in the cathedral there, he was buried beside his father in Riverside Cemetery. Except for a family house in Denver, his estate was a $5.25 bank account in Salt Lake City.

The Church had grown in Spalding's time to a total of three parishes and twenty-one missions with approximately fourteen hundred communicants. Friends and foes praised the forty-nine-year-old bishop's courage, lively intellect, advocacy of workers's causes, and his outspokenness. But when the tears were shed and the eulogies shelved, the question is, what would have happened had Spalding lived? Despite his pastoral skills, Spalding's socialism alienated him from many mainstream Episcopalians. Numerous establishment figures in the East and in Salt Lake City kept their checkbooks closed during Spalding's last years, and those, like Spalding, who questioned the war effort were on a collision course with a broad segment of church membership, as Spalding's successor soon discovered.

Independence Hall, Third South near Main Street, Salt Lake City. The adobe building originally housed a "Gentile" Young Men's Literary Association that attracted non-LDS settlers engaged in business, banking, or transportation. The Episcopal Church held services there after the arrival of its first missionaries in May 1867. *Used by permission, Utah State Historical Society, all rights reserved.*

St. Mark's Cathedral, 231 East 100 South, Salt Lake City. Richard Upjohn, 1802–1878, designed the building, which included the city's first church bell. Its cornerstone was laid on July 30, 1870. Bishop Tuttle was elected cathedral rector November 18, 1870 and consecrated the building on May 14, 1874. The vestry said the bishop "should always be, ex officio, the rector of the cathedral parish." *Used by permission, Utah State Historical Society, all rights reserved.*

Daniel S. Tuttle, first missionary bishop of Montana, Utah, and Idaho, 1867–1886, bishop of Missouri from 1886–1923, and presiding bishop of the Episcopal Church, through seniority, from 1903–1923. The rugged, upstate New York native was initially responsible for a jurisdiction of 340,000 square miles. By his estimate Tuttle traveled over 40,000 miles by horse, stagecoach, or train in the missionary district and missed only two Sunday services in twenty-seven years because of illness. *Diocesan Archives.*

Rowland Hall School, first known as St. Mark's School for girls, opened in 1881 in Salt Lake City through a gift of Virginia Lafayette Rowland of Philadelphia and her daughter, in memory of Benjamin Rowland, husband and father. Three old dry goods stores and a half-ruined adobe bowling alley on Main Street were previous sites for Episcopal schools. Tuition costs were a constant problem, and Tuttle raised over 500 scholarships of $40 each to help fund Rowland Hall and church schools in Salt Lake City, Odgen, Logan, and Plain City. *Diocesan Archives.*

The building of church schools, like St. Mark's Grammar School, was central to the ministry of Utah's first missionary bishop, Daniel S. Tuttle. Tuttle said, "Out from the training in church schools may emerge in a most wholesome manner and degree, faith that is not afraid to reason and reason that is not afraid to adore." St. Mark's, a day school for boys and girls, first opened in July 1867 and moved to its own building on 100 South in 1873. *Diocesan Archives.*

A late nineteenth century's artist's rendering of St. Paul's Chapel, at the corner of Main Street and Fourth South, Salt Lake City, where ground was broken in April 1880. Money for the "semiGothic" structure came from the Mount family of New York City, whom Bishop Tuttle had known as a Sunday school teacher-seminarian in the 1860s. As the church's original site became increasingly a commercial neighborhood, the congregation moved elsewhere, and the original structure was torn down in 1918.

The interior of St. Mark's Cathedral in 1903. The stained glass windows behind the altar, were destroyed in a 1935 fire. The canopied bishop's seat, or cathedra (left), reportedly came by ox cart from San Francisco after a sea voyage around the Cape of Good Hope in the 1870s. It represents the place and authority of a bishop as head of a diocese or missionary district. *Diocesan Archives.*

St. Mark's Hospital, one of the West's leading early medical institutions, originally opened in May 1872 in a rented adobe house in Salt Lake City. It was funded largely by dollar-a-month dues from local miners. In 1892 a new hospital and a nursing home were built at 800 North 200 West. *Bulkley Photo Collection.*

St. John's Chapel, Ninth East and Logan Avenue, Salt Lake City, began life in a barn, and in 1890 moved to a small wooden building seating forty persons. In the early twentieth century a larger church building was added, and in 1910 Sara Napper organized an active parish program for women and children. Parishioners sent funds and sewing to Alaska, China, and Armenia. By the early 1940s membership had declined to forty-six persons and the property was sold for $8,500. *Diocesan Archives.*

Rowland Hall School at its new site at 205 East First Avenue in 1906. *Diocesan Archives.*

James and Lydia Luceila Webster Gillogly lived in a freight car for several months after their arrival at Ogden on July 18, 1870. Gillogly originally held services in the Union Pacific Railway passenger room. He died in 1881 and his wife, pregnant with their fifth child, remained in Ogden for seven years as a music teacher. Gillogly built the Church of the Good Shepherd, which was consecrated on February 6, 1895. *Thelma Ellis Photo Collection.*

St. Peter's Chapel, originally the chapel for St. Mark's Hospital, was founded in 1891, then physically moved in 1907 to 657 North Second West Street near the new hospital. "The Friendly Little Church on the West Side" was an active parish in the early twentieth century, but its numbers declined, and it closed in the 1950s. The Rev. A. Leonard Wood served the chapel from 1928 to 1957. Wood was a British veteran of the Boer war and a former newspaper cartoonist. *Diocesan Archives.*

Bishop Abiel Leonard, 1888–1903, second from left, front row, with clergy and lay leaders of the Montana, Utah, and Idaho Missionary District, which Leonard called "one of the most extensive and difficult in the American church." Leonard, who died of typhoid fever at age fifty-six, spent much of his time on the road. His letterhead contained the message, "If you do not receive a reply to your letter within thirty days, you may know that I am absent on a visitation. Always address me at Salt Lake City." *Diocesan Archives.*

A Native American wedding party at the Mission House, Randlett, 1905. Episcopal Church Native American work in Utah began in 1894 with Bishop Leonard's appeal for $3,000 to build a chapel and mission house on the Uintah Reservation. *The Spirit of Missions* (October, 1905): 63.

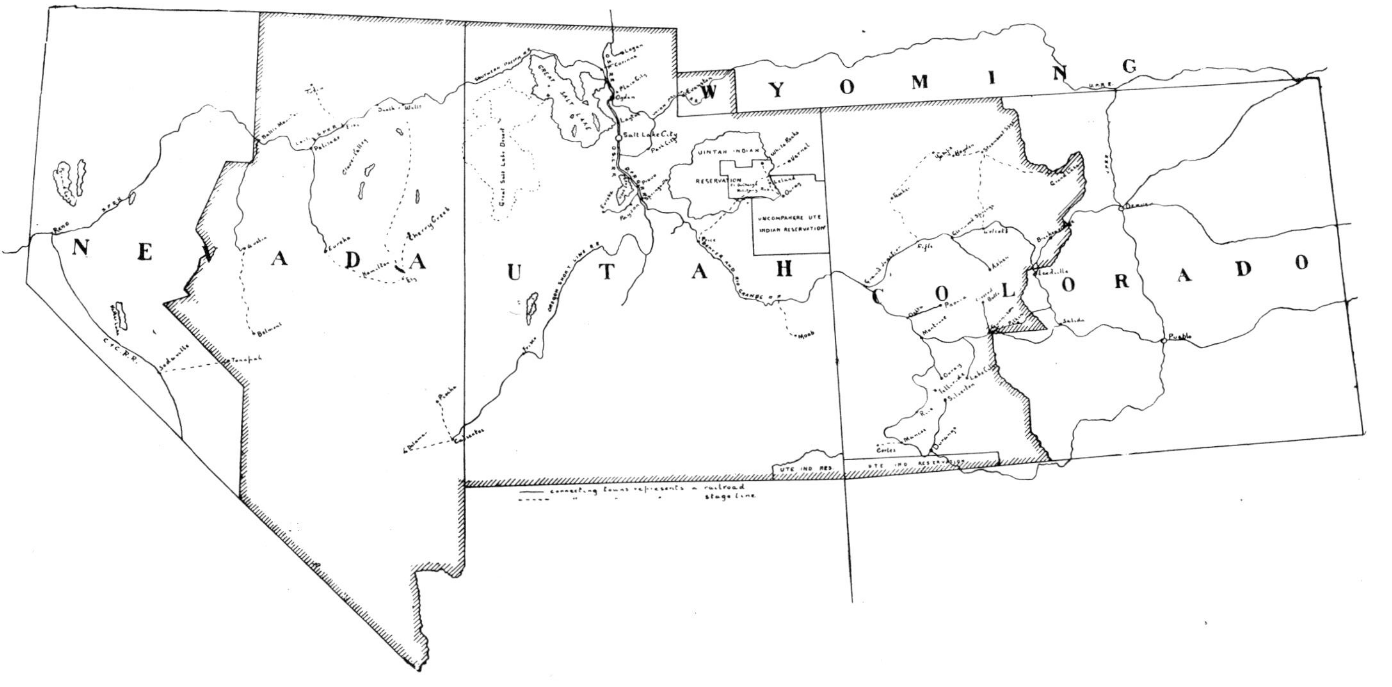

Map of the Missionary District of Salt Lake, 1903. *Diocesan Archives.*

Franklin Spencer Spalding, missionary bishop of Utah, 1904–1914. Spalding built up academic missions at St. John's House, Logan, and Emery House, Salt Lake City. As a Christian Socialist and Social Gospel advocate, he preached at the Cathedral of St. John the Divine in New York City and at London's Westminster Abbey during the Pan-Anglican Congress of 1908. Spalding's *Joseph Smith as a Translator* (1912) argued that the Latter–day Saints founder's translations of early Egyptian documents were spurious, and created considerable controversy among LDS readers. *Diocesan Archives.*

Bishop Franklin Spencer Spalding shown in the bow of a boat carrying the U.S. Mail and rowed by Native Americans. Spalding traveled frequently in the vast Utah Missionary District, including to the Ute reservations east of Salt Lake City. The journey to Whiterocks took four days by stagecoach, train, or on horseback. *The Spirit of Missions* (October 1909): 874.

Franklin Spencer Spalding (center, with cap) was a member of the first party to climb western Wyoming's Grand Teton peak. The three climbers, led by Billy Owen, an experienced guide from the Colorado Mountain Club, began their ascent at 5 A.M. August 11, 1898, and reached their destination eleven hours later, following what was afterwards called the Owen-Spalding route. Spalding called the view "a grand sight, one of the grandest on earth." A Spalding Falls is located at the Meadow campsite at the Middle Teton Glacier. *Denver Public Library, Western History Collection, F-6770.*

St. Mark's Cathedral decorated with American flags on December 12, 1912. Utah became increasingly patriotic as World War I approached. Bishop Franklin Spencer Spalding, 1904–1914, spoke against the war, as did his successor, Paul Jones, 1915–1918, a socialist and pacifist. J. Walcott Thompson, son of the commandant of Fort Douglas, a local attorney, and a cathedral vestry member for forty-seven years, led opposition to Jones, which resulted in the latter's resignation as bishop. *Used by permission, Utah State Historical Society, all rights reserved.*

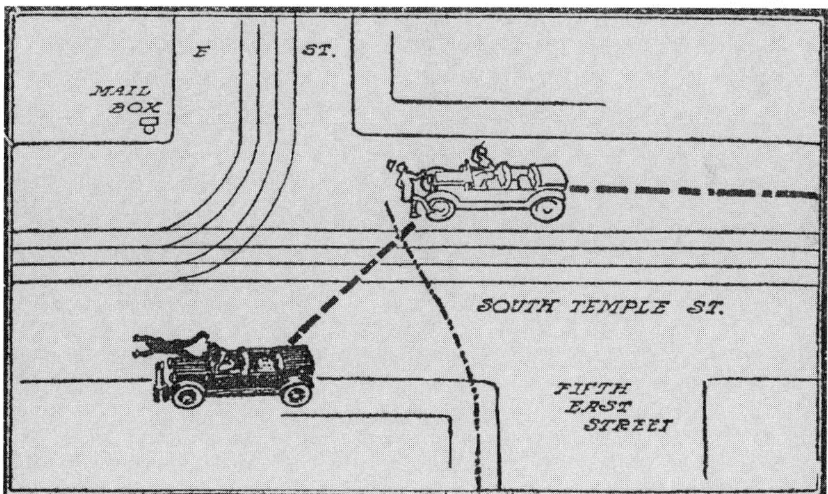

Bishop Spalding was killed while crossing Salt Lake City's South Temple Street from Fifth East on the night of September 25, 1914. He was struck by a two and one-half ton Lozier touring car driven by Adrienne King, a speeding teenaged driver and local judge's daughter who was never charged in the accident. Miss King was severely bruised and the car dragged Spalding fifty feet until it struck a pole carrying electric and trolley wires. 'So heavy was this impact that the uprights of this steel tower were bent and one was snapped," a newspaper account stated. The photo and diagram of the accident are from the *Salt Lake Herald-Republican*, Saturday, September 26, 1914.

J. Wesley Twelves set out by horseback from St. Paul's, Vernal, to make his pastoral rounds, c. 1916. Twelves and his wife, Elizabeth, stop for lunch (lower photo). Missionary district transportation was mainly by horseback, stagecoach, wagon, or train until the 1920s, although some clergy hitched local rides on government "mail cars." The missionary district debated the advisability of providing clergy with automobiles and telephones. *Elizabeth Twelves Miller Collection.*

Chipeta, "White Singing Bird," wife of the Uncompahgre Chief Ouray and a Ute leader in her own right. She was reputed to be the only woman allowed to attend Ute tribal meetings, was an active member of the Episcopal Church, knew the bishop, and was buried in an Episcopal funeral service at her death in 1924 near Montrose, Colorado. *Used by permission, Utah State Historical Society, all rights reserved.*

Rosa Camfield, an English woman, worked in Whiterocks, Randlett, or Vernal, from about 1907 until her death in 1935. Much of the church's work among the Utes in eastern Utah was done by women missionaries, whose salaries were less than half those paid the male missionaries. The women were schoolteachers and taught Bible lessons, cooking, sewing, and hygiene. They were nurses and social workers, and provided refuge for battered women and orphaned children. *Bulkley Photo Collection.*

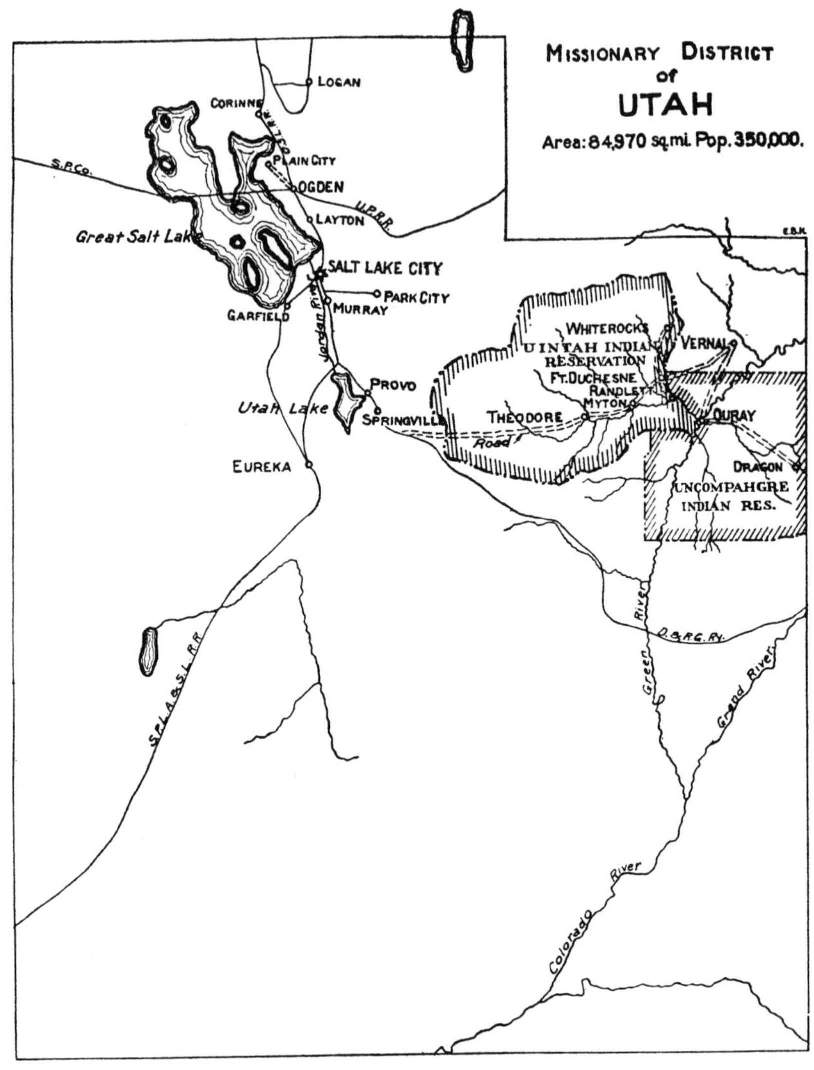

Boundaries shifted during the missionary district's history and only in the twentieth century were state and missionary district coterminous. The original Missionary District of Montana, Idaho, and Utah existed from 1867 to 1880. Next it was the Missionary District of Idaho and Utah, 1880 to 1886, followed by the Missionary District of Nevada and Utah, 1886 to 1898. The Missionary District of Salt Lake, 1898 to 1907, became the Missionary District of Utah (shown above) from 1907 to 1971, when the National Church made Utah an independent diocese. The state's southeast corner was ceded to a separate Navajoland Area Mission in 1977. *Diocesan Archives.*

The bishop's residence, 444 East First South, Salt Lake City. Bishop Spalding, 1904–1914, kept his office here and shared the house with his sister, who worked as his secretary. Bishop Moulton, who arrived in 1920, lived in a second floor apartment, with his wife and two children. His office was on the ground floor, and his secretary occupied rooms on the third floor. *Diocesan Archives.*

St. Paul's Church, Vernal, originally met as a congregation in 1900 in Jake Workman's Opera House, then in the Odd Fellows Hall. First services in the Gothic Revival church shown here were held on September 13, 1913. St. Paul's Lodge, next door, was completed in 1912 as a residence for single women attending schools in Vernal. It later became a hospital, then a clergy residence, and finally a parish hall. *Diocesan Archives.*

St. Elizabeth's, Whiterocks. An initial church service was held at Fort Duschene in 1894 at the invitation of Colonel J. F. Randlett, post commandant, acting Indian agent, and active Episcopalian, who gave the church land for a mission. Bishop Abiel Leonard began St. Elizabeth's congregation in 1897, and the building was erected in 1904. *The Spirit of Missions* (September 1921): 574.

Holy Spirit Episcopal Church, Randlett. The Episcopal church was designated to take charge of Native American educational and religious work among the Utes in 1885 when the U.S. Congress divided such work among several denominations. Bishop Abiel Leonard built the church and rectory in 1896. *The Spirit of Missions* (September 1923): 9.

Indian schools were an important part of the Episcopal Church's missionary work with Native Americans. A Bureau of Indian Affairs boarding school was established near Fort Duschene in the late 1880s and then moved to Whiterocks. In the 1920s it housed two hundred Native American children drawn from various Ute clans. Possibly these two photos of young Native Americans were taken at Whiterocks in the 1930s. They were part of the collection of Archdeacon William F. Bulkley, who visited there frequently with Bishop Moulton. *Bulkley Photo Collection.*

4

Paul Jones

The Pacifist Bishop

(1914–1918)

> It seems abundantly manifest that an end has come to the usefulness of the bishop of Utah in his present field, and that no earnestness of effort on his part will suffice to regain it.
>
> —Tuttle Commission Report, December 12, 1917

> Expediency may make necessary the resignation of a bishop at this time, but no expediency can ever justify the degradation of the ideals of the episcopate which these conclusions seem to involve.
>
> —Bishop Paul Jones, 1917 Convocation Report

If a writer of Greek tragedies had lived in early-twentieth-century America, and sought material for a next play, the encounter of Paul Jones, Utah's pacifist bishop during World War I, with the Missionary District Council of Advice and the House of Bishops of the Episcopal Church, would have provided rich subject matter. All the ingredients were there: wartime patriotic fervor; Jones, the idealistic and uncompromising bishop; and the unyielding local and national church leadership. All sped toward a collision, doing what they did in God's name, led by Daniel S. Tuttle, a character of biblical proportions and founder of the missionary district, who presided over the removal of his successor. And, as in a tragedy, forces once unleashed led a life of their own which the protagonists could not control.

The story could begin with a snapshot that captures a moment in Utah church history. The fiftieth anniversary of the missionary district was commemorated on June 10, 1917 at St. John's, Salt Lake City. Daniel

S. Tuttle, Utah's first missionary bishop, who had come west in 1867 and worked tirelessly for nineteen years to build the missionary district, returned for the event. He was presiding bishop now, by virtue of seniority, and had been bishop of Missouri since leaving Utah in 1886. The eighty-year-old Tuttle, a bishop for fifty years, stands for a moment not far from his younger colleague, Paul Jones, thirty-seven, a bishop for barely two-and-a-half years. The angular, thin Jones stares confidently ahead, as does Tuttle, forty-three years his senior. The passing shot suggests the future encounter between the two that would play out over the next nine months, resulting in Jones's resignation, and raising questions about free speech in the church unanswered until decades later.[1]

Paul Jones (1880–1941) spent twelve years in Utah, first in 1906 as codirector of St. John's center for college students, Logan, then as archdeacon, or principal assistant, to Bishop Spalding in 1913. After Spalding's death in 1914, he was named missionary bishop until forced to resign because of his anti-war activities in 1917.

Jones was more than a one-issue antiwar activist. A gifted pastor and administrator, he adroitly managed such assets as the district possessed, and frequently visited with the dozen diocesan clergy scattered throughout the state. He urged that women be elected as convocation officers, an advanced idea for Utah and the Episcopal Church in 1915, and one not acted on for nearly a half-century. Articulate in offering the Episcopal Church as an alternative to Mormonism, during his three-year episcopate he also worked to outlaw the use of peyote, a hallucinogenic drug employed in Native American rituals, and defended Prohibition. In both latter instances, the church took a stand on public policy issues, and in doing so removed the wind from the sails of some of Jones's opponents, who argued the church should say nothing about politics.

The bishop sought to raise clergy stipends, which averaged $1,200 in 1917 and provided no retirement insurance. "These men are expected to dress well, keep open house, hold their own often among people of wealth, educate their children and exercise leadership in their communities. It is obvious that eighty percent of them cannot be expected to save enough money to provide for old age," Jones wrote.[2] He endorsed a Church Pension Fund proposal to provide clergy annuities of half the clergy salary at age sixty-eight, and a widow's annuity of half that sum. Jones urged the missionary district to raise $5,000 to launch the program, and collected $1,035 from his own clergy for it. The bishop also made some attempts at national fundraising, but his eastern contacts were limited. Further, World War I was in the air, and his pacifism closed many of the Episcopal Church's traditional doors to the impoverished missionary district.

The new bishop had little interest in ritual or ceremony; his daybook contains an entry for December 14, 1915: "Midnight celebration at St. Paul's Church—assisted and preached. Incense used for the first time in the Episcopal Church in Utah."[3] He also supported a short-lived ministry to Utah's four to five thousand–member Japanese community. The Rev. P. C. Aoki was hired in 1917 to hold services and teach English in three cities.

As archdeacon, Jones had traveled about the state at Spalding's behest. In a swing through southern Utah he held services in dance halls and school houses, braved dust storms, hitched rides on grocery vans, took trains with erratic routes and schedules, and twice had his bag with vestments, prayer books, and hymnals lost. He described a service in Modena, normally a town of fifty persons, whose size swelled in the spring when pens were set up to shear 125,000 sheep. Two church members working for the weather bureau arranged for services in a dance hall. Seats were planks laid on boxes and oil cans, a pump organ was carried from a nearby house, and notices were hastily tacked up in the saloon and store. Once more Jones's bag failed to arrive, and he spent Sunday afternoon copying the words of hymns on a typewriter. At the announced hour more than seventy persons gathered in the dimly lit room, and an LDS organist who could only play by ear led the hymns until she reached "Jesus, Lover of my Soul," when she whispered loudly, "How does it go? I've forgotten!" Jones hummed the tune for her, and what was probably the first Episcopal service held in Modena continued.[4] LDS strongholds like St. George, Cedar City, and elsewhere reported "no welcome for the Gentile visitor." In Cedar City, "the fire marshal refused to allow the City Hall to be used for a service, and it was necessary to pay for the use of the tabernacle even though so few came out to the service that it had to be given up and a few hymns sung instead."[5]

Later, when he was bishop, Jones calculated that on one trip to the Uintah Basin, which covered 807 miles, "416 miles was by standard gauge railroad, sixty-two by narrow gauge, fifteen by horse drawn stage, ten by sleigh, one hundred seventy-four by auto-stage, fifty-seven by private team, thirty by private auto, thirty-five on horseback, and eight on foot."[6] He held eighteen services that time, in churches, halls, schools, a YMCA, and outdoors.[7]

The vicar of St. Paul's, Vernal, owned two horses, and later a Model T Ford. In 1917 he purchased a motion picture projector, which was shipped weekly with a film to various outlying congregations. The trip from Vernal was by "stage," a reconstructed Buick car used for carrying mail and passengers in isolated regions. Green River was crossed by ferry, but during high current a single person and the mail were carried across in a basket suspended from a cable.[8]

As with Spalding, nothing in Jones's background suggested the intensity of his later views on social questions. Jones graduated from Yale University in 1902, and from the Episcopal Theological School in Cambridge, Massachusetts, in 1906. At home in the Pennsylvania mining country during college vacations, he spent a summer as a strike-breaker in a coal mine, and another in a tax office, learning the skills with numbers that would aid him in church administration. He grew up, he said in a phrase that could have come from F. Scott Fitzgerald, "with right-thinking people of the best type," adding, "My years at Yale did nothing to shake those sound conclusions . . . wealth as evidence of individual probity, punishment as the only possible treatment for crime, the foreigner to be kept in his place and to be treated kindly, but firmly, the army and navy as the loyal defenders of the nation, the worship of the church as the proper expression of all decent and respectable people—all these conceptions were mine by ordinary training and association."[9]

During Jones's last year at seminary, Bishop Spalding made a recruitment trip to the Episcopal Theological School seeking two clerics to establish a community house for young men at Logan's two colleges. The salary was $75 a month, less than an elevator operator would make, but Jones and a classmate, Donald K. Johnson, volunteered. Many of Jones positions on social and economic issues bear the influence of conversations with Spalding, but he was his own person, whose intellectual formation came a generation later than Spalding's.

Jones knew the work of the English Christian Socialists F. D. Maurice and Charles Kingsley. The Social Gospel, emphasizing the church's role in redeeming economic inequities in society, was taught in Cambridge, and Jones had heard the Bible spoken of as "a dangerous and dynamic book, radical, and revolutionary."[10] He "came to see that Christianity and socialism were not contradictory but supplementary," a biographer of Jones wrote.[11]

The young clergyman arrived in Logan in 1906. Eventually his salary rose to $90 a month, allowing him to marry Mary Elizabeth Balch, a New Englander and a pacifist herself, whom he had met on a trip to California. Their honeymoon was a covered wagon trip up Utah Canyon. Jones also staked out an eighty-acre isolated farm property in Box Elder County. When he had spare time in Logan, he took the train to Brigham City, transferred to the Southern Pacific heading west to Kelton, then rode another ten miles by horse to the farm. Jones cleared sagebrush and raised grain crops on the isolated property, until he moved to Salt Lake City. Years later, his grandchildren gave part of the property to St. John's, Logan.[12]

The Logan community center was a success. A "Common Room Club" was formed with a small chapel, gymnasium, classrooms, and club space. Discussions, lectures, and "smokers" were its weekly fare. A seasonal membership cost five dollars, and after two years, women members were accepted. The center had several sleeping rooms, the only library in town, with nearly a thousand books and thirty periodicals, a pool table, shuffleboard, and tennis courts. The "Knights of King Arthur" for young men was eventually replaced by a Boy Scout troop, the first such recognized troop in the western United States. Jones was its scoutmaster, and it attracted several future community leaders. The lawn tennis court could be rented for ten cents an hour. A current events publication, *The Portal*, was published from 1908 to 1913.[13] Its commentary on national and international political and social questions was of a high order. It promoted a Sportsmen's Club to protect fish and game, and asked the local Commercial Club to open a room where farmers and their families coming to town could rest and warm themselves during the winter. *The Portal* urged streetcars for Logan, a modern sewer system, the piping in of pure spring water, and bringing Chautauqua cultural programs to the growing city.

Jones and Johnson preached on Sundays, attracting sizable congregations of young LDS men and others.[14] When Bishop Spalding visited Logan, he wrote, "Jones and Johnson are doing splendidly. . . . It is wonderful what impression they have made on the town. It's the first time really well-educated gentlemen have been sent there. I'm hoping for great things for Logan."[15]

Jones's approach to problems was cerebral and analytical. His pamphlet, *Points of Contact: A Consideration for Dissatisfied Latter-day Saints*, was tightly argued for an audience of questioning or disaffected Latter-day Saints. Jones said nothing negative about the Latter-day Saints, but succinctly compared the Book of Mormon and the Episcopal Book of Common Prayer on points such as the sources of authority, the plan of salvation, God, revelation, and the intermediate state of the soul following death. It was unfortunate that the Episcopal Church was not represented in the smaller towns of New York State, such as Palmyra, in the 1830s, he said. Had that been the case, Joseph Smith might have found a welcoming denomination and not felt a need to organize a new church. "In many of his early ideas, his desire for an authoritative ministry . . . where he was out of harmony with the denominational Christianity around him, he would have found himself at home in the Episcopal Church. It is there that the Latter-day Saint today who has lost his faith in Mormonism may hope to regain and refresh his faith in God's work in the world."[16]

In 1913, Jones was named archdeacon of Utah and vicar of two small congregations in Salt Lake City. A newspaper account said, "his appointment was attributed chiefly to his executive acumen, his wide grasp of church matters and his organizing ability."[17] Jones gradually added a number of administrative roles, including secretary to the Episcopal Missionary District of Utah, clergy recruiter, and member of the religious education and social service committees. Spalding was bishop, but Jones was increasingly his second in command.

The new archdeacon and his wife, expecting a child, moved in with the bishop in the latter's large house in downtown Salt Lake City. "It will be grand to have a baby in the house because I've always loved babies," the unmarried bishop wrote his mother, shortly before his death on September 25, 1914.[18] Paul and May's baby was born on Spalding's birthday, March 13; they named her Barbara Spalding Jones.[19]

The House of Bishops, at a special meeting in Minneapolis on October 8, 1914, elected Jones, then thirty-four, as missionary bishop of Utah. The House in all likelihood saw continuity between Spalding and Jones. However, J. Walcott Thompson, a cathedral vestry member for over forty years and a Council of Advice member, found Jones immature and would have preferred a "bishop from the east with a big reputation" who would have access to wealthy donors.[20]

As bishop, Jones was unwavering in his Social Gospel–pacifist beliefs, but they were presented in a matter-of-fact way, along with the rest of his religious convictions. He joined the Socialist Party, because socialism "seemed to represent the most honest effort in sight to apply Christian principles to the social order."[21] The bishop's social theory was a straightforward, action-oriented response to Christ's New Testament teachings. The Gospel provided practical solutions to correct inequities in the social order, he believed. Marxist theorists would find such writings puzzling deviations from their doctrine, for Jones never advocated anything but traditional American forms of government.

Jones lacked Tuttle's forceful personality and Spalding's range of interests. He was tall and thin, with angular features and an acerbic personality. Under attack he responded with a barrage of pointed questions. If he had stayed a socialist, he probably could have made it, but he was a vocal pacifist as well at a time of patriotic fervor, an explosive combination of forces. At that time, there were only seven Episcopal clergy nationally who were declared pacifists; Jones was the only bishop.[22] When he came under heavy attack later that year, Thompson called him "a mere nobody."[23] Thompson, a local attorney, engineered the bishop's removal, aided by the clerical and lay leadership of the cathedral and St. Paul's parish. An irony is that flanking the high altar of St. Mark's Cathedral are large memorial windows to the wife of Thompson, son of the commandant of Fort Douglas, and Bishop Spalding, a socialist and outspoken antiwar cleric.[24]

The pacifist controversy took place in a growing church, and needs to be viewed in perspective. To read the four annual reports on Jones's episcopacy is to read of a church gradually expanding despite difficult circumstances. Jones delivered all his annual reports in person, except for the 1918 one, read after his resignation. It would take careful reading between the lines to discern some of Jones's political views, for he did not mention them, except for a brief statement at the time of his resignation. Meanwhile, church membership was little affected by the controversy. The number of communicants increased from 1,426 to 1,461, and Sunday school enrollment rose substantially from 1,289 to 1,629. The number of missions grew from nineteen to twenty-four from 1915 through 1917, including new missions in Helper, Castle Gate, Kenilworth, and Standardville, struggling mining or railroad centers.[25] The parish and mission budget was $19,838 in 1915.[26] At the time of Jones's departure it had slightly decreased, to $17,851.[27]

Of the world situation in 1917, Jones said that some people believed war was terrible but inevitable, while others believed that Christian love should triumph, even if it resulted in an individual believer's death. The two viewpoints were irreconcilable, Jones believed, but a greater responsibility fell on Christian clergy than on the general public. It was their role to quicken the consciences of their people—to speak out fearlessly and adhere to a higher standard of ethical behavior—even in the face of opposition. "To ask that a priest or bishop modify or emasculate his preaching of the gospel, as some would do, is to strike at the one ground of hope that we have for continued upward progress of the Christian faith."[28]

Also, during this time Jones sought to continue the basic relationship with St. Mark's Cathedral, formulated by Tuttle in November 1870, and by Leonard in a joint declaration of February 7, 1895, and again on September 11, 1909 by Spalding. The bishop would be ex officio rector of the cathedral, although parochial care of the cathedral congregation would be delegated to the dean. "Whenever a vacancy occurs in the office of Dean the wardens shall give notice thereof in writing to the bishop. The Vestry shall then proceed to the choice of a Dean but no election of a Dean shall be complete until it is confirmed by the bishop," Article Four of the Joint Act stated.[29]

Women in the Utah Church

Women were instrumental at every level in carrying on the church's work in Jones's time. Busily and without fanfare, they held the struggling churches together. Except for celebrating the Eucharist, several were priests in everything but name. Sara Napper, social worker and diocesan registrar, and Deaconess Frances B. Affleck kept the small missions of St. John's and St. Peter's, Salt Lake City, alive during interims between clergy, and Margueritte Schneider began missionary work on the city's lower west side. St. Mark's Hospital struggled with finances because of the war, but the hospital's operating rooms were upgraded and a chaplain was hired, aided by women volunteers from the cathedral. Fourteen women's groups reported at the Convention.[30] Speaking of the role of women, Jones said, "there is no question, I think, but that our parishes and missions are kept up very largely by the devoted efforts of the women through their guilds and other organizations." He then proposed that the canons be interpreted "to include women as well as men" as elected members of the annual convention. The proposal did not carry then, as it had not in 1889, when the three women from St. John's, Logan, appeared as delegates and were turned away.[31]

Jones continued Spalding's work in Utah's coal camps and mining towns. Helper was a stop near Price on the Salt Lake City–Denver route of the Rio Grande railroad, named for the "helper" engines attached to carry trains over Soldier's Summit. Local railroad officials had erected a small chapel there and, since one railroad official was a Presbyterian and the other an Episcopalian, the two denominations alternated Sunday services. But the churches always led a tenuous existence and within a few years the basement became a machine tool shop and the church a bunkhouse. By 1917, services were resumed at St. Barnabas's mission, Helper, which continued until the 1940s. Five miles up from Helper, high in the canyons, were the coal camps. "They are comparatively new towns; none over five years old. The coal company owns everything there except the lives of the men and their clothes," a priest who visited them wrote. "The company store gets back on an average about forty percent of the wages each month. . . . The people, on their side, have no interest in erecting a church where they cannot buy the ground."[32]

Many of the miners came from England, but there were sizable Greek, Italian, and other European populations as well. Mine work was hazardous; safety standards were poor and cave-ins and equipment accidents were frequent. In Castle Gate, the first service was held in 1916 in a schoolhouse, the only available building since the community hall was used on Sunday nights for a picture show. The building was crowded, and those who could not sit at children's desks sat on top of them. Many of the English people had not attended such a service since arriving in America fifteen years ago. "A elderly lady said, 'It does me good to see the bit of white surplice again.'"[33]

On the following Sunday sixteen children were baptized, gathering around the teacher's desk as an altar. One child was named "Paul" in honor of Bishop Jones. The men, with English and Welsh names, were unaccustomed to attending church, and gathered in front of the store until the service began. One parishioner asked that the service not take too long, as "The Submarine Secret" was showing at the cinema that evening and "we have not missed one in the series."[34] Advent Mission, Standardville, and Trinity Church, Castle Gate, continued their existence until the 1930s, Ascension Mission, Kenilworth, until 1949. By then the mines had played out and those who could moved on.

To the west of Salt Lake City were the copper mines, which Spalding had targeted for attention, and where Jones supported an active ministry. The minister there was Maxwell F. Rice, who spent a decade in Utah, first among the miners, and then at Emery House, near the University of Utah campus, and as chaplain to St. Mark's Hospital. Rice described life in the Magna camp, part of the Garfield copper mining complex: "On the right of the road are rows of houses possessing baked alkali yards for lawns, with not a blade of grass nor a tree." Rice, who helped build the church with his own hands, remembered "hiring a boy to sit on the ridge pole of our mission in this camp with a pail of water to cool the sheets of corrugated iron which I was nailing on the roof. There was no place for children to play except in the shadeless slop-soaked yards or the dusty roads until we built a playground."[35]

More than 2,000 men worked at Garfield; Rice called it "a steam shovel project larger than the Panama Canal." At nearby Arthur, church services were held in the Odd Fellows's Hall, and a Sunday school in Sunflower Hall. "No where was one more needed than at this settlement where the children were running wild in a vicious environment."[36] In response to local need, the company erected an attractive church, used by several denominations, and a clubhouse. Rice also started a Garfield Club to keep men out of the pool hall and saloon.

Sunday school teachers were hard to come by during the summer, so Rice had children act out different biblical scenes each week. In the Good Samaritan story, two boys portrayed robbers, the priest was dressed in an acolyte's robe, and the Good Samaritan arrived in a Boy Scouts' uniform, and applied his recently learned first aid techniques. Commenting on the meaning of the parable in the Garfield context, Rice wrote, "The scene at the inn gives us the opportunity to bring out the lesson. The Good Samaritan is thanked for having saved the robbed boy's life at the risk of his own. He promises not to call foreigners 'Dagos' 'Greasers' 'Bohunks' etc. but to think of them as *neighbors* [italics in the original]."[37]

"Our Christmas is often shrouded by smelter, smoke, and the angels' song confused by the roar of machinery," Rice wrote of the five Christmas services he held in 1918.[38] The tree the missionary had bought had been given to the manager of the Garfield plant. A gymnasium full of children gathered for the celebration and the manager "sent his machine forty miles to bring it to the children." Next the tree was moved to the church for Sunday services, then to a camp for soldiers. Meanwhile, services were held at nearby St. Andrew's, Ragtown. "Candles on many cakes lighted up forty very happy faces gathered about tables at the mission." Refreshments gave way to Christmas songs and stories, and later to the lighted tree. Next, Rice headed for a motion picture theatre in Greek Town, watching red-hot slag pour down a long dump at a smelter, as he led two cars full of children to the next Christmas party. "The tree for the children of this Greek and Austrian settlement was smaller than the others, but it bore more presents and more candy for each child and was quite the wonder of their big black eyes."[39] The Christmas celebration was difficult to arrange in the midst of the mills and smelter, Rice concluded. "Yet strange to say, we felt almost at the outset the mighty Spirit that gave birth to Christianity sweeping before us accomplishing what we ourselves could not have done." A year later, Jones reported a new community church had opened in Garfield, supported by several denominations, and built with company funds. Bishop Spalding's eastern friends provided its furnishings as a memorial to Spalding.

By 1917 St. John's House, Logan, which Jones had helped found a decade earlier, would soon close. Most male students were off to war, the town had a new public library, and emphasis in Logan shifted to a regular parish ministry.[40] Emery House at the University of Utah had thirty students in 1915, and enjoyed a few more years of active life.

Native American Work

Jones was interested in Native American ministries and, both as archdeacon and bishop, traveled to the eastern Utah reservations. In his sparse but observant prose, he described a 1915 winter hillside funeral near Ouray where a Native American was burying his infant daughter in the hills, a remarkable passage in religious writing:

> Half a mile up from the road we found the others gathered. Two Indian girls, one the mother of the baby, were huddled over a fire. Wissi-up, Ah-choop, and Buckskin Jim had just finished digging a grave in the hard gray shale. A dead horse, half eaten by coyotes, lay nearby pointing his feet to the sky, and on one side an old squaw sat in a wagon, while the saddle horses stood around. First the tent in which the child had died was placed in the grave. Then the body, wrapped in quilts, blankets, and shawls, was put in position with the head resting on a pillow.

> While Mr. Hersey read a part of the burial service we stood with bared heads, and even Wissi-up and Ah-choop took off their hats, though they were none of them Christians. When the words of the service were ended the missionary told them of the little burying ground chapel at Randlett, where there would never be any danger of their loved ones being disturbed, as they might be up in the hills. Then the baby's playthings were put in the grave, while one of the men broke up the dishes and pans that had been used in the tent, for the Indians bury with the dead all the articles that have been associated with the person that has gone. We turned to our team and went on our way, feeling that something had been done to bring that family closer to the Kingdom.[41]

Also in 1915, Jones participated in a brief effort to bring together the Episcopal churches of Utah, western Colorado, Arizona, and New Mexico at Four Corners, where the four states later comprising the Navajoland Area Mission met. Three bishops, and a clergy representative from Arizona, stood in their respective states and a communion service was held. An observer wrote, "The service was impressively reverent throughout, and no cathedral, with organ, choir, stained-glass and other embellishments, could have made a more glorious scene than did this open mesa, surrounded with the great mountains of the four states, with its rude stone altar, with the bishops in their Episcopal robes, and a congregation composed of Indians, sheep dippers, [and] a Mormon post-trader."[42] Jones, and the other church leaders, recognized the need for the Episcopal Church to work among the Navajo, principally through a medical or educational ministry. But a lack of resources and the coming of World War I left the vision unachieved.

The growing use of peyote among Native Americans was a mounting concern of missionaries. Native Americans who went north and south in Wyoming and Montana were active, both in using the drug during religious services and selling it to local people. By 1916, peyote use on the Uintah Reservation in Utah was estimated at fifty percent. One of the carriers was a Sioux named Sam Lone Bear, a trick roper and bronco-buster. While some Native Americans supported its use, others opposed it and approved of legislation outlawing its use.[43] In his 1917 report, Jones noted that drug use among the Utes had dropped after the peyote cult had been outlawed. "A number of those who had been loyal to the church dropped away and all those who took up with peyote refused to have anything to do with us." Of nineteen Utes on the Randlett mission list, eight never used peyote, two were doubtful, and six used the drug but gave it up. One person who used the drug died, two still used it. "When Mr. Hersey held his Easter feast for the Indians, after an interval of two years, there was good attendance of

Indians and an excellent spirit manifested. I think we safely feel that the worst of that trouble is over."[44]

Meanwhile, Milton J. Hersey worked hard to gain Native American support for traditional Christian feast days. At Christmas, boxes of gifts arrived at the nearest railroad station, sixty-seven miles away, from Chicago, St. Paul, and elsewhere. Once the missionary had assembled the gifts at the church, an invitation went out by word of mouth for people to gather. A visitor wrote, "Shaggy, obstinate-looking Indian ponies, with every kind of saddle-cloth, from Navajo blankets to old pieces of canvas, are tied in front of the church; comfortable family parties come in wagons and strange-looking sleighs. The church is filled, the squaws and children in front, the bucks by themselves in the rear."[45]

Missionaries wanted Native Americans to adopt non-Native American dress, cut their hair, wash, and learn English. The painting of faces is common to many cultures, but the missionaries discouraged Native Americans from adorning themselves this way. "Here and there a painted face, but not many in this church, for the Rev. Mr. Hersey stops at such a one in his progress down the aisle, and ridicules it with gentle irony," a missionary magazine reported.[46]

Gifts were piled about the front of the church, and Hersey read the Christmas story, explaining the gifts came, not from him, but from others, after which he and his wife distributed them to each person. While the white children were eager to open their gifts and see what others got, the Native Americans showed "no loud talk, no boisterous laughter! A gentle smile of satisfaction lights the faces of older Utes as the children receive their gifts. . . . In this distribution of gifts one thing is noticeable; no envy or jealously is shown or felt." The author noted that sharing of possessions was a part of Ute culture, and "no Ute can be truly prosperous, for what he has another may claim of his hospitality."[47]

Hersey's reports suggest he was a hard worker, going long distances by buggy to make calls, often in harsh weather, distributing food and clothing, holding services, and attending to the mission schools and small infirmary. He got along well with bishops. Leonard pointed to him as an ideal missionary; Spalding spoke glowingly of him, as did Jones. After almost two decades among Native Americans, Hersey concluded it was time now to think of recruiting native catechists and clergy, but no indigenous church leadership was raised up until after World War II. The family of Floyd A. O'Neil, a scholar of Native American history, grew up on the reservation where Hersey worked. "Dad knew him," O'Neil recalled. "His name resounded for years and not always was the resonance affirmative."[48] Hersey's mentality fit that of the Indian Rights Association, a group of

Philadelphia Quaker and Episcopalian reformers whose motto was "Kill the Indian and Save the Man." Native Americans who sided with the reformers were called "progressive Indians" and were rewarded materially, as were "Rice Christians" in the Orient. But others were left confused and resentful of the system.

The search is in vain among such reports of Hersey's as remain for any appreciation or defense of indigenous culture or beliefs. He was hard working and generous, as was his wife, who died at his side in 1916. But his aim was to "elevate the Red Man" —convince Native Americans to accept "Anglo" ways, abandon traditional roles of food gathering for sedentary farming, reject traditional religious beliefs and accept Christianity—with no effort to explore points of compatibility or incompatibility with existing belief systems. Hersey was representative of missionaries of his era; pious, long-suffering and hard-working, they dedicated their lives to civilizing the Native Americans, while simultaneously contributing to the destruction of Native American culture.[49]

If few records exist about what Episcopal missionaries thought about the Utes, an unanswered question is, how did the Utes view Christianity? Three different responses are possible. First, some Utes became devout Christians, adopting the new religion out of conviction while also hoping it would improve their lot. Second, many people engaged in passive resistance, avoiding the church, opposing its teachings, and finding in drugs, alcohol, or cynicism a defense against the intruder. Third, there was the large community of dualists, those who subscribed to traditional beliefs and practices at home, and sang Christian hymns fervently at church. It was not difficult to live in the two worlds, and many Native Americans found this the preferred way. "The gradations are mind-boggling. Some accepted, some succeeded, some died, some withdrew, some became violent," O'Neil reflected. "The quality of interaction varied so differently. Families were caring and took care of the church, like the Pawwinnees; they were just fine Christian people. Then there were those associated with the church more informally. I think this was the biggest group. You cannot make a generalization."[50]

War Clouds, the Drive to Remove Paul Jones as Utah's Bishop

The Latter-day Saints, vilified for opposition to the federal government in the nineteenth century, outdid themselves as patriots in World War I. Enmity toward Germany and its allies was widespread. Salt Lake City's German Avenue was renamed West Kensington, sauerkraut became "Liberty Cabbage," and persons with German names kept a low profile. This was not a nuanced world. Fort Douglas became an internment center for three hundred German nationals; pacifists, Socialists, and other peace activists were held there as well.[51]

A Salt Lake Tabernacle rally attracted ten thousand persons on March 26, 1917, and the "loyalty, unity and solidarity" of all Americans was urged "in support of whatever course becomes necessary." Bishop Jones spoke the next day at a Socialist rally attended by five hundred persons at Unity Hall, voicing support of President Woodrow Wilson, but decrying the "hot-headed pseudo-patriots of today" who "put democracy, loyalty and truth in terms of guns, fighting and bloodshed, terms that this new world, if not the old, has grown beyond."[52] Jones spoke at a time when war fervor was mounting; the United States would declare war on Germany and its allies a few weeks later, on April 3, 1917.

Response from Jones's opponents was swift, triggering the unrelenting pressure that forced his resignation by the year's end. The engine of opposition was the Bishop's Council of Advice, six men with only consultative powers, except when the missionary district was vacant. Five of the six members were from St. Mark's or St. Paul's, the city's largest parishes. They included Dean William W. Fleetwood, recently arrived at the cathedral from Ogden, Morris L. Ritchie, senior warden of St. Mark's and a three-term district judge; J. Walcott Thompson, junior warden of St. Mark's who would be a vestry member for forty-seven years, J. Herbert Dennis, Rector of St. Paul's, Professor George M. Marshall, secretary to the vestry of St. Paul's and a lay leader there for over forty years, and William F. Bulkley, since 1914 assigned to St. Mary's, Provo.[53] Missionary district vestry offices were not high turnover positions, yet Thompson and Marshall, the leaders of the anti-Jones movement, appear to have been record holders in their respective parishes. Bulkley, who said little during the controversy, and who would be the missionary district's archdeacon for two decades, was the Socialist Party's candidate for State Treasurer in 1916, collecting 4,621 votes out of 283,896 cast.[54]

The resolutions against Jones sent to the House of Bishops all originated with St. Mark's, 385 communicants, and St. Paul's, 300 communicants, the historians Sillito and Hearn note.[55] Thompson was the leader, with Marshall his dutiful scribe. He had come to Salt Lake City to join his father, the commanding officer at Fort Douglas, after graduating from Yale Law School. Thompson composed the following prayer, read by Bishop Tuttle at the cathedral during his June 1917 fiftieth anniversary commemoration. The occasion was dedicating a flag given in memory of Thompson's son, Captain Edwin Potter Thompson, who had died at Camp Bliss, Texas, on September 29, 1916, one of 665 young Utah men who died among 25,000 from the state who served during World War I.[56] It is always dangerous to turn political disputes into prayers, but with careful phrasing, Thompson stated his differences with Jones in liturgical language.

> Almighty God, our refuge and strength, in this time of strife of war, we turn to Thee in humility and faith. Endue those in authority over us with courage and wisdom and thy holy fear. Strengthen and protect our defenders by sea and land and suffer no dishonor or crime to stain our arms. Accept at our hands, we humbly pray Thee, this flag of our country given to the cathedral. To the thoughts of our hearts and the guidance of our lives may it ever be unfurled in peace when peace is righteousness, for liberty when liberty is law, or for justice, when justice is unselfishness. Protected by it and protecting it may we stand fast, we beseech Thee, true Americans, true lovers of our country and true helpers of the world. In honoring and serving the flag, may we in hearts and lives honor and serve Thee, through Jesus Christ our Lord.[57]

The prayer, an intimate statement of grief and patriotism, and the various written communiques of Jones and the Council of Advice, portray two positions on a collision course. The Council's opposition was unyielding. Jones and Thompson apparently never tried to discuss their differences, no easy task in any case, for the two positions were irreconcilable. The challenge was not unlike asking Creon and Antigone to try and make common cause.

Tuttle, who had unsuccessfully urged Jones to soften his position, tried to offer something to both sides in an August 1917 "Letter from the presiding bishop," written shortly after his visit to Utah. What greatly pleased him on returning to Salt Lake City was "the Americanism everywhere evident," as demonstrated in public enthusiasm for the Liberty Bond and Red Cross drives. "As an American, I am proud of Utah. She furnished her fighting men, and good men they were too, for the Spanish War. She is furnishing men for the war we now have on our hands. And she is furnishing food as well as men. And money too." But Tuttle was also generous to Jones. He noted with pride that Utah now had fifteen clergy and 1,445 communicants, and "the bishop is kindly, peaceful, faithful. The clergy are earnest, active, hopeful. May God's guidance, grace and blessing be upon them and their important work."[58]

St. Mark's vestry began the offensive against Jones on March 28, noting "with keen regret your recent utterances in reference to the present National Crisis" and requested the bishop "to issue a statement over your own signature . . . that your opinions are those of an individual and should not, by reason of your official position in the Church, be attributed to the

Episcopal Church nor to any members thereof." Jones replied tersely two days later: "At the time of my consecration, I promised to exercise myself in the Holy Scriptures, and call upon God by prayer for the true understanding of the same. No mention was made of calling upon St. Mark's Vestry for guidance. . . . As my stand in the matter of war is based upon what I believe to be the clear teaching of the Scriptures, you can understand that I feel no necessity to make the statement you request."[59]

Marshall and the Council consistently misrepresented local church sentiment. Widespread support for Jones existed among the non-Salt Lake clergy and laity, if not agreement with his antiwar views. The Council of Advice, however, presented itself to the national church as representing the entire missionary district. It gave no evidence of talking to anyone but its own members or those supporting its position; its written briefs contained only anti-Jones arguments. In April 1917, Maxwell W. Rice, of All Souls', Garfield, compiled a petition signed by a majority of clergy outside Salt Lake City, stating, "While we may not agree with Bishop Jones in regard to his view on this subject, we do emphatically assert that he is not only within his rights but that it is his duty as bishop to speak his convictions on subjects of such vital moral and spiritual consequences to the welfare of our country. We hereby record our disapproval of any attempt to curtail this privilege which the Episcopal Church grants at the consecration and ordination of its bishops and clergy."[60] Another supporter was J. Wesley Twelves, a Philadelphia Divinity School graduate, who came to Vernal in 1916, attracted by Jones's Social Gospel beliefs.[61] Charles F. Rice, priest-in-charge of St. Andrew's Church, Eureka, a mining district parish, wrote on July 31, "when the dean, wardens, and vestrymen of St. Mark's presume to speak for the 'rank and file of the Episcopal Church in Utah,' they are getting out of the bounds of their jurisdiction."[62]

That summer, the Convocation of the Missionary District of Utah was held at St. John's Chapel, Salt Lake City, June 7 and 8. It was business as usual, the only mention of the war issue coming late in the bishop's address: "We clergy must then preach according to the light that has been given us with the hope of leading men on to the goal which we all desire."[63]

Despite the growing controversy, Jones maintained a sense of humor. He recalled receiving two anonymous letters from Salt Lake City. One warned him that God might bring him to an untimely end for speaking against Mormonism, as it had his predecessor. The second letter said Jones would become an LDS member in ten years unless he committed suicide. "I am not expecting either event," Jones responded.

That fall the Council of Advice took its case to the national church, prompting a reply on September 28, 1917, from Bishop Arthur S. Lloyd, head of missionary programs for the Episcopal Church, to Thompson: "Why don't you do as the fathers did and assemble together men like yourself and ask God to do the thing men will never be able to accomplish—that is to help our friend to see and discriminate."[64] "The man is so fine," Lloyd told Thompson, "and I know whatever the appearance may be—I read some clippings which criticized him pretty severely—there never was a clearer-minded man, or one with more single purpose for what is right and what he believes is Christian."[65] Lloyd most likely believed that if Jones would be more politic and soften his pacifist rhetoric, his episcopacy might be saved and the white heat of opposition be abated. But such compromise was not possible for Jones, whose bedrock religious convictions were on the line.

Tuttle, as presiding bishop, now watched things deteriorate in the missionary district he had spent almost two decades building. Without spite or underhandedness, he joined with those seeking to remove Jones.

On October 2, Jones was in Los Angeles on a family visit, and attended a local peace rally. When protesters appeared, the small group of people moved to a different house. *The Salt Lake Tribune* inaccurately headlined the story "Swarms of Police Chase Bishop Jones, War Veterans Keep Christian Pacifist on Run in California." The vintage yellow journalism reporting of that era said:

> The Rt. Rev. Paul Jones, bishop of the Episcopal Diocese of Utah, did not get far here today in his prayer for [German] peace. He was interrupted by civil and Spanish war veterans, citizens of Eagle Rock, a suburban community, who sang "The Star Spangled Banner" with such determination that the meeting of Christian Pacifists which Bishop Jones was calling on the Lord to bless, broke up in disorder and the delegates hied themselves by automobile to another part of the community, to meet in another private building and start all over again, hoping against hope to shake off the swarm of police and government operatives.[66]

Jones called the newspaper story "totally inaccurate," and presented a different version of the story. He said he had been in California, not to attend the meeting, but to pick up his daughter who had been spending the winter with her grandmother.

> The meetings were quiet and harmonious, given to the discussion of aspects of the question of the conflict between war and Christianity. No objection was made by the secret service men present to anything that was said. There were no interruptions, and no attempt was made to break up the meetings. Having then to leave the city, I cannot speak for

> what happened at other sessions, but considering the inaccuracy of the reports of those two, I should not be inclined to put much faith in the accounts which appeared.[67]

The Council of Advice asked for Jones's resignation, stating on October 4, "your affiliation with various seditious organizations, the shame and embarrassment experienced by the flock committed to your Episcopal care through persistent promulgation of unpatriotic doctrines, your steadfast refusal to heed the advice and remonstrances of your brother bishops and your clergy and laity in this matter, and the injurious consequences of your course upon the life of the Church in this state, have convinced your Council of Advice that your usefulness as bishop of the Church in Utah is at an end."[68]

Jones replied four days later with a set of questions for council members, such as "Please state the names of any seditious organizations that you know of which the bishop of Utah has been affiliated" and "Please state, what, if any, unpatriotic doctrines the bishop of Utah has, to your knowledge, persistently promulgated, and the occasions on which he has done so."[69] It was a strategy Jones often employed, stripping away the emotional language aimed at him and asking for specifics, and it infuriated his opponents. "This is no time for academic discussion," an irritated Professor Marshall replied. "If you have been able to travel over your jurisdiction, to read the public press, to listen to the Council of your coworkers, to read the solemn request of their Council that you resign and yet not be able to answer each of the ten questions you ask us to answer, we feel that it would be useless for us to do so."[70]

The Council of Advice next wrote Tuttle, on October 5, urging the House of Bishops "to send in his place an efficient man in whom all the West and all the Church can have enthusiastic confidence and whose aggressive loyal, and churchly leadership we can unqualifiedly support."[71]

The House of Bishops took no action at its October meeting in Chicago other than to chide Jones for indiscreet speech. Marshall then wrote, on October 19: "The churchmen of this city, with rare exceptions, so rare as to be ignored in proportional influence, read with dismay the report in the morning papers that the House of Bishops saw in Bishop Jones's attitude toward the war and in his utterances nothing more than indiscretions and that he was likely to return to Utah and continue to lead the church here. He is preaching and teaching exactly what known traitors and German sympathizers are preaching and teaching. The careless or ignorant child with a gun may kill as surely as the deliberate murderer." Marshall continued, "The most bitter opponents of Bishop Jones's sentiments here cast no imputations against his personal or Christian character—he is above reproach. . . . We are not asking for his deposition, or the disgracing or humiliating of him in any way whatsoever. We're simply insisting that his usefulness to the church in Utah is at a complete and permanent end."[72]

Intensifying their efforts, the Council sent a letter to all local clergy and missions on October 25, asking about "what the atmosphere or feeling of the city is regarding Bishop Jones and the action taken by the Council of Advice and House of Bishops. We know that it is a hard thing for any of you to act against a friend, especially one who has been so fine a friend as Bishop Jones but this is a time when personal feelings must be put in the background and the good of the church in the district and the needs and good of the nation be brought forward."[73]

Both support and opposition to Jones were voiced in the responses, but once more the Council never included the comments favorable to Jones in its reports. They also actively solicited anti-Jones mail; several surviving replies refer to a letter sent by the Council, with Walker's law office the center of activity. Rice of Garfield had already written to back the bishop, and Edwin T. Lewis, from St. John's, Logan, wrote, "the affair has been one of passing interest and surprise but of absolutely no influence or effect whatever. Neither the Church's position not my own has been affected. Bishop Jones's many friends have been much surprised by his attitude, but I believe I am right in saying that there were many more surprised by the request for his resignation. It was always a clear matter that the bishop expressed his personal opinion only. . . . Bishop Jones's usefulness here in Logan is certainly not seriously impaired."[74] Backing for Jones was voiced from the mission in distant Vernal. "I do not know of but one person in the community who thoroughly agrees with the bishop, on the other hand I do not know of one person who heartily condemns the bishop," wrote J. Wesley Twelves, vicar of St. Paul's Church and Lodge there, adding, "There is general feeling of admiration for him in this particular instance. . . . Of course there are people here as there are in Salt Lake City who do not like the bishop and this is simply an opportunity to show their hatred, this is not due to anything the bishop has done." Twelves continued: " A large number of people outside the Church have an idea that the Council of Advice is a body which controls the appointment and actions of bishops and that they having asked for his resignation, therefore it must be that he is in the wrong. Naturally I have corrected them and informed them that the body is simply his own appointed advisory board."[75]

An additional source confirmed popular support for Jones. On October 8, Jones sent a letter and questionnaire to 180 church members throughout the missionary district, asking them the same questions he had put to the

Council of Advice, requesting a reply in time for him to present the results at the House of Bishops meeting in Chicago on October 17. What use Jones made of the responses is not known, but a 1934 tabulation disclosed that 114 of the 180 questionnaires were returned, an unusually high sampling. Essentially 35 percent of the respondents agreed Jones should resign, 45 disagreed, and the rest did not fit either category. What is significant is that when the Salt Lake City sources of opposition to Jones, St. Mark's and St. Paul's, were filtered from the sampling, only 8 percent believed the bishop should resign. And apart from the clergy members of the Council of Advice, "only one of the remaining twelve clergymen of the District did not support the bishop."[76]

On October 19, the House of Bishops requested the presiding bishop to call a commission to look into affairs in Utah, "so that the bishop of Utah may govern his action by their advice." The bishop of Missouri and presiding bishop, Daniel S. Tuttle, the bishop of Texas, George H. Kinsolving, and the bishop coadjutor of Iowa, Harry S. Longley, became a commission of inquiry. It smacked of a Star Chamber proceeding. The bishops first met alone on Nov. 7 with Fleetwood and Thompson in St. Louis without Jones being present, then again on December 12, when it summoned Bishop Jones to appear "when ever occasion demanded," which meant briefly at the hearing's end.

Jones again adopted his strategy of asking his interrogators pointed questions. He saw clearly this was a struggle of truth, as he understood it, versus church power. Jones was not interested in institutional power, and constantly kept the issue at a biblical–ethical level. His questions were answered cryptically:

> Q. Does the Commission find that the allegations of the Council of Advice are justified (a) That I have been affiliated with seditious organizations?
>
> —A. The Commission does not charge seditious organizations, but does say questionable organizations in respect of loyalty to the Government.
>
> (b) That I have persistently promulgated unpatriotic doctrines?
>
> —A. The Commission is not satisfied that you have persistently promulgated unpatriotic doctrines; but the evidence shows that on occasions you have promulgated such doctrines.
>
> (c) That I have injured the life of the Church in Utah and elsewhere?
>
> —A. Yes, it seems to the Commission that you have injured the life of the Church in Utah and elsewhere.

> Q. Does the Commission find that I have exceeded my prerogatives in coming to the conclusions I have in regard to war and Christianity?
>
> —A. The Commission is of the opinion that in our free country you are not to be officially restrained in your maintenance of opinions which you hold as an individual; but it also thinks that weighty responsibility attaches to pronouncements by a bishop, and that thoughtfulness and reticence on his part are exceedingly desirable.
>
> Q. Does the Commission believe that I should accede to the request of the Council of Advice and resign?
>
> —A. Yes.[77]

Finally, the Commission wrote that most church members believed the war with Germany would lead to a "sound and lasting peace," and any expression against the war "should not come from an Episcopal representative of this Church." They concluded, "it seems abundantly manifest than an end has come to the usefulness of the bishop of Utah in his present field, and that no earnestness of effort on his part would suffice to regain it.[78]

Jones believed that Tuttle, the report's main drafter, old and deaf now, had completed it before their meeting. Bishop Longley of Iowa, to whom Jones had sent his own survey results, arrived late; his train was delayed, and the pro-Jones material sent him was never included in the document. Jones was ushered into Tuttle's dining room, where the brief inquiry was held, and the report was read to him. Jones was not allowed to address the Commission in his own defense, only to comment on the completed document.[79]

The most chilling conclusion the Tuttle Commission advanced was "the making of such an Episcopal proclamation should be preceded by the withdrawal of the maker from his position of Episcopal leadership."[80] That argument, if accepted by the House of Bishops, would severely restrict free speech in the church, and provide a convenient way to limit any future controversial positions taken by bishops on public issues. World War I was the central issue now, but the Church was beginning to explore race relations, and other contentious issues were soon in the wings. Jones should resign, the Commission concluded, on or before March 12, 1918.[81] The Commission knew it was seeking the resignation of a colleague against whom no canonical charges had been filed. Its action should not be seen as precedent setting, it noted, only a response to "an excited condition of public opinion."[82]

Jones was on his way out. A newspaper report from St. Louis said the bishop, reached at Union Station while boarding a train for Salt Lake City, said he would comply with the resignation request, although he had not changed his viewpoint on war. "I think this action reflects more on the church than it does on me," he remarked. "I will admit that if any war could be a righteous war, this one is it, but I can not believe there is such a thing as a righteous war. I have no sympathy for Germany. I am of Welsh descent." Newspaper accounts also quoted Tuttle as saying this was the first time in the history of the American Church that an Episcopal bishop was asked to resign for reasons not concerned with questions of religious faith or doctrine.[83]

Resignation, December 20, 1917, Effective April 11, 1918

The end came swiftly. On December 20, 1917, Jones submitted his resignation, which then must be approved by a majority of dioceses. His parting shot to Tuttle was

> I had hoped that, notwithstanding the 'excited condition of public opinion' referred to by the Commission, there might be room in the Church for a difference of opinion on the Christianity of warfare and ways of attaining peace, and that, if so, it was preeminently the duty of one supposed to be a leader of the Church to voice his convictions on those subjects. But the commission makes it perfectly clear in its report that a bishop should resign before venturing to differ from others on such a Christian problem, or to express opinions at variance with the Government. To me, that seems evidently to mean that the bishops of the Church should be followers and not leaders, and I have no desire to remain in such an anomalous position.[84]

Jones sent the Council of Advice a short letter on the same date, enclosing an official authorization "to act as the Ecclesiastical Authority of the District" and offering to meet with them to allow a smooth transition.[85] At the end of his 1917 convention address, he gave one of the few statements to the local church of his views on the effort to remove him from office:

> I do not care to criticize the action taken by the Council of Advice. No doubt the Council acted according to its best judgment, and time will show the wisdom or folly of that judgment. . . . Expediency may make necessary the resignation of a bishop at this time, but no expediency can ever justify the degradation of the ideals of the episcopate which these conclusions seem to involve.[86]

The same report contained a chronicle of the actions, inserted by the Council of Advice "profoundly moved by a sense of their responsibility," detailing their steps to force the bishop's resignation. They expressed no positive comments on his twelve years of active ministry in Utah.[87]

The Council next passed a ponderously self-congratulatory resolution on March 29, 1918, urging the House of Bishops to accept Jones's resignation. "The developments since said resignation was requested, have emphasized the correctness of their judgment and the wisdom of their actions," the council concluded, urging the bishops to send "a strong loyal man, from without the District, to be the bishop of Utah."[88] A non-controversial pastor and "big Easterner" fundraiser is what the Council wanted.

It fell to the House of bishops, meeting at the cathedral of St. John the Divine in New York on April 10, 1918, to write the closing chapter in the Jones saga. Bishop Tuttle was at work as well. Aware of criticism of the Commission Report for violating due process and seemingly limiting the power of a bishop to speak out on public issues without first resigning, Tuttle stripped all such language from the document. The new report contained a single argument, "that the utterances and associations of the bishop of Utah had impaired his influence in promoting the peace and welfare of the Church in Utah to such a degree as virtually to destroy it."[89]

Tuttle hoped to move the matter quickly, but his plan backfired. When the Jones resignation came to the floor, several bishops asked that a Special Commission be appointed to examine the matter further. Documentation for and against Jones was appended to the record, and next day the bishops met in executive session. The bishops accepted Jones's resignation, but before doing so passed a resolution supporting the government of the United States for obeying "the law of moral necessity in seeking to stop a war of deliberate aggression by the only means that are known to be effective to such an end." Free speech should be balanced with responsibility; members are "entitled to the same freedom of opinion and speech as any other citizen of the United States," but "should be guided by a deep sense of the responsibility which rests upon one who occupies a representative position." This was a less restrictive position than Tuttle had advanced earlier in his report, which said "the making of such an Episcopal proclamation should be preceded by the withdrawal of the maker from his position of Episcopal leadership."[90]

Finally, referring to the December 12, 1917, report, the House of Bishops said it was "unwilling to accept the resignation of any bishop in deference to an excited state of public opinion, and therefore declines to adopt the Report of the Special Commission or to accept the resignation of the bishop of Utah for the reasons assigned by him in his letter of December 20, 1917."[91] That reason for Jones's resignation was declined, but the issue was moot because part of the deal was Jones would still resign. The actual resignation was delivered a day later in a one-line letter, "I desire to present to you my formal resignation as bishop of the Missionary District of Utah." The missionary bishop of Western Colorado, Frank Hale Touret, became acting bishop, at Tuttle's request, until 1920, when a new missionary bishop of Utah was named.

In retrospect, the encounter between the Council of Advice and Jones can only be described as brutal, and the action of the House of Bishops as lacking courage. The Council attacked the bishop relentlessly, and the House of Bishops failed to support one of their own who took a stand on a controversial issue. The bishop's equivocation raised troubling questions for the church. Jones was never tried, yet the commission's basic assertion was he was disloyal to the national government. But there was no state church in America, and free exercise of speech was guaranteed by the Constitution. The language the bishops used to muzzle Jones could just as easily apply to another church leader advancing any controversial issue of national policy, such as civil rights, the Vietnam War, or the place of women in the church. The larger question remains, what would have happened had Jones not resigned? He could not have been removed from office. The war would soon be over and he would have resumed his episcopal role, albeit with diminished support from some powerful Salt Lake City Episcopalians at St. Mark's and St. Paul's. Still, a majority of the Utah clergy and laity stood by him, and the missionary district could have weathered its crisis. Jones's resignation was effective on April 11, 1918; the war ended seven months later, on November 11.

What does the church do with a thirty-seven-year-old bishop without a diocese? Jones never faced a trial, nor was he deposed. A bishop for life, he was given a voice but not a vote in the House of Bishops. Although he temporarily did supply services in some parishes for a bishop friend in Maine, Jones never held an episcopal appointment again. He became executive director of the Fellowship of Reconciliation, a peace activist group, where he stayed until 1929. He also spent six months filling in as acting bishop of Southern Ohio. Nearby was Antioch College, Yellow Springs, Ohio. Its president, Arthur H. Morgan, former head of the Tennessee Valley Authority, invited Jones, whom he had long admired, to become the college's chaplain. A fixture on the college campus, Jones was voted Antioch's most popular professor. He was sometimes called "Bishop to the Universe" because of his wide interests. William B. Spofford, later bishop of Eastern Oregon (1967–1979), was a student at Antioch from 1938 to 1942, and remembered Jones. "One female student and I were in his class—which was mostly two hours of reflection and discussion. Very dull but quite obviously a 'saint' of peace, gentleness, and courage."[92] An outspoken early advocate for equal treatment of Jews and African Americans, Jones ran for governor of Ohio on the Socialist ticket in 1940.[93] He lost, but stayed on at Antioch until his death of multiple myeloma in September 1941.

As The Wheel Turns: Paul Jones Is Added to the Episcopal Calendar

The last hurrah did come to Jones, however. In 1991, the General Convention of the Episcopal Church asked the Standing Liturgical Commission to add his name to its Church Calendar of Christendom's venerated and respected leaders, in a class including Martin Luther, Hildegard of Bingen, Thomas Becket, C. S. Lewis, Dietrich Bonhoeffer, and the Martyrs of El Salvador. The action was completed in 1998. September 4, the date of his death, was marked as a day of special commemoration, and a collect was provided to commemorate the life of Paul Jones, bishop of Utah and pacifist.

> Merciful God, who sent your beloved Son to preach peace to those who are far off and to those who are near: Raise up in this and every land and time witnesses, who after the example of Paul Jones, will stand firm in proclaiming the gospel of the Prince of Peace, our Savior Jesus Christ, who lives and reigns with you and the Holy Spirit, one God, for ever. Amen.[94]

The ordeal of Paul Jones had come full circle.

5

Arthur W. Moulton

The Lean Years

(1920–1946)

> The East which has given lavishly in the past is discovering that the West is rich too… and that it is probably true that this rather lusty youth should take over its own responsibilities for the support of religion.
>
> —Bishop Arthur W. Moulton, 1938

> The District needs a new plan and a new spirit but most of all a new spirit….to divert the attention of the clergy, in particular, from their own local difficulties and jealousies towards a common cause to which all may give their best.
>
> —F. W. Bartlett Report, 1928

The first half-century of Utah church leadership produced such seminal figures as bishops Tuttle, Spalding, and Jones, and the missionary district's history would rival that of any Episcopal diocese for lively interest. After the latter two bishops, Utah sought a less politically controversial leader. Arthur Wheelock Moulton, beloved rector of a large New England congregation, fit the bill as a pastor, but his episcopate coincided with the Depression and World War II, giving a different cast than anyone could have anticipated to the Episcopal Church in Utah. The 1920s and 1930s were two decades of struggle and survival, followed by World War II, when new members poured into Utah for defense industry and military installation jobs, and demands for new churches arose. And in 1951 Moulton made world headlines as one of the first recipients of the Stalin Peace Prize.

Tall and affable, Moulton looked the part of a New England patrician bishop; in reality he came from humble circumstances. His father was a men's store clerk and Moulton sold shoe products door to door to work his way through college and seminary. He also took care of his mother, who had been left a widow at an early age. An engaging conversationalist and attentive listener, he was a welcome addition at any gathering. "He attracted attention anywhere he went," his granddaughter, Jane Moulton Stahl recalled. "He was kind and gentle and funny, able to engage sincerely with bootblacks and hat check girls as well as Salt Lake City's elite. He really believed in his job. I never heard him say anything negative about it."[1] Moulton prided himself on his ability to remember children's names, and was genuinely solicitous of every member of the missionary district. The Moultons kept a dime box at home, and at the end of a visit children were allowed to reach for a handful of dimes (and sometimes silver dollars). The lanky prelate could pull chalk out of his ear, and his family remember him as an expert Old Maid player, slapping his knee while sitting on the spacious screened in porch of the bishop's residence. At a civic send-off after his election as fifth missionary bishop of Utah, the mayor of Lawrence, Massachusetts, said, "Bishop Moulton is a man who never asks what another's creed is when help is asked."[2]

Moulton was a Phi Beta Kappa graduate of Hobart College in 1897, and a member of Sigma Chi fraternity. He attended General Theological Seminary, and graduated from the Episcopal Theological Seminary in Cambridge, Massachusetts, in 1900. Ordained in 1901, his entire parish ministry was spent at Grace Church, Lawrence, Mass. Moulton was an active community leader, and in 1912, when immigrant laborers struck to protest poor wages and working conditions in Lawrence, Moulton publicly sided with them, despite the owner of one of the major mills being an active member of Grace Church.

It was William Appleton Lawrence, his predecessor as rector at Lawrence, and later bishop of western Massachusetts, who nominated Moulton for the vacant Utah missionary bishop position. When the appointment was offered him in 1919, Moulton took six months before accepting it. He would be leaving a successful parish and Utah was a long distance away. But once he agreed to accept the position, Moulton's enthusiasm was unrelenting over the next quarter-century. He was consecrated bishop at his own parish church on April 29, 1920, with the ubiquitous Bishop Daniel S. Tuttle as one of the consecrators. The future bishop was chaplain to the First Battery of the Massachusetts Field Artillery from 1905 to 1910, and during World War I was a captain and chaplain of a base hospital in Orleans, France, for which he was named an honorary citizen of the city and a colonel in the French army.[3] During his time in France, Moulton saw the horrors of war first hand, and became a staunch supporter of international organizations and an advocate for world peace.[4]

Mrs. Moulton, Mary Corinne Prentice, of Milford, Massachusetts, was remembered as a woman who kept to herself, and who figured little in church life. She was Moulton's second cousin, the only daughter of a successful feed and grain dealer. Mrs. Moulton resisted moving to Utah, and when she did, rarely left their house, although she maintained an active interest in her husband's life and cut out newspaper clippings for him. She subscribed to the Milford, Massachusetts, *Daily News* until her death in 1968. "She was not an asset to his career," their granddaughter recalled. "In a passive way she never assumed the role of a bishop's spouse. She was socially ill at ease and did not turn up for ceremonial events."[5] Income from her inheritance allowed the Moultons to hire a cook (whom Moulton drove home each night after dinner), and for the family to live more comfortably than on a missionary bishop's salary, which was $4,200 in 1920. The couple delighted in simple pleasures, and spent much time at the bishop's residence. "Ahrt" and "Daisy", as they called each other, enjoyed Sunday afternoon drives around Salt Lake City, and lunch on the roof garden of the Hotel Utah. Moulton was accustomed to treating himself to a cigar and glass of beer at home after dinner.[6] The Moultons had a daughter, Mary Caroline, who stayed in Salt Lake City, wrestled with alcoholism, held several short-term jobs, and took care of her parents in their old age. A son, John, an Episcopal priest, spent two years at Good Shepherd, Ogden, and became chaplain of the Iolani School in Honolulu, and later canon at the Cathedral of St. John the Evangelist, Spokane, Washington.

"Moulton's gestures reminded me of the actor Walter Hampton," Betty Dalgliesh, a local priest, said of the bishop, adding, "He personally knew every child. When my husband and I were in New York in 1944 and it was time for our daughter to be confirmed she said, 'I don't know the bishop of New Jersey. I want to go home to my own bishop whom I know and love.'"[7] Thelma S. Ellis remembered Moulton from his visits to Good Shepherd, Ogden. "He knew everybody by name and something about them. Once when I was in California he was preaching in a church, so I went. When he saw me coming through the reception line he threw up his hands and said, 'Here's Utah!'"[8]

Contact between the LDS leadership and the Episcopal bishop was limited but cordial during the Moulton era. Moulton got along well with the LDS leadership, and when the Province of the Pacific met in Salt Lake City in May 1928, it was invited to hold a Friday evening service in the LDS Tabernacle. The Tabernacle Choir sang and President A. W. Ivins of the First Presidency spoke.[9] The other example of such a tabernacle service came when the Archbishop of York visited Salt Lake City in 1949. (The Rt. Rev. Arthur F. W. Ingram, Lord Bishop of London visited Ogden for half an hour between trains on November 7, 1928, and spoke for ten minutes at Good Shepherd Church before continuing to San Francisco.)[10]

A touching anecdote about a Moulton–LDS encounter is contained in the diary of David O. McKay, president of the LDS Church. On McKay's seventy-eighth birthday, September 8, 1951, Bishop Moulton, also seventy-eight that year, had called to offer birthday greetings. The LDS leader was tired and under doctor's orders to rest. When he learned of Moulton's call, he immediately visited Moulton at the latter's apartment, saying, "'It was not right for me to let your gracious, considerate call go unheeded, so I am here to pay my respects to you, and to thank you for your consideration in calling at my home today.' . . . The Reverend [Moulton] was visibly moved and he repeated, 'Why I have never had anything so nice happen to me before. Won't you please sit down and visit with me?' . . . As I picked up my hat to leave the Reverend came over to me, put his hands upon my shoulders, bowed his head, and gave me a blessing. I reciprocated by giving him a blessing." The head of the LDS Church left "feeling satisfied that I had done the right thing by repaying his visit of this afternoon, and that much good would result from the contact we had with each other this day."[11]

Despite cordial personal relations with its hierarchy, Moulton regarded the institutional LDS as "an enormous religious force, fired with all the fanaticism that goes with ignorance and power . . . this monstrous Mormon incubus."[12] Moulton, like his predecessors, sprinkled his reports to headquarters with "Mormon menace" language hoping to gain additional funds. But by the 1930s the arguments had diminished appeal. Mormonism had become more mainstream American, and Episcopalians looked increasingly to China or Africa as mission fields.

Moulton had few skills as a fundraiser, and the 1920s and 1930s were a difficult time for raising money. Nor was he skilled as an administrator. Notwithstanding, he built a new church, St. Martin's, in isolated Roosevelt, supported a mission in Duschene, found money for the Uintah Native American programs, supported a mission among the miners, and turned the Helper YMCA building into a chapel–social center for railroad workers. The cathedral sacristy was rebuilt after a 1935 fire, and a parish hall was added. St. Paul's, Salt Lake City, also moved to a new building. But otherwise the Moulton years were lean times for the Missionary District of Utah. "This is a hard and challenging field," the bishop wrote in 1928. "It is unique and abnormal."[13] When the Diocese of Western Massachusetts became vacant in 1937, Moulton indicated his willingness to be nominated for it, but it went instead to another candidate.

In 1929, Moulton asked the national church for an emergency grant of $25,000; for three years he had been taking out loans to cover faculty salaries at Rowland Hall and a bank threatened foreclose.[14] Church properties bought but not developed by Spalding and Jones were sold to raise money. In 1933, the national church sent a representative to survey the district's financial affairs and found it $58,782 in debt, although Moulton had pledged $10,000 of family money against a $11,465 debt for the Helper mission. Bookkeeping methods were makeshift, large overdrafts by one employee had been allowed, checks bounced, and loans were left unpaid. Bad as conditions were, the national church representative concluded, the District was in better condition financially than when Moulton took charge after a three-year absence of any resident bishop.[15]

Moulton defended his administration against critics. Before he arrived, debts had mounted, properties were run down, and church employees were demoralized, he said. Utah was like a foreign mission field, he concluded. Moulton had erased the $30,000 debt of St. Mark's Hospital, kept Rowland Hall School functioning during the Depression, and Emery House alive despite dwindling numbers of students. The Helper Mission proved costly, but "it was our opportunity and our duty and I took it and did it." Although an Episcopal Church presence in southern Utah came later in the twentieth century, Moulton hoped to fund an itinerant missionary and mission car to travel between Cedar City and St. George, hold meetings, and distribute literature. At one point Moulton compared the Episcopal missionaries to David slaying Goliath. In less colorful language, he stated his missionary philosophy: "We must not be shabby or run down, or ungenteel, or dingy, or ragged. We must be a little ahead in architecture and beauty and culture and of all things in Christian character, and in the long run (and that after all is what missions means) we shall win out in a splendid way."[16]

Rowland Hall was a success story against all odds. Enrollment shrunk during the lean years, and to survive after the cut in church funding, the school incorporated as an independent, nonprofit institution with a self-perpetuating board of trustees. Despite financial difficulties, it maintained a strong academic program and placement record. Each student took two years of Latin and three years of French, plus English, mathematics, history, and science. At the same time, athletics had moved from lawn croquet and gentle walks to more rigorous basketball, swimming, tennis, ice skating, and field hockey. Boarders could only leave campus with a chaperone, but were allowed to visit day students on weekends, and attend one movie a week with other boarders.[17]

Though not as outspoken as Spalding or Jones, Moulton took clear stands on domestic and international issues. His was a simple, unvarnished patriotism. "Americans never give up," he was fond of saying. An internationalist, during World War II Moulton was active in the Save the

Children Federation, the English-Speaking Union, Russian War Relief, and British War Relief. After the war he became Chair of the United Nations Association of Utah. Obert C. Tanner, a local business and community leader, worked with Moulton in the organization, and noted the "Cold War antagonism made grass roots support for the U. N. very difficult to obtain." Utah's governor led local opposition to the international body in the 1950s. "We had to dig deep to find within ourselves the strength that could support the U. N.," Tanner recalled, echoing a sentiment similar to Moulton's.[18]

In his first report to the missionary district, the bishop announced he would list the names of those who had died during the past year at the beginning of each annual address, and in some years that was the speech's most memorable section. Otherwise, a sameness pervades his reports over a quarter-century. Affable and rambling like the man himself, they lack focus, and the reader's tendency is to comment "Moulton meant to say . . . ." Here is Moulton, in 1923, on the church and society: "You can account for socialism, Sovietism, the Ku Klux [*sic*], syndicalism, communism by the fact that men have believed in sufficient numbers that real and intolerable abuses have existed which could only be wiped out and away by some form of direct organization and direct action. If now there be allowed to grow up within this country—to go no further—a generation denied the privileges and safeguards of a sane and efficient religious education. I tell you that the times ahead when you and I are grandfathers will be very trying to the souls of men."[19]

Moulton's public statements bear examination, because he attracted national attention in the late 1940s and early 1950s as a leading member of a Communist-front organization. Moulton was no Communist; what he said was mainstream American, but would be considered extreme in Utah. Moulton wrote in 1937: "I decline to be stampeded by the alarmists who are having so much to say about Communism. I think there is no doubt that Communism is on the way. So is Social Security on the way. So is the 'Mormon' Church on the way. . . . Communism is a theory of social life and living and as such will probably grow. . . . While Communism cannot be stopped it can be directed and that is where you and I fit in, that is where the Christian Church comes into play."[20] Elsewhere, he added, it may not be the business of America "whether the French get their coal or the Germans refuse it, whether this or that Sultan remains in power and the size of his harem regulated. But it most certainly is our business, if we can trace any part of the suffering, poverty, perplexity, burden, and the threatening menace of a new and more terrible world war to the absence from boards of deliberations, and councils of advice, and assemblies of nations, of the richest, mightiest, and I think most seriously religious of all the countries of the earth."[21]

The Bartlett Report: "A Real Salary for a Real Man with a Real Job"

During the late 1920s and 1930s, the national church experienced declining revenues, and cut its subsidies to Utah. Should it continue to support a missionary district that showed so little progress? "With but 1,500 communicants after fifty years of effort it would seem to an observer that the Church had not received adequate returns on its investment,"[22] a 1928 national report stated. At that time Frank B. Bartlett, Executive Secretary of the national church, visited Utah and made a frank analysis of church conditions there. Bartlett's report and Bishop Clark's 1946 survey are the two most comprehensive appraisals of the Episcopal Church in Utah in their time. Bartlett, who became bishop of Idaho, 1935–1941, found widespread incompetence among the clergy, poor morale, and little appetite for mission. Bartlett wrote, "The District needs a new plan and a new spirit . . . to divert the attention of the clergy, in particular, from their own local difficulties and jealousies towards a common cause to which all may give their best."[23]

The key to an active missionary district was effective clergy, without which Utah would continue to flounder. Bartlett wrote,

> Begin at once the elimination of the men who are not effective. I am giving the bishop the names of the men who, in my opinion, should be sent elsewhere. Also the reasons why they are no longer useful to Utah. . . . Get the best possible men on the new salary, honor them for their devotion to the Cause of Christ as they serve in the hard and lonely places; put away forever the heresy that the town and country work of the church is the place for failures or for those who are on trial, or for those who have outworn their usefulness elsewhere. Let your whole policy resolve about the idea—'A real salary for a real man with a real job.'[24]

Many of the Utah clergy were lazy and of low intellectual and emotional caliber, the report found. Bartlett was blunt:

> I found a lack of a whole-hearted loyalty; a tendency to be hyper-critical; a willingness to seize upon any alibi for the lack of achievement. Here and there men appeared to be absolutely incompetent and ready to accept subsidies as if the church owed them a living. There is no place for such men in the church. They should be eliminated as soon as possible. On the other hand I found men who are devoted to their work but without the personality or equipment to do their work successfully. Such men cannot be permitted to block the way of progress. Furthermore,

> funds allocated to the District, given in trust, cannot be used to pay the salaries of such men, if we are to be faithful to our trust. I feel that individuals must be sacrificed if they stand in the way of the extension of the Church's work. With all loving kindness, but with no sentimentality, they should be sent on their way.[25]

For Bartlett, salaries were the heart of the problem. Current $1,800 clergy salaries should be raised to $2,400, with housing in addition. "There are some men in the District who may not be worth more than $1,800. If that be true they are a hindrance to the work and should be replaced. There are others whose salaries should be raised." The church lagged behind in some communities because "we are trying to do big work with $1,800 men."

The 1928 survey presents a sobering picture of the state of church work in Utah. Among the problems were the mining towns. Park City, a perennial problem site, was an active mining community of about four thousand persons, including twenty-two church families. Bartlett wrote: "Social conditions—terrible; drunkenness, prostitution. People accustomed to low standards. Church people seem powerless to make any change. To face this situation our Church has poor equipment; a dirty church building; no hall for social work. No men to help. A few loyal women. . . . The wretched Church on the hill is never going to make an impression on that godless town."[26] Eureka was another mining town of four thousand persons. Possibly twenty Episcopal families lived there, and another fifty were scattered in outlying communities. There was "much immorality, a 'tough life' for boys and girls," with only a Scout troop for boys and "nothing for girls, except what the LDS Church does for its own."[27] The church building could be remodeled and serve as both a church and social center, and if a "red-blooded man" was sent there to work with young people, the community would raise $600 toward his salary.[28] In the coal fields, in places like Helper, Kennilworth, and Castle Gate, the climate was "morally rotten, prostitution, gambling, and boot legging encouraged by those who dominate the community. Foreign-born in control of politics and business. Church people don't seem to count. . . . Find a man who has some experience in dealing with hard problems and 'Hard-boiled men.' He must have what is popularly called a 'punch.'"[29] In Provo, site of Brigham Young University, "young men and women are beginning to ask embarrassing questions regarding the Book of Mormon, etc. One LDS bishop admitted that these youngsters were a real problem to the Mormon leaders. Herein lies our greatest opportunity."[30]

As for Salt Lake City, Bartlett noted diminished work in St. Peter's Mission and at St. John's, both small, struggling congregations in communities where they failed to grow. He recommended locating a new church in the expanding Sugar House district. Of the main churches in Salt Lake City, St. Mark's Cathedral and St. Paul's, Bartlett said, in language Clark would use two decades later, "I sense a lack of enthusiasm and optimism; the lay people, particularly the men, do not seem to be tied to any definite program. Are these churches in Salt Lake only to serve a small group of nice people, called Episcopalians, or have they a mission to all people? Simply to hold services does not justify the existence of a Church. The test of a church is its Output. What is the Episcopal Church putting into Salt Lake City?"[31]

Lean Times and the Great Depression

Progress was modest during Moulton's episcopate; it could hardly have been otherwise, given the conditions he faced. In 1920 there were six clergy, in addition to the bishop, plus four women workers, and 1,420 communicants, almost a thousand of them in the three largest parishes. The church's nearly twenty other missions averaged from eight to thirty members. The adverse economy resulted in further cuts. Clergy were removed from the key parishes in Vernal and Logan, and the Vernal lodge for girls was leased as a hospital. It was not reclaimed for church use until 1950. By 1931 there were eleven regular clergy in the district, including the bishop, $25,563 in locally raised funds, and 1,822 communicants.[32] Moulton juggled his meager resources. His office was a back room on the first floor of the bishop's residence 440 East First South Street, which he shared with a secretary, as had Spalding. "We keep plugging away and are making progress slow though it be," Moulton the habitual optimist reflected. "Perhaps that is the best kind of progress."[33]

Moulton's years as bishop coincided with the Depression and a severe downturn in Utah's economy. All the numbers went down. With the end of World War I, government contracts in mining and rail freight industries terminated abruptly, and support of American farm product sales to Europe halted, all directly affecting Utah. The large Utah Copper Company's Garfield smelter plant, scene of an active Episcopal ministry for many years, closed in 1921, and by 1934 some 206 out of each 1,000 persons in the state received welfare support.[34] The desperation of the times is captured in an encounter between a labor inspector and a worker.

> One day I thought I was doing a man a favor by telling him when his shift ended, that he had completed twenty-eight hours [of a thirty-hour work quota] and that he need not come back the next day. I simply did not think it would be worth coming ten miles to work two hours and get ninety-six cents. He didn't say anything at the time. About 8 P.M. the

> fellow showed up in my backyard. I happened to know that he lived five miles from my home. He asked if he could not come out the next day and get the ninety-six cents to which he was entitled. He told me he had walked all the way from his home and planned on walking back. That's how much he needed the money, and that is what he was willing to do to get it—walk ten miles and work two hours, plus find some way to get another ten miles to work and the same ten miles back.[35]

For the Episcopal Church, it was a time to circle the wagons around the campfire. In 1934, the national church ordered Moulton to dismiss eight of his clergy, calling Utah work static. Moulton found places for some of them, and when an eastern clergy friend sent a generous check, Moulton applied it to clergy salaries.[36] With an earlier check for $500, Moulton provided each clergy member with a year's subscription to *The Atlantic Monthly* and a modest collection of contemporary religious books.[37] He sent his benefactor, Howard Chandler Robbins, dean of the General Theological Seminary in New York City, excerpts of clergy letters responding to the salary cuts. One said, "I was not altogether surprised at receiving your communication telling of another cut in my salary, but did not dream that it would be so drastic. This may be a drastic way of reminding the church in the West that she must expect herself hereafter to bear some proportionate share in meeting missionary stipends."[38]

The small churches rallied as best they could, with worship services conducted as regularly as clergy presences would allow. Activities led by women were at the core of any parish's existence. Sewing, canning, and cooking brought women together, but they also watched after the sick and needy, fed the hungry, kept an eye on children, and prepared the church for festive times like Christmas and Easter. The Church of the Good Shepherd, Ogden, used to make and sell St. Michael's Pudding at Christmas in the 1930s. This recipe was preserved in the church archives and makes 148 pounds before steaming: "Raisins, twenty pounds; Currants, eight pounds; Citron, eight pounds; Bread crumbs, thirty-two quarts; Eggs, eight dozen; Milk, sixteen quarts; Brown sugar, thirty-two pounds; Suet, sixteen pounds; Soda, thirty-two teaspoons; Nutmeg, twelve teaspoons; Cinnamon, fifteen teaspoons; Cloves, fifteen teaspoons; Cider, five quarts; Ginger, fifteen teaspoons; Salt, fifteen teaspoons. (Steam for four hours)."[39]

St. Mark's Hospital shelved its upgrading plans, missions in the Uintah Basin and mining camps were closed, and clergy doubled up to serve several missions and churches. Archdeacon William F. Bulkley literally drove all over the state in his Model T Ford, holding services. In one annual report he listed nine visits to the reservation and several to the coal camps, plus sending over 800 hand-written post cards to scattered church members.[40] Roads were mostly graveled, and sometimes were only two ruts through underbrush. Once, while returning from Nevada, Bulkley hit a pothole and broke a front axle, after which he hitchhiked into Delta. He spent the night there, and phoned a mechanic in Provo, who shipped a new axle by the morning train to Delta. Bulkley then hitchhiked back to where the car had broken down, and installed the new front axle.[41]

Bulkley spent most of his life in rural ministry, and was a founder of the Society of the Rural Workers Fellowship, a Canadian and American clergy and laity group specializing in rural ministry. An Easterner and 1905 graduate of Trinity College, Hartford, Connecticut, and Berkeley Divinity School, Middletown, Connecticut, he came west in 1908 to improve his health. For six years Bulkley was chaplain to St. Mark's Hospital and vicar of All Souls', Garfield, ministering to the large community of industrial workers there. On Valentine's Day 1914 he married Fannie Lees, superintendent of nurses at the hospital, and from 1914 to 1929 was vicar of St. Mary's, Provo. Moulton brought him back to Salt Lake City as archdeacon, and Bulkley spent the next two decades on the road most Sundays, until his retirement in 1949, holding services in parishes without regular clergy and founding Sunday schools in places like Park City—which he visited monthly for several years—Duschene, Eureka, and Whiterocks.

In Salt Lake City Bulkley's sister-in-law, Ellen Lees, was a district visitor, a title given women missionaries. She wrote, "Many of the 'newly-poor' have been so perplexed over the sudden plunge from comfort to need, that the necessary procedure in applying for aid has utterly confused them. It has been possible to help them over the rough and humiliating spots. . . . Many visits to the Agency with, and for, those needing help, eased over some trying moments."[42]

Thelma S. Ellis was a member of the vestry at Good Shepherd, Ogden, during the Depression. When John W. Hyslop, Good Shepherd's rector, retired in 1934, the vestry sent him monthly checks, sometimes as little as $15, for two years until his back salary was paid.[43] "We did everything ourselves. We struggled. We prioritized our bills, the ones that had to be paid, and the ones that could be paid later. We saved everything, used everything that could be used. When we didn't have food, my father went up in the canyon and fished until he brought us back our supper."[44] But the perspectives of churchwomen were not insular. The missionary district's Women's Auxiliary sent gifts to African-American children in Charleston, South Carolina, and to Japan. At its 1936 meeting, participants heard a talk on bills before Congress in which they were especially interested, including legislation against lynching and bills to ease the plight of sharecroppers.

The meeting went on record favoring a neutrality bill to prevent the United States from being drawn into war.[45] Moulton said little about the Depression in his annual address to the Church in 1932. "Will you forgive me if I do not say anything about the Depression or tell you when it is going to end? I go to the theater once in a while and can see no diminution in numbers; it appears to be just as hard to get a seat. I discover just as much difficulty to find a parking place for my car any morning or afternoon on the street. Stores were filled with crowds this Christmas."[46]

By 1924, there were 1,265 communicants and the missionary district's budget was $62,000; its investments swelled to $30,000. The number of communicants rose to 2,065 in 1935, despite an exodus of more than 143,000 workers from Utah seeking jobs elsewhere.[47] In 1936, Moulton lamented the steady decline in appropriations from the national church, resulting in a corresponding decline in mission programs. He sensed what was coming. Utah could no longer compete with the foreign missions in China or Latin America as a fundraising draw for donors. The West had been conquered, and except for a certain fascination with Native Americans, little else from Utah was reported in the pages of church publications. The missionary districts in the West "will never again receive the generous assistance which in the past has built them up," Moulton told Utah Episcopalians. "The East which has given lavishly in the past is discovering that the West is rich too. . . . It no longer has to be carried. . . . It is probably true that this rather lusty youth should take over its own responsibilities for the support of religion."[48]

What Moulton lacked as a commentator in the public area he made up for as a hands-on bishop, visiting the far corners of his missionary district in a rickety automobile over wagon trails that were gradually becoming roads, and making periodic fundraising trips East as well. The bishop's published list of his official acts for 1924 covered eight pages and contained little down time, a schedule that would exhaust a modern senatorial candidate, and he kept at it, year after year. Moulton made two lengthy trips to the reservations and one to the coal camps that year, and visited every functioning mission or parish at least once each year. He confirmed twenty Native Americans, including Black Otter, 100 years old, addressed the St. Paul's Parish, Salt Lake City, annual meeting, visited St. Mark's Hospital and Rowland Hall, gave the Phi Beta Kappa oration at the University of Utah, and addressed a local gathering of prison chaplains. All this while running an office and visiting parishes. Since he was acting bishop of Nevada for part of the period, he traveled there several times, and spent January to April fundraising in Massachusetts and Chicago. In October and November he returned to the same places, sometimes speaking in two or three churches a day to audiences more receptive than rich.[49]

Economic recovery came slowly to Utah. In 1936 Moulton wrote, "We have managed to get through the year in some way or other. It is due to the fact that many of our clergy have been willing to keep on with their work at greatly reduced stipends."[50] Recalling the state of clerical finances, a church member said that one night Moulton arrived for dinner with a flat tire. When the host, a staunch Presbyterian, went down to help him, he saw that all four tires on Moulton's car were bald. While the others had dinner, the host took Moulton's car to a tire shop for a new set of tires.[51]

Eventually, the tide turned. Relief switched from direct handouts to public works programs. In 1935 Alwin E. Butcher, the English-born rector of St. Paul's, Salt Lake City, responded to a letter to church leaders from President Franklin D. Roosevelt, inquiring about conditions in the community. Roosevelt had attended services there as a presidential candidate in 1932. Butcher said life had improved in Utah. There had been an upswing in mining and farming; the poor were being attended to with food and clothing; but the "white collar class" was the most hard hit, people "too proud to go on relief, many of them doubled up with other members of families," but whose savings had been depleted and whose home purchasing possibilities vanished. He asked Roosevelt "for this great nation to work out a plan to forever banish unemployment" through public works programs.[52]

Automobiles became increasingly numerous in Utah in the 1930s. Dangerous mountain trails were straightened, and a ribbon of paved roads soon connected distant cities. In 1928, more than 10,000 new motor vehicles were registered in the state. Postal service expanded, and in rural areas postbags were hung from metal bars or on tree limbs. Lacking vehicles of their own, clergy sometimes rode with the mail drivers from one mission to another. The early cars frequently had to be pushed up steep hills and pulled through swift streams; tires wore out quickly, and punctures were frequent. Moulton's accounts are laced with reports of frequent breakdowns. A typical entry (from Eureka): "About 10:00 o'clock we thawed out the car, lifted it out of the mud into which it had frozen, and started out for Provo. Never was there a more beautiful sight. The city lights were twinkling on the mountainsides, the moon was brilliant in the cloudless sky and those great hills stood out in sharp relief against the heavens. The spotlight of the car, the hair pin curves, the sharp turns, the startled rabbits leaping across the road, and then the blizzards blinding us and forcing us to creep along the white streets; the arrival home at 2:00 in the morning."[53] The Church wondered about providing cars for its clergy. The gift of a car to a clergy member could mean the recipient having to spend up to $500 from a meager salary for gas, oil, and repairs. Instead, increase clergy salaries and let missionaries buy their own vehicles, Bartlett suggested. "It will increase the men's self-respect. It will free them from the possible charge they are using the church's property for personal pleasure. . . . It will put them on par at least with the laboring people of the community in their ability to get about whenever and wherever they please."[54]

Commercial airline passenger service came to Utah in 1927, easing the state's isolation. Telephones gradually replaced the telegraph; indoor plumbing was now a feature in newly constructed homes. In 1922 KZN (later KSL), Salt Lake City, went on the air with a half-hour of programming each evening. On July 15, 1929, the first broadcast of the Mormon Tabernacle Choir was aired. Gradually, Utah became a tourist attraction, and southern Utah became the setting for Tom Mix, John Wayne, and other western films. Motion picture theatres took away the business of popular dance halls, like the Saltair Pavilion.[55]

New Deal programs also helped change the state. On the eve of World War II, 11,000 persons annually were employed by the Works Progress Administration program. Dams and water storage facilities were built at a cost of $22 million, the Rural Electrification Administration brought electricity to isolated rural communities. This allowed iceboxes to be replaced by refrigerators, resulting in a revolution in the way foods were preserved. Labor unrest was rampant in mining communities, and gradually the trade union movement reestablished itself in Utah.[56]

St. Mark's Hospital and St. Mark's Cathedral

The 1920s and 1930s were years of struggle for St. Mark's Hospital, yet it gradually grew. One ward was closed for lack of nurses. The hospital scrambled for funds, and its annual list of donors contained such entries as: St. Mark's Cathedral Association, making of four night shirts; St. John's, Logan, $15; Mr. A. H. Cowie, subscription to fifteen magazines; War Workers, twenty-five eye bandages; Rev. H. E. Henriques, six sets of fancy salts and peppers and one case of oranges; Mrs. George Y. Wallace, jelly; Staff Doctors—for Nurses' Christmas, $70, Deaconess Shepherd, one quart fruit.[57]

The hospital budget was $122,000, and the medical director, Dr. F. S. Bascom, noted competition came from two additional medical centers, the new state-of-the-art LDS Hospital and Holy Cross Roman Catholic Hospital. St. Mark's had been expanded to 150 beds, and the nursing school averaged forty-five students at a time.[58] Mining contract patients declined, but the number of private patients rose sharply, representing a future trend. By 1925, fifty physicians were admitted to practice at the hospital, and twenty-two others had associate status. Doctors were among the first to abandon horses for automobiles, house calls became common, and a motorized ambulance was purchased for the hospital.

The hospital's chaplain in 1931 reported that, of 2,524 patients, sixty-six percent were Latter-day Saints, others were mainstream Protestant and Roman Catholic church members, plus Greek Orthodox and Buddhists. The chaplain accompanied five patients into the operating room at their request, held 88 services, made a constant round of visits, and distributed hundreds of books and magazines.[59]

Despite various moves, the hospital remained in a poor location, while demands for its services increased. It was located next to a railroad and an oil refinery, and a 1921 fire at the Utah Oil Works forced the hospital to move its patients to other institutions for four days. St. Mark's activity increased despite economic hard times, from 2,852 patients in 1920 to 2,976 in 1930, and the number of charity cases increased as well, from 2.8 percent to 6.9 percent. In 1933 Olive Waldorp, nursing school director, became hospital superintendent, and a member of the hospital's board of directors. A doctor said she "ran the hospital out of a desk drawer. . . . Everything ran like clockwork."[60]

Utah experienced a major outbreak of polio, and in 1940 employees of the American Smelting and Refining Company purchased an iron lung and respirator for the hospital. During World War II the School of Nursing expanded, funded in part by government grants, and by 1945 was enrolling 135 students in a two-and-a-half-year program. All costs were borne by the federal government, in turn for which the women were assigned to military or civilian hospitals. A new five-story wing was added in 1944, increasing the hospital's bed capacity from 151 to 224.

St. Mark's Cathedral made it through the 1930s with both a disastrous fire and the building of a new parish hall and offices. By 1933, cathedral membership was 601 persons, of whom only 150 pledged money for its upkeep; pledges brought in only $6,000 in 1932, and it was necessary to let staff go. At one point, the cathedral vestry asked to meet with the dean about ways to reduce his salary. By 1934, the cathedral elected two women to its vestry. The issue was not gender equality; Mrs. H. W. Dascher and Mrs. J. W. Collins were both wealthy parishioners, and during the lean 1930s the parish's women assumed responsibility for the costly task of keeping up the building and grounds.

On March 31, 1935, an early morning fire caused by a defective furnace nearly destroyed the cathedral sacristy. The organ was ruined; fire melted six memorial windows, and destroyed the chancel's elaborately carved wooden paneling. Seventy-five firefighters battled the blaze for nearly two hours before bringing it under control, after which the cathedral's Boy Scout patrol removed the damaged items. Insurance covered most of the $50,000 loss, and Bishop Moulton secured the old Victory Theater organ as a replacement for the cathedral's instrument. After the fire Roman Catholics, Jews, Christian Scientists, and Presbyterians all offered their worship space to the St. Mark's congregation.[61]

Bishop–Cathedral Relations: Their Historic Continuity

Should St. Mark's Cathedral be a leading Salt Lake City church, or the central church of a district-wide ministry? The question had been raised several times in the missionary district's history. An agreement was negotiated between cathedral and missionary district in 1925. The cathedral should be a powerhouse, Moulton believed, a place that laity and clergy of the scattered, isolated district could claim as their home, while it exercised a leading educational, musical, and liturgical role. "A cathedral that functions properly is harnessed up to the whole District. The circumference knows that it is part of the center and, in a missionary district there is always a circumference. The outposts, some of them very weak, ought to be helped to understand they have a foothold. The missionaries ought to have an opportunity to come home and a home to which to come."[62] Of St. Mark's in-house advocates of an independent, self-contained cathedral, Moulton wrote: "Parochialism, while not yet dead, is dying. Anything we can do to hasten its demise would be permanently constructive. It has been the curse of the church. This Church is an Episcopal Church, but all over the country we have been a long time discovering it."[63]

Bishop Moulton served as acting cathedral rector from 1929 to 1931, and from 1934 to 1936; it was common for missionary bishops to serve parishes during such long vacancies. Moulton, aided by other clergy, also served as rector of St. Paul's from 1942 to 1945 during World War II.

On January 10, 1935, the cathedral filed an updated Articles of Incorporation with the State of Utah. This was not the result of any change in the bishop's long-established status as rector, but a pro forma boilerplate provision of the 1933 Revised Statutes of Utah that required nonprofit organizations to update their registration with the state.[64] The document was a fill-in-the-blanks form that changed nothing in missionary district relationships. "The Rector of St. Mark's Episcopal Cathedral in said Parish shall be the bishop of Utah, who shall delegate the parochial cares to a Dean," Article 6 stated. "Vacancies in the office of Dean shall be filled by call of the Vestry by and with the consent of . . . the bishop of Utah" (Article 17). The basic bishop–dean relationship had not changed since it was established at the cathedral vestry's first meeting on November 18,

1870, when the bishop was elected permanent ex officio cathedral rector.[65] The relationship was reaffirmed in a Joint Declaration of February 7, 1895, during Bishop Leonard's time, by Bishop Spalding and the cathedral in a Joint Act of September 11, 1909, and by the same parties in a Joint Act of January 18, 1917, during Bishop Jones's episcopate. Years later, the updated Articles of Incorporation of St. Mark's Cathedral, filed on August 30, 1985, stated (Article 7), "The Rector of the Cathedral Church of Saint Mark shall be the bishop of the Diocese of Utah who shall delegate the parochial rights and duties to a Dean called by the Vestry with the consent of the bishop."[66]

In 1937, the cathedral borrowed $7,500 to build a parish house, funded in part through the sale of 500 ten-dollar bonds paying three percent interest.[67] The new Bishop Spalding Memorial Hall cost $35,000, and in February 1938 the cathedral celebrated with a Great Two-day Carnival with a "delicious dinner each evening at 6:30 o'clock" costing seventy-five cents per person. Dancing and a "big bridge party" and children's activities followed, and there was a parcel post counter, country store, and fortuneteller.[68]

It was time for St. Paul's to move. Commercial buildings had surrounded its previous downtown location not far from the cathedral, and the church followed many of its parishioners to the suburbs. St. Paul's had purchased a lot on the northeast corner of 300 South and 900 East on March 5, 1917. Services were held in the new parish hall from 1920 to 1927, when the new Tudor Revival building was completed. The design, popular with churches, country clubs, and upscale housing developments of the 1920s and 1930s, was suggested by Professor George M. Marshall, who taught English at the University of Utah, and who was a longtime church member. The *Salt Lake Tribune* said the work of the local architectural firm, Ware & Treganza, was "pronounced one of the finest in the state from an artistic standpoint."[69] The old church property was sold for $192,500; the new building and grounds cost approximately $75,000, with the remaining sum going toward an endowment. During the first forty-four years of its existence, St. Paul's had twelve rectors, one of whom stayed only six months. The longest tenure was that of the Rev. Alwin E. Butcher, who stayed nineteen years, from 1923 to 1942.

St. Paul's had long enjoyed a close relationship with the Masons, and on April 24, 1927, the grand master, Dana T. Smith, relaid the original cornerstone, with the dean of the cathedral, William W. Fleetwood, joining him on the platform in Masonic regalia. Masons from all over the state marched from the nearby temple. On the first Sunday of Advent, November 27, 1927, the new building was consecrated. With its eye for clerical color, the *Tribune* wrote, "The vestments of the officiating clergy will reflect the dignity of the celebration. Bishop Moulton and Bishop Moreland will wear capes of white, lavishly embroidered in gold and lined with crimson silk."[70] The preacher was Bishop William Hall Moreland of Sacramento, in whose diocese Butcher had recently served.[71]

World War II

Utah's location helped shape its response to World War II. Distant enough from the Pacific to avoid the threat of attack, it was an ideal site for Army training camps and Air Force bases. Its isolation made it an attractive place to keep German prisoners and Japanese detainees. A dark stain on national and state history was the presence of the Topaz relocation center for Japanese Americans that opened in 1942. Approximately 8,000 Japanese American men, women, and children spent three years in confinement at a site thirteen miles northwest of Delta, part of the 110,000 Americans of Japanese ancestry who were forcibly relocated, mostly from the West Coast to the interior.[72] Utah also became a center to store and test atomic weapons, with disastrous consequences unforeseen at the time to "down-winders," the thousands of residents living in the path of atomic radiation.

Across the state at least 49,500 new jobs were created. Fort Douglas became headquarters of the Army's Ninth Service Command. Between August 1942 and October 1943, more than 90,000 airmen took basic training at Kearns Army Air Base, which became a quickly growing community. Flight crews that dropped the atomic bombs on Hiroshima and Nagasaki trained near the Utah–Nevada border at Wendover Air Base, the world's largest site for training bombers. The Utah General Depot, near Ogden, employed 4,000 persons and held 5,000 prisoners of war. Hill Field, also nearby, was built as a WPA project, and soon it employed over 15,000 civilians and 6,000 military.[73] No less important, though smaller, were the Tooele Army Depot, a 1943 offshoot of the Ogden base, and the Deseret Chemical Depot, a top-secret storage site for chemical weapons. By the mid 1940s, approximately 28 percent of the state's income came from government work; the numbers would reduce to 20 percent in 1978, but Utah remained one of the most dependent states in America on defense-related employment.[74]

As defense industry employees swept into the state, their numbers included Episcopalians, or potential church members, who would gradually contribute to the rise of several new parishes in the post-war period. From 1940 to 1943, employment increased from 148,000 to 230,000, and per capita income, once 20 percent below the national average, soon surpassed it.[75] The state's population grew 25 percent between 1940 and 1946. This growth from 555,310 to 688,862 persons was largest along the Wasatch Front, where most defense industries and population centers were located.[76] These would be the sites of future Episcopal churches in the 1970s.

Native American Work: The Utes

In addition to other demands on his role as bishop, Moulton maintained an active interest in Native American work, especially among the Utes. He visited the reservations as often as he could, and shared his limited resources. The total population of the reservation in 1932 was 1,250 persons, down from 6,000 in 1880, yet numbers of Native Americans baptized and confirmed remained significant, even during times when there was no resident missionary priest.[77] Moulton was intrigued by the Uintah Basin reservations, which he spoke of as "my basin" and church publications called the "Bishop's Basin." Encounters with Native Americans were infrequently commented on, and little was written about their life, only that they came, danced, were confirmed, and went away. His reports differ little from those of other western missionaries. Photos of him with the Whiterocks or Randlett congregations show tall, rail-thin Moulton towering over local people, sometimes dressed in full Native American beadwork and feathers. His position appeared to be that the basic goodness of traditional native society need not conflict with Christianity, as in this passage.

> One morning as I was walking across the field I noticed an Indian man standing alone in front of the altar. His hat was in his hand and his head lifted toward the cross. He was a picture indeed—black braided hair, brilliant red shirt, bright blue overalls, yellow moccasins. All alone, he stood there motionless for twenty minutes. . . . I hope and I think he realized that in the new religion which we were presenting to him was to be found all that was best of his old life and ever so much new inspiration for the days to come.[78]

Moulton described a confirmation service elsewhere as including "the crowded church, the altar ablaze with many colored lights, the sunflowers massed about the sanctuary, the Indian dog that got caught in the altar rail and could not get through, the braves with their colored handkerchiefs over their heads which I carefully removed, the Indians kneeling on the floor in honest devotion waiting in humble faith for the Gift, the Indian policeman, and the big white leader. They were all there and I confirmed them every one. They stayed through the afternoon, lying on the rectory lawn, all colors, all ages, old men and maidens, young men and children, ponies tied to the fence and the dogs sleeping under the trees."[79]

The women missionaries among the Utes remained a sympathetic and lasting presence demonstrating an evangelism of service and contact. Living in near poverty themselves, they taught local women to read, sew, prepare foods, and adopt more healthy lifestyles. Rosa Camfield continued her long work at Whiterocks. One Christmas she wrote: "Out on the back porch stands a new kitchen range, ready to be placed. . . . The old range was the trial of my life. Had I been given to profanity I certainly should have indulged at times." Other presents were "things like sugar, canned fruit, apples, oranges, stockings and handkerchiefs, some money presents, material for dress and waist."[80] Hers was a busy life in all seasons. She helped local people write letters, and read the letters they received. Clergy came to hold services only once a month, so she led worship services as well. On Tuesday evenings she taught sewing to Native American girls; on Fridays, reservation boys came to play checkers and other games. A ten-member white Women's Guild met on Tuesdays; a five-member Native American Girls' Friendly Society met weekly as well. Camfield showed people basic sanitary and food preparation measures, plus "helping the sick and more than once I have buried the dead. When I go to bed I never know but that some one will call on me for various reasons—perhaps the husband has been drinking lemon extract and the wife is afraid to stay with him. I have women stay two or three days sometimes. . . . Sometimes a girl will come to evening service and does not like to (nor should I like her to) go back to her home"[81]

In Whiterocks, a Native American elementary school housed 200 children, thirty-two of them Episcopalians. The local Episcopal vicar, whom Bartlett in his 1928 report called "tactless, dogmatic, and dictatorial," feuded with the Indian Agent.[82] A community hall was needed because local people "loaf and gamble through the winter months." Possibly someone might be raised up to be "a missionary to his people," one of the first references to the possibility of native ministries.[83] The Utes were taught the skills of deep irrigation by an English missionary couple, Mr. and Mrs. O. K. Richards, who also managed the Whiterocks school. At Randlett, the Church owned thirteen acres of land and had a church building and almost a hundred members, including both Native Americans and a handful of whites. A woman worker held the church together, Bartlett wrote, "The greatest power in the basin is Mrs. Richards. Every week a large group of women, white and Indian, meet at the rectory for sewing and instructions. Mrs. Richards keeps them together and her quiet, loving influence is felt far and wide."[84]

Logan Revived in the 1940s

Despite the influx of new persons during the war, church growth was most evident in Logan in the post-war period. For several years during the early 1940s, Walter Preston Cable, a lay reader, maintained a lonely but active presence in keeping the miniscule Logan congregation alive. Cable's correspondence with Moulton records a series of small victories: the roof or windows of the church were repaired, a new family showed up for services, a few persons volunteered for an activity—not the dramatic statistics or stories that made headlines, but telling evidence of a small, caring community.

Cable's first service was on December 13, 1942. Of the thirty names from the parish list he inherited from the 1920s, only twelve or thirteen could be located, and five were in the pews that Sunday. Cable opened a church where "windows were shuttered, furniture broken and the whole so besmirched with the accumulated dirt of the years as to be almost blasphemous."[85] His May 1943 report listed five services. Attendance was between three to eight persons; the collection was $1.85. The long-unused building was now clean, and soon its roof was repaired, Cable noted. "The church, all lighted up on Wednesday evenings, has aroused considerable interest among passers-by; one lady, more valiant of heart than the rest, ventured in to participate in the service with me. And several of the parishioners have remarked how good it seems to see the windows aglow once more."[86] Cable recorded a total of nineteen services held between November 1942 and May 1943. Average attendance was six persons per service, and the monies raised amounted to $150, of which $50 came from Bishop Moulton. On Good Friday, Cable held a three-hour service with recorded music. "Sir John Stainer's oratorio 'The Crucifixion' was chosen as being entirely proper and of high quality. To make this music available, a small electric phonograph and amplifying unit was obtained together with the complete records."

Also keeping St. John's alive was Major Ben B. Blair, an instructor in the University's Military Science program, who lent his organizational skills and enthusiasm to building up the small congregation. During the summer of 1945, a seminarian, Jimmie McClain, was assigned to Logan. McClain starred on the long-running NBC "Dr. IQ" radio show. As a benefit to raise money for a church organ, he put on a "Dr. IQ" live program at Logan's Capitol Theater on July 18, 1945, and raised nearly a thousand dollars.

Moulton's Later Years; The Stalin Peace Prize

The last year of Moulton's twenty-six-year tenure was 1946. In 1945, on the eve of his retirement, a national church officer observed: "The bishop's inertia in the past and present—an apparent inability or refusal to act . . . has proved disastrously discouraging to clergy and laity alike. They are dispirited and now show evidence of hopelessness, even of a certain fearfulness of any action, which is deeply disturbing. They think the security of their own future is at stake! They admit that the Church's work in Utah has been 'coasting downhill' for the past five years."[87]

Still, there was considerable progress to report. The number of parochial clergy, including the bishop, was eleven, six of whom had arrived in recent years. There were now twenty-five churches or missions, including the Navajo mission H. Baxter Liebler opened in 1943, and a short-lived Japanese mission at Layton in 1944. Despite the hard times, church numbers rose from 1,737 in 1931 to 2,631 in 1946.[88] Moulton retired on September 13, 1946, after reaching the mandatory retirement age of seventy-two. At his retirement, the Missionary District Convocation passed a resolution. "We have parted with the faithful bishop . . . but we shall ever be united to him in spirit because we do actually believe in the Communion of Saints. Bishop Moulton is indeed a saint in spiritual things and always a gentleman in his relation to his fellow clergy and to all mankind."[89]

On April 6, 1951, during the height of the cold war, the first Stalin Peace Prize winners were announced from Moscow. The sole American was Bishop Arthur A. Moulton of Salt Lake City. The Russian equivalent of the Nobel Prize, the awards commemorated Josef Stalin's seventieth birthday and included a gold medal bearing Stalin's likeness and 100,000 rubles, roughly $25,000. The seven recipients included Prof. Frederic Joliot-Curié, Nobel Prize winner and former head of France's Atomic Energy Committee until dismissed for his Communist party ties, and Hewlett Johnson, popularly known as the "Red Dean" of Canterbury Cathedral.[90] Moulton, seventy-eight, and retired for five years, told a newspaper he was taken "completely by surprise. The only award I want in working for peace is peace."[91] Such public recognition by the Soviet Union would usually go to an avowed communist or high-profile supporter of the Soviet Union; Moulton was neither.

Moulton's tie to the Soviet Union was through the American Committee for the Protection of the Foreign Born, one of several Moscow-funded and directed front organizations that capitalized on legitimate American interests, in this case due process for foreigners facing deportation. The second honorary co-chair was Professor Louise Pettibone-Smith, who taught Biblical studies at Wellesley College.[92] The ACPFB was founded in 1933, and registered some success in opposing the capricious deportation of the foreign born, a perennial concern of church and civil liberty groups. Its Executive Secretary was Abner Green, a long-time Romanian communist now resident in New York City. Green probably nominated Moulton for the prize. He would have seen Moulton as a prestigious figure—an Episcopal bishop would look good on the letterhead—and someone who would not interfere with the organization's policies, all of which originated in Moscow.

Moulton's name also appeared on a December 1949 news release of the Committee for Peaceful Alternatives to the Atlantic Pact, which claimed membership of about a thousand clergy, educators, writers, civic and labor leaders, "including seven Protestant bishops and two Nobel prize winners." The Committee urged President Truman "to propose an agreement whereby the atomic bomb should not be used as an instrument of international warfare."[93]

The retired bishop never attended any meetings of the ACPFB, nor did he visit its New York offices, or write the turgid prose mailed out under his name in its press releases. A congressional investigation report stated that Moulton knew absolutely nothing about how he was selected and elected as co-chair.[94] "The first that he knew he was being considered for honorary co-chairmanship was when he was advised he had been elected. He implied that he accepted the office 'to help out and be nice' and testified that 'I didn't ask any questions.'"[95]

A member of the peace activist group, the Fellowship of Reconciliation, which Jones once headed, Moulton spoke in Madison Square Garden in 1949 at a cultural and scientific conference for world peace, but was not a delegate to the Soviet World Peace Council. "I have never been across the seas in any interest of that kind," he said, adding, "I am convinced that America, upon whom the leadership of the world has been thrust, should lead in peace as well as in other lines. I want to see America arise as a great spiritual ideal."[96] The FBI developed a thirty-three-page file on Moulton, largely based on rewrites of local newspaper clippings from 1949 to 1951, plus a sighting with a luncheon guest at the Alta Club. The final entry noted his death on August 18, 1962, at age eighty-nine.[97] "He was not a communist," James W. Beless, Jr., a former FBI agent and diocesan chancellor said, adding, "He was very badly used."[98] "There was no money, no medal, nothing ever turned up as a result of it," his granddaughter remarked. "He never got anything from it but a lot of grief."[99]

As Stalin's harsh rule became widely known, and the 1956 Russian invasion of Hungry shocked international public opinion, the ACPFB lost membership and influence. By 1958, its key public activity was an annual picnic, and members were encouraged to send eighty-fifth birthday greetings to Bishop Moulton.[100] Moulton was Utah's third successive bishop to actively support international peace initiatives, succeeding Spalding, the socialist, 1904–1914, and Jones, the pacifist, 1915–1918.

6

Stephen C. Clark

A Promising Episcopate Cut Down by Death (1946–1950)

> He was a visionary and a careful planner.
> —James W. Beless, Jr., Chancellor

> The fifty-mile circle is obviously our best future.
> —Bishop Clark, in his 1949 Ten Year Program

The shape of the modern Episcopal Church in Utah is largely due to the careful planning of its most unknown bishop, Stephen Cutter Clark, whose promising episcopate began in December 1946. Stricken with a stroke in January 1949, he died in November 1950. Clark's name is rarely mentioned, but his clearly enunciated vision and careful planning for the church's growth over the next decade provided the blueprint from which his successor, Richard S. Watson, built several churches. Clark was a person of unvarnished evangelical faith, hard working, and a details-oriented leader. His accounts of life in the missionary district leave a candid picture of the local church struggling for shape and definition in the immediate post-war years.

Institutional church life was on hold during Moulton's later years, and the western bishops sought as his successor someone who would give new life to the missionary district in the post-World War II era. Stephen C. Clark, the first westerner nominated for the post, was such a person. He had been elected by the western provincial council of bishops who selected him over another candidate, Arthur C. Lichtenberger, who later became bishop of Missouri, and still later presiding bishop. Plain-looking and plain spoken, Clark conducted a no-frills ministry in an energetic, able manner. He was fifty-two at the time of his consecration, and had been rector of St. Paul's, Pomona, and then St. Mark's, Pasadena, for twenty years. Born in Pasadena on August 6, 1892, he attended Occidental College, graduated from the University of California in 1914, and from the Episcopal Theological School, Cambridge, Massachusetts, in 1917. Ordained a deacon that year, he became a priest in 1918. Clark knew Utah, having served as priest-in-charge of St. Luke's, Park City, for a year and a half. Clark married the former Helen Marcia Moodey in 1917, and they had four children. The future bishop held several responsible positions in the Diocese of Los Angeles, including membership on the Standing Committee, and editor of the *Los Angeles Churchman.* He was also assistant secretary of the House of Deputies for the 1940 General Convention.

Clark's consecration took place on December 6, 1946, at St. Paul's Cathedral, Los Angeles, by the presiding bishop, Henry St. George Tucker, assisted by Bishops Bertrand Stevens of Los Angeles and Arthur Moulton of Utah. Eight other bishops participated in the service; gifts included a pectoral cross, Bible and Prayer Book, a Communion service, luggage, and a briefcase. Crosiers had not yet gained usage in Utah, and copes and miters remained in the back pages of church apparel catalogues. The missionary district Clark entered was composed of twenty-five hundred communicants, three parishes, and twenty-one missions.[1] "He was a businessman," Thelma S. Ellis of Good Shepherd, Ogden recalled, "but he didn't remember people's names. Once he and his wife spent New Year's Eve with a prominent couple from our parish. When he came on a visitation the next week he couldn't recall their names."[2]

In 1947, the national church allocated $19,435 for work in Utah, and the missionary district was expected to raise an additional $5,095. Shortly after arriving in Utah, he was officially seated at the cathedral on January 26, 1947, as part of the missionary district's annual convocation. Within three months he visited every parish and mission, traveling over 6,000 miles by air, train, car, jeep, horseback, and auto stage-cars that carried U. S. Mail and passengers to rural areas. Here is Clark emerging from a car stuck in the sand during a 1946 visit to the Navajo mission in southeastern Utah.

> The mesa was unmistakable; I could keep that in mind and in sight, and took courage. Another of those sharp descents, a trail sometimes six to eight inches wide, with precipices one dared not look at, a deserted hogan—again vast wastes of stunted sage and rabbit grass, another descent as steep as the last, but below us a lovely green valley, with three or four Navajo houses of the palisades type, with windows, doors, and chimneys. Water—would there be water to drink? Padre [H. Baxter

> Liebler] reached the houses first—no, not a soul about! But in the distance ahead of us a covered wagon. "Summer camp of these people," he said, and so it was. There was water, and there were melons and smiles of welcome; we tarried only a few minutes. We had passed the pointed mesa with the long talus slope; the Padre looked at his watch. "One o'clock. I'll have you at the Mission by two, or break every switch on the Reservation in the attempt." Slickrock, sandy slopes, cobble stones; narrow trails, washes.[3]

Shortly after arriving, the bishop prepared a basic talk about Utah. "Come with me in my car as I drive over the District of Utah in a quick trip assessing its needs." The first stop was the state's southeast corner, home of the Navajo where the missionaries "live in conditions you and I would not have the courage to face. Dirt floors—rationing of water—none of the comforts we so easily lay hands on, do they have access to."[4] Next came Moab, Monticello, and Crescent Junction, cut off from the church except for two or three services a year. Carbon County was the site of busy coal mines. "By day the miners work in the darkness of the mine—at night they come out of the pits to face a community, artificial, from its blazing neon lights to all the desperate evils men can cling to when their souls are dark," including prostitution and gambling.

To the east, the Ute reservations held a "different people entirely from the Navajo. They are more like the Indians we have read about in childhood. They are stolid and cold and slow and unresponsive." In Park City, a retired priest held services twice monthly for a congregation of twenty in "a cracker box, thirty feet long and twenty feet wide—a little white shed, literally hanging on the side of the mountain." "More men—more money—if only we had the tools in terms of persons and money to do this job!" was a constant refrain. Clark's snapshot of Utah church conditions was realistic. Parishes and missions were isolated, qualified clergy hard to come by. Episcopalians were rarely in larger income brackets, and the LDS presence was pervasive. Clark said the Latter-day Saints represented "a powerful organization largely controlling most aspects of the state. Its theology is vague, nebulous, and uncertain." Like some of his predecessors, he saw signs of its disintegration; the day was not far off "when a great apostasy will come and people will begin to leave the rank and file of Mormonism. Now is the time, during this weakening period, for our Church to strike, and strike hard and fast."[5] Clerics since Tuttle's time had been finding the cracks, but LDS numbers and influence continued to grow.

During the late 1940s the LDS Church made cautious efforts toward cooperative relations with other denominations. When the Archbishop of York stopped in Salt Lake City on his way to the Episcopal Church's general convention in San Francisco on September 23, 1949, a service for 4,000 persons was held at the Mormon Tabernacle. The LDS leadership participated and the Tabernacle Choir sang.

The Ten Year Plan: Focus on a Fifty-Mile Radius from Salt Lake City

Clark's set speech was a prelude to a comprehensive ten-year plan he devised after a year and a half in Utah. Its findings shaped Watson's building program a few years later, and represented the only systematic future survey of church conditions in Utah since Bartlett's 1928 study. Clark believed Utah's future population growth would be mostly concentrated in a fifty-mile zone radiating from Salt Lake City, framed by the Wasatch Mountains and the Salt Lake desert. Purely rural areas would not be productive places for church work; most were strongly LDS and defectors who tried to join the Episcopal Church faced social ostracism and economic ruin. But around Salt Lake City it was different. Clark estimated the 1949 population of Utah at about 600,000 persons, 480,000 of them Latter-day Saints, and 120,000 "Gentiles," of whom 100,000 lived near Salt Lake City. Possibly ninty-five percent of Utah's non-LDS population lived within a fifty-mile radius of the state capitol. "The so called 'jack' Mormon, or lapsed member, is very prevalent in the city areas. They have lost both faith and interest in the teachings of their Church, but four or five generations of history, which is constantly glorified, plus the general inertia in changing one's religion, keeps most from leaving the LDS Church."[6]

The Episcopal Church had built no new churches in Salt Lake City in fifty-nine years, although the city's population had grown six-fold during that period. Here is where it should concentrate its resources. One of the first new postwar churches was All Saints' Mission, a growing suburban congregation of a hundred people who would build its own building in Clark's successor's time.

The early years of All Saints' history read like the wanderings of the Children of Israel in the desert, a member reflected. In 1948 a group of mothers, several "war wives" among them, asked the bishop to help establish a Sunday school in southeast Salt Lake City. The church was launched on August 30, 1948, during a weeklong summer church school for seventy-seven children in the garage of Mr. and Mrs. F. H. Moreland at 1771 South 200 East. A Sunday school then followed in September, and continued until cool weather set in and another family offered a heated basement. A meeting of interested persons was held near All Saints' Day, and Bishop Clark suggested

All Saints' as a name for the parish. Robert Rusack, a seminarian and later bishop of the Diocese of Los Angeles (1974–1986), served as parish lay reader from February to May 1949. A women's guild of eight persons gathered on the evening of January 6, 1949, and soon three guilds comprising 115 women were launched.[7] The church found a temporary home in the American Legion clubhouse, the Weasku Inn, a restaurant at 2263 East 2100 South, a brief period at Westminster College, then Fairmont Park (1951), followed the post guardhouse at Fort Douglas where the Sunday school met in a jail cellblock. Soon services moved to the post chapel; by then over 200 young people gathered for Sunday school in the post's administrative building and officer's club.

"Morale was high and All Saints' was a 'happy ship,'" one of the organizers recalled.[8] Land at 1700 South and Foothill Boulevard was donated in 1952 by James A. Hogle, a business entrepreneur, with the provision that a driveway and parking area be shared by All Saints' and its neighbor, the Jewish Community Center. "It was at this spot in August 1948 that Bishop Clark, Ellsworth Stone and the F. H. Morelands met and were inspired by the view," Mrs. Moreland wrote. "Salt Lake City surrounded by mountains with the waters of the Great Salt Lake shimmering in the far distance, nothing close by but the unimproved ground which gave a feeling of strength and permanence."[9]

Clark wanted the Episcopal church to expand, especially in the city's south and west ends and immediately south of the city, where the population had grown to over 35,000 persons. Clark had a seminarian visit door to door to obtain a list of Episcopalians or persons interested in supporting new missions. "If this succeeds, next spring a mission should be opened, and if possible a priest found to live there."[10] A new mission was needed west of the railroad tracks, where 15,000 persons now lived, if $25,000 could be raised. Struggling St. Peter's Mission, a small congregation next to St. Mark's Hospital, should be closed. "The Church is rickety, and held together by iron tie rods. The basement is poorly lighted, poorly ventilated, and in winter damp and smelly."[11]

The bishop was concerned about the insularity of the two main Salt Lake City parishes, St. Mark's Cathedral and St. Paul's, both "very strong and very parochial." "They have become so self-centered, and so interested in developing their own equipment, that they do not give generously in any missionary way, and they fail to attract progressive minded Church people moving into the city. Since the strength of the church is here in the City, the change of the mindset right here is the most serious problem facing the bishop."[12] Elsewhere he told the national church: "morale of the District has changed noticeably in the last six months, and if I could possibly find the opportunity to change the leadership in my two city parishes and secure cooperative rectors, I believe we might make quite fast progress in the greater city programs. That is the immediate mission field ahead, but it is likewise my hardest problem to meet because the city is where we have had the greatest amount of loafing and horse-play for many years past."[13]

Parish status would soon come for St. Mary's, Provo, which had eighty-four communicants in 1950. Provo represented "our best and most neglected opportunity in Utah," Clark believed. With new leadership, St. Mary's could raise a budget of $4,000 a year. Of the incumbent, William J. Hawes, Clark said, "I have tried everything with him, and he simply has not the stuff."[14] In Garfield, for thirty-five years the Episcopal Church occupied a community church built by a local copper company. The church's heyday had been in the period up to 1918, when industry was booming. In more recent years, membership dropped sharply, but the work of two different enthusiastic seminarians raised numbers to over 115 children for a vacation Bible school.[15]

Further outside Salt Lake City, the Church of the Good Shepherd, Ogden, "was the most nearly normal functioning church when I came into the District," possessed of "the best missionary vision of any of our three parishes." Clark had closed "the little broken down church in Plain City." It had only two communicants now and only six non-Mormons lived in the town. Clark had an eye on the growing space between Salt Lake City and Ogden, still mostly farmland, but with 10,000 persons living there. The sprawling communities of Clearfield, Layton, or Farmington would be logical sites for a mission, possibly in conjunction with a Japanese congregation, although that never happened. There were 3,000 Japanese in the state, 300 Christians among them. Most came as railroad workers in the nineteenth century and stayed on as farmers. A mission for the Japanese, Holy Cross, Clearfield–Layton, was called by Clark "my most difficult and mysterious problem." The priest-in-charge had the congregation buy him a house in Salt Lake City, but Kenneth W. Nakajo rarely visited the mission and lost the congregation's confidence. "He roams the state here and there, jumping from one community to another, and after four years of work has found only twenty-four communicants and perhaps forty Christians," Clark wrote, while noting that a new generation of Japanese preferred to join English-speaking churches.[16]

Clark wanted to focus on a few strong missions, "rather than to see how many names I can put on a list. I feel that in Utah and even worse in neighboring Wyoming we have built too many small almost unused buildings"[17] Scattered services were still maintained at Helper and Kenilworth;

the region's coalmines attracted English miners some of whom were Church of England members. Clark's juggling included placing a talented young seminary graduate and his enthusiastic wife in Kenilworth, "where we have a bit of a tradition," with the backing of the Independent Coal and Coke Company manager, William J. O'Conner, an active Episcopalian. The bishop's long-term goal was a church in Price, a city of 7,000 persons, centrally located among the scattered mining communities.[18]

Work resumed in Logan, where the church retained a small core of twelve to fifteen families. "I am very happy over Logan," Clark said. The State Agricultural College with its 4,500 students was a big draw, but "the lost ground of forty years abuse and neglect is hard to regain." The Logan church's roof needed replacement, and an aging furnace poorly heated both church and rectory. The Women's Auxiliary raised $1,250 for needed repairs, and the bishop secured the services of a priest from Nebraska, Willis Rosenthal, who also taught part time at the college. Between fifty and sixty students attended discussion groups at St. John's House, including "two eastern Orthodox from Lebanon, an Indian who is a Hindu, a Mohammedan from Egypt, a Chinese Christian . . . from Shanghai (incidentally singing in the choir) and Episcopalians from Maine, Ohio, Washington, Idaho, and several other States."[19] Clark thought more people would come to the Episcopal Church in Logan because the local Presbyterian minister constantly attacked Mormons. Also, "Mrs. Rosenthal keeps open house, all day and all week, with a pot of coffee always on the stove and the boys love her baby. Why don't we salary good parson's wives?"[20]

"I know Park City best because I lived there a year and a half thirty years ago," Clark wrote, "and it was a fair town then, even if tough. It is still tough, in fact tougher."[21] Its former deacon tried to revive services there, aided by the now elderly William F. Bulkley, but with little response from the community.

The Clark plan was bold, but without resources to realize it. Clark's report was interlaced with minute accounts of moving small sums about to build here and there. Sell an unused church property in one place, add part of the retiring archdeacon's salary to another project, ask the national church for a grant for a third. He managed to increase Utah's budget from the national church to $25,495 in 1950, and set $2,400 as the minimum salary for married clergy, plus $180 a year for each minor child. His own salary was $6,000. He estimated he covered 20,000 miles a year. The missionary district allowed clergy seven cents a mile for official travel, and Clark's travel allowance was about $700.[22] It was also Clark who saw the possibilities for Camp Tuttle, a former Girls' Friendly Society camp, and planned for its upgrading, work that continued under his successors.

The Uintah Basin

The Clark report divided Uintah Basin work into the "white field" and the "Indian field." In the former, Roosevelt and Fort Duchesne had shrunk in importance as farming decreased. Prospects were better in Vernal; oil had been discovered in nearby Colorado, but it remained a difficult, isolated field. Church services had been reduced to one afternoon a month in Fort Duchesne; no services had been held in Roosevelt in three years, and the church property was sold to the state government. The Vernal rectory had also been sold, and the Church was used by a Southern Baptist congregation. Clark dismissed the resident deacon, ordained by Moulton, who also doubled as a Congregationalist minister; he then moved to another state where he came out as a full-time Congregationalist.[23] Bad luck ran in streaks. The bishop sent a new candidate to Vernal; this one launched a youth program, but left a string of unpaid debts, butchered the rectory with amateur carpentry, antagonized the local community, and was "perhaps my worst mistake to date in Utah, but I did inherit him, with some doubts, and now have more."[24]

Notwithstanding the difficulties, Native American work was "my happiest spot in Utah," the bishop observed. The Whiterocks and Randlett missions had been almost closed down, but an active priest, Joseph F. Hogben, known locally as "the buckaroo parson," was recruited for work there. "Father Joe" had a horse called "King" and a car called "Pilgrim." Hogben spent seventeen years among Native Americans in Nevada, Idaho, and Utah, and estimated he traveled over 60,000 miles on horseback. A World War II chaplain, he arrived in Utah 1946 and stayed until called up as an Army chaplain in the Korean War. Hogben was priest at both Whiterocks and Randlett, and is remembered for founding the White Rock's Posse that rode in eastern Utah parades and for Bishop's Day. They did precision riding and trick roping. Hogben "does much of his calling on horseback—a few sandwiches in his saddle bags—visiting the sick—baptizing—and carrying our Lord's message," a local commentator observed.[25] In a year's time after his arrival, 99 persons were presented for confirmation, a church school of 150 persons was organized at Whiterocks, and $60 raised toward the priest's salary. The local Native American community painted the decrepit rectory and the Women's Auxiliary contributed $1,500 for a woman worker. A half-ton truck was bought for the mission, and when Bishop's Day was held at Whiterocks, 550 Native Americans and 200 whites gathered, the largest assembly of its kind for anything outside the Sun Dance or Bear Dance.[26]

The automobile once more figured in church planning. In towns and mining communities, potential church members were moving to small farms up to fifty miles distant and commuting to work. This meant smaller local congregations on Sunday mornings, and Clark believed the Church should no longer should plan on separate sites less than twenty-five miles apart. He found merit in working with Protestant "Comity Councils." The idea was that if a particular church was strong in a town, others would support it if they had no congregation of their own in that location. But there was a down side to the combined churches as well. The doors may be open, but competition soon surfaced in the pews, and the movement produced few success stories. In communities where there was no Episcopal Church, Clark tried "personally to visit several times a year (by invitation) and hold an Episcopal communion service at 8:00 A.M. for our few scattered communicants, and then preach at the regular morning service." In some places, "I shall have to carry on a program in competition, probably in a private home, and in one or two places I shall probably invade the territory if we find enough people not properly churched."[27]

The entire missionary district's clergy staff was eleven persons, including the bishop, and twenty-six churches or missions, most of them small and struggling. Only the two largest Salt Lake City parishes contributed over a thousand dollars each to the missionary district's budget; the rest raised $100 or less. Clark said salaries were "pitifully small all over the church and tragically small in Utah." The total assets of the Corporation of the Episcopal Church in Utah were $49,152 at the end of 1946. Notwithstanding the difficulties, there was modest growth. The Committee on the State of the Church noted that numerical growth of the Episcopal Church was 0.97 percent in 1946 and 2.83 percent in the Province of the Pacific, but 3.54 percent in Utah.[28] Most of it came from defense-related employers coming from out of state.

Clergy recruitment was the main problem facing the missionary district, Clark believed, as it had been since its inception. The national church was short a thousand priests in the late 1940s. The bishop visited eight seminaries in his recruitment efforts, and created a summer seminarian's program to attract promising young recruits. He was pleased that some Utah parishes pledged $325 a month toward clergy salaries if he could find the priests. He hoped to initiate a program of lay readers to assist vacant parishes and revive the Girls Friendly Society, which once had seventeen branches. *The Episcopal Churchman of Utah* was launched, one of five district or diocesan publications issued at various times in the Utah church's history.[29]

Clark also found new living quarters. The church had owned two different downtown houses since Tuttle's time, used variously as bishop's residence and twenty-five offices, but downtown Salt Lake City was fast becoming commercial, and the Clarks moved to a dwelling on the Rowland

Hall school grounds, 233 First Avenue, on the corner of B Street. Diocesan offices occupied the ground floor, and residential space for the bishop and family was on the next two floors.

Clark also prepared a modern set of Canons, approved by Presiding Bishop Henry Knox Sherrill, since Utah was a missionary district. They were passed in 1949 at the missionary district's Forty-Second Annual Convocation. Each parish and organized mission could send a delegate to the annual convocation for each fifty members, but no congregation could send more than five delegates, an effort to keep the cathedral and St. Paul's from dominating the convocation. An Executive Council would assist the bishop in carrying on the work of the church. The bishop was its president, and also appointed three of the group's nine members. The archdeacon, chancellor, and treasurer were also voting members.[30]

St. Mark's Hospital was in solid shape. It added an operating wing, paid for mostly through federal funding, and "now has the best operating facilities between the Mississippi and the Pacific Coast."[31] The hospital called 1946 its "greatest year;" 6,486 patients were admitted and 951 babies were born there. An endoscopic clinic was added, and a medical amphitheater built, allowing medical students to watch surgical procedures. The Chaplain made numerous calls on patients, administered baptisms, held services of Holy Communion, and distributed sixty-five copies of *Life* magazine. In 1948 the average length of stay was eight days, slightly above the national average, partly because of the number of orthopedic and long-care cases. Ultraviolet lights were added for surgery, and several oxygen tents were purchased. The School of Nursing began a cooperative program with Westminster College, with fifty-three students. Rowland Hall School for Girls was recovering from the Depression and was carrying on "in spite of several tragic mistakes (one by the present incumbent) in the selection of Headmistresses."[32]

As for Emery House, "This is no longer an institution, only a poor building rented to the city for a second rate youth program. It is a tragedy from any angle. First, that Bishop Spalding's vision of an institution on the edge of campus, seems to have been outmoded almost before the building was finished."[33] Only a handful of the two hundred Episcopalian students at the University attended programs, and an interdenominational "Fellowship House" was no more successful. Clark wanted to sell Emery House and use the proceeds toward a new mission church in Salt Lake City.

The bishop gave only three convocation addresses to the district, largely reflecting themes from the Ten Year Plan. Clark at that time also presented the advanced idea of recruiting lay readers from established parishes to serve as missioners in places without clergy, a program he never had time to develop, and one his successor did not favor. There was also the reality of even less financial backing from the national church. "I have been told in no uncertain terms that my task is to work for some self support, especially in the matter of the vicar's stipend, from every place, large and small," he told the convocation. Three years later the convocation passed a resolution deploring the failure of the Provincial Synod to seat women delegates. "It seems to me that we are crippling our efficiency by not using the wonderful woman power we have in the District," the bishop remarked in 1947.

But all was not well. Clark, the determined executive, knew what he wanted to do, and ruffled feathers in the process. Divisiveness was identified as a problem among the Utah clergy by Bishop William F. Lewis of Nevada, who became temporary administrator of the missionary district after Clark's death. Lewis, in an address to the missionary district, said, "Emphasis on partisanship—on minority prejudice of the small group as opposed to the larger fellowship. These things are the stuff which produces the chaos of hell!"[34]

Death Comes to the Bishop

In January 1949, while in San Francisco for a meeting, Clark was stricken with a stroke. After several weeks hospitalization there and in Utah, he was eager to resume his work, but illness persisted, and he died on November 30, 1950. Following Clark's death, his widow received a $500 a year pension. Clark's time in Utah was brief, slightly more than three years of productive work, and clearly represented a transition from the old to the new. Church growth would increasingly concentrate on the Salt Lake City region, the automobile would change the shape of parish boundaries, and women would assume increasingly important roles in church governance within a decade. Native American work continued fitfully but earnestly, while Utah became of less interest to the national church. The day was not too distant when a new independent diocese would tumble into being.

The Navajo Mission and H. Baxter Liebler

The following section discusses the Navajo mission of H. Baxter Liebler, which began in 1943, late in Moulton's episcopacy, although Moulton and Liebler had little contact. Clark visited Liebler and was actively interested in the mission. Watson would have liked to exercise episcopal oversight in Navajoland, but distances were considerable, and Liebler played the loner's game, keeping the mission under his personal control until, with age and shrinking funds, it was necessary for him to turn over its deed to the missionary district. After Liebler retired in 1962, the mission struggled on, to be replaced by the Navajo Area Mission with a Navajo bishop in 1979.

> The New England bishop's wife and two ladies stopped for gasoline at the isolated Utah desert crossroads. At the same station was a man with a dust-covered black cassock and weathered face in a rusty Jeep.
>
> "Are you, by chance, an Anglican?" asked the bishop's wife.
>
> "Not by chance, madame, but by sincere conviction," came the answer.

The story's authenticity cannot be verified, but it is part of the legend built up around H. Baxter Liebler, one of the Episcopal Church's most colorful missionary figures. He came across the solitary desert by pony, and returned in 1943 to settle at Bluff, Utah, in Navajoland, where he opened St. Christopher's Mission. Soon it included a modest school, living quarters, a common room, and medical dispensary.

H. Baxter Liebler (1889–1982) was fifty-three when he headed west, with his wife, Frances; two Anglican Franciscan monks, Brothers Juniper and Michael; a nurse, Esther Bacon; and Helen Sturges, a social worker. Liebler began daily services the day of his arrival, and gradually his Navajo improved, the mission was built, and its ministries expanded. The mission's parish bounds covered approximately 1,800 square miles of mostly desert and grazing land, where 2,000 Navajos led a hand-to-mouth existence. The founder of St. Christopher's retired in 1962, moving to a solitary retreat center sixty miles away at St. Mary of the Moonlight, Oljeto. By the time of his death in 1982, the Navajoland Area Mission assumed responsibility for continuing, albeit in a different manner, the work this pioneering priest had single-handedly begun almost forty years earlier.

"Father Liebler," that is the only thing to call him, was born in New York City on November 26, 1889, the son of a successful second-generation German American Broadway theatrical producer who held the rights to the American production of George Bernard Shaw's plays. Educated at the Horace Mann School and Columbia University, Liebler spent summers in Connecticut where he read Henry Wadsworth Longfellow's *Hiawatha* and James Fenimore Cooper's *Leatherstocking Tales*, and talked with Ernest Thompson Seton, a New England neighbor and author of *Two Little Savages* and other period works for young people.

Liebler attended Nashotah House Seminary, an Anglo Catholic institution in Wisconsin, then for twenty-five years worked weekdays in New York City, running his wife's family business, a company that made wooden artificial limbs. He commuted weekends to Old Greenwich, Connecticut, where he literally built St. Saviour's Church and served as its long-time nonstipendiary rector. For many years he spent vacations in the Southwest, planning eventually to move there. Liebler wrote Bishop Moulton in 1942, asking permission to set up a mission in southern Utah among the Navajo. Moulton replied that the southern Utah Native American lands were not part of his jurisdiction. Liebler tactfully pointed out some were within the missionary district. As Moulton gradually became more welcoming, Liebler became warmer, closing his letters with *in Domino* and eventually "cordially *in Domino.*" The Connecticut priest wanted to find a place where Native Americans had never encountered any missionaries, thus allowing an unalloyed encounter between church and indigenous people. The Navajo had had at least perfunctory contact with Christianity through the early Spanish Franciscans, and in 1923 two Episcopalian women missionaries had already been at work among the Navajo. Laura M. Parmelee and a Miss Ross had established a brief-lived medical dispensary at Bluff, treating 928 dispensary cases and receiving over 1,400 Navajo visitors.[35] Still, for Liebler, this was the place, and he pitched his tents and began to build the settlement that would soon become St. Christopher's. A complication was that Liebler did not hold clear title to the land, which belonged to the U. S. government and was sold to him by two men who did not own it. Liebler mustered his supporters to contact their Congressional delegations, and in 1948 both houses of Congress passed a bill selling the land to Liebler's Southwest Mission for $1.25 an acre.[36]

The Native Americans called Liebler "the one who drags his garment his-garment-is-long" or sometimes "Sore Guts," after he mistakenly drank alkaline water from a desert pool. He became a respected figure in the small missionary district, and was twice elected a delegate to national conventions. His relations with Utah's bishops were calculatingly correct; he scrupulously kept good relationships with four of them, three of whom dreamt about what they would do with the Mission when he retired, and he sometimes peppered bishops with letters on arcane points of Anglican practice, such as whether or not baptism by sprinkling water was valid. Salt Lake City was a long way off, the roads were poor, and Liebler didn't mind it one bit. "Father Liebler never paid any attention to bishops," another priest who knew him well remarked.[37] He also kept his distance from the national church's Office of Indian Affairs, and spoke against their efforts to "civilize" Native Americans by abolishing their traditional culture and beliefs. Later, when national church policies shifted toward affirming indigenous cultures, he saw it as a vindication of his efforts.[38]

Liebler was a gifted publicist. A prolific and skilled writer, his periodic newsletters reached a direct mailing audience of 30,000 persons, and raised over a million dollars to cover mission costs. Dressed in the garb of a Spanish padre or of a Franciscan monk, he was the natural subject of photographs and had an unerring ear for collecting insightful snippets of conversation to work into his books and articles. He encouraged working groups to spend time at St. Christopher's, produced film footage and radio shows, and maintained a multi-year correspondence with donors. Liebler's habits were simple, as were those of his followers, and he died with few possessions or savings. Helen Sturges (1897–1985) had a modest inheritance that tided the mission over in difficult times, but money was otherwise in short supply.

Liebler's letters were laced with humor. Once he received an unsolicited brass cross and candlesticks followed by a frantic letter asking for their return. The objects had been given to the Episcopal cathedral in Fargo, North Dakota, as a memorial but were removed when a disgruntled dean left and sent them to the Navajo mission. When the irate original donor demanded their return, Liebler, who had never opened the crate, wrote, "I am only sorry that this headache has come upon you. I hope that this time General Convention will enact a canon stating that when a memorial or other gift is given, it is given and the donor relinquishes all right and title to its use or non-use. I once suffered under an atrocious stained glass window, but never summoned the nerve to heave a brick through it."[39]

The Anglo Catholicism Liebler promoted all his life disappeared in the 1960s with Vatican II and the liturgical reforms leading to a new Episcopal Prayer Book.[40] Yet for Liebler, the Episcopal Church represented a continuation of the ancient Catholic Church, untainted by the Protestant Reformation. "The pagan Navajo has of course none of the prejudices of Protestantism, and it would seem worse than futile to present him a religion in any way tinged with that divisive force which has done so much to weaken the life of the Church," he wrote. His was the Latin missal mass and the daily offices said from his Latin breviary. When low-church Bishop Clark discovered that Liebler included the Latin canon of the mass said silently by the celebrant as part of the Episcopal eucharist, he ordered Liebler to discontinue the practice.[41] Clark was uncomfortable with Liebler's extreme ritualism and hoped that, since Liebler was advancing in age, the mission might soon come under missionary district supervision, but Liebler outlasted Clark and his successor, Watson. Liebler was no ecumenist, although he cooperated unhesitatingly with other denominations on service projects that would advance Navajo interests. Still, he noted, "the Navajos are unspeakably confused by the presentation of variant forms of Christianity which, obviously, are irreconcilable with one another."[42]

A decade after arriving in Bluff, Liebler articulated his accommodationist policy toward Navajo religion. He was far ahead of most missionaries of his generation; in 1954 he wrote, "St. Christopher's does not strive to make Navajos into White Men. Cultural assimilation must come at some time, but it is far off. Deepest respect for Navajo ways and traditions is a part of the Mission's basic attitude, and excepting only such elements of Navajo culture as are opposed to sound hygiene or Christian morals, those ways and traditions are encouraged."[43]

While many missionaries denounced traditional religion as pagan, a word Liebler sometimes used, he saw in it the deep beliefs and symbols that held a society together. "The lines of the life of the Church and the life of the American Indians were parallel lines, but they met in infinity which is God," is how he summarized his position in 1972.[44] Liebler's inclusivist perspective was influenced by the viewpoint of a teacher at Nashotah House, Canon Winfred Douglas, a gifted church musicologist and specialist on Native American cultures, who urged the church to respect the worth, beauty, and sanctity of Native American life instead of trying to destroy it.[45] Thus Liebler was content to share the same hogan with traditional healers, and pray with the sick after they had prayed with them. Although he attended Beauty Way and Enemy Way ceremonies, and participated in the corn pollen rite, a traditional form of blessing, he never incorporated any such rituals in his own services.[46]

Liebler found ancient sources for his accommodationist policy in a letter from Pope Gregory to an early missionary to Britain.

> The temples of the idols in that country should on no account be destroyed. He is to destroy the idols, but the temples themselves are to be aspersed with holy water, altars set up, and relics enclosed in them. For if these temples are well built, they are to be purified from devil-worship, and dedicated to the service of the true God. In this way, we hope that the people, seeing that its temples are not destroyed, may abandon idolatry and resort to these places as before, and may come to know and adore the true God.[47]

Liebler spoke Navajo, and sometimes used traditional sand painting to illustrate sermons. His original sermons were drawn from an early set of Franciscan instructional talks in Navajo. The Navajo sometimes spoke of him as the person "who spoke Navajo with a good accent but had few words." Liebler joked that it took him six weeks to prepare a sermon and six minutes to deliver it. He wore his hair long, tied in back with a ribbon, Navajo fashion. When he celebrated mass, he let his hair flow freely, so that the good forces would circulate easily through it and not become trapped. Children at the mission school were also encouraged to let their hair grow, something not allowed at government schools.[48]

Christmas was a festival already known to Navajos, and St. Christopher's mission made much of it, sometimes attracting several hundred families.

Liebler's creche included Navajo figures, except for the wise men from the East, who were Comanches in war bonnets. A plaster statue of the Virgin Mary depicted a Navajo woman holding the Christ Child in a traditional cradleboard.[49] Liebler's successor, Wayne L. Pontious, ran the mission from 1962 to 1972, and said of the mixture of Navajo culture and Anglo Catholicism: "We were a natural outgrowth of the native culture, because a new generation of medicine men were not being formed. We used music, they used music. We used incense, they used incense. We practiced healing, they practiced healing."[50]

Although the original St. Christopher's Church was decorated with priceless local rugs, Liebler made no use of Navajo colors and designs in liturgical vestments, preferring the traditional fiddleback Roman Catholic chasubles then in use. After Pontious became vicar, he attended a church meeting in New York City and happened upon a Fifth Avenue Native American crafts store, where he spotted a colorful set of vestments using Navajo designs. They were made at St. Michael's Roman Catholic Mission in northern Arizona, not far from Bluff. Pontious took the vestments back to Utah, had them blessed at a traditional Navajo sing, and used them at the mission.

A decade after the mission's founding, Liebler called attention to startling changes in Navajo society. Uranium and vanadium, a mineral used in strengthening steel, were found on the reservation, bringing revenues to the Tribal Council and jobs to young men. Used car dealers and moneylenders multiplied. Liebler wrote, in 1953, "people hardly knew a clutch from a radiator, today may have owned and wrecked three or four cars, have learned to tinker and keep them running and drive them over a sandy trail you would think impassable." At one time the name of Jesus Christ was known only as "the White Man's most powerful swear word," but now missionaries from competing denominations were at work and "radio stations from four points of the compass blare forth confusing and divisive variations on the Christian theme preached by hired Navajos." Traditional religion was dying, indigenous healers who died were not replaced, and "no young men are learning the ceremonies and chants. What is to take its place?" he asked. He hoped for a Christianity that "can be a world-wide religion that commands the respect of the best thinkers of all cultures. But it could well be a welter of confusion leading either to bitterness or indifferentism."[51]

Liebler included Native American music for the sung parts of the mass, and his successor added drums and rattles. The mission used two hand-printed music booklets, one contained "Amazing Grace," "What a Friend We Have in Jesus," plus the Marian hymn "Ye Who Claim the Faith of Jesus". *The Mass of St. Isaac Jogues* (1607–1646), named for the

French missionary to the Mohawks, was adapted for local use. Liebler, an excellent musician, had written an opening Kyrie using a melody from a Hopi snake dance. The Gloria was composed of several Plains Indian melodies, the Creed from a ninth-century plainchant, the Sanctus was an Omaha melody, and the *Agnus Dei* came from the Zuni. The mass ended by singing "The Navajo Mountain Song," which Liebler wrote on a trip to Navajo Mountain.[52]

An after-mass prayer in Navajo was used, translating roughly,

Jesus Christ, young man chief,
Being God's son,
Now I've made your offering, now I've made smoke.
Today I became your child.
Today I became your grandchild.
You speak just to me.
I will do your commandments.
I will follow as I pray to you, you do it, you watch over me.
Stand for my defense,
Stretch out your hand for my defense,
Plead in my defense.
Wood streams bring peace to me,
Grass under me, bring peace to me,
Gentle breezes bring peace to me,
Passing rains bring peace to me,
Passing thunder, bring peace to me.
Let dew fall near me.
Let pollen form near me.
Before me, peace; behind me, peace.
May I have long life walking, and afterwards peace.
Peace has returned. Peace has returned.[53]

What would the Navajo make of such a service? Their own music differed from that of the Hopi or Plains Indians, and was based on repeated rhythmic intensity rather than melody for effect. Navajo cosmology represented a systematic view of all creation, with which the new Christian religion intersected only in places. But, even if the Navajo's own belief system differed from Liebler's, they respected him for his sensitive appreciation of their religion, as he understood it.

The Navajo were caught between two worlds, Liebler believed, and (here he is writing from a Navajo perspective), instead of advancing their own self-interest,

> we the Navajos, are doing a great favor to Washington by sending our children to Washington schools. In the same way, we are doing the missionaries a great favor by attending church services, and in return for this free gift that we are making to the missionaries we expect certain conditions and favors.[54]

How real was the depth of conversion among the Navajo? Many habitually covered their bets and "made the rounds" of several Christian missions, confused by the variety of doctrines preached, but willingly taking food and clothing from several sources. "Navajo religious acceptance was layered," remarked William J. Hannifin, who worked closely as a chaplain to the Navajo at the Intermountain School in Brigham City. "They lived in both worlds. Among the Navajo they were Navajo, among the White Men they were like them. I prefer to think of it not as either/or but both/and."[55]

In talks to eastern audiences and articles on culture and religion, Liebler explained traditional Navajo beliefs, the agonizing dynamics of the Native American–white encounter, and the need for both traditional beliefs and Christianity to coexist. Navajo religion and Christianity did not easily intersect. Death was feared by the Navajo and there was no talk of the afterlife, making explanations of the Resurrection difficult. Gods and spirits existed, but intercessory prayer was unknown. Sacraments were harder to explain. Baptism became "head-top water," confirmation "our interior-standing (or soul) being made strong," penance "our sins taking-away," and the eucharist "our mouths into, a thing is put."[56] Lustral water, used as "holy water" in blessings, might be employed to expel skin walkers, malevolent spirits that prowled about doing harm.

Summary: Sustaining an Atmosphere of Worship

Despite its chapel being partially burned down in 1950, and being destroyed by an arsonist, Donald Marshall, in 1964, the mission thrived for over a quarter-century. Its twelve-bed clinic had five thousand patient names in its files. Children were born there, tuberculosis, a deadly disease among Native Americans, was combated, and an emergency airstrip was built to evacuate those who could not be treated locally. Distant mission stations in Montezuma Creek and Monument Valley were added. A bridge spanned the San Juan River, thanks to Mission lobbying, and wells were drilled, allowing families direct access to water.[57]

The isolation took its toll on many visitors, but not on the ascetic Liebler, who was as positive as any Desert Father about the mission. He recalled the psalmist, "The lot is fallen unto me in a fair ground; yea, I have a goodly heritage."[58] His was a solo virtuoso ministry, one of sustained high achievement without leaving deep roots. Neither native priests and lay leaders nor lasting local church organizations resulted from his work. It is not that Liebler did not consider such matters, but he realized that strong family and clan loyalties existed among the Navajo; a priest raised up from one clan would have difficulty being accepted by others, and organizations seeking cross-clan support would require immense amounts of work with no assurances they would succeed. And it would be difficult to find a Navajo priest who could fit himself into the pre-Vatican II Anglo Catholic mold, the only model of ministry Liebler could personally accept.

Hundreds of persons were baptized and thousands came in contact with the Mission. Liebler never saw his work validated by numbers, but by encounters of a more spiritual nature. It was an atmosphere of worship he strove to create, one different from any other meeting of people.

> The mass was open to all who wished to attend, and in countless instances fulfilled the words of Christ, "I, if I be lifted up, will draw all men unto me." The most completely uninstructed Navajo, entering our church for the first time, knew at once that he was confronted by *worship.* This was no grazing meeting, no debate or gabfest; it was a group intent upon the Way that draws all men to the Infinite.[59]

In another instance, Liebler was asked to baptize a three-year-old dying child. It was the mission's first baptism.

> As we approached the hogan there was the unmistakable sound of a medicine man at work—song and rattle. . . . There was hardly a bit of flesh left on the poor wasted body. The medicine man looked up at me with a welcoming smile, summoning his best English. "Me make prayer good. You make Jesus-talk." Holding up two fingers closed jointly together, he added, "Two good make strong good." . . . I explained what baptism means—the regeneration of the soul, the pouring in of sanctifying grace, incorporation into the Mystical Body of Christ. . . . So I told the medicine man that I would make Jesus-talk which would make the baby's soul holy and ready to meet our Creator.
>
> All of the traditional ceremonies were used—salt, oils, white cloth, candle—in addition, of course, to the essential water and form of words. The flickering light of the fire was reflected in the silver coins and buttons on the mother's velveteen blouse and in the eyes of the other children, the medicine man and the parents. It was a sight never to be forgotten—the first baptism. And the mode seemed prophetic of

> our whole approach to this people: the cooperating medicine man, the simplicity of surroundings, together with a scrupulous observance of traditional details of ceremonial.[60]

What is the balance sheet on Liebler's nearly forty years among the Navajo? He left meticulous documentation in books and archives. It is almost as if Liebler anticipated most questions a historian would ask, and had an answer for them. It was an impressive legacy of consistent achievement he rendered in Navajoland. The mass was central to it, and the priest as dispenser of sacraments in the Catholic tradition was at its heart. But he raised a functioning school and a modest clinic as well, and Liebler and his small band of associates were constantly at work as advocates of Navajo interests.

He did not find any native candidates for the priesthood; after his retirement, Father Wayne Pontious, his successor, departed in 1972, and the mission atrophied. Eventually, in 1979, the Navajoland Area Mission was formed by the Episcopal Church, coterminous with Navajo lands in Utah, New Mexico, Colorado, and Arizona. Steven Tsosie Plummer, born in 1944, became the first Navajo priest, and later bishop in 1990. He was a member of one Navajo lineage, his wife of another, and acceptance across clan lines remained a challenge. Plummer, seeking to accommodate different Navajo allegiances, moved his office to Bluff, Utah, although diocesan headquarters were in Farmington, New Mexico.

Robert S. McPherson, who conducted extensive oral interviews among the Navajo, said he never heard any real criticism of Liebler. The Navajo were intrinsically polite in their comments about people who came to aid them, and Liebler did not force his religious views on others, offered medical care, food and clothing, and assistance with burials. "To a people who had very few other places to turn for help," McPherson concluded, "his brand of missionary work was not invasive, and he consciously worked on social relations as much as he did the more philosophical religious aspects."[61]

In 1962, shortly before his retirement, Liebler ended his newsletter with a paragraph that provided a summa for his own twenty-year ministry among the Navajo:

> Yes, we praise autumn and the blessings it brings. Cool nights and brilliant days. The Mission bell crisply ringing. Chanting the psalms for the day. Our Holy Sacrifice early in the morning. Steaming oatmeal for breakfast. The yellow flash of the school bus for Bluff. Children's voices. The sound of hammers. Jeep rides to outstations. Children's faces in the religious education classes. Visiting the people. New things learned. Vespers at evening. Supper chats. A tiring day. Peaceful sleep.[62]

7

Richard S. Watson

Bishop of a Growing Church

(1951–1971)

> What did I see? I saw a new Church emerging. That is what I saw. I saw the Holy Spirit at work. I saw the leadership passing out of old hands into young hands. I saw the courage passing out of old minds into young minds. I saw a new Church emerging.
>
> —Richard S. Watson, 1970

> Say a bead for me.
>
> —closing line to numerous Watson letters

He worked first as a vaudeville actor, and the instincts never left him; then as a lawyer, priest, and bishop. Richard S. Watson, missionary bishop of Utah from 1951 to 1971, could look up from his desk like an executive in a 1950s movie, fire off demographic statistics, and unroll blueprint drawings of churches he dreamed of building. Nine new churches or missions were established in places as distant as Moab and Brigham City, and others given new life, an amazing feat considering the 1959 diocesan budget was $396,640. Watson's long episcopate was a time of steady growth. And despite a demanding regimen of local and national travel for fundraising, he found time to play Beckett in the 1959 Rowland Hall production of T. S. Eliot's "Murder in the Cathedral."[1]

Richard S. Watson was born July 14, 1902, in Del Norte, Colorado, and as a young man toured the West with a vaudeville company on the old Orpheum Circuit to raise money for college. "I found five-a-day too much of a strain however, and then went into stock company playing both leads and character parts in plays which were then popular on Broadway."[2] The future bishop also worked nights as a hotel clerk and YMCA manager. After graduating from the University of North Dakota in 1925, he practiced law, but sold his modest practice to follow the love of his life, Rachael Virginia Sumners, to Dallas, Texas, where he found work as an assistant credit manager with the Pittsburgh Plate Glass Company.

Richard's father was a priest, as were Rachael's two brothers, and, upon his father's death, Richard decided that was the career he would follow, so he attended Virginia Theological Seminary. In a frank letter to a prospective seminarian, Watson acknowledged the difficulties of returning to study after several years in a job, adding,

> I have never been quite certain as to what constitutes a 'call.' Some men have felt that they are literally hit over the head by a club which God holds in His hands. Most of us, however, have a restlessness of spirit, together with an inner desire to do something with life which has real meaning, and which is concerned with helping people. In my case, it was definitely these two factors. I was restless of spirit, although happy in the work I was doing. It just did not seem to me that I could continue on much longer in a job, which while necessary to a business, had so little to do with God's purpose for mankind. So, I went to seminary that first year with many misgivings, because I was not certain. With my bishop I had an understanding that I would try it for one year, and at the end of that year, if direction had not been crystallized, I would check out.[3]

In 1932 Watson graduated cum laude and married Rachael (married couples were not allowed in seminaries in those days). The couple headed for a church in Sherman, Texas, then Tuscaloosa, Alabama, where they spent seven busy years. Following a brief stint at a Dallas, Texas, parish Watson was named dean of the cathedral in Seattle, Washington, where he stayed seven years. The cathedral had been seized by a bank for nonpayment of a mortgage and a total debt of $450,000. "Three top men, including the former presiding bishop, Arthur Lichtenberger, had turned it down," Watson recalled. "When they reached the bottom of the barrel, they came up with me."[4] The dean worked hard to pay off the cathedral's bills, and the Watsons became fixtures in an attractive, supportive community.

The death of Bishop Stephen C. Clark on November 30, 1950, had left the Utah missionary district vacant. A new missionary bishop—the last for Utah—would be elected by the House of Bishops on nomination of the bishops of Province 8, the bishops of the western states. Bishop Karl M. Block of California suggested Watson, a popular figure among west coast church leaders, and by now a member of the Episcopal Church's National Council. The election, held in El Paso, Texas, was unanimous, but presented a wrenching decision for Watson, whose salary would be only slightly more than half of what he received in Seattle. On March 6, 1951, Watson wrote his friend and mentor, Stephen Fielding Bayne, bishop of Olympia, and one of the leading voices of twentieth-century Anglicanism, that he was resigning as dean "with heavy personal loss" from a community "we have come to love with real affection." May 1, 1951, was set as the new bishop's consecration date in Utah.[5] "We are asking a man to give up the warmth and feeling of his own congregation, never again to have his own congregation. We are asking him to give up the easy ways of a pastor for far harder and more lonely ways. . . . Advancement? Not advancement—servant to all,"[6] a colleague wrote.

The presiding bishop, Henry Knox Sherrill, who years earlier Bishop Spalding had tried to interest in St. John's, Logan, came west to lead the service. Bayne, who a decade later become executive officer of the Anglican Consultative Council, was the preacher. The consecration coincided with a three-day regional synod, so most of the West Coast's Episcopal Church leadership was present.

A color film was made of the ceremonies, which began with a procession from the nearby First Congregational Church of Salt Lake City and ended at St. Mark's Cathedral. The processing dignitaries and the district's ten active clergy were flanked by a cordon of Boy and Girl Scouts. Television cameras both carried the program live and relayed it to an overflow crowd in Spalding Hall.

Bayne, who was invited to Utah often by Watson to lead conferences, wrote in the consecration program: "You will see neither the honoring nor the transformation of a mortal man; you will rather see him entrusted with the authority and the holiness of the Christ and His Church, and you will hear the prayer that he may be worthy of what is committed to his charge. He will be *your* shepherd, God willing; and needs and asks your prayers now and as long as he lives, that he may rule mercifully and guide wisely and bear the witness of the Church with courage and understanding."[7]

The local clergy gave the bishop a pastoral staff made of African mahogany. It was a shepherd's crook on which a large Utah beehive, made of local copper by the Kennecott Corporation, had been superimposed. A dove was carved from wood and the staff's remaining metal parts were silver, lead, and zinc from Park City mines. Such a staff is carried before the bishop in procession, and held by the bishop when blessing or exercising a pastoral office. The staff was stripped down by Bishop Charles, but still used by Utah's bishops a half-century later. The pectoral cross, of Celtic rope design with five amethysts set in it, was the gift of a Seattle parishioner. The clergy of the Diocese of Olympia gave Watson an amethyst ring, with the seal of the missionary district carved on the stone. The bishop's six-year-old son, Richard, was vested as an acolyte and presented his father with the ring.

The state's population was 700,000 and growing rapidly. The missionary district Watson came to in 1951 was composed of three self-sustaining parishes and thirteen missions. The total number of communicants was 2,751. There had been 289 baptisms in that year, 179 confirmations, 46 marriages, and 112 burials.[8] Clergy salaries were $2,400 a year, and turnover was high. Watson had received thirteen turndowns in his first year as bishop. One clergy candidate was identified as "a bit queer with a checkered past," another "at his best is not too active." "At present my hands are tied," the bishop concluded, lamenting the lack of funds to hire more qualified clergy. Meanwhile, responsible lay leadership was a plus; 103 persons attended one Salt Lake City gathering "and a more enthusiastic crowd I never saw."[9]

Finding clergy for small, isolated missions was always difficult. Watson described work in Carbon County in a 1964 recruitment letter: "Dragerton is a small coal mining community where we have a small but fine congregation. They have recently built a beautiful new church with their own hands." The vicarage was attractive, and

> being a coal mining community, a large part of the population is non-Mormon and gives considerable hope. Thirty miles away lies Price, which is the county seat and also one of the major points for the Denver and Rio Grande Railroad. About ten miles away is the community of Helper, whose former congregation is amalgamated with the Price congregation. This is a small but loyal congregation, but the potential of growth here, too, is great.[10]

Clergy who knew him remembered Watson as a caring pastor who stayed in touch with retired staff members. In 1959, he passed on a check to Deaconess Frances B. Affleck, now nearly eighty and in ill health. Affleck, who had spent many years in Utah, replied, registering "disappointment over the failure of the House of Bishops to provide a small pension for the twenty-five elderly Deaconesses who did not come under Social Security or other pension systems. We were told that the bishops who objected wanted further study to be made, but by then most of the twenty-five may have inherited their Heavenly Mansion and will not be in need."[11]

Appalled by the low level of giving from church members, Watson told parishes they must pay their clergy more before he could ask the national church for additional funds. The bishop asked clergy to keep travel reimbursement vouchers to a minimum to save money, and exclude hospital, convention, and clergy meeting travel. He worried about the high cost of living. “Rents are out of sight” in Salt Lake City, Watson wrote. “It will cost a cool $100 per month for a small house.”[12] Once he wrote a clergy member saying he could no longer keep paying the priest’s health insurance out of his own salary, as he now had his son’s college tuition to pay.

The bishop claimed no special skills as a fundraiser, but it became one of his main activities. “I’m not a good money raiser,” he told the convocation. “I squeeze it out of people and get it, but I’m not happy about it and the people aren’t happy about it either.”[13] In Utah he visited the manager of a copper company, and successfully raised funds for a seminarian after having crossed a picket line where two of his clergy were protesting the mining company’s wage policies.[14] The new bishop mixed easily with Utah’s Episcopalians, but few were of means, and, a westerner like Clark, he had no ties to eastern donors. Instead, he worked the halls of the national church headquarters and sent chatty, attentive letters to those who held the purse strings. If he heard of money for a new program, Watson applied for it. To those whom he knew, he closed the letter with “Say a bead for me” or “Love and kisses.”

One of the bishop’s initial goals was to upgrade the missionary district’s camp, costing $40,000. Utah was a state of scenic splendor, and the church since Spalding’s time had sponsored summer camps for young people, eventually acquiring extensive acreage in Big Cottonwood Canyon east of Salt Lake City, which Watson and his successor, Charles, promoted for widespread church use. The whole spring-to-autumn period, he hoped, would be filled with conferences for adults and young people, plus retreats, parish vestry conferences, and choir, altar guild, acolyte, and clergy gatherings. Title and water rights to the old Girls’ Friendly Camp near Brighton, now called Camp Tuttle, were acquired from the United Park Mining Company at Park City. Lay people did most of the work to improve the meeting and dining rooms and individual screened cabins. It was life in the rough, but church members looked forward to it.

By 1955, Watson could point to considerable progress. The church in Logan was reviving under new leadership. In Carbon County, missions in the small coal communities of Dragerton and Kenilworth functioned. St. Peter’s mission in Salt Lake City was closed, as were the longstanding Helper and Garfield missions. Garfield’s smelter had closed, and little was left of the town.[15] He was pleased to tell the national church that by 1957, All Saints’ had secured $90,000 in pledges to build the first portion of its church, and the cathedral had pledges of $125,000 to add a new story to the Parish

House, refashion the building's front, and create office space for the bishop and dean.[16] A few months later, Watson announced the commencement of work in Bountiful, Kearns, and Moab. Given the funding constraints the church faced, it was an amazing sprint of growth. On September 17, 1967, the cathedral dedicated a 44-rank 2421-pipe Holtkamp Centennial Organ, with a program prepared by Maurice Abravanel, music director, the Utah Symphony, and organist Jeanne Rugg Clark.[17]

In 1959, the Mission District's number of communicants rose to 3,599, and total income was $396,640. Local support accounted for $213,681, more than half that total.[18] Watson noted, "As a missionary bishop my salary is the lowest of all the bishops." He said that on $8,000 a year he could not contribute to a portrait of the retiring presiding bishop, and "it will take all I can scrape up to even come to Dallas" for a church meeting.[19]

Watson is remembered as an exceptional preacher, careful in preparation, thoughtful in delivery, and in easy contact with congregations. His improvised sermon on violence in America minutes after he learned of the shooting of Martin Luther King, Jr. was recalled years later. "He would build his sermons to a dramatic climax. You could see it coming. Then he would end and turn out the light in the pulpit as a final punctuation mark," a cathedral parishioner recalled.[20] Each December 29, on the day commemorating the life of the twelfth-century martyred archbishop of Canterbury, Thomas Beckett, Watson read Beckett's farewell sermon from T. S. Eliot's "Murder in the Cathedral" at a cathedral service.

"He had a difficult job. He was supposed to fill a role in the community, but there was never any money for him to do that," his chancellor recalled. Each year Watson was lent a Cadillac from an Episcopalian auto dealer. Though an impeccable dresser, the onetime actor sometimes wore shoes with holes in their soles to make a point.[21] Finally, as chairman of the board of St. Mark's Hospital, he was paid $5,000 a year, which allowed the Watsons to entertain. James W. Beless, Jr., who served as chancellor to the missionary district, remembered working with Watson on three or four clergy sexual misconduct cases between 1963 and 1970, and two or three cases of clergy with debts scattered about the small communities in which they lived. In one instance, Watson held a farewell party for one of the clergy he was forced to remove. "Watson was honest, he was decent to work with," Beless recalled.[22] The bishop had a quick temper. There are several accounts of his presenting a budget at convocation. If there were questions, his reply was, "I raised the money, I can decide where it is spent." Persistence in questioning would result in Watson "turning as purple as his robes" and gaveling the convocation to a recess.[23]

Cathedral–Bishop Relations

The heart of Watson's 1955 address was about the prickly state of cathedral–bishop relations, a concern of other Utah bishops as well. Watson wanted to open up the cathedral, the flagship parish of the missionary district, to be the center for diocesan church activity. He laid before the convocation the basic question—should the cathedral be the mother church of the district, or just another parish church? Clearly he favored the former, a place were convocations and ordinations would be held, a teaching center that would attract great preachers and teachers from all over the church, a place where choirs and acolytes could be trained, and a daily round of liturgical prayer held. To make this happen, a change in the canons was required. Watson said, "We should have a loyalty to our own parish or mission church of which we are a member. That is a prime loyalty. But we should have a second loyalty, and that is to the other church to which we belong: our cathedral church, and it is our cathedral, as I say; or it isn't our cathedral, one of the two."

Watson proposed expanding St. Mark's parish vestry to become a broadened cathedral chapter with representation from the entire missionary district. There would be a two-track process. The dean as rector and the vestry as parish council would continue that function, but "the Dean will be more schizophrenic than he is at the present time," dealing with both chapter and vestry.[24] Watson still talked about ways to implement the proposed canonical revisions two years later, while the cathedral leadership, opposing any change in roles, silently continued on its way.[25] Adroit at the ancient game of church politics, the dean and vestry derailed the bishop's plans.

Bishop of Northern California, or California?

With no advance warning, and with no effort on his part, in 1956 Watson was elected bishop of a much larger diocese. Bishop Archie W. N. Porter of the Diocese of Northern California (1933–1957), had been stricken with a heart attack and called for the election of a successor. Watson won by a wide margin. "Your greatest asset is your ability to be a real pastor to the clergy, and that is what we need so badly here," one priest wrote him.[26] Calling it "the most difficult decision I have ever had to make," Watson declined the election; he told Porter he was "turning the corner here in Utah and the door has been opened much wider in the last two years. It just did not seem the right thing for me to do to leave at this moment."[27] In fact, Watson had his eye on a much larger episcopate.

The Diocese of California would come open in 1958, when Bishop Karl M. Block (1941–1958), who had advanced Watson's name for Utah, would retire. Some of the San Francisco clergy told Watson he was a leading candidate; the other was James A. Pike, dean of the Cathedral of St. John the Divine in New York City, an internationally recognized, controversial figure.[28] Well known from his successful deanship in Seattle and impressive Utah work, Watson was one of four candidates advanced by the forty-member nominating committee for the February 4, 1958, election of a bishop coadjutor, the person who would become diocesan bishop when the latter retired. Four additional candidates were nominated from the floor. Watson was stunned to receive only one clerical and one lay vote, and withdrew after the third ballot. Pike, always ahead, secured the election on the sixth ballot with 53 clergy and 221 lay votes.[29] "He [Watson] was never the same after the election," a Utah priest observed.[30] But fourteen years of hard work lay ahead.

Doctrine and Liturgy, Caught Behind the Eight Ball

In matters of doctrine and liturgy, Watson represented the low churchmanship of his era. He emphasized clear preaching and a simple service done with dignity. In this, he mirrored the style of many bishops of the 1950s. Morning Prayer was the standard Sunday service, with the bishop arriving shortly before it began, preaching, conducing a confirmation, then leaving soon after a parish luncheon or reception. Although the liturgical movement was gaining momentum throughout the church, Watson viewed it cautiously from the sidelines. He sometimes spoke of the bishop as being caught behind the eight ball, between advocates of change and traditionalists. Conference photos show him attired in moiré silk cassock, tugging on his pectoral cross, striking a pose that could have graced a theatrical handbill. He told a potential recruit: "There is no extreme churchmanship amongst us save at one Indian Reservation. We all wear Eucharistic vestments and our congregations are accustomed to them."[31]

In 1965, Watson sent a circular to all clergy, upset that in several congregations clergy had altered the communion service, saying the Prayer of Humble Access and the Thanksgiving together instead of having the distribution of bread and wine in between them, as was accepted practice. The issue for Watson was church order. "If anyone wishes to change any Rubric in the Prayer Book, permission must be asked for in writing and given in writing by the bishop. . . . It is not that I object to these things being done, it is the principle involved. If any priest changes any Rubric to suit his own personal wishes, every other priest has the right to do the same. This way ultimately leads to chaos."[32]

By 1968, Watson agreed to a five-month use of the church's new trial liturgy. He wanted the book of proposed services in contemporary language to be introduced in parishes with proper instruction, then evaluated. His mood was cautious but accepting.[33] He balked at the use of laity to administer the chalice at communion. "I want the clergy to know . . . I shall authorize this usage, only where there is a real need. I shall not authorize it simply for the purpose of allowing a layman to administer the chalice."[34]

Following a clergy conference to discuss liturgical change and norms for worship, Watson issued several directives. *Open Communion*—"It is the consensus that there should be no invitation announced from the chancel to persons not communicants of this church."[35] *Authority of the Book of Common Prayer*—Collects, Epistles, and Gospels for the day must be used, with no substitutions without the bishop's permission. Lay readers could not read the Epistle, but special allowance was granted for young people to read the lesson and part of the service on Youth Sunday, Boy Scout Sunday, and similar occasions.[36] *Perpetual Deaconate*—"The bishop announced that the bishop and Council of Advice have decided that the Perpetual Deaconate is not to be created in Utah."[37] *Lay Readers*—"There is a danger of over using them and using them where they should not be used. . . . Clergy should not shrink their own duties just to allow glorified participation by lay readers."[38] *Mormon Baptism*—Although most of Watson's predecessors had accepted Mormon baptism, he reversed this trend, requiring at least a conditional baptism by converts.

> Even though water and the words are used there is a distinct difference in interpretation of the words. We do not mean the same thing theologically and consequently, cannot accept the baptism. In addition to this, the Mormon Church holds to the position that it is the one true church. Since all other churches are false, it intends to baptize into the one true church and not into the Church of Christ as we believe. . . . Most persons request that we do not conditionally baptize, but rather that we have the full Church baptism since they feel they have not been properly baptized before.[39]

Local church music was ragged to Watson's ear, and Episcopalians didn't know how to act in church. The place of music was raised in his 1956 address. "We live in the midst of a people who sing—they sing with all their hearts and with their voices. We may differ from them theologically . . . but we must stand in admiration for a people who sings its faith with its lips and with its hearts." Then, in contrast, "I wish you could know the feeling almost of desolation which comes upon me as I journey about from church to church and hear the weak and insipid singing by our congregations and even by some of our choirs, and this is not directed at any particular choir, but I am just amazed at how we fail to sing what we know. . . . We mutter our responses, some of us do not even open our lips to the words of the hymns. It is a sad commentary, my people." He urged church musicians and parishioners: "Do something, I don't care what it is, whatever you do will be for the better . . . do something for the music of the church in our district."[40]

The irreverent atmosphere in churches also upset the bishop. He asked how priests could lead worship when people bombarded them with unimportant questions just before the service. "Acolytes are stirring about under foot, Altar Guild people are still trying to get things ready, choirs are in the way. He doesn't have a bit of a chance to relax and to look at himself in the sight of God before he comes in to face his people. Something must be done to our sacristy manners. . . . Again I'm not talking about only one, I'm talking about all, without exception, every single one of our churches."[41] When he came to a church to do a service, such as confirmation, it was "his service, and the loose offering was for his discretionary fund," which was as low as $400–$500 in some years.[42]

Watson was deeply engaged in his Utah work from the start. He wrote a family friend in 1957: "We could not possibly be any happier any place than we are right here. We have just moved into a new home, which has a wonderful backyard or 'garden' as Rachel is trying to train me to call it. Nearly every evening we have people in and have barbecues on the lawn. I have become an accomplished outdoor cook believe it or not, and we have lots of fun."[43] Later the Watsons held an open tea from 4 to 6 P.M. every Thursday afternoon, when any Episcopalians in town or visiting from outside were invited for "a cup of tea, a cup of coffee and a bit of conversation and a cookie."[44] The Watsons had the entire ten-person clergy staff over for dinner once a month. "He was a good cook, he loved to do steaks. We were very much like family in those days and the Watsons helped promote that," a clergy member of the 1960s recalled.[45] Clergy and laity of the era also remember Rachael Watson with affection. A woman with dignity and warmth, she presided over the silver teapot at Spalding Hall receptions, was an easy friend with other clergy and community wives, and a compassionate presence in her own right.

"For all purposes we are really a foreign field," Watson wrote another bishop in 1958. "The State of Utah is dominated and controlled completely by the Church of Jesus Christ of the Latter-day Saints. Politically, economically, educationally, and socially, this Church officially calls the tune throughout the State. . . . Many of our communicants hold to the faith of the Church in the face of deep pressures, job-wise, economically and socially. Very few of our people are in what the Episcopal Church likes to call the 'upper class.' We are miners, laborers, and office workers. Our percentage of executives is extremely low."[46]

Watson was proud of Rowland Hall, and in 1956 reopened St. Mark's school for boys, closed for over a half-century, in what had been the bishop's residence on First Avenue and another building. Rowland Hall was a flagship institution, with 250 day and 30 boarding students, and "our graduates win scholarships everywhere in the country." St. Mark's opened with seventh, eighth, and ninth grades; and by 1959, a full secondary program was in place. The school weathered a shaky first year, but soon enrollment exceeded a hundred students. Enrollment at the church schools represented a cross-section of the community, and college placement levels were impressive. About forty percent of the student body came from church families, thirty percent were Latter-day Saints, and the rest were Jews, Roman Catholics, or other Protestant groups. In 1963 the two schools combined, and in 1964 a fence separating the two institutions was removed, completing the merger.[47]

Each Friday, when he was in town, Watson held services at Rowland Hall, breakfasted with students, and led a class on religion. Watson delivered his impromptu talks walking up and down the chapel aisle, engaging the students (St. Mark's boys joined the congregation on Friday mornings).[48] Tony Larimer, one of the school's English teachers, once cast Watson as Thomas Beckett. "People talked about the play for years. I wanted to cast him as the judge in 'Andersonville Trial,' but he had to be on the road. In those days the bishop traveled a lot. There was no money." Larimer, as drama instructor, and Francis L. Winder, as chaplain, worked together on several creative initiatives, such as staging medieval mystery plays or contemporary plays with religious content. Religious activity was visible in the school's life. Each year a crucifer or principal Cross-bearer was elected from the student body, student readers participated in worship services, and courses probed biblical and ethical issues, with ample time for free discussion.[49]

Watson actively chaired the St. Mark's Hospital board of directors as well, and the hospital continued to expand in the postwar period. A psychiatric ward was added in 1946, and a pathologist and laboratory director in 1949. St. Mark's also hired a full-time anesthesiologist, and in 1960 the x-ray department added a nuclear medicine unit, including state-of-the-art devices to provide radiation therapy and oncology treatment. Then, in 1970, the hospital appointed Francis L. Winder as a full-time priest–counselor and Katherine Getz as a social worker, two programs that would later expand and become models of their kind for other regional institutions.[50]

Native American Work

Watson left work among the Navajo to Liebler, with his high church eccentricities. Liebler raised his own considerable funds, which Watson could never duplicate. Watson worried that Liebler, who retired officially in 1962, might hand St. Christopher's Mission over to the Roman Catholic Church at some point, as Liebler periodically hinted. "Technically this Mission is under the oversight of the Missionary District of Utah. Practically, however, we are in the peculiar position of having little official relation to it," Watson wrote.[51] Calling Liebler "a tower of strength in working and advising the whole Church on its missionary work with the Indians," yet "a man of changeable moods and ideas," Watson said Liebler was a "one man show," and "no priest has ever been able to work happily in assisting him."[52] Liebler micromanaged every aspect of the mission's life, skillfully presenting a compelling image of its work in his steady stream of newsletters and correspondence. Mass began each morning at 6:30 for the small community. Since the chapel was unheated, Liebler kept a hot water bottle wrapped in a towel on the altar to warm his hands.[53] "He was an opportunist. Liebler held himself out as part of the missionary district when it was helpful, otherwise he was pretty independent," Watson's chancellor recalled. As Liebler grew old and funding problems increased, the missionary district was forced to take over payment of its many unpaid bills. Then the chancellor discovered that the Navajo Mission had been incorporated in New York State as a personal holding by Liebler, who finally ceded title to the missionary district.[54]

Ministry to the Utes was largely a small pastoral ministry, and Watson's diocesan addresses announced the coming and going of several clergy who left the reservation lands after a short stay. The Native Americans called them "fly by night missionaries." Some missionaries, like Sterling J. Talbot, who retired in 1946 after twenty years's work on the reservations, and Joseph F. Hogben, were remembered for their positive contributions. But not all clergy left such memories. Watson "had a priest some years ago who left . . . under a cloud with the work a shambles"; another lay worker was sentenced to three years in prison by a federal court "and turned out to be a homosexual and a pervert of the worst sort."[55] At one point the Church Army, a lay evangelical movement within the Episcopal Church, sent workers to the Ute reservations. They held church services, taught religion courses, trained acolytes, ran youth groups, and sponsored basketball teams. Watson tried hard to obtain $5,000 from the national church to purchase a bus for the mission, which had five basketball teams engaging over sixty Ute young men, but the national church did not pay for vehicles. Eventually enough money was raised locally to purchase a second hand bus.

From 1965 through 1967 Captain William Roberts of the Church Army led an active ministry on the Ute reservations. His salary, with uniform allowance and Social Security, was only $373 a month. It was a ministry of small, scattered, but real achievements. Some entries from his reports provide a snapshot of the demands of church life at Whiterocks:

> Car broke down, burned out a piston, in shop a week, very expensive to repair. Our Little Belles were champions in their division of the basketball tournament—each took home a trophy. (April 1966)
>
> We left Whiterocks Saturday evening, September 3, following the funeral here at St. Elizabeth's. . . . We returned on September 23rd to find our house had been broken into repeatedly during our absence with considerable loss and damage. (September 1966)
>
> Buried a two month old boy and then four days later baptized a two month old girl. Had a House Blessing service on the 15th so the parents and brothers and sisters of the infant who died could return to their home and live. It used to be that a house was burned down or boarded up if someone died in it. (If death was anticipated the person was placed outside to die.) Now that a house with all its rooms can be blessed, the family can return and 'start over.' (November 1966)
>
> Made a number of 100 mile round trips to Ouray at the southern end of the reservation over Christmas weekend to comfort Doris Comacots whose 22 year old son Alex froze to death two days before Christmas. His car failed as he was en route home; he was unable to start it, tried to walk home, but froze to death in the snow. We have had below zero weather, down to minus eighteen, since mid-November, and deep snow, which has affected church attendance; the men make daily trips up the mountain for wood and the women can not leave the wood stove fires in their houses or they will go out. Few have adequate clothing for this kind of weather. Christmas Day attendance [194] was good. (December 1966)
>
> Bishop Watson made his visitation to St. Martin's [in Roosevelt, Utah, where an Episcopal Church operated from 1914 to the 1960s with support from the reservations and the church in Vernal]. . . . I presented three lay readers who were licensed for one year and sixteen who were confirmed. . . . On Saturday planes were grounded and the Bishop's car was turned back at the pass because of deep snow, but he was able to get to us by bus on Sunday. Praise God. (April 1967)[56]

Watson believed there was much worth in traditional Native American belief that could be affirmed by the Christian churches: "We have adopted the theory that many aspects of the native religion have the possibility of a Christian impact. Rather than taking the old line of discarding everything the Indian understands and loves, we are attempting to make use of the fine spiritual strength of the Indian religion in a Christian way. Sometimes the results of this approach are quite surprising and gratifying."[57]

The Bishop Pike Affair

The Episcopal Church in the 1950s and 1960s was stirred by the presence of James A. Pike, first as dean of the Cathedral of St. John the Divine in New York City, then as bishop of California in San Francisco. In the staid Eisenhower era, Pike sped like a comet through the ecclesiastical landscape. When the Pike–Blake plan for unity between Episcopalians and Presbyterians was announced at Grace Cathedral, San Francisco, in 1960, it was a bombshell to both denominations. The initiative of two accomplished church leaders, it caught their respective deliberative bodies by surprise. Watson was no admirer of Pike, to whom he had lost the 1958 California episcopal election. He wrote a colleague, "I am becoming more and more concerned over Jim's desire for personal publicity, which is calculated in every move he makes. . . . He is brutal, and so ambitious that he is already running to be the next PB [presiding bishop] or, preferably, the head of the 'Reformed Catholic Church.'"[58]

On October 5, 1966, Watson was one of twelve bishops who signed a presentment against Pike, who "for the past several years held and taught publicly and advisedly [through both the written and spoken word] doctrine contrary to that held by this Church." Watson said, "I am not at all certain that this is the way to deal with the matter. For one thing, I am convinced nothing will give Jim better satisfaction than to be made a martyr."[59] Watson was right; Pike was a gifted self-publicist, eagerly sought by the media as a source of lively interviews and stories. Disenchanted with the Episcopal Church, Pike resigned as bishop in 1966, and continued a personal quest that caused him to comment on most issues facing the modern church, from civil rights and racial justice to the influence of psychics and mediums.

1967–1971, Watson's Final Years

The Utah Episcopal Church was one hundred years old in 1967, and Bishop Bayne was invited back to lead a centennial conference in April on "The Ecumenical Outlook–1967." His two addresses were followed by remarks from other religious leaders. All Protestant and Roman Catholic clergy in the state were invited to attend.[60] Presiding Bishop John E. Hines came to

Utah October 13–15 to speak at the Bishop's Dinner, held in the Prudential Federal Auditorium and at the Sunday Convocation Eucharist at the Valley Music Hall north of Salt Lake City. In 1961, Watson brought the well-known anti-apartheid figure, Trevor Huddleston—at that time Anglican bishop of Masasi in Tanganyika—to Salt Lake City for the missionary district's annual convocation.

Clergy turnover remained a constant problem. In his 1967 address, Watson noted the arrival of five new clergy to replace those who had left, especially those working among the Native Americans and in smaller, isolated congregations. Two years later, he said that even with clergy salaries of $4,800 he could not find recruits, and requested his convocation to add an additional $700 so that he could be in the "lowest bargaining market."[61]

The church's general convention in 1969 fully accepted women as delegates. Opposition was raised, but the arguments had "lost their sharpness and their meaning," and now women "are full partners in the life and work of the church."[62] Of the role of women in the Utah church, Watson said, "I can never find the words to say about the church women and the work they are doing. . . . The women in the church both nationally and in every Diocese and District, seem to be able to give to the church the greatest spiritual inspiration we receive. . . . Thank God the women do somehow find the time and set us an example that we would do well to follow."[63]

The church's mood was changing swiftly in the 1960s. Watson worried that the Episcopal Church in Utah was "becoming a congregation of Protesters." The national church had met in a special convocation at Notre Dame, Indiana, in 1969 to discuss racism and announce a costly program of reparations and remedial actions. Watson noted, "vicious personal attacks were laid on me as though I were somehow the sole architect of this Frankenstein."[64] C. Matthew Gilmour, active as a lay leader at the cathedral and in the national church, recalled Watson as "very, very cautious" on public policy issues. Gilmour, an attorney who crafted several of the national church's social policy statements, said, "he never held me up, but he never did much to help me either."[65]

The Utah missionary district was moving toward independence. Watson told the 1969 convocation delegates, "the whole temper of the House [of Bishops] when I came into it was that 'Poor Utah' will never be a Diocese and certainly if it ever is, it will be the last one in the Episcopal Church."[66] He wanted Utah to raise its own annual budget so that "we can present the next bishop as his consecration gift, a missionary district which is ready for diocesan status."[67] The bishop's salary was now $12,000, plus travel, utilities, and modest pension premiums. The Discretionary Fund was raised to $2,000.[68] After two decades of hard work, Watson had moved the Utah church from penury to a cut above poverty. In 1970 there were sixteen clergy apart from the bishop, ten of whom had been in the state less than five years.

The Watsons, accompanied by St. Mark's Dean Richard Rowland and his wife, attended the Lambeth Conference of 1968 and visited England. Their trip was paid for by May Dascher, a wealthy widow and cathedral parishioner. Mrs. Dascher later developed Alzheimer's disease, and sometimes became lost walking in the Second Avenue neighborhood several blocks from the Watson's residence. The bishop and Rachel, pastor and ultimate caretakers, frequently drove through the neighborhood until they located her.[69]

Watson, age sixty-five in 1967, noted he could retire in three years or face mandatory retirement at age seventy-two. He hoped to leave his successor a Church which, if it is not a self-supporting Diocese, would be one within two years. Working the corridors of the national church until the end, he wrote, "Is there any possibility of getting some monies to cover the moving expenses of the new bishop?" Finally, "I don't suppose you have any monies to help an old bishop move to someplace to retire?!"[70]

The life of a missionary bishop was grueling, filled with opportunities but limited by resources, and Watson's health was declining. Roads were precarious; three times during one winter his car was pulled out of ditches. As he aged his face became fuller, his glasses thicker, and his hair snow white. The bishop was operated on for cancer in 1958.[71] Watson sought frequent comfort in alcohol. In April 1958 he wrote a friend in Dallas: "It was a rather hectic stopover. Your bottle of Scotch helped to relax me and also to make me do a bit of thinking, and I appreciate it."[72] In 1960 he wrote, "Christmas Eve I drove down to Moab for a seven P.M. service where we had eighty-six persons with sixty-eight communions. Then I drove to Price for the eleven P.M. service where we had forty-eight communions. I got a couple hours sleep—or rest—in the motel and at four A.M. was on the road for Salt Lake City arriving here at seven A.M. Christmas morning. I find I am getting a bit old for this rat race, but it was a truly glorious Christmas Eve for me."[73] A blood clot on his right leg resulted in a lengthy 1961 hospital stay, and the discovery of high blood pressure, blood sugar, and cholesterol. He presided at that year's convocation from a wheelchair with a propped-up foot.[74]

On January 22, 1971, Watson submitted his resignation to Presiding Bishop John E. Hines. He would soon be sixty-nine years old, had been a bishop for twenty years, and would live on until July 16, 1987. "Ill health has plagued me and I have not been able to meet all of my responsibilities or commitments. Covering a territory of nearly 85,000 square miles, particularly during the long winter months is something which needs a much younger and healthier bishop."[75] A portrait of Watson, and one of his wife, were painted by the leading Salt Lake City artist, Alvin Gittens, to hang in church headquarters; and on the twenty-fifth anniversary of Watson's consecration. the Diocese gave a portable wooden altar to the cathedral. The bishop and Rachel moved to a two-room apartment in La Jolla, California, but his church pension was not enough to pay their rent and living expenses. The difference came from twenty-five-dollar monthly contributions of eight Utah friends, not all church members. Roy Gelder, treasurer for many years, was a main contributor.[76]

A newspaper article announcing the bishop's resignation noted his successor would be nominated and elected locally for the first time in the missionary district's 103-year-old history. The bishop's advice to his successor was to "be a good and faithful pastor to his priests and second to have infinite patience with himself and all of his problems."[77] Watson enjoyed a reputation as a gifted pastor to his clergy, but the infinite patience he spoke about eluded him.

1958–1969, A String of New Churches

Clark was the planner, Watson the builder. "I have just established my sixth parish," Watson announced in 1969, "making three in the last eighteen months where we had three prior to that for sixty-five years."[78] This chapter concludes with snapshots of several Utah Episcopal churches that achieved their critical mass in the 1950s and 1960s. The availability of historical sources was uneven, but locally kept documents, oral interviews, and Parish History Days conducted with individual congregations provided most of the material for this section. No attempt is made at presenting complete histories of each church. Hopefully, other writers and individual parishes will undertake that task.

Many of the mid-century churches have similar early histories: a small congregation of outsiders, often composed of defense contractors or other government employees, came from the east or the west coast and wanted to establish places to worship. Some congregations met initially in basements or home recreation rooms; one held Sunday school classes in a jail cell. As numbers grew, they moved to larger quarters, such as dance studios, restaurants, and social halls, surrounded by tables of goods on sale or stuffed animal heads. Finally, when money was raised, a building was erected, and a priest hired or provided by the missionary district. But this was never a smooth path. Numbers and money came slowly, while the determined laity held the small, slowly expanding congregations together.

At least ten parishes were in gestation; St. Luke's, Park City, became active again in 1964, and work was temporarily revived at St. Stephen's, Kearns and Granger, in 1962, and St. Martin's, Roosevelt, in 1964. Elsewhere, efforts were undertaken to establish missions in Kanab and Green River.

Joseph F. Hogben, formerly vicar at Whiterocks, returned to the missionary district after the Korean War. Watson offered him the post of archdeacon, but Hogben preferred parish work, and helped with the transition at All Saints' in 1955. Hogben's own spirituality was deeply influenced by his work with Frank S. B. Gavin, a well-known spiritual director and teacher at General Theological Seminary, where Hogben graduated in 1935, and by membership in the Roman Catholic Archconfraternity of Joan of Arc. He wrote Ingrid Bergman, who played the lead role in the 1948 film *Joan of Arc*, and the actress sent him the cloak she wore in the film, which Hogben hung on his living room wall.[79]

Bishop Watson dedicated the new All Saints' building on January 23, 1955. The Denver and Rio Grande Railroad contributed an engine bell for the new structure. All Saints' new vicar, Elvin Gallagher, arrived that year, and within three years the congregation was debt-free. On November 23, 1958, All Saints' became the first new Salt Lake City church admitted to parish status in the missionary district in the twentieth century.[80] Although the roof was barely on and the paint hardly dry, Watson urged the All Saints' community to help start a new congregation several miles away in the growing Salt Lake City suburbs. The Rev. Peter H. Jones, who became All Saints' vicar in 1962, was also asked in May 1963 to head the new St. James's Mission, meeting at that point in the Cottonwood Mall.

In Salt Lake City, St. Paul's parish grew considerably in the postwar period. For twenty-two years its rector was Carl R. Ericson, who arrived in 1957 and retired in 1979, after which he was active for several years as a supply priest in numerous parishes. A low churchman with a strong singing voice, church members decades later also remembered him as an able administrator of a large parish and a faithful pastor who spent considerable time calling on the parish sick and shut-ins, and on other people parishioners would recommend. A native New Yorker and graduate of City College of New York, Ericson was ordained a priest in 1935, and served in several parishes in Colorado, including All Saints', Denver, Spalding's former parish, before coming to St. Paul's.

The church had come to Carbon County early in the 1900s, when the Denver–Rio Grande Railroad built a small chapel at Helper. Several denominations held services in the building, set over a repair shop. In 1927, Bishop Moulton organized Episcopal services in a refurbished YMCA building there, and a chapel was constructed in nearby Kenilworth. For many years a determined archdeacon, William F. Bulkley, traveled monthly in his sturdy Model T Ford to Helper and Kenilworth. Then, in 1947, a mission was started at nearby Dragerton, in the Sunnyside Library, using an orange crate for an altar. (Orange crates and packing cases were sometimes used as church altars in isolated church buildings.)

By May 1948, the Dragerton congregation had purchased the J. W. Galbreath & Company clinic building for a dollar. A train bell was donated, as was the case for several Utah churches, and a cross was made in the Carbon County Railroad shops. The Dragerton work was now spearheaded by Stuart Fitch, a priest, and his wife, Nan. Fitch had supplied in Carbon County missions for two summers before being assigned there from 1954 to 1958. Since the two communities of Helper and Kenilworth had shrunk in numbers with the decline in coal mining, Fitch consolidated the two congregations into a single mission at St. Matthew's, Price. Members of Trinity Church, Dragerton, continued to worship there until the congregation built a new structure in 1964. The vicar, H. Wayne Mars, Fitch's successor, designed the building and a local industrial engineer completed the plans. As they finished their shifts, coal miners stopped by to work on the structure. Company electricians and plumbers also donated their services, and construction kinks—like a five-foot ceiling in the men's room—were corrected. Bishop Watson consecrated the new church on April 18, 1964.

The active church body lasted until the 1980s. "It was a real community. We lived in the church. Period. That was it," a long-time member recalled. Funeral dinners became community events, as were money-making spaghetti suppers. A few Greek Orthodox and several Roman Catholic families attended Trinity. Periodic rummage sales allowed immigrant families to purchase clothing for children at twenty-five cents an item. The church worked hard for a new community high school, and when it was built "we took some of the Hispanic kids up to the school and got them enrolled," Virginia Cochrane, who lived in East Carbon since 1948, recalled.[81] The small, tightly knit church community continued active until the early 1980s. By then the railroad had moved elsewhere and the Kaiser Coal Company had closed. The fine building, once so welcoming, was rarely used, and its handful of remaining, aging members pondered its future.

St. Matthew's Church, Price, purchased property for a new church building in 1960. The Price congregation's growth was due in part to the determination of Dr. Roy Robinson, doctor to the Independent Coal & Coke Company, and his new bride, Marion Robinson, a former University of Utah French major. The Robinsons had come to Kenilworth in 1926. When the mine closed in 1959, the couple moved to Price, where Marion played the piano and organ and taught Sunday school. The church had no resident priest from 1970 to 1984. In June 1984, St. Matthew's merged with Ascension Lutheran Church. A Lutheran pastor, Perry Francis, served both congregations from 1984 until 1989, but with the coal industry's decline, Price's population dropped from 10,000 to 7,500 persons, severely affecting the combined congregation.

Courtney A. Shucker II, an Episcopal priest from Nevada who had been a Lutheran church musician, was called to lead the congregation in September 1998. On St. Matthew's Day, September 2002, Allan C. Bjornberg, bishop of the Rocky Mountain Synod, Evangelical Lutheran Church in America, and Carolyn Tanner Irish, bishop of the Episcopal Church in Utah, dedicated a strikingly attractive modern church, set high on a hill on twenty acres of ground overlooking Price. The Episcopal Diocese's Project Jubilee had funded the building. Ascension–St, Matthew's had about fifty-five families, and included a new category of "Affiliated Members," who joined the church but were neither Lutherans nor Episcopalians.

The Church of St. Francis, Moab, was founded in 1954, when six persons gathered in a home and were determined to start a church. The Episcopal Church could trace its Moab origins to 1889 when a missionary, Sarah Elliott, started a Sunday school for eighty students at her own expense.[82] The class met in Woodman Hall, long since torn down, and when the Community Baptist Church, the first organized non-LDS congregation established in Moab, was founded in the 1890s, Ms. Elliott joined, but remained an Episcopalian. She also founded the town's Women's Literary Guild.[83]

Mid-twentieth-century clergy included Stuart Fitch, who during the 1950s frequently made the long trip from Price to hold services, Roger H. Wood, Joseph F. Hogben, who had also spent time at Whiterocks and All Saints' in Salt Lake City, and Sanford E. Hampton, who also was at St. James's, Salt Lake City, and was suffragan bishop of Minnesota from 1989 to 1995. A church building was constructed in Moab in 1963, then expanded in 1990 to include worship space for over a hundred persons, and a parish hall that was widely used for community activities. The discovery of uranium in the 1960s added to the city's wealth and numbers, and the region, situated on the Colorado River, was a popular site for filming Western movies. Although it faced economic hard times in the 1980s, Moab became a tourist center and a site for cultural festivals, some supported by the church. Charles McCormick, a local priest, provided eucharistic services during the church's several interims without a permanent vicar, and also led an active Episcopal Social and Pastoral Ministries program, primarily with prison ministries and with drug/alcohol programs. A Blessing of the Animals service around the time of St. Francis's Day, October 4, and a St. Patrick's Day Dinner in March became "traditions." James R. Tendick, a more recent rector, organized a Hispanic ministry at the church, and often acted as advocate for the Hispanic community with local officials. The Spanish-speaking priest was asked to preside over the funeral of a Mexican worker denied burial in the local Roman Catholic Church. His attentiveness to the family, and the support of other members of the St. Francis's community, resulted in a growing number of Spanish-speaking Christians feeling welcome at St. Francis's.

On May 15, 1960, St. Mary's, Provo, became a parish after fifty-three years as a mission. The Rev. Phillip Kemp, its vicar from 1949, was determined to see the church reach parish status, and died a day after that happened. Roger H. Wood, a former lawyer, later ordained as an Episcopal priest, took over parish leadership in January 1961. Wood was active in prison ministries; an expanded parish hall was built; and by the time he left in 1966, membership had grown to 237 communicants. St. Mary's drew heavily for membership on families employed by the Geneva Steel Corporation, doing so for several decades until the plant closed.[84] The parish was a representative Episcopal "oasis" church. The population of Utah County, home of Brigham Young University, was ninety-five percent Latter-day Saints.[85] For much of its history, a small band of lay members held St. Mary's together. John Howes, a high church priest, was vicar from 1937 to 1948, during which time a set of twelve stained glass windows, believed to have come from France, were installed, as were several statues of saints and other church adornments, which a later low church successor relegated to the church attic. Howes had originally been stationed in Randlett, and continued to make monthly visits there after coming to Provo. By 1950, the church had 117 baptized members and eighty-four communicants. And in 1970 it was given a 274-pipe tracker-action organ, made in the Netherlands, as a memorial to James Jay Morrow, a former parishioner. Two decades later the world-renowned violist, William Primrose, joined St. Mary's when he was a faculty member of the Brigham Young University Music Department. Primrose, former first violist with the NBC Symphony under Arturo Toscanini, lived in Provo from 1979 until his death in 1982. He played Bach's "Jesu, Joy of Man's Desiring" at a Lenten communion service in 1980, and with his wife, Hiroko, and daughter, Mana, followed a 1981 Advent Choral Evensong with a Beethoven Trio.

St. Peter's, Clearfield, began life when more than a hundred persons gathered at the Pioneer Elementary School, Clearfield, on September 21, 1958. In one classroom Joseph McGinnis, rector of the sponsoring church, Good Shepherd in nearby Ogden, led services. Next door a parish member, Phyllis Larson, held a nursery school where there were "prayers, singing, recitations, Bible reading, lots of hand-clapping, picking up, and loving." Mrs. Larson worked with the small children for twelve years, bringing bags and boxes of toys with her each Sunday.[86] Meanwhile, a planning committee had canvassed restaurants, bars, and a funeral home as possible meeting sites.

A surplus Navy piano was obtained through a "midnight requisition" at the base, and church women raised additional money by selling home-cooked meals on Fridays in downtown Ogden. On January 25, 1960, Good Shepherd's vestry purchased five acres of land for $7,000 for St. Peter's. The church could not afford a lawnmower, so a local farmer grazed his sheep periodically on the church lot, keeping the high grass and weeds under control. When it was time to build, men and boys worked evenings and weekends to haul stone from nearby Ogden Canyon. Unfortunately, the vicar and architect, also a church member, changed the building plans without consulting the parish, and a nasty division was created that lasted several years.

Bishop Watson consecrated the completed church on a cold, foggy night, January 17, 1965, with 238 persons present. A captain's chair from a local restaurant was borrowed each time the bishop visited, and became the episcopal seat. Stones for the new altar came from Good Shepherd's building. During its first forty-years, the church was the site of 366 baptisms, 316 confirmations, 92 marriages, and 57 burials. It was difficult to find a permanent vicar for St. Peter's, and almost twenty clergy served it in a twenty-year period. Congregational turnover was high, as well, since many parishioners worked for the government or in defense-related industries.

Bishop Watson dedicated St. Michael's, Brigham City, on Sunday, November 17, 1963. The vicar, William J. Hannifin, had been serving at St. John's, Logan, and as chaplain to the Intermountain Indian School, which included many students who had been raised as Episcopalians. The small congregation, which included several recently-arrived families employed by the Thiokol Corporation, builders of a solid-propellant rocket motor for the U. S. Air Force's Intercontinental Ballistic Missile program. The congregation was launched on October 17, 1957, when at least nine persons met at a local home with the priest. Soon they began meeting in the local Community Presbyterian Church, where the first eucharistic service was held in November 1957. The Episcopalians arrived first on Sunday mornings, in coats as it was sometimes freezing cold. "And everyone was very careful how they moved about because the seats were rife with slivers and protruding nails."[87] Next, in April 1959, the small congregation moved to the Protestant Youth Center, near the Intermountain School. Marian and John Higginson, the Thiokol manager and his wife, gave a property near the school, and a building campaign was launched on April 16, 1962. A simple but attractive church structure was built for $59,000, and dedicated by Bishop Watson on November 17, 1963. "Many of the kneelers were booby traps," a member recalled. "Often loud noises would be heard as the person too close to an end hit the floor with a bang when the other person rose before he or she did."[88] The completed and paid-for building was consecrated by Bishop Otis Charles on November 18, 1973.

St. Mark's Terrace, a thirty-two–unit elderly housing project run by the Episcopal Management Corporation, was built near the church a year later, and some of its residents joined St. Michael's. When employment at Thiokol dropped from 6,000 to 1,800 persons, St. Michael's membership decreased as well, to thirty-one families in 1981.

On May 16, 1976, Allen Smith and Frank Giles, the first sacramentalist priests of the newly independent diocese, were ordained by Bishop Charles to serve the local congregation. Their names were originally pulled from a hat. Parishioners were asked to nominate others whom they believed could assume priestly roles. Giles was surprised by the nomination, believing he was eminently unqualified. But once he accepted the call, he plunged himself into a round of parish activity, especially with the vicar's departure. Giles, a fulltime Thiokol employee, completed a three-year theological education by extension course from the University of the South. Smith, a charter member of the congregation and a flyway biologist with the U. S. Fish and Wildlife Service, was a bookish person with a gift as a teacher who ministered at St. Michael's until his death on September 14, 1980.

A ship's bell had been informally acquired by a resourceful parishioner from a Navy gun plant near Pocatello, Idaho, and moved to Brigham City. Discussions about where it should be placed, and experimental hangings and tests, extended several years before the bell, eventually given the named "Edgar," was securely mounted in a belfry and rung for services.

* * *

In the late 1950s, several families of Episcopalians in southern Davis County, many of them with government-related industries, wanted to form a church. Wesley Frensdorff, dean of St. Mark's Cathedral, was encouraged by Bishop Watson to sponsor the fledgling mission, and various cathedral clergy held services in church members's homes. By 1961, the congregation had grown to about fifty persons, and met regularly at the Bountiful Jeep Posse, a volunteer search and rescue organization. Two stuffed buffalo heads flanked the altar, and numerous other animal heads hung from the walls.[89] In 1966, the Episcopal congregation moved to the chapel of Bountiful Community Church, a long-established United Church of Christ congregation. A new building was constructed for the two congregations; St. Mark's Cathedral contributed four acres of land for the new church.[90] The Rev. Quentin F. Kolb, St. Mark's curate, agreed to spend half time working with the Bountiful congregation, and to be part of the UCC church staff during an experimental year, until April 1967.

The two congregations agreed to hold monthly joint communion services, and gradually the congregations merged. So successful was the venture that the Episcopalians sold their original land purchased by the diocese, and "bought into" the new community church. A common board of directors exercised church governance following a May 27, 1973, agreement, and multiple joint programs were launched, such as scout troops, a women's fellowship, Alcoholics Anonymous groups, and a square dance social club. Worship, other than on the first Sunday of the month, was generally a 9 A.M. Episcopal Choral Eucharist, followed at 10 A.M. by a United Church of Christ preaching service, but Congregationalists often attended the Eucharist and Episcopalians the preaching service. The Rev. Donald Procter, who became UCC pastor in 1972, was authorized by Bishop Charles to preside at the Eucharist.

While the two congregations fairly quickly settled on common social and community outreach programs, much time was spent arriving at protocols for the joint communion service, including detailed congregational study of the two communion rites. Finally, Episcopalians would come forward to the communion rail and kneel to receive the bread and wine. Congregationalists remained seated as cups of grape juice and cubes of bread were passed. At the same time, Episcopalians strove to uphold their traditions and teach them to newcomers. The Rev. Cass Nevius, vicar from 1979 to 1982, was a gifted teacher. Shrove Tuesday pancake suppers were instituted, and on Ash Wednesday members were marked with the sign of the cross on the forehead, something new in Bountiful. A parishioner, returning home by car from the Ash Wednesday service, was struck by another vehicle. "My

God, what has happened to you?" the second driver asked, on seeing the cross of ashes on the first driver's forehead.

The union of the two congregations was always tenuous, depending in large measure on the church's ordained leadership on both sides leaning over backwards to cooperate. Episcopalians regarded Proctor, the UCC pastor, as someone who wanted to be in control, and strains developed.

On April 23, 1993, the Bountiful Episcopalians, encouraged by the diocese, voted to form a separate church. The two congregations met together for the last time that August. Two lay members of each congregation spoke of what the time together had meant to them, gifts were exchanged, and the separation was competed on September 1.[91]

The rupture was a bittersweet experience. Probably it was inevitable, members believed, but it still left strains. Hall Blankenship, an active lay leader in the Episcopal congregation, said in one of the farewell talks, "We've learned to love one another; learned to laugh and cry together; we've baptized our children and buried our dead." He recalled the shared "miles of fund-raising spaghetti and gallons of spaghetti sauce" and his babysitting the church's temperamental furnace one cold Christmas Eve and morning.[92] Worship space for the separate Episcopal congregation was found in the vacated First Interstate Bank building in neighboring Centerville. Its thick-doored bank vault was used to store vestments and altar hangings, while the bank's drive-in window served as a backdrop to the altar. In May 2002, building a modern church was completed and the new church was consecrated. A forty-two-year chapter in the Church of the Resurrection had ended, and a new one begun.

Like many other new or expanding Utah Episcopal churches, St. James's, Midvale, began life with about twenty-five suburban families in 1963. The church was an offshoot of All Saints'. No sooner had that church started in the early 1960s, than Bishop Watson encouraged it to assume a mission role in the expanding city's suburbs. An east–west line was drawn at 3900 South and church members who lived south of the line were asked to join the new congregation.

St. James's held its first services on May 5, 1963, in the Cottonwood Mall. The Sunday school met in an upstairs dance studio, and the congregation in the mall's auditorium. Midweek eucharists were sometimes held in the laundry room of the vicar's home. In 1965, the mission moved to the Shalimar Reception Center on 6200 South, but the space was small and its owners "were worried that we either spill wine on their carpet or set their fake aspen trees on fire with our candles," Paula Patterson, an early member, recalled.[93] The congregation returned briefly to All Saints', then to the Wasatch Presbyterian Church, the Holliday Community Church, and the Southeast Christian Church, sharing that building consecutively with St. Thomas More Roman Catholic Church and Southeastern Unitarian Church. St. James's moved into its permanent location at 7486 Union Park Avenue, Midvale, in 1993.

From 1967 to 1972, Sanford Hampton was vicar. It was the time of the Vietnam War. "Some thought it was a poor idea, some thought it was good. Father Sandy marched against it—some marched against him right back to All Saints'."[94] In January 1979, Richard and Anne Thieme shared a joint ministry there. Anne Thieme left in 1983, following the couple's divorce; Richard in 1984. By then the church had grown to 711 communicants. In one instance the youth group prepared an "infamous Mexican dinner" for the parish, at another time they left the bottle of communion wine for Sunday's services partially filled with grape juice. The suburban parish always featured a strong program for young people, which included the Cockleshell School, a preschool, and in 1983, the parish held an Easter Eve cross-country ski trip to Camp Tuttle for the Easter Vigil.

A Listening Post anonymous call-in line for teenagers was popular at the church for a few years. Intergenerational fellowship meals were always a feature of church life, and an annual Italian Dinner became a fund raising Mardi Gras event.

Despite its closeness and energy as a parish, St. James's experienced several low points, such as when a married priest ran away with the married choir director. The personal and doctrinal rigidity of Bruce Moncrieff, rector for a brief eight months during 1984–1985, was called "the most stressful period for St. James's with deep and painful divisions."[95]

St. James's still uses a bent processional cross from its first service. "In the finest Anglican tradition, the priest used that cross to triumphantly knock three times on the door to open our first place of worship. As can only happen at St. James's, the cross went right through the door and our landlords presented us with our very first damage bill."[96] Thirty years later, almost to the day, an impressive new building was dedicated by Bishop Bates on a nearby five-acre site in the expanding south end of Salt Lake City, and the church began to consider its own future missionary role.

The West Valley's sweeping farmland was quickly giving way to housing developments, and in 1962 Francis L. Winder, at that time the missionary district's clerical pinch hitter and later archdeacon, met monthly with Episcopalians to start a congregation in the steadily expanding Salt Lake

City suburb. At first the twenty-some members met in a basement recreation room, then in a former dry cleaning establishment, and later in the Taylorsville Recreation Hall. Money from the national church allowed for the purchase of several acres of land, and gradually a cinder block multipurpose building was completed. Men of the church did part of the construction work to keep costs down. Given the absence of regular clergy for most of its early years, St. Stephen's was kept alive and growing through committed lay leadership. St. Stephen's also claimed Utah's first woman lay reader and chalice bearer, Marjorie Black, later ordained to serve the congregation as a local priest. Like many isolated startup parishes in an alien setting, St. Stephen's gradually created its own traditions in a setting of recently built housing developments and shopping malls. Members made mince pies on "Stir up Sunday," named for the Advent Collect that began "Stir up they power, O Lord, and with great might come among us." On Maundy Thursday the parish held a traditional Jewish Seder meal, and, as a fundraiser, organized an annual pit barbeque that took eighteen hours to prepare.

Dorothy Alley, one of the original members, especially recalled an Easter Vigil in the 1980s. The Easter lessons were read, the Paschal candle lit, and as dawn came over the mountains Eileen Burton, daughter of members Carlye and Barbara Burton, was baptized. Bazaars, spaghetti dinners, and socializing were important ingredients of parish life for the small congregation. Stanley Daniels, like many members a former Hercules Engineering employee, commented on the cultural isolation of being an Episcopalian in an LDS setting., "It was like being disenfranchised. Minority voices are not heard in this state. It is a theocratic island in the midst of a country that is otherwise pretty representative."[97]

On Christmas Eve 1966, fifty-seven persons gathered in a recently moved Army chapel in Tooele, 35 miles west of Salt Lake City. Founded in 1963, St. Barnabas's congregation began as twelve families meeting in the Moose Lodge, the Smelterman's Hall, and a Roman Catholic social building, led by Mrs. James Anderson and John Wilson Traver. Gradually the congregation raised three thousand dollars in savings from fundraisers and pledges. When the nearby Deseret Army Depot offered to sell a surplus military chapel for seven hundred dollars, the congregation was in business. St. Mark's Cathedral provided an interest-free loan, allowing the new congregation to purchase a lot from the City of Tooele and prepare it for the new building.[98] Two clergy, Paul Taylor and Charles W. Preble, served as vicars of both the Tooele church and St. Stephen's Mission, Granger, in the late 1960s. Later, when the church was without clergy, as was frequently the case, Bishop

Charles ordained eighty-one-year-old Frank Bowman, former mayor of Tooele, as a local priest. Bowman had been a lay reader for fifty-seven years, and Charles reduced the usual waiting time for ordination from deaconate to priesthood from one year to two weeks.[99]

As with other new parishes, church furnishings were donated from several sources. St. Mary's, Provo, gave eighteen pews, and the men of St. Barnabas's had to unload 120 bales of hay from a borrowed truck to transport them.[100] St. John's Church, Stockton, California, Taylor's new parish, sent St. Barnabas's an attractive candelabra set, that "glistens and glows and catches every facet of light," the warden wrote the donor.[101] "So many groups have sent us candles that we will be able to get by without purchasing these for sometime to come."[102] The church's altar had belonged to the long-closed St. Peter's Chapel in Salt Lake City, and had been found weather-beaten and stored under a chapel building at the church's camp in Brighton. Mission members also saved Gold Strike stamps, Gift Stars, Green Stamps, and Betty Crocker coupons to acquire tables, silverware, and plates. "Even five cent gasoline savings coupons were saved and used to obtain a beautiful punch bowl and cups, and a can opener."[103]

The old church of St. Paul's, Vernal, grew slightly in numbers in the 1950s and 1960s. Its fresh-from-seminary vicar, Alan C. Tull, remembered his 1958–1961 period there as "the last years of the inland frontier. The oil business was thriving." Possibly thirty persons attended Sunday services, and the congregation worked hard to make the historic St. Paul's building attractive. Civic activities included the vicar's sponsorship of the town Hot Rod Club for youth who "did not fit in LDS society. It gave them a place where they were accepted."[104] Citizens in Vernal kept in touch through a well-informed telephone operator who might tell an inquiring caller, "The doctor isn't there today, it's his day off."

Not all churches were led by permanent clergy. In addition to a corps of locally ordained clergy, a distinctive feature of the Utah church was the steady work of its committed laity, especially women. The 1951–1952 minutes of the Women of St. John's Church, Logan, provide an insight into how this band of eight to fourteen members helped hold the small church community together. They cleaned and decorated the church, made several $40 contributions to purchase a piano, prepared cookies and sandwiches for Sunday school Christmas programs, sold shampoo, and made kneelers for the church. The women were also interested in the world beyond their doors. They were active in the community's annual World Day of Prayer, studied life in Brazil, and heard a talk from a member who had visited there. Internationalist in outlook, they did not want U. S. government appropriations to the United Nations slashed, and agreed to find housing for two international students.[105]

In the 1950s and 1960s, several clergy came and went at St. John's, Logan, five years being a long stay for most. William J. Hannifin alternated between Logan and Brigham City between 1957 and 1962. Paul J. Habliston was vicar from 1969 to 1971, and after a conflict with the parish, resigned to found the Cache Cleaning Service, Home and Office Care.[106]

St. David's, Page, Arizona

Strictly speaking, St David's, Page, Arizona, joined the Diocese of Utah much later, receiving parish status in January 2004. But it is included in this section on the Utah church's expansion, for the congregation actually began in 1957. The small town of Page originated about this time as home for construction workers building a dam on the nearby Colorado River. "There was nothing in Northern Arizona but rock, sand, and sagebrush, with a herd of Navajo sheep now and then in the distance," wrote lay reader Fred S. Finch. Finch regularly traveled one hundred twenty miles from distant Kanab to hold services for the small community that met in the trailer and later the clinic waiting room of Dr. Ivan Kazan, the town doctor.[107] Page's city planners offered free land to churches on Lake Powell Boulevard, in the town's as yet unbuilt downtown, and ten denominations accepted the offer. The church cluster attracted national attention when the radio broadcaster Paul Harvey told audiences about Page's unique "church row."

The Episcopal Church completed its cinder block church and fellowship hall in 1959. Geographic isolation affected the small community and attendance remained in the teens for many years. Page became part of the Diocese of Arizona, but contact with diocesan headquarters in Phoenix was minimal. A combination of local lay readers and visiting clergy from distant Arizona cities kept the church together. Tragedy struck the small community as well. Dr. Kazan was killed in an airplane crash. His son, Tim, later vicar of St. David's, and his wife, were killed in an auto accident while returning from Arizona Diocesan Convention.

Finally the Diocese of Arizona approached the Diocese of Utah in 1999 to consider a transfer. Utah began supplying clergy for Sunday services and St. David's became part of that diocese in 2000. In 2001 Stephen Keplinger, who had just completed ministerial studies at the Church Divinity School of the Pacific, and his wife, Jean, went to Page, where Keplinger held his first service on January 21. Originally attracted to the southwest by the natural beauty of the red rock regions of southern Utah and northern Arizona, Keplinger found a job with a printing company in St. George and was active in the small Episcopal community there, plus doing freelance writing, before attending seminary.

And numbers grew at Page. Average Sunday attendance in 2003 rose to fifty persons. A community food pantry became a major form of outreach at St. David's. Although the town has only 7,000 persons, the food pantry served 2,000 monthly. The town depended heavily on tourism for income and most jobs were service related, which made for high unemployment in off-season or when tourist numbers were down. St. David's also operated the town's main social service agency, the Circle of Page, which provided both financial and counseling aid. The parish received a boost when Keplinger was tossed out of the conservative-dominated local ministerial association for holding a workshop on centering prayer and supporting the local gay community. "This public rejection of me was aired in the local press, causing a backlash effect, which attracted many more people to St. David's," he remarked.[108]

Such growth as the Episcopal Church in Utah experienced does not invite a neat summary or easy comparisons; it was more like an eruption, the Pentecostal stirring of wind and spirit described in the Acts of the Apostles. Members invited strangers to join them for Sunday worship. Persons with demanding jobs and limited incomes gave freely of their time and money; others spoke boldly of what the new communities meant to them, and banded together as strangers in the closed religious culture surrounding them, which bishops since Tuttle's time described as a foreign country. No conventional wiring diagram would explain how St. James's and All Saints' both cooperated at times and at others moved out to establish their own lively missions, or the enthusiastic but resource-limited St. Stephen's community in West Valley City actively aiding the small, struggling Episcopal mission in Cedar City, which in turn assisted the emerging Episcopal congregation in St. George, or how congregations sprung up in Tooele, Brigham City, Clearfield, and Centerville. All were "welcome[ing], proclaiming the kingdom, and teaching about the Lord Jesus Christ with all boldness and without hindrance" (Acts 28:30) as the Episcopal Church in Utah entered a new era.

St. John's House, Logan, was the jewel in the crown of Bishop Spalding's educational programs. Based on his experience as a student at Princeton University, Spalding wanted to create centers for Christian young men to discuss moral and civic issues, stage cultural events, hold "smokers," and attend chapel. Paul Jones, later archdeacon and bishop, ran St. John's House from 1906 to 1913, along with Donald Johnson, another Yale University and General Theological Seminary graduate. *Special Collections and Archives, Utah State University.*

In 1910 Archdeacon Paul Jones made a trip to southern Utah. He held services in the town dance hall in Modena, invited there by two church members who worked in the weather bureau. "Seats were made with planks laid on boxes and oil cans, an organ was carried over from one of the houses, and notices were put up in the saloon and store." *The Spirit of Missions* (April 1911): 305.

Bishop Paul Jones, 1914–1918, came to Utah as codirector of St. John's House in 1906. Bishop Spalding brought him to Salt Lake City in 1913 as archdeacon, and after Spalding's death a year later, Jones was elected bishop by the House of Bishops meeting in Minneapolis. His brief episcopate coincided with the coming of World War I. Jones was a Christian Socialist and a pacifist. Under pressure from the Salt Lake City–based Council of Advice and from the House of Bishops, Jones resigned on December 20, 1917, effective April 11, 1918. *Dalgliesh Photo Collection.*

Bishops Daniel S. Tuttle (with beard) and Paul Jones are shown at St. John's Church, Salt Lake City, in June 1917 on the fiftieth anniversary of the missionary district. In his capacity as presiding bishop, Tuttle worked for his successor's resignation. In 1998 Jones was added to the Episcopal Church's calendar of figures who led exemplary or saintly lives, or who endured persecution for their beliefs. His commemorative day is September 4. *Used by permission, Utah State Historical Society, all rights reserved.*

Helper was named for the extra engines that helped trains climb the 6,000-foot grade of Price Canyon. Railroad officials originally established a church there that alternated between Presbyterian and Episcopal services, the denominations of the two managers. At one time St. Barnabas's, Helper, supported three branch missions: Trinity Mission, Castle Gate; Advent Mission, Standardville, which met in a dining hall; and Ascension, Kenilworth, which met in an amusement hall. *The Spirit of Missions* (May 1917): 327.

The YMCA building, Helper, Utah, was purchased by the Episcopal Church in the late 1920s and used as a center for young men working in the Carbon County mines or for the railroad. Helper was a stop on the Rio Grande railroad's Salt Lake City-Denver line. The YMCA building contained a chapel, library, beds for thirty-nine men, and showers. Bishop Arthur W. Moulton pledged $10,000 of his own funds as collateral to purchase the building. *Western Mining & Railroad Museum, Helper, Utah.*

Arthur Wheelock Moulton served the longest tenure of any Utah bishop. He led the church during the economic hard times of the 1920s and 1930s. To his surprise, he was named in 1951 one of the first recipients of the Stalin Peace Prize. A World War I ambulance driver in France, Moulton had experienced the horrors of war and was a strong advocate for peace and the United Nations, but he was not a communist. *Diocesan Archives.*

Shown here in Native American garb, Moulton periodically visited the Ute reservations. The total reservation population in 1932 was 1,250 persons, down from 6,000 in 1880, yet numbers of Native Americans baptized and confirmed remained significant. *From a period scrapbook, Diocesan Archives.*

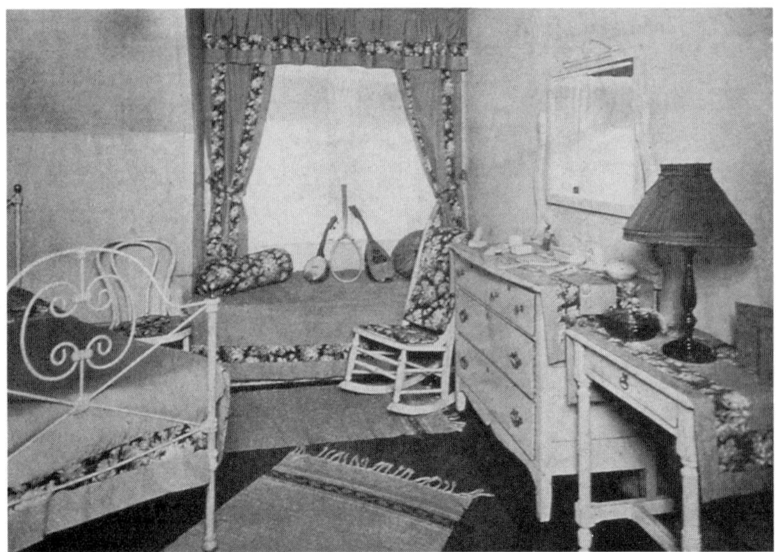

A students' room at Rowland Hall in the 1920s. Pennants and unframed pictures were not allowed on the walls, and residents were not permitted to use the telephone without permission. Tuition was $750 a year for boarders. Courses were English, Latin, French, Bible, mathematics, history and civics, physics, home economics, music, stenography, and typewriting. *Bulkley Photo Collection.*

Emery House, adjacent to the University of Utah, Salt Lake City, was a 1913 gift of Mrs. Thomas J. Emery of Cincinnati as a memorial to her son. The resident center housed twenty men, few of whom were Episcopalians, and contained a chapel, swimming pool, gymnasium, tennis court, and a dining hall with two servants. The center, completed just before World War I, struggled during the Depression. It became a municipal boys' club and was sold to the Roman Catholic Church in 1948 to become a Newman Center. *Bulkley Photo Collection.*

William F. Bulkley and his Model T Ford were inseparably identified in rural Utah. Archdeacon Bulkley came to Utah in 1908 and retired in 1948. He served as chaplain at St. Mark's Hospital, vicar to All Saints', Garfield, and vicar of St. Mary's Provo. A 1916 Socialist Party candidate for state treasurer, Bulkley spent the next three decades traveling all over the state, holding Sunday services in parishes without clergy, organizing Sunday schools, and keeping in contact with rural Episcopalians. *Bulkley Photo Archives.*

St. Paul's Church, 261 South 900 East, moved to its present Salt Lake City location in the 1920s. The period Tudor Revival church was consecrated by Bishop Arthur W. Moulton on November 27, 1927. Several Masonic groups participated in the service, as they had for its predecessor. *Diocesan Archives Photo.*

St. Mark's Cathedral sustained extensive damage in a March 31, 1935, fire caused by a defective basement furnace. Much of the sacristy was destroyed, along with several memorial windows, the organ, and altar furnishings. Cathedral membership in the early 1930s was about 600 persons; pledged income in 1932 was $6,000. *Used by permission, Utah State Historical Society, all rights reserved.*

Stephen Cutter Clark, a California native and rector of St. Mark's, Pasadena, was elected missionary bishop of Utah in 1946 and died in 1950. Hard working and plain spoken, Clark devised a ten-year plan for church growth in the post–World War II period which resulted in several new parishes being built. *Used by permission, Utah State Historical Society, all rights reserved.*

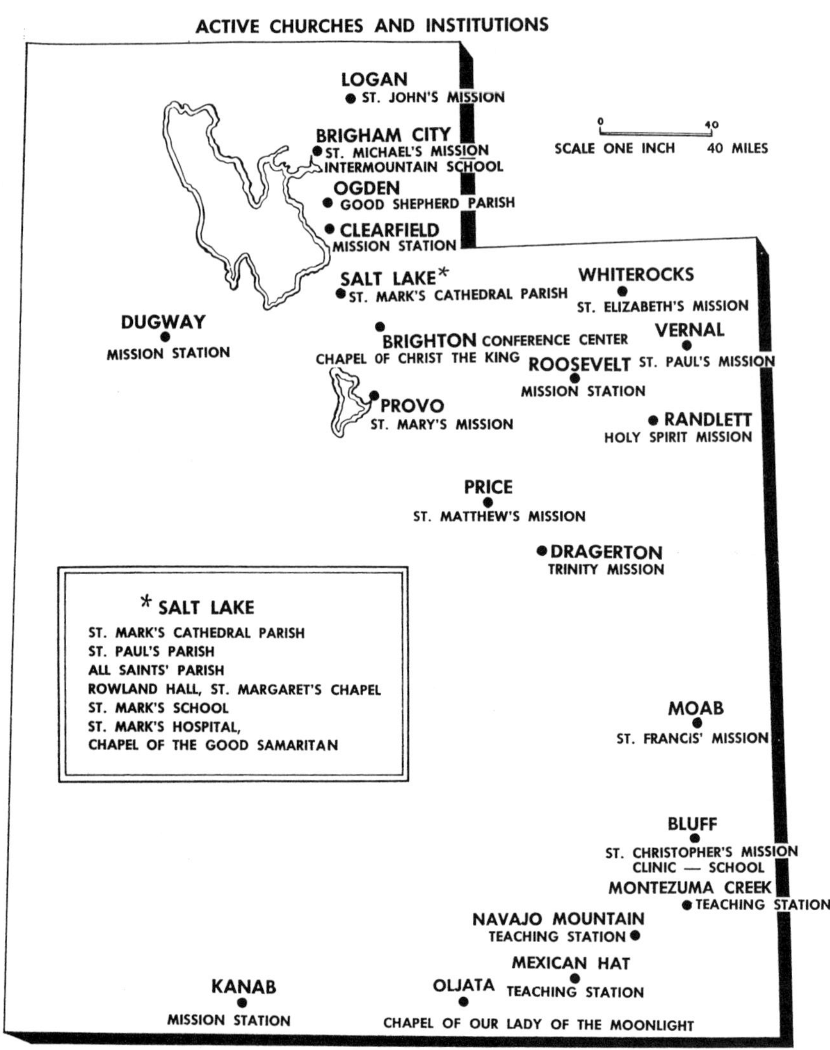

Active churches and institutions of the early Watson era. The missionary district contained three self-sustaining parishes, fourteen missions, several mission or teaching stations, and 2,751 communicants. *Diocesan Archives*

Wilbur Cuch, Archdeacon William F. Bulkley, Jasper Cuch, Jr., and Vincent Cuch. Ute dancers participated in the consecration service of Richard S. Watson as missionary bishop on May 1, 1951. Watson wrote, "Rather than taking the old line of discarding everything the Indian understands and loves, we are attempting to make use of the fine spiritual strength of the Indian religion in a Christian way." *Used by permission, Utah State Historical Society, all rights reserved.*

Richard S. Watson, front row, in moiré silk cassock, was Utah's last missionary bishop, 1951 to 1971. Watson worked his way through college as an actor, then became a lawyer before attending Virginia Theological Seminary. He built nine new churches or missions in Utah on a shoestring budget. *Diocesan Archives.*

Joe Hogben, "the buckaroo priest," with flag, on his sorrel horse, "King," leads the Whiterocks Posse in 1950. The Native American horsemen did precision riding and trick roping and appeared in civic parades in eastern Utah. Hogben was vicar of St. Elizabeth's, Whiterocks, and Holy Spirit, Randlett. The penciled caption of this photo said "he does much of his calling on horseback—a few sandwiches in his saddle bags—visiting the sick—baptizing—and carrying Our Lord's message." *Used by permission, Utah State Historical Society, all rights reserved.*

The Whiterocks Posse in formation for a Bishop's Day program, Whiterocks, 1950. Senior Queen Arita Taveapont is in the foreground on a horse, Father Joe Hogben (with flag) was vicar of the two Ute reservation churches. *Used by permission, Utah State Historical Society, all rights reserved.*

The quickly expanding churches after World War II, pressed for space, met in basements, homes, dance studios, and social halls. Here the Sunday school of All Saints' is shown in 1951 meeting in the former Fort Douglas cellblock before a new church was built on Foothill Drive. *Utah State Historical Society Photo.*

Bishop Watson (with shovel) broke ground in May 1954 for All Saints' Episcopal Church at 1710 Foothill Drive. Watson was the first Utah bishop to carry a crosier, a wooden bishop's staff, at ceremonial events. Watson's staff (visible to right) contained a Utah beehive made by the Kennecott Utah Copper Company and a lead dove from the Park City lead mines. His successor, Otis Charles, kept the crosier but removed the symbols. *Diocesan Archives.*

H. Baxter Liebler was fifty-three years old when in 1943 he left a New York City business career and a church ministry in Old Greenwich, Connecticut and drove west to found St. Christopher's Mission to the Navajo in Bluff, Utah. He officially retired in 1962, moving to a trailer at St. Mary of the Moonlight, Oljeto, a retreat center sixty miles away. Liebler died in 1982. *Special Collections and Archives, Utah State University.*

The chapel and high altar, St. Christopher's Mission, Bluff, Utah, in 1948. Navajo themes, such as a circular design, open space at the top, and local rugs, were incorporated by the founder, H. Baxter Liebler, who also made widespread use of Native American music in services. The chapel was burned in a fire in 1950, and was destroyed by an arsonist in 1964. *Special Collections and Archives, Utah State University.*

The first bishop of the independent Diocese of Utah, E. Otis Charles, 1971–1986, was a leader in liturgical reform in the Episcopal Church. The innovative Charles also launched a program of ordaining clergy to local ministries without formal seminary study. Charles championed social justice issues, including nuclear disarmament and opposition to deployment of the MX missile. In 1986 he became dean of the Episcopal Divinity School, Cambridge, Mass. Charles, after retiring, openly announced he was homosexual. The father of five children, he divorced his wife of forty-three years in 1994. *Diocesan Archives.*

Anne Campbell Thieme, the first woman priest ordained in Utah (May 25, 1979), was co-rector of St. Peter's, Clearfield, from 1977 to 1979, with her then husband, Richard. The couple transferred to a larger parish, St. James's, Salt Lake City, serving there from 1979 to1981. Campbell later moved to Seattle, Washington, where she became a nurse with the aged and the dying. *Used by permission, Utah State Historical Society, all rights reserved.*

Francis L. (Pete) and Bonnie Winder, leaders in the Utah church for nearly half a century. Winder, ordained in 1957, served as canon missioner at St. Mark's Cathedral, chaplain at Rowland Hall–St. Mark's School, and chaplain at St. Mark's Hospital, and archdeacon. From 1972 to 1986, he was in charge of Good Shepherd Church, Ogden. A longtime Sunday school teacher, Bonnie Winder became diocesan director of Christian education and a member of the Standing Committee. *Photographic Poetry by Wixom.*

W. Lee Shaw, ordained in 1992, founded the St. Chad Society, a ministry for people who had left the Latter-day Saints Church. He also helped establish Integrity, a support and advocacy group for gays and lesbians. "I do not consider myself to be a 'gay' priest," Shaw said, "Rather, I am a priest and pastor who is gay, among other things in my life, and am trying to live out my baptismal covenant and ordination vows as I serve the Episcopal Church." *Diocesan Archives.*

George E. Bates, bishop of Utah from 1986 to 1996, is most remembered for selling St. Mark's Hospital, founded by Bishop Tuttle in 1872. The December 1987 sale made one of the church's poorest dioceses one of its richest. The Binghamton, New York, native was rector of parishes in Oregon and New Mexico before being elected second bishop of the independent diocese on June 20, 1986. Plagued by ill health, he retired on June 29, 1996, and died on March 30, 1999. *Mitch Mascaro, The Herald Journal.*

St. Stephen's, West Valley City, is one of the post–World War II expansion churches built by the Episcopal church along the Wasatch Front. In turn, its congregation helped found a new mission in Cedar City, which then helped a small congregation in St. George grow. *Diocesan Archives.*

A cold Easter dawn in the desert, 1959. The Rev. Adams Lovekin of Williams, Arizona, standing behind the lectern, holds the first Easter sunrise service for the small Episcopal Church of St. David's in Page, Arizona. The isolated congregation became part of the Diocese of Utah in 2001. A more recent rector, the Rev. Stephen Keplinger, and his wife Jean, helped expand the congregation and created a food pantry and counseling service to serve the community of seven thousand persons, which faced widespread unemployment. *St. David's Archives.*

Carolyn Tanner Irish, a Utah native, was elected bishop coadjutor, successor to Bishop Bates, on December 3, 1995. The sixth woman elected as a bishop of the Episcopal Church, she became the fourth woman to lead a diocese. Raised in a prominent Latter–day Saints family, she studied philosophy at Stanford, Michigan, and Oxford universities. Irish was ordained a bishop on May 31, 1996, and took charge of the diocese on June 29 of that year, with her predecessor's retirement. She is shown with the Most Reverend Desmond Tutu, Nobel Prize laureate and former archbishop of Capetown, during the latter's visit to St. Mark's Cathedral, February 10, 2002. *Kevin Lee, Deseret Morning News.*

8

E. Otis Charles

The Independent Diocese (1971–1986)

> The future of the church will rest more and more with the total community of the baptized and, as bishop, I will hope to make my place in the midst of the community as its encourager. Above all as one who seeks to share and inspire the love of God which sustains our life together.
>
> —Bishop Charles, 1971

> Truth is always a good thing. I could not imagine living the rest of my life in a deceptive way.
>
> —Bishop Charles discloses his homosexuality, Camp Tuttle, 1976

The thick white hair and thin, slightly lined ascetic face suggested someone who prayed a lot, and the merry, piercing eyes bespoke pastoral warmth. If the casting director of a 1970s film sought someone to play the role of bishop, on sight they could have easily settled on E. Otis Charles, first bishop of the independent Diocese of Utah. Charles was a right-side-of-the-brain person, an E in the Meyer Briggs personality test. He could have been a theatrical director, had he chosen another line of work.[1] His vestments were colorful, and the liturgies he designed gave careful attention to music, movement, and lay participation. They were far from the plainness he inherited.

The Charles era, 1971–1986, was one of rapid change in almost every domain of church life. It went surprisingly well in Utah, major innovations swiftly following one another, with general acceptance and little opposition from church members. The buttons distributed early on said it all, "Episcopalians, one-half of one percent but we make a difference."

Women were ordained, and for the first time the church discussed the place of homosexuals openly. Active lay ministry was encouraged, and Charles ordained a corps of local deacons and priests, called "sacramentalists." Not since the time of Spalding and Jones did a bishop speak out on so many public issues; with Charles it was about the death penalty and nuclear waste storage in Utah, disarmament, Watergate, and the draft. Nationally known figures like William Sloane Coffin and Harvey Cox were invited to discuss topics like the arms race and human sexuality.[2] A synergy was created with a series of progressive cathedral deans who were articulate voices on religion and public-life issues.

A new prayer book and hymnal were introduced—Charles chaired the national church's Standing Liturgical Commission. It was a creative time at the cathedral as well. The bishop choreographed the full splendor of the Easter Vigil service, and the cathedral's brilliant young organist, Clay Christianson, led a multi-choir performance of Bach's "St. Matthew Passion." Charles less successfully tried several innovations in church governance, including brief-lived regional deaneries and inter-parish cooperation programs. A plan for house churches never materialized. Clergy and laity freely discussed their dreams and visions for the new diocese. Yet, for all its creative energy, Utah was a poor diocese, and Charles's achievements were accomplished on a shoestring.

Those who knew him give Charles high marks as a pastor. He remembered the aging H. Baxter Liebler on the anniversary of his ordination, making Liebler an honorary canon. The files of several churches contain solicitous letters from the bishop to a priest, or sometimes to a vestry helping a church through the difficult process of removing a less-than-competent clergy leader. Charles was an intense participant in everything he did. "He had the sort of personality that either engaged you or you wanted to distance yourself from him," a contemporary acknowledged, adding, "Otis and I duked it out a number of times."[3]

What was Otis Charles like? "Real is the first word that comes to mind," Anne Campbell, the diocese's first woman priest, recalled. "He carried our bags from the airport when we came to Salt Lake City. That is not what you would expect of a bishop. He was someone with his own vision, but was willing to listen to others. He was very pastoral." Of the diocesan clergy in the late 1970s and early 1980s, she recalled, "we were a tiny, incredibly intimate group at that time, eleven priests. All congregations in Utah were small and broke. We lived in a state where religion was a hot issue. We were a marginalized people and one big happy family. You knew everyone's warts and bumps. I never knew what a gift that was until the hospital was sold and things changed."[4]

Charles was forty-four when he was elected bishop of Utah, with its less than 3,500 communicants. Born in Norristown, Pennsylvania, on April 24, 1926, he grew up in Audubon, New Jersey, where his father was a teacher in the Camden schools. Neither parent was interested in religion, but two neighboring women took young Otis to church school at St. Mary's, Hadden Heights, New Jersey, where he was baptized. Only confirmed children could stay for the full service. Otis thought he was missing something, and badgered the rector to allow him to attend confirmation class. St. Mary's was a Morning Prayer parish, and one of the women took Otis with her each Sunday by bus to mass at St. Clement's, Philadelphia, a well-known east coast high church parish. His high school graduation coincided with World War II. Charles joined the Navy and, as part of his military training, was sent for several weeks to a course at Trinity College, Hartford, Connecticut. The splendor of its Gothic chapel deeply impressed the youth, and after the war, he returned to Trinity, graduated in 1948, and decided to attend seminary.[5]

At New York's General Theological Seminary, Charles discovered a growing passion for liturgy that would be pivotal throughout his life. The church in the 1950s was also discovering urban ministry, and Charles was attracted to the work of Dorothy Day and the short-lived French worker–priest movement. Charles had met his wife, Elvira, at General, where she came to work on a summer project. A 1948 graduate of Hunter College, she had decided that a career in fashion with Lord & Taylor was not for her, preferring instead to help the poor and marginalized in society. They were married on May 26, 1951, at the Church of the Resurrection in New York City and began married life in an urban parish in Elizabeth, New Jersey, and in 1953 moved to Beacon, New York, a mid-Hudson Valley town on the opposite side of the river from Poughkeepsie. St. Andrew's sat on the fault line between Beacon's black and white communities. It was the civil rights era, and Charles actively recruited African American parishioners, many of whom came from Southern Baptist churches, so there was plenty of singing. "Those were great years," he recalled; by now the family included five children, and the next-door rectory had become a parish hall for the growing congregation. Bishop and Mrs. Paul Moore, leaders in the 1960s church reform efforts, lent the couple their house near Kent, Connecticut, for a summer vacation. Then a nearby parish, St. John's, Washington, Connecticut, asked Charles to become its rector.[6]

The period of Charles's stay in Connecticut coincided with the Vatican II renewal movement in the Roman Catholic Church. Nearby in Litchfield, Connecticut, were the Montfort Fathers, an unreconstructed missionary order. Vatican II resulted in the closing of many small, isolated seminaries.

In this case, four of the monks wanted to found an ecumenical center. Charles left his parish in 1968 to join them. At the same time, he became executive secretary of Associated Parishes, a liturgical renewal movement within the Episcopal Church.

Prayer book revision and liturgical experimentation were widespread all over the United States in the late 1960s and 1970s, and Charles, by now a member of the Standing Liturgical Commission of the Episcopal Church, flew about the country holding workshops on creative forms of worship. One such stop in 1970 was in Utah, where a classmate from General, Wesley Frensdorff, was dean of the cathedral. Charles led a conference on "Introducing the Green Book," the Episcopal Church's trial usage volume. He later chaired a conference in Loveland, Ohio, on the proposed baptismal rite attended by William J. Hannifin, a longtime Utah priest. In 1971, Charles was one of three candidates nominated to be bishop of Connecticut. A letter and questionnaire had come from Utah at the same time. "I put them on the dining room sideboard and they sat there. Elvira said, 'I knew it was our future.' After I lost the Connecticut election, I wrote the Utah diocese. Bill Hannifin, representing the clergy, and Bob Gordon, a lay leader, came to Connecticut to interview me. I was told I was a candidate."[7]

1971—A New Bishop, an Independent Diocese

The election of a new bishop was one sign of Utah's becoming an independent diocese, after being a Missionary Diocese for 103 years. At its 1970 General Convention, the Episcopal Church had made many domestic missionary districts independent dioceses, responsible now for raising their own budgets and electing their own bishops. Charles, one of seven candidates, was elected on the fifth ballot on May 16, 1971, at the special convention of 105 persons from the new diocese's nineteen congregations.[8] His salary was $12,000 a year, with a $10,000 life insurance policy, $4,000 for travel, $1,000 for representational expenses, and a $2,000 discretionary allowance.[9] Extending the insurance policy to the bishop's family required a convention vote.[10] The median total compensation for Utah's thirteen full-time clergy in 1972 was $9,700. The national median was $10,500. Utah was seventy-third out of ninety-two dioceses.[11]

The consecration service, scheduled for September 12, 1971, was a signature event in Charles's episcopate. The bishop requested a two-day retreat with diocesan clergy beforehand at Holy Trinity Abbey, a Roman Catholic Trappist monastery in Huntsville, Utah. Father Emmanuel, the abbot, had a close relationship with many Episcopal clergy. Presiding Bishop John E. Hines was the principal consecrator. The service was set for 10 A.M. on a Sunday at the University of Utah's Special Events Center, with all Episcopalians in the new diocese invited to attend. (There were no other Sunday services in Utah that day.) Charles designed his own vestments, which a newspaper account described as "brilliant psychedelic hues in red, orange, green, yellow, and black."[12] More than forty yards of red Thai silk were ordered for clergy vestments, but arrived too late for use. (Charles had to find the money first.) Musicians strolled about the grounds and a "festival potluck" followed the service. Everyone attending was asked to bring extra food.[13]

Balloons decorated the building, but the planning committee nixed a suggestion to let loose a cloud of doves following the service. The preacher was C. Kilmer Myers, bishop of California, whom Charles had known for his pioneering work in urban ministry in New York. Charles provided the bread and wine for the celebration, and the new Second Order communion rite replaced the traditional 1928 Prayer Book service. The Ordination Service for a new bishop was one Charles had helped write. Hymns not yet widely used, such as "Take Our Bread," were introduced. Charles knelt on a Navajo rug to receive the laying on of hands. Diocesan clergy were con-celebrants with the new bishop, and each was presented with a matching stole. The bishop's pastoral staff had been refinished for the event, and its beehive and seagull, two classical Utah and LDS symbols, were removed. The bishop selected a plain gold signet ring, a traditional symbol of authority, which was presented to him by the clergy. He wore Bishop Leonard's pectoral cross until he could select one for himself.[14]

In 1971, the new diocese had fifteen parochial and institutional clergy, including the bishop. All but five had come within the last five years.[15] Liturgically, Morning Prayer had long given way in Utah to a parish Eucharist in most churches. Support for liturgical innovation was widespread. Dorothy Gordon, a parishioner at St. Mark's Cathedral, was one of the authors of the prayer book rite for the Reconciliation of a Penitent.[16] The service of celebration of a new ministry was field tested at St. Stephen's, and the Burial of the Dead was patterned on one used at the Huntsville Abbey.[17] Reflecting on the place of the Episcopal Church in a heavily LDS setting, Charles observed, "One of the remarkable things about Utah is that it is a very open diocese. The church is a bit of a counter culture. Everyone got pushed to the left of where they were. We did not have the difficulties other places did with the new prayer book or the ordination of women."[18]

At the October 1971 diocesan convention, Charles unveiled his plans for the new diocese. He saw his ordination as a visible transition from an old to a new order. During the previous century, "the strength and survival of the church depended to a large extent upon the capability and vision of the bishop and those most closely identified with him."[19] In the coming century, "the future of the church will rest more and more with the total community of the baptized and, as bishop, I will hope to make my place in the midst of the community as its encourager."[20]

His program was "to create an environment within the diocese in which each person has an opportunity and feels able to express his or her particular needs, concerns, hopes, aspirations; an environment in which all of these form the ingredients of our discussion and debate; an environment in which decisions reflect a consensus of opinion."[21]

The newly independent western missionary districts met to form Coalition 14, named for the fourteen member dioceses. They represented 450 mostly small, rural congregations covering thirty-six percent of the landmass of the United States.[22] C-14, as the group called itself, agreed to pool a single annual request for funds from the national church. Previously, each of the twenty-some missionary bishops made frequent trips back east to seek their own funds. A C-14 publication called that process "a really weird mixture of paternalism and individual initiative."[23] It announced a minimum clergy salary of $7,200 as a goal for the dioceses, plus a $1,200 car allowance, housing, utilities, and insurance. The activist Charles worked hard with the new group, and Robert Gordon, his lay assistant, carefully prepared the new diocese's numerous requests, most of which were supported by the Coalition.

Organizationally, Charles tried several initiatives, some of which he later abandoned. Four regional deaneries were created, but Utah was a large state, churches and clergy were notoriously parochial, and the regional idea never got off the ground. Neither did an inter-parish cooperative plan, where larger parishes would help smaller ones. The idea of a joint council was launched, including a twenty-one member standing committee (fifteen of them lay members), to which were added former members of the corporation and executive council.[24]

Two years later Charles said, "Our meetings have been long and often tedious. We have gone home exhausted and with headaches."[25] "He had an ass of stone," a colleague later recalled, "because he could sit in meetings forever." But Charles was committed to process the way a seventeenth-century Calvinist might be wedded to Predestination. "I have always been trustful of process, believing that what comes out of it to be good," he remarked later.[26] Newsprint sheets were tacked up on meeting room walls as a way of soliciting lay and clerical nominees for various positions. Nominations of women were specifically encouraged. Extra time at convention was spent in intense small group discussion.[27] These were followed by parish conversations, a Eucharist, and a business session Sunday morning, at which a budget and resolutions were adopted.

The pattern Charles established was repeated in future gatherings over the next decade. The files contain thick sheets of notes penned in his bold artist's hand, with words like "total ministry" and "inter-parish partnership" underlined. It was the heyday of "process" management; consultants and trainers appeared with newsprint and magic markers. They guided people sitting at circular tables through their responses to questions like "Dream how to best use the bishop" and "When I see the word 'Diocese' I immediately think of . . . ."[28] Canons gradually evolved out of the discussions, although they were clearly of less interest to the bishop than the process of engagement with clergy and laity. "I didn't perceive myself as being in a power struggle with the clergy or others," he reflected. "First, there were only fifteen of us. We worked together, went on retreats together. Utah was a great place to be a bishop."

An observer in a future generation would wonder how Charles accomplished all he did, for his staff was one executive assistant, Robert Gordon, a former oil company employee and insurance salesman, and a secretary, Marjorie Black, who turned the bishop's scattered notes into finished statements.

As for relations with the cathedral, Charles saw them as harmonious, but a close observer said, "Otis impinged on the cathedral a lot. His office was over there and there were lots of hard feelings. He was always interested in changing the liturgy or was hanging up art pieces nobody liked."[29] Frensdorff, cathedral dean since 1962, had cautioned of tension between himself and Watson and in his December 1971 vestry report added, "we were never able to define the roles and relationships involved."[30] At one point, when the cathedral leaders tried to remove him as pro forma rector, Charles threatened to move the cathedra, the official seat of the bishop, to St. Stephen's mission, West Valley City, and make the newly-completed cinderblock building the diocese's main church.[31]

Church growth was not a priority for the new diocese. St. Luke's, Park City, continued its fitful existence. The mining town had become a ghost town during the Depression, and from 1947 to 1964 the church had been deconsecrated. It was revived briefly, and a priest from St. Paul's, Salt Lake City, held periodic services there. But the congregation was always small, and the structure badly in need of repair. Bishop Charles deconsecrated it again on July 15, 1978, and helped carry out the altar. Still, a determined core of five parish families would not give up, meeting at a Holiday Inn or in one another's homes for worship. Within a year the needed repairs on the old building were completed, and Lincoln Ure, a Salt Lake City hospital chaplain during the week, made the Sunday journey to Park City where, without stipend, he held weekly services for several years.

Anne Campbell Thieme, Utah's First Woman Priest

In his 1973 convention address, Charles reminded the diocese that at the previous year's national convention in New Orleans, he was among those voting for the ordination of women.[32] At the 1976 Minneapolis General Convention, women were admitted to all three orders: deaconate, priesthood, and episcopacy.[33]

Anne Campbell Thieme was ordained as Utah's first woman priest on the Feast of the Ascension, May 25, 1979, at St. Peter's, Clearfield.[34] Born on May 12, 1945, Campbell attended Northwestern University as a journalism major. She took degrees in 1965 and 1967, met her husband, Richard Thieme, married in a Jewish ceremony, and lived in England for two years, where Richard converted to Christianity and decided to attend seminary. Anne, the mother of three small children, joined him at Seabury Western Seminary in Evanston, Illinois.

"We wanted to be a tandem couple but our only work was cleaning an office building in Evanston," she recalled. After graduating in 1977, the couple was selected by St. Peter's, Clearfield, to fill two half-time jobs. Was there hostility at Anne's being a woman priest? "The parish bought into it from the start. Men were willing to accept me pretty easily. It took longer for some women, but people were gracious when they met me in person." In September 1979, the Thiemes became co-rectors of St. James's, in an expanding Salt Lake City suburb, but the marriage soon came apart, and Anne overdosed on over-the-counter sleeping pills. She later reflected: "We were co-rectors and there were no role models. If something went wrong at the office, we would both bring it home in the evening. I was avalanched with positives, lionized, made a member of the Standing Committee and Commission on Ministry six months after I was ordained. The relationship took a competitive edge."

Anne later married Peter Maupin, a priest who had done an interim ministry at St. James's. The couple spent six months in Vernal, Utah, then moved to Seattle, Washington. Anne became a family therapist, served part-time in a parish, divorced, and later lived with a community of Roman Catholic sisters and became a nurse with the aged and dying.

What does she remember most about her time in Utah? The desert.

> I came to love the Red Rock Desert. It is a holy place. It is not surprising to me that so many of the world's great traditions had birthplaces in the desert. That's my image of my journey in Utah. It's the glory of the desert journey with the intensities of heat in the wilderness of large perspectives, the big sky, the joy of shade and the intimacy of a cave

> or an oasis surrounding a water hole, the extraordinary flash of beauty when the rains come and the wash, the blaze of wild flowers where you thought there was just desert sand.[35]

Ecumenism: Francis L. Winder and the Ogden Covenant

Ecumenical activities were rare in Utah, but in 1976 Francis L. Winder went against the tide. His 450-member Good Shepherd Parish, active since the 1870s, was left landlocked amid the parking structures and cement buildings of well-intentioned but poorly conceived downtown redevelopment in Ogden. Nearby St. Joseph's Roman Catholic Church was in similar straits. Winder had gotten to know his Roman Catholic counterpart, and from their contact the two parishes explored possibilities for shared activity, leading to a covenant drafted and signed on Trinity Sunday, 1977, for the two denominations by Bishops Charles and Joseph L. Federal, the Roman Catholic bishop of Utah, 1960–1980. The document was filled with hope. The "highest leadership of the Roman Catholic and Anglican churches have expressed a desire for reunion." It was time now to pray for one another, periodically attend each other's worship services, seasonally hold joint worship services, and sponsor action programs in everything from social justice to cultural events.[36]

During the next two years, cautiousness and coolness turned to warmth and boldness as a small segment of members of both parishes began to act together. Neither parish had the resources to run a preschool, but combined they launched the Ark School, led by a skilled teacher, Bonnie Winder, the rector's wife. Experiencing the frustration of sharing church life together but not being able to share communion, many parishioners from the two congregations petitioned the Vatican and archbishop of Canterbury to work more zealously for full communion. Canterbury replied with a handwritten letter expressing his own distress at the failure of reunion efforts. The Vatican secretariat said only that the message was received and noted. Six years into the Covenant, the two parishes designed an ambitious joint project to aid the transient poor through volunteer advocates. St. Anne's Center was founded in an unused Roman Catholic school. Later, as archdeacon, Winder was largely responsible for founding the Community of Churches in Utah and other collaborative programs with the Roman Catholic and other Protestant churches.

Strategy for Ministry and Mission in the Diocese of Utah

Five years after his ordination as bishop, Charles reflected on progress in his convention address. He saw the bishop's role having moved to "a participatory style of life. . . . We have consciously set aside a rigidly hierarchical organization. Differences in relationship have been based on function rather than rank, wealth, size or prestige."

The bishop voiced enthusiasm for the Charismatic movement, as he had the Cursillo movement earlier, and as he would for other such possibilities appearing on the horizon. He recalled a 1960 Agnes Sanford School of Pastoral Theology gathering, where he had asked for her prayers. "As I left the room where we had been praying, I was filled with an overwhelming sense of joy. The only word I know to describe it is hilarity. All my upbringing said, 'This is no way to behave in public.' So, I did what seemed proper. I went to my room. There, on my knees, I fought to control the bubbles of joy. I pushed my feelings down inside as though putting them back in a box."[37] A quarter-century later, Charles recalled the event in almost the same language, but this time said, "What I experienced was that I am all right who I am. After that it will be a question of living with myself."[38] By which Charles meant the discovery of his homosexuality.

Evaluation was the stepsister of innovation, and in 1974 Charles participated in a self-evaluation workshop. He listed his strengths as confidence in his own personal abilities, a willingness to learn, and adaptability in understanding the positions of others. His self-catalogued weaknesses "too often short circuit[ed] my own process in making decisions": wishing to impose his own goals, and entering situations only at the point of crisis.[39] Evaluations of the bishop by others mirrored his own assessment. One said he was capable of "giving and withholding authority simultaneously." A priest wrote, "sometimes I think you have your own agenda and are blind to where others are coming from, though you try to see the other side." Another identified Charles's leadership style as a "subliminal benign dictatorship."[40]

Charles faced daunting organizational challenges with few resources. He did not launch brand new missions, as Watson had, believing the new diocese faced enough demands in supporting and financing its existing programs. One of the few mission initiatives of the 1970s occurred in Utah's south, but was not the result of any central planning. The Episcopal Church in Cedar City began life in the fall of 1977 when James and Katherine Mittenzweis, a lay couple, hung up a sign in their yard that said "Episcopal Church Meets Here." Bishop Charles told the story of heading through southern Utah and nearly driving off the road when he saw the sign; no one from Cedar City had any contact with the diocese.

For many Sundays, the living room congregation was Jim Mittenzweis, who worked for the FAA, his wife Kathy, and their daughter Rebecca, who Bishop Charles licensed as a lay reader at age eight. They were joined by Dr. Sonja B. Wycoff, a Los Angeles physician now working in Cedar City, and a few other families. The new congregation of St. Stephen's, West Valley City, began supporting the even newer Cedar City Episcopal community. Father James A. Martin, priest in charge of St. Stephen's, and various church members made the nearly 250 mile trip to Cedar City every six or eight weeks. They gathered for Saturday evening potluck, and fellowship evenings, spent the night as guests of various church members, and worshipped as a community on Sunday mornings. The Cedar City Episcopalians periodically came north to St. Stephen's as well.

In November 1978 Otis and Elvira Charles spent a weekend with the Cedar City congregation, talking late into the night about people's hopes for the future. The initial five-family Cedar City congregation gradually expanded, sometimes joined by students and faculty from what eventually became Southern Utah University. The Mittenzweises were transferred to Gallup, New Mexico, and in 1984, an orange-walled shopping mall archery shop became a store-front church. The congregation, informally named the Episcopal Mission of Southwest Utah until 1983, called itself St. Jude's, after the first century Roman Catholic martyr and saint, patron of hospital workers and desperate or lost causes.

Dr. Wycoff said, "St. Jude's has never waited for help or even permission from headquarters in Salt Lake to move ahead and do what needs to be done. We've been too far away and alone for too long."[41] Chairs of various sizes, shapes, and colors were assembled in the six hundred square feet of store space. Drapes in the colors of the church year were ordered from Sears and Roebuck, except for purple ones used during Advent and Lent. Since these liturgical season colors were not carried in the Sears catalog, Dr. Wycoff found the appropriate choices in a Las Vegas custom drapery shop. Her description, "I found a remnant of purple satin which appeared to be left over from decorating a brothel. I wasn't sure there was enough so I asked the man if he had any more of it. He said, 'God, I hope not!' But he made us a pair of drapes for $56—and that's the story of our custom-made drapes."

Evicted on short notice when the shopping mall changed owners in 1987 the congregation moved to a house at 354 South 100 West, where it stayed for several years, then, with diocesan help, it purchased the former Roman Catholic Church of Christ the King in 2001. Even as it was in formation, St. Jude's was a mission-minded church. As St. Stephen's helped St. Jude's, the latter helped launch Grace Church, St. George, in the early 1980s. By then Fred Cedar Face, a Lakota Sioux and lay reader, and his wife, Mary Jane, had joined St. Jude's. It was Cedar Face and Mittenzweis who alternated holding services and helped jump-start Grace Church, St. George, in its early days.

St. George existed as a small congregation since July 3, 1966, when a service of Holy Communion was held at the home of Nello and Eleanor

Beckstead, 781 East 100 South. The Becksteads, formerly of St. Paul's, Salt Lake City, had recently moved to St. George. They found sixteen Episcopalian families in the St. George, Cedar City, and Washington, Utah, area. The celebrant at the first service was the Rev. Lawrence Kern, chaplain of St. Mark's Hospital, Salt Lake City, and priest-in-charge of St. Luke's, Park City, a former "timberline circuit" priest from Colorado. St. Mark's Cathedral provided prayer books and hymnals for the small congregation. A communion service was arranged every two months in St. George. Nello Beckstead would read Morning Prayer each Sunday morning in the interim.[42]

A "Sacramentalist" Ministry

Life was never dull in Charles's time. In 1973 the bishop introduced a controversial program to ordain local deacons and priests. First called "Auxiliary," then "Sacramentalist" ministries, they finally became Canon 8, later Canon 9, clergy. The idea was to raise up deacons and priests with limited responsibilities in every parish. "Sacramentalist" clergy could celebrate the Eucharist in their own particular parish, but were not supposed to preach, make house calls, participate in community ministries, or wear clerical dress outside the church. They would receive no payment, retirement, or medical benefits. At church conventions they had at first no clerical vote, then a half clerical vote, and eventually a full vote.

For Bishop Watson, life had been a continual struggle to find and pay for a priest in each parish. His successor said, "this is ridiculous; I'm spending all my time and energy in raising money to keep a seminary trained priest in each church." He found precedents in the writings of Roland Allen, the mid-twentieth-century Anglican missionary and champion of locally ordained clergy, and in the example of such local ministries already employed in Alaska by Bishop Robert Gordon. Utah's size, and the isolation of many of its churches, led him to launch the new program. "A congregation must not be deprived because it is small or poor. A congregation must not be prevented from making Eucharist week by week—even day by day—because it cannot afford a professionally trained priest." Each congregation was asked to identify individuals suited to become priests and deacons under the program.[43] He set no training standards for participants, and some were better prepared than others. Charles believed that ordination came first, and participants could improve their skills later.

After several years of experimentation, in 1978 the requirements for locally ordained priests and deacons were codified. The Canon 8 priests had limited responsibility, and would be part-time, non-stipendiary volunteers.

(Several later sought retirement and medical benefits for their work, and Bishop Bates quietly put some on the diocesan payroll.) Such priests had a decidedly supportive role, and would not serve as vicars or rectors of congregations, nor would they exercise general pastoral, administrative, or educational oversight of a congregation. Prospective local clergy should have skills at leading worship, and a "good speaking voice, poise, grace, and attractiveness." They should "be known as a person who is continually growing."[44] By 1974, one such priest was functioning in Tooele, and others were in training at St. Francis's, Moab; St. Michael's, Brigham City; and All Saints', Salt Lake City. A search was conducted to find candidates for the Uintah Basin in eastern Utah, and for the Church of the Good Shepherd, Ogden.[45] In 1978 there were eight such priests functioning in six Utah congregations, with four others in various stages of preparation.

Some of the local priests remembered the discrimination they faced from seminary-trained colleagues. Sometimes it was shown in a patronizing manner. "You talk about a cutthroat thing," Elizabeth Dalaba, a local priest at St. Peter's, Clearfield, recalled twenty years after her ordination in 1981. "I remember one clergy member telling me 'You're not educated.' I said 'I have my degree,' most of us had degrees. It was absolutely outrageous, but these men were so jealous of their prerogatives."[46]

Many of the Canon 8 clergy were ordained in their sixties and seventies, near or after the age when other clergy were retiring. Some were reluctant to lay down their ministry with advanced age. Others were identified in their communities as "regular" clergy and were asked to join ministerial associations, and participate in community ecumenical services. Pastoral and preaching demands soon came their way, as well. Also, some became fixtures in parishes with their own loyal followers, especially during the long interims between seminary-trained clergy. When a new priest arrived, the local clergy often remained forces to be reckoned with.

The Canon 8 program had positive and less positive results: At its most basic level, it was the people of God making Eucharist, the fundamental act of worship of the church. But in the church structure, the sacramentalist clergy moved from positions of lay church leadership to the bottom of the clerical pecking order, below the seminary-trained priests, at least during the program's initial years, when clergy collegiality was distinctively two-tiered. Also, many of the participants were among the parishes' strongest lay leaders, thus depriving the small, emerging diocese of some of its most able independent lay voices, an absence noticeable decades later.

A reader whose experience with ministry is only the traditional seminary-trained model might look skeptically at the Utah program, but it served an important purpose, even with its improvised quality. Utah was a small, poor, isolated diocese, whose scattered churches were often deprived of sacramental services. The locally ordained clergy filled a vacuum, offering the bread and wine to the small communities gathered from Vernal to Tooele, from Cedar City to Logan.

Betty Dalgliesh and Dovie Hutchinson

Among the locally ordained clergy was Betty Dalgliesh (1904–2004), who spent almost a half-century in first lay and then ordained ministry at St. Paul's, Salt Lake City.[47] Dalgliesh left Philadelphia in 1933, during the Depression. Jobs for historians were hard to come by, and her husband, Harold, found a one-year appointment in the three-person University of Utah History Department. Driving across the United States for thirteen days in their $200 Buick touring car, the couple headed down out of the mountains toward Salt Lake. Betty asked, "I wonder if there will be an Episcopal Church here?" "I certainly hope so," said Harold.

Harold taught European History until 1971, and then was historiographer of the diocese, meticulously collecting and cataloguing the missionary district and Diocese's historical records. Betty, a Phi Beta Kappa graduate of the University of Pennsylvania, taught history for a term, worked at the University's Middle East Center for seventeen years, and was copyeditor of a scholarly journal for fifty-one years, while raising two children—Bill, a local attorney who eventually served as Bishop Charles's chancellor, and Margaret, who later lived in California.

On May 10, 1986, at age eighty-two, Dalgliesh was ordained a priest at St. Paul's. "I was called by my congregation to be a local deacon," she recalled, "but I decided I didn't want to be a deacon. I had been doing everything a deacon does for several years. If I was going to do anything, it would be as a priest." For nearly fifty years at St. Paul's, she had taught Sunday school, been part of St. Martha's Guild, led discussion groups, visited the sick, trained acolytes, cooked parish dinners, been a delegate to four General Conventions—whatever it took to support an active parish and diocese.

St. Paul's advanced four persons for ordination, but Dalgliesh was the only one to complete the process, which she described as being like "a two year Oxford–Cambridge tutorial" with Donald P. Goodheart, St. Paul's rector from 1980 to 1988. "The fact is he pushed me, challenged me," she recalled. "I knew church history, anyone whose specialty was England from 1400 to 1600 would know that. But I didn't know theology. Don was very practical, willing to reduce issues to points where they could be studied."

Goodheart, later rector of a large church in Winston-Salem, North Carolina, said of Dalgliesh: "She was a person of incredible energy, a real take-charge person. I remember once we were taking the day to do home communions, one every hour for eight or nine hours, with half an hour for lunch. I was totally wiped out at the end and said, 'It's time to call it a day' and Betty said, 'How about just one more?'"

Brigham Young's great-granddaughter, Dovie M. Hutchinson (1914–2003), was another locally ordained priest. Raised up by the Church of the Resurrection in Bountiful, Hutchinson was one of two persons the parish presented to Bishop Charles for the ordination process from her parish. (The other candidate declined, and moved to Florida.) Peter Chase, vicar of the Church of the Resurrection, designed a work-study program for the past-seventy widow and mother of five children. Physical and psychological examinations were followed by practical training in pastoral calling and biblical studies. Hutchinson remembered reading and discussing *The Cloud of Unknowing*, Stephen Neill's *Anglicanism*, and Marion J. Hatchett's *Commentary on the American Prayer Book*. "I poured over those books line by line," she recalled a quarter-century later.[48] Ordained in Bountiful on June 26, 1988, she actively served at Resurrection after her official retirement in 1995 until her death in 2003. "I felt comfortable that I could do the work, preach, celebrate, visit the sick, help people in the community," she recalled.

Charles and Liturgy

Liturgy was central to Charles's ministry, in a way that administration and fundraising never were. It was his work with Associated Parishes that brought Charles to the attention of Utah, and his time spent as a leader in liturgical reform allowed the diocese to introduce the 1979 Prayer Book and 1982 Hymnal with little opposition. Two breakaway congregations led brief existences in Salt Lake City and Logan but died of natural causes, and a few letters in the Charles-era archives objected to the changes, one linking them somehow with communism.[49]

Each Monday when he was in town, the bishop held a 5 P.M. Eucharist at the cathedral. He asked one parishioner, Frances Wilson, to promise to be there so there would be a congregation. Before long, the numbers increased to over twenty persons. Gathered at the chancel steps for the Service of the Word, people read and discussed the lessons, then moved to a freestanding altar, where they formed a circle. The basic service was the new Rite III liturgy, an experimental rite with full congregational participation.

All of the splendor of worship came together in the Easter Vigil service, as the church moved from darkness to light, from death to life. The lighting of the new fire and Paschal candle, the baptisms, singing of the Exsultet, and Easter communion were all combined in the Anglican tradition's most glorious worship services at the cathedral. Charles focused on it with all his creative intensity. The records contain his lighting instructions. In bold script he wrote: "At the time of the ALLELUIA, CHRIST IS RISEN, as the bishop says 'Alleluia' the brown switch is turned up. As the Dean at the High Altar says 'Alleluia' the chancel (4 from left) switch and Nave 3 (extreme right) are turned up."[50] Many LDS persons, coming from a church that did not emphasize liturgy, were drawn to the cathedral, especially for its festive Christmas, Easter, and other seasonal celebrations.

Wider Questions

What was it like to be the leader of the Episcopal Church in a state dominated by the Church of Jesus Christ of Latter-day Saints? "It was like being a black pastor in a white community. It was like being a minority and not being able to affect anything around you. In Rome, you pay attention to what is going on in the Vatican; in Salt Lake City, it is with the Mormon hierarchy." Charles sought a meeting with the First Presidency, the LDS Church's ruling triumvirate, to discuss LDS baptism. Joseph Fielding Smith, the First President, was elderly and slept through most of the meeting; his counselors, Nathan Eldon Tanner and Harold B. Lee, led the discussion. The meeting was held in a large room, with the three LDS officials seated at the head of a T-shaped table; Charles was given a chair facing one of the wings, and a stenographer sat nearby. Lee said there was no point in discussing the issue of baptism, because Episcopalians did not have the Holy Spirit; hence, Episcopal baptisms were not valid.[51]

Basically Charles, like most of his predecessors, accepted the baptism of Mormons joining the Episcopal Church, unless they sought to be baptized again, which many did. The position adopted on LDS baptism by the diocese and enunciated in Charles's time continued to be held by the Episcopal Church in Utah for the rest of the century. Charles wrote, "no baptized Mormon whose life has been lived in faithful commitment to the Lord, and who comes to the Episcopal Church as a result of maturing Christian awareness is required to be rebaptized or even conditionally baptized." He stated that Episcopalians could accept the fact that Mormon baptism was by water and the Holy Spirit, in the name of the Father, Son, and Holy Spirit, adding, "since the validity of baptism was never dependent upon the proper belief of the one who administers the sacrament but upon the desire of the one baptized, it is my belief that to require even conditional baptism is a violation of the individual's conscience."[52] Charles was aided by his theological adviser, Alan C. Tull, a Utah cleric who spent many years as chaplain to Trinity College, Hartford, Connecticut. His paper, "On Mormon Baptism: A Report from Hippo," argued that Mormon baptism could be found acceptable through acceptance of St. Augustine's conclusion that the sacrament of Baptism remained valid, "however polluted and unclean its ministers may be."[53] A similar position was taken by Francis L. Winder, who urged Episcopalians not to confuse LDS theology with a wider vision of the church.[54]

Wesley Frensdorff, Robert M. Anderson, and William F. Maxwell, Cathedral Deans

The cathedral was a center of religiously informed social and political activism in the 1970s and 1980s, and St. Mark's was sometimes a stepping-stone for cathedral deans to become bishops. Such was the case with Wesley Frensdorff, dean from 1961 to 1972, then bishop of Nevada from 1972 to 1985. After his retirement, he served as assistant bishop of Arizona until his death in 1988, in a small plane crash over the Grand Canyon. Frensdorff, of German Jewish ancestry, was an early advocate for what later was called "Total Ministry." His essay, "The Dream," written while he was in Nevada but based in part on his Utah experience, remained in print decades after it was written. The totally ministering church was a place "in which the sacraments, free from captivity by a professional elite, are available in every congregation regardless of size, culture, location, or budget." It was a place where "all sheep share in the shepherding," where "the law is known to be a good servant but a very poor master." A church "affirming life over death as much as life after death . . . as concerned about love in all relationships as it is about chastity, and affirming the personal in all expressions of sexuality." A church "so salty and so yeasty that it really would be missed if no longer around; where there is wild sowing of seed, and much rejoicing when they take root, but little concern for success, comparative statistics, growth, or even survival."[55]

From 1972 to late 1977, Robert M. Anderson was dean of St. Mark's Cathedral. Born on December 18, 1933 in Staten Island, New York, Anderson graduated from Colgate University in 1955, and in 1961 from Berkeley Divinity School at Yale University, where he was a Danforth Fellow. He married Mary A. Evans in 1960, and she was an active participant in most of his public ministry. Anderson served parishes in Stamford, East Haddam, and Middle Haddam, Connecticut, before coming to Salt Lake City in 1972.

Although Anderson had a reputation for social activism, it was his strong prayer life and passionate interest in liturgy and religious arts that informed his public presence. The cathedral's Holtkamp organ, a state-of-the-art instrument in its era, brought music lovers to the building. Cathedral music programs included an annual Bach organ concert on New Year's Eve that filled the building, liturgical dance as part of the services, and an annual arts festival coordinated by G. Edward Howlett, a cathedral clergy member and university chaplain. Mary Anderson organized the Mustard Seed, a Christian bookshop, and an active lay worship committee worked closely with the clergy in planning experimental services.

Tall, affable, and an engaging speaker who sometimes delivered sermons with minimal notes and carefully told stories to a rapt congregation, those who heard him remembered Anderson's ready laugh and sense of humor, someone who could work easily with those holding differing views. He served as president of the Utah Council of Churches from 1974 to 1976, and as a member of the Standing Committee from 1974 to 1977. It was also Anderson who gave intellectual buttressing to many of Charles's public policy utterances.

The cathedral congregation to which Anderson came was a decidedly liberal one. At the annual parish meeting in January 1977, some seventy-two percent of the fifty persons responding to a questionnaire opposed capital punishment, and more than ninety encouraged the clergy to become involved in social issues and exercise their own consciences in addressing social concerns.[56] The 1977 Gary Gilmore capital punishment case, Utah's most notorious execution since that of Joe Hill in 1915, triggered vocal opposition to capital punishment. A telephone call from Presiding Bishop John M. Allin caused Anderson to become active. Bishop Charles was out of the country at the time, and the presiding bishop, articulating the church's opposition to the death penalty, asked Anderson to carry a message to the state. Anderson was the only local church leader to do so; the Roman Catholic Church did not speak to the issue, and the Latter-day Saints supported blood atonement.[57] Meanwhile, the issue attracted national attention, and demonstrators poured into Utah.

Gilmore, who had spent eighteen of his thirty-six years behind bars, was shot by firing squad at 8:08 A.M. on January 17, 1977, at a Draper, Utah, prison. He was the first person sentenced to death in the United States since the death penalty had been reintroduced in 1976. Advocating life imprisonment as an alternative to the death penalty, Anderson and Charles both spoke out publically. In retrospect, Charles wished the church had voiced its opposition earlier, before the execution was set. He recalled visiting the governor at home, but the chief executive would not stay the execution. Charles said publicly he hoped "we can deal effectively with perpetrators of heinous crimes and still eliminate the death penalty." The bishop also objected to the trial's speediness, including Utah Attorney General Robert Hansen's late night flight to Denver to argue against a federal appeals court granting a stay of the Gilmore execution.[58]

Although bishop–dean relations were sometimes frayed, Anderson and Charles got along well. Both had been active in the liturgical reform movement in Connecticut, and it was Charles who nominated Anderson as one of the candidates for the cathedral dean's job. Then, at age forty-four, Anderson was called to be bishop of Minnesota. He stayed in Minneapolis from 1978 to 1993, and after retirement became an assisting bishop in the Diocese of Los Angeles.

William F. Maxwell, St. Mark's next dean, arrived in 1978, and continued the cathedral's social–political activism. A former dean of St. James's Cathedral, Chicago, Maxwell was a graduate of Seabury Western Seminary, and chaplain at Northwestern University, who also led large parishes in Texas, Montana, and Oklahoma before coming to Salt Lake City.[59] A highlight of Maxwell's time in Salt Lake City was a service for 600 persons at the cathedral to mark the arrival of the NAMES Project AIDS quilt in Salt Lake City in 1987. The service concluded with a candlelight walk to the nearby Salt Palace, where the quilt was displayed publicly. Few in the LDS community would acknowledge the presence of AIDS, and the cathedral launched a public education program. "Folks in the cathedral ceased to be upset and anxious about gay issues after the service. It stopped being an issue and the cathedral congregation came together in a really lovely way," Maxwell remembered. Gay men served on the vestry and one served as senior warden. A gay man was elected head of the altar guild, and for two years a group of gay men and married couples met weekly and were open about their relationships.[60]

Maxwell also hired an assistant, Bradley S. Wirth, later rector of All Saints', to work with the homeless and start a food bank. Groups like Utah Issues, a public policy advocacy group, were housed in the cathedral basement. A cathedral-backed Utilities Task Force petitioned the legislature not to allow the utilities of the poor to be cut off in winter for nonpayment of bills.[61]

With his own strong interest in liturgy, the dean helped organize a yearly Good Friday service in which over a thousand persons processed in downtown Salt Lake City—from Roman Catholic to Presbyterian, Methodist, Greek Orthodox, African Methodist Episcopal, and Episcopal churches—led by a large wooden cross, after which they heard Bible readings for the day and sang Passiontide hymns.

The MX missile proposal was a Carter-administration program designed to build on Utah's defense-related industrial base; by 1969 nearly 4,900 persons were employed locally in the missile industry, including active members of many Episcopal parishes.[62] The Salt II treaty had been signed in June 1979, and the $60 million to $100 million project was dangled before Utah and Nevada, with its more than 20,000 new construction jobs. The down side was that with over 200 mobile missile launchers, these two states would be instant targets in case of war. Hundreds of thermonuclear warheads would be moved among thousands of thick silos covering a vast desert landmass, leaving the Russians to guess their location. The desert would be webbed with concrete roadways, and its fragile water system would perish. The Chairman of the Joint Chiefs of Staff summarized the complex issue in a sentence: "We're sorry that someone has to be the bull's-eye, but you're it!"[63]

Charles sought LDS cooperation on opposition to the planned deployment of the MX missile in Utah, and the U. S. government's proposal to deposit nuclear waste in the Utah and Nevada deserts. Gordon B. Hinckley, who later became president of the Church of Jesus Christ of the Latter-day Saints, was a first counselor at the time. "He was just great to work with," Charles recalled, "carefully gathering the facts and asking a lot of questions." Throughout the winter of 1980, Charles and other church representatives met with their LDS counterparts. The number of persons on each side of the table gradually grew. Finally the Mormons asked them to make a presentation, but said their schedule was busy and they would not have time to make a response. Then, that spring, the announcement came from the First Presidency. They opposed the MX missile deployment in Utah, and later the nuclear waste deposits as well. "That was the end of that," Charles recalled. "I realized later what an internal struggle it must have been for them, because they were committed to supporting the lawful authorized authority in the state. The MX deployment would have been the largest public works project in the country."[64]

The bishop's most extensive public statement was in 1982, on the thirty-first anniversary of nuclear testing in southern Nevada. He urged a strong arms control treaty, a comprehensive test ban treaty, a freeze on further development, testing, and deployment of nuclear weapons, and a reduction of the existing stockpiles of nuclear weapons; "in short, by giving up the notion that we can create a safe world by reliance on the threat of nuclear war," he said.[65] At the same time, the Standing Committee supported the idea of a bilateral, verifiable nuclear weapons freeze. J. A. Frazer Crocker, Jr., an Episcopal cleric, accepted the chair of Utahans for a Nuclear Weapons Freeze, seeking to obtain 100,000 signatures on a petition urging a halt to nuclear arms testing.[66]

The cathedral also hosted an ecumenical statewide meeting on "The Arms Race and the Human Race," keynoted by William Sloane Coffin of

Riverside Church, New York City, on April 12, 1980. At the service Charles likened the people of Utah to Moses, who would rather have not been called on to lead his people out of Egypt, but who accepted the call. In this case, Utah's citizens faced a similar call to oppose the MX missile.[67]

Combining his interests in liturgy and public policy, the bishop arranged for a 1978 cathedral service commemorating the Saints and Martyrs of Our Time, including Martin Luther King, Jr., the martyred Ugandan Archbishop Janani Luwum, Jonathan Daniels, an Episcopal Theological Seminary student shot in Alabama in 1965 while helping in a civil rights campaign, and Dietrich Bonhoeffer, a German Protestant theologian who was hanged in 1945 for his resistance to Hitler.[68]

Elsewhere, Charles supported a General Amnesty for Vietnam draft resisters, urged impeachment proceedings against Richard Nixon, and, with Anderson, opposed any further presidential pardons. "Let mercy follow justice," he wrote President Ford, opposing a Nixon pardon.[69]

Native American Ministries

It was clear to Bishop Charles that something had to be done with the Navajo mission. Father Liebler had retired in 1962, to a trailer sixty miles distant from St. Christopher's, where he founded St. Mary of the Moonlight retreat center, along with Brother Juniper, Helen Sturges, and Joan Eskell, whom he would marry on October 27, 1979, after his wife, Frances's, death on October 4, 1977. Charles called Liebler an "incredible person," whose sole flaw was his rigid model of pre-Vatican II Anglo Catholic priesthood. By the 1970s, St. Christopher's mission was running up sizable deficits, and failed to raise up any indigenous clergy.[70] Father Wayne Pontious, whom Liebler groomed as his successor, had never held a parish or managed a complex institution before. Charles asked him to leave when conditions failed to improve, and a series of priests came for short periods, while work at the mission atrophied.

By 1975, a new mission strategy was called for, including the idea of carving out a "Navajo Area Mission" with its own bishop. The Utah Diocesan Convention passed a resolution to this effect, and in 1979 the General Convention created the Navajoland Area Mission, comprising Native American missions from the dioceses of Utah, Arizona, and Rio Grande. Charles was suggested as first bishop of the Navajo Area Mission, but the post went instead to Bishop Frederick Putman, then retiring from Oklahoma. At that time the Rev. Steven Tsosie Plummer was the only Navajo priest, having been ordained on July 25, 1976.[71] Plummer became bishop of Navajoland in 1990.

Meanwhile, the Ute missions had come to a virtual standstill. In 1983, Iva O. Cutshaw, warden of St. Paul's Church, Vernal, reported the historic church building at Whiterocks was falling apart because of vandalism, and advised it should be razed and the debris hauled away. But the Church waited, and Bishop Bates resumed a ministry to the reservations several years later. In the meantime, lay leaders like Nancy Pawwinnee kept the small congregations alive. "When I became an Episcopalian, I did away with everything else. That's how I felt about it. I was a traditional Episcopalian, a 1928 Prayer Book Episcopalian," she said. The Church of the Holy Spirit, Randlett, was the center of her religious life for over a quarter-century. Not someone caught between two cultures, for Nancy there was no connection between traditional religion and her Christian beliefs. The Sun Dance was a place to meet friends; its religious significance was nil. "Our dad didn't believe in it, so we didn't believe in it," she recalled.[72]

Born in Ouray, Utah, on October 9, 1921, Nancy was one of ten children of a Ute sheepherder and his wife. Life was happy for the young woman, and continued that way. Her earliest recollections were of the family moving with the herds to summer pasture. There she ran barefoot, swam, and played. "It was a wonderful childhood," she recalled. "We couldn't even remember the Depression, because we lived the same way we had before because we were well provided for." She attended the Ouray Indian School in 1929; the three-year course took Nancy and her sisters four years, since they spoke no English. From 1931 to 1936 she was a student at the nearby Whiterocks Boarding School, where Bishop Moulton baptized her in 1931. Next came the Sherman Indian School in Riverside, California, from which she graduated in 1940. During World War II, Nancy returned to Utah, and in September 1942 went to work for a Salt Lake City commercial sewing company. Shortly after retiring and returning home in 1977, she agreed to lead Morning Prayer services for the small Randlett congregation until a resident priest was found, which took until 1987. Meanwhile, she and a handful of other Native American women kept the church alive, teaching children, visiting the sick, and preparing the altar when an occasional priest came to hold a Communion service.

Clifford Duncan and St. Elizabeth's, Whiterocks

Clifford Duncan, a Ute healer and Whiterocks church member, bridged both religious worlds, Christian and Native American.[73] At funerals he was able to chant both the traditional Native American prayers in a liturgical setting and participate in the Episcopal Church's burial service. Duncan explained that Ute prayer requires facing the four cardinal points of the compass. Life is divided into patterns of four, "talking to all creation." In the morning "light gives all things birth." It is a time of cleansing, oblations, and preparation for the day ahead. Evening brings the end of the day and presages life's end. It is also a time of forgiveness. "We ask all things to be corrected so that we can begin the new day." Midday is the time of healing. "You have light on both sides, morning and evening. . . . We are not the ones that possess healing. It has to be a spirit that is outside of us."

Born at Whiterocks in 1933, Duncan remembered his great-grandfather coming to church each Sunday by horse, and his mother taking him there, a mile's walk to St. Elizabeth's. The youth attended the local Native American boarding school until his father was transferred to Fort Duschene with the Bureau of Indian Affairs. Duncan graduated from high school there in 1952. After two years as a tank driver with the U. S. Army, he became a consultant helping various government agencies locate and preserve Native American sacred lands in several states.

His interest in traditional religion was heightened by participation in the Sun Dance as a young person, and later by being asked to lead such ceremonies. The last of the Ute traditional healers had died or had ceased to practice by the 1930s, but elders shared their knowledge of their past and their beliefs with Duncan. Both the annual Sun Dance and the more frequently conducted sweats "give you an insight into who you are and why you are here." Both rites were avenues to expiation, purification, and restoration, compatible with similar church ceremonies. Duncan found Episcopal mission clergy to be generally accepting of Ute religion, and believed the Episcopal Church has played a positive role among Native Americans. Still, church ritual "needs more of a Native American interpretation" as a way of showing the comparability of biblical and Native American religion.

St. Mark's Towers, the Schools, the Hospital, and Camp Tuttle

In 1975, the U. S. Department of Housing and Urban Development (HUD) launched a nationwide program for low-income elderly and handicapped persons. Occupants were required to pay thirty percent of their income for rent, and the federal government would pay the rest. Charles liked the idea of such a program and applied for a grant to help house the elderly in Salt Lake City. To his surprise, a letter arrived from Washington saying $3.6 million had been set aside for a local housing program.[74] An Episcopal Management Corporation was set up to oversee the venture, and an unused property at 650 South 300 East was purchased for one dollar from the Salt

Lake City School District. It took three years of negotiating before ground was broken, and on December 19, 1979, the first tenants moved into the ten-story building with its 100 one-bedroom apartments.[75] Total expenditure to the Diocese: $23.

Basic funding for St. Mark's Towers was the three million dollars plus a low-interest loan payable over forty years from apartment rentals, after which the building would become diocesan property. HUD then told the diocese additional funds were available for another project. Without skipping a beat, Charles and Robert Gordon, his principal lay assistant, prepared plans for a seventy-two unit garden-style apartment complex on five acres in suburban Kaysville. Two million dollars was allocated from federal funds for that project. St. Mark's Terrace, Brigham City, a thirty-two unit million dollar project, followed in 1988. Then came St. Mark's, Millcreek, in south Salt Lake City, costing almost a million dollars for twenty-four units set next to a park. In 1993, the Northern Utah Labor Council decided to remove itself from the housing business and transferred to the Diocese ownership of Union Gardens, a $1.5 million fifty-unit project in Ogden.

By the twentieth century's end, the 228 units of housing in five developments under Episcopal Church auspices were worth an estimated $26 million; they had cost the church only $20,000. Lisa M. Jones, operations director for Danville Development Corporation, which managed the properties, observed that from the early bricks-and-mortar approach, HUD became aware of the problems of "aging in place," and funded service coordinators who initiated craft activities, outings, and recreational and educational programs.[76]

On April 30, 1970, groundbreaking took place for a new St. Mark's Hospital. The old location, next to an oil refinery, had been added to for a half-century plus, and it was time to move.[77] The new site was a spacious suburban location in the heart of the expanding valley's population center at 1200 East 3900 South. The $15 million structure on a twenty-acre site was dedicated in April 1973, and within a year its 251 beds claimed an over ninety percent occupancy rate. The new location and state-of-the-art facilities contributed to the hospital's success, and soon private medical clinics and offices were built nearby. The hospital provided over a million dollars worth of free care each year to the poor, added an MRI unit and other new technologies, plus an expanded community health education program and a pastoral care program directed by Lincoln Ure, an Episcopal priest and professional counselor, whose Clinical and Pastoral Education program attracted students from around the country.

But the hospital's move coincided with the beginning of a new era of demands on private hospitals. Sweeping changes were in store for most such institutions, leading to the sale of many. Costs rose, government regulations increased, and hospital management became a specialized industry in America. By 1984, St. Mark's occupancy rate had dropped to sixty-four percent. Hospital stays were shorter, costs rose, and more patients visited doctor's offices for treatment, reducing demands for hospital care. St. Mark's joined an association of nonprofit hospitals as a way of sharing information and achieving economies, but the wave of the future was acquisition by one of the growing number of for-profit professional medical management corporations. That was just over the horizon.

Charles was also interested in Rowland Hall–St. Mark's School, helping it to affirm its continuing role as a school with a distinctive moral grounding. A watershed event was his moving from chair of the board to becoming a board member in 1984, thus giving the school a dotted line rather than a direct tie to the Episcopal Church. In 1976, the school had closed its boarding facilities, ending a ninety-six-year tradition. During the 1980s a new headmaster, Thomas Jackson, faced the daunting task of raising $2.5 million in a capital campaign to move the near-bankrupt institution to solvency. Meanwhile, the student body more than tripled, from 240 to 840 students, and it acquired the former Roosevelt Junior High School on Lincoln Street as classroom space for grades seven through twelve. The lower grade classes remained at the historic Avenues campus, but major renovations in 1984 allowed for building a new wing to the main building.[78]

Coming Out: The Bishop as Homosexual

It was the summer of 1976, and Charles was spending a weekend at Camp Tuttle with his wife and their friends, Bishop William C. Frey of Colorado and his wife. At Compline, an agitated participant said to the small group of six persons seated in a circle, "Otis has something he wants to say." "We're not here to talk about Otis," Frey responded. But the participant had released deep, long-suppressed emotions within Charles. "There is something I need to say," the bishop replied, and went to his cabin to ask Elvira, his wife of twenty-five years, to join him. He then disclosed he was a homosexual. "At that time it felt like a good thing," he recalled. "Truth is always a good thing. I could not imagine living the rest of my life in a deceptive way." Charles had been aware of his sexual leanings since at least seminary days. At General, he prayed for a sign from God, and when Elvira appeared, he took it as a sign of what his future state should be. They were married and raised five children, and had nine grandchildren. Elvira was his constant companion, hard-working in the diocese as a volunteer at the cathedral, and an active hostess at the bishop's residence as well as in many other service organizations. Almost all of his letters welcoming others to Utah include the phrase "Elvira and I."[79]

The bishop was torn between two tendencies: to openly acknowledge his homosexuality, discovered over a quarter-century earlier, or to keep it private. After the 1976 Camp Tuttle disclosure, he discreetly informed the head of the Standing Committee and a few others of his leanings. Experiences at earlier retreats affirmed for him that it was permissible to be who he was, but this fractured his relationship with his wife, and eventually lead to a divorce. The issue never became public while he was in Utah, and Charles resigned in 1985 to accept a prestigious appointment as dean of the Episcopal Divinity School in Cambridge, Massachusetts. Elvira went with him, but after his retirement in 1993 they separated. Their divorce was final a year later, and Charles moved to San Francisco, where he became an influential presence in the gay community there.

Elvira remembers the Camp Tuttle encounter and its implications differently than her husband. She was asleep in their cabin, she recalled, when Otis awoke her to say he was gay. "That really was hell," she said, "You realize that the next day something is going to change. We didn't do anything. He just wanted to live with himself. Besides, I had a poor self-image. I was a volunteer, what could I do on my own?"[80] Elvira continued to shield her husband as bishop, herself, and her children. "It was a different era," she recalled. "There were prohibitions that don't exist now. I felt responsible, which was true of women of my generation." Otis also returned from a lengthy Ignatian retreat, convinced the couple should stay together. And in the 1980s Elvira's aged parents, who had lived in Spain, settled in Salt Lake City. After Charles retired from EDS, Elvira moved back to Washington, Connecticut. Of the divorce, she said, "We just sort of knew he would go his separate way. It just happened." She displayed no bitterness toward "Deac," saying of their life together, "I thought I had the most blessed, positive life going. I was never angry at the church the way some people are when their relationships come apart." Then, "I don't need to see him. It's too toxic."

On April 24, 2004, the bishop's seventy-eighth birthday, he and Felipe Sanchez Paris, sixty-two, a four-times-divorced retired professor and political organizer and the father of four, invited friends to join them at "the consecration of their life together" at St. Gregory of Nyssa Episcopal Church, San Francisco. Charles thus openly affirmed his commitment to his same sex partner in a colorful two-hour service ending with the couple being carried out of the church in separate chairs by well-wishers. A week later, following considerable publicity about the service, Bishop William E.

Swing, head of the Diocese of California and a supporter of the election of openly gay Bishop Gene Robinson of Vermont, revoked Charles's license to function in any clerical capacity in the West Coast diocese. Charles, who in retirement had been an assisting or part-time bishop in California, said the ceremony was "done with the bishop's knowledge and done according to his protocols." Swing said, "I was entirely clear with Otis about what would be permissible and what would not. Bishop Charles chose to override my decision and proceed on his own authority."[81] Long retired, Charles had not lost an ability to attract headlines.

9

George E. Bates

The Bishop Who Sold the Hospital

(1986–1996)

> George was an enigma.
>
> —Bishop William P. Spofford, bishop of Eastern Oregon

> Barbara—having lost a son much, much younger than Andy, we cannot even imagine the horror you are going through. But, we can taste it. And it is awful. Love, Sue and George.
>
> —telegram, n.d.

When the colorful, activist Charles moved on to his Cambridge deanship, the Utah diocese sought a less dramatic personality in its next bishop. George E. Bates fit the bill. Tall, at 6 feet 6 inches, and looking like a bishop, he was the experienced rector of two significant parishes, one in Oregon, the second in New Mexico, before becoming Utah's ninth Episcopal leader. Bates could be a textbook pastor in one-on-one situations, compassionate with those facing grief or reversals, and quick to respond to clergy and laity needs when made aware of them. For parishes in conflict with their clergy, he stayed the course, clarified issues, insisted on openness, and helped resolve emotionally laden disputes. He had an abiding interest in the poor, the marginalized, and those recovering from substance abuse, and gave generously to such causes once the diocese sold St. Mark's Hospital in December 1987. This watershed event in the history of the Episcopal Diocese of Utah resulted in a distinctly different before and after diocese, and the sale's implications remain to be sorted out years later.

Bates did not mix easily with the state's leadership, nor did they seek his advice beyond the obligatory civic boards expected of someone in his position. Some of this was due to his shyness, but he also had consciously taken the Episcopal Church out of the policy arena shortly after his election. He was most at home with known quantities, "the good old boy network," a close associate recalled, and he frequently called those he valued most "good brother" or "good friend" in letters.[1] He was possessed of a constant faith that saw him through the dark hours of "the journey of life," a favorite phrase of his.

His own struggles, first with sobriety, then with daunting medical problems, were discussed openly. Bates, once a heavy smoker, was treated by radiation for cancer of the throat during the summer of 1988. He left the state for sick leave in a more humid climate, then returned to Utah to resume part-time work while recuperating.[2] His regimen included three hours a day in a hyperbaric chamber for oxygen therapy.[3] "I have no plans to resign or to take a disability retirement," he told the diocese that year. "There is more than one way to proclaim the Gospel and preach the Good News. I hope that acceptable liturgical alternatives may be found regarding the voice of the bishop while I am learning new methods of communication. As Corporation Sole, I also have a great deal of unfinished business."[4] Bates used a torpedo microphone to speak as his voice weakened, and he spent increasing time in hospitals, working at home, or on medical leave, reducing his availability to parishes and clergy.[5] His right shoulder was operated on in 1992 for the third time. He had six knee replacements, and four hip replacements on the right side.[6] The bishop took medical retirement on June 29, 1996, at age sixty-three, and died three years later.

Sale of St. Mark's Hospital

The sale of St. Mark's Hospital had not figured in either the diocesan profile or discussions with candidates for bishop in the 1986 election, but once it was sold, the character of the Utah diocese changed dramatically, affecting basic ideas about the roles of congregations and clergy, and their relationship with the bishop. This before and after quality of the diocese marked new differences as sharply defined as the state's geology.

The idea of selling the hospital originated with Otis Charles.[7] A western Episcopal diocese had sold its hospital to a nonprofit corporation for one dollar, and Charles liked the idea of doing something comparable with St. Mark's, but was absorbed by the multiple demands of his office and never followed through. Shortly after Bates came to Utah, Albert Colton, a lawyer–priest and hospital board member, asked the bishop if he wished to pursue the option. Bates liked selling the hospital, but not for one dollar.[8]

By the 1980s, St. Mark's ran with little church influence. Its Episcopal Church identity was derived primarily from its historic name, nursing school, church-supplied chaplaincy, and Clinical Pastoral Education Program. The day of the independent hospital was fast fading, and two other local institutions, Holy Cross Hospital and the Latter-day Saints Hospital, were being sold; St. Mark's, a well-run regional hospital and an attractive investment opportunity, soon followed.[9] Several bids were considered, and after tough negotiations, the buyer was the Hospital Corporation of America. HCA was a for-profit hospital management company founded in 1968 by a Nashville, Tennessee, father-and-son medical team turned business entrepreneurs, Drs. Thomas Frist, Sr., and Thomas F. Frist, Jr., who later became a U. S. Senator from Tennessee. At the time St. Mark's was purchased, HCA was restructuring and had recently sold 104 hospitals. Its remaining flagship properties were 82 large general hospitals and 225 hospital management contracts.[10] Hospital management had become a big business in America.

In an August 28, 1987 press release, Bates announced the pending sale, saying it would allow the church to concentrate on "building up the body of Christ," fulfilling its charitable responsibilities and missionary work, and providing seminary-trained clergy throughout the diocese.[11] The bishop stated, "economic competition, government regulations, declining Medicare reimbursement and the high cost of medical services have limited the ability of St. Mark's Hospital to act as an effective agent of this Church's charitable outreach."[12] The State of Utah challenged the hospital's tax exemption as a charitable institution, and the county government saw opportunities to collect tax revenues as well.

Vocal opposition to the sale came both from hospital employees and within the diocese. Bates wrote hospital employees on September 2, 1987 to assure them St. Mark's would not be closed, and that the nursing program at Westminster College and the St. Mark's chaplaincy programs would continue, as would an irrevocable trust of several million dollars providing health care for those who could not afford it. Grateful patients and their families had contributed to the fund through the years.[13] Shortly after the sale was completed, however, fifty-five employees were dismissed as part of the hospital's restructuring.[14] Lincoln Ure, director of St. Mark's Pastoral Care Center and the diocesan priest most affected by the changing relationship with the hospital, remembered his encounters with Bishop Bates over the sale of St. Mark's. The hospital staff voiced concern that the institution's commitment to indigent care be maintained. Bates assured them that would be the case, but Ure recalled that monies in such programs gradually diminished to those specifically designated in bequeaths for that purpose. "It was a promise he forgot as time when on," Ure remembered.[15]

Lawsuits and settlement negotiations took almost three years to complete, even after the hospital was officially sold on December 31, 1987.[16] HCA and a later owner kept the name "St. Mark's" for the hospital by agreement, but later added it to other medical facilities without diocesan permission.[17] A convoluted Medicare settlement of $2,700,000 and malpractice claims of $1,331,822 complicated the transaction.[18] "Though not popular with everyone, it was a good move," Bates reflected on the sale, "a giant learning experience for me, and [it] provided considerable money for the poor and the homeless. Also, Utah, which was almost a 'destitute' diocese in terms of finances, now has the resources for parish development and increased diocesan staff."[19]

Reflecting on the new money now available, William F. Maxwell, dean of St. Mark's Cathedral from 1978 to 1990, observed: "We needed a theology of affluence. We had a pretty good theology of penury. We were like the Beverley Hillbillies. We had money rolling out our ears and it was exciting."[20] "The money was a two edged sword," lay leader Barbara Losse reflected. "There were a lot of wonderful things you could do with it, but it also went to George's head."[21]

Once the sale was completed, the impoverished diocese became wealthy. Newspaper reports put the sum at around $100 million dollars. No one in the parishes knew how much it was or what the bishop would do with it, and Bates was slow to provide answers.[22] The bishop had an initial reason for not disclosing details. The sale was complicated, took time to sort out, and was hindered by lawsuits. Finally, on the Feast of the Annunciation, March 25, 1988, he announced a $600,000 grant to the Salt Lake Men's Shelter and Homeless Program to complete its 235-bed downtown facility. After presenting the check to Mayor Palmer De Paulis at a cathedral service, Bates spoke of the Annunciation. "The announcement was made to a poor young girl in a remote village of a country occupied by a foreign power. At the time of Christ's birth, Mary and Joseph had to seek shelter in makeshift quarters, for there was no room for them in the established places of rest. Essentially, the Holy Family was a homeless family."[23]

The $600,000 was part of over a million dollars distributed in the first round of annual charitable grants announced by January 1, 1989.[24] Another major grant was $150,000, divided among seventeen Utah parishes to support their ministries. Additional money went to the Holy Cross Hospital AIDS program; Project—Utah; Campus Christian Center, University of Utah; Spouse Abuse Victim Assistance Project; Legal Aid Society of Salt Lake; and Odyssey House, Salt Lake City. The diocese supported groups committed to alleviating the burdens of poverty, abuse, chemical dependence, illness, and those with disabilities.[25] Absent from the list were social or political advocacy groups of the sort Charles had supported, in spirit if not financially.

As word of the church's affluence spread, requests for funds multiplied. In 1993, the diocese received more than $1,610,080 in requests for aid, but had only $250,000 to allocate through the Charitable and Educational Grant Committee. The spread of grants to those in need was: poverty, fifty-three percent; disabilities, thirty-two percent; chemical abuse, six percent; and physical and mental abuse, nine percent.[26]

The Corporation of the Bishop

With the hospital's sale, the Utah diocese, one of the church's poorest, became among the richest church institutions in America. Before selling the hospital, Bates had looked carefully at other Episcopal dioceses with large endowments, and was anxious to avoid the mistakes made by some. The Diocese of Rochester had lost $25 million by promising money to various groups without protecting its core assets; others had invested in resort hotels or risky securities. Bates pursued conservative investment policies, and wanted to keep the money in safe financial instruments. He also controlled the assets himself, while seeking investment advice from outside experts. The mechanism he employed was the Corporation of the Bishop, a Corporate Sole that under Utah law gave complete control to the person in charge of the corporation.[27] This long-established Utah law allowed the head of any church to acquire, hold, sell, mortgage, or exchange property without any authorization of the members.[28] Bates kept the money in several accounts, including the Bishop's General Fund No. 1, Bishop's Fund No. 1 (different from the Bishop's General Fund No. 1), the Bishop's Special Fund, the Diocesan Development Fund, Charitable and Educational Fund, Indigent Health Care Fund, and the Real Estate Transaction Account.

Bates's nondisclosure of the extent of assets and their use frustrated the diocese. A few people supported leaving the entire matter in the bishop's hands, but others wanted transparency in the management of diocesan assets, adding these were not private monies, but church property gradually accumulated through the years from the time Bishop Tuttle founded the hospital in 1872.[29] In his 1989 diocesan address, Bates said the Corporation of the bishop's assets were $74,283,278 in fixed income investments. "Only a portion of the interest income may be expended," he told the diocese.[30] "This money is an enormous benefice to be celebrated and cherished and guarded and loved, as it represents the years and years of work by so many, many people—Episcopalian and non-Episcopalian."[31] The names of the

Corporation of the Bishop's investment committee and Charitable Advisory Board were disclosed at the convention. "It's people who make it work," Bates said. "Offer those persons to God in daily prayer as they preserve the corpus, the principal of this money."[32] The members, however, played only a limited advisory role, and the Corporation was structured so that decision-making authority was in the bishop's hands, aided by a few close advisers.[33]

Bates never publicly disclosed the Corporation's full assets and how they were spent. He said, in 1991: "If I open this Pandora's box, I am inviting direct questions about the present posture of assets. Because of the market, the volatility of the same, because of the fact that everything isn't settled, and much more to the point—because I do not want to become involved in revealing that kind of information as Corporation Sole, I am again reticent to do anything that would go beyond the statement I have written."[34] A year later, the bishop told the diocese the biblical reasons why he was reluctant to discuss the subject of money further. "I became uneasy with this posture when I reread Matthew 6:1–4" about giving alms in secret. The church monies did not compare in size with other large foundations in Utah, and "more to the point for me as your bishop, I think our posture of quiet and mostly anonymous work is appropriate."[35] "Be proud, be humble, be alert, above all, be thankful!" Bates told Utah Episcopalians, who still awaited a comprehensive statement of the diocese's assets and how they were spent.[36] "Most people in the diocese did not know anything about the financial capacity or the management of resources in two-thirds of the financial part of the church,"[37] Stephen F. Hutchinson, later its Chancellor, observed.

A partial reconstruction of diocesan finances is possible from documents available in the post-hospital-sale period. The stated goal for income from the Trust was seven million dollars in some years.[38] In the Bates administration, about a third of the total annual trust income went toward the annual diocesan budget, another third was controlled directly by the bishop, and the remaining money went to various grant projects or to what was then called Episcopal Social and Pastoral Ministries. For example, the 1990 diocesan budget of $2,722,948 included only $144,604 from congregational giving.[39] By 1992, the diocesan budget had risen to $3,310,358, of which 93.4 percent came directly from a grant from the bishop. Congregational giving amounted to only five percent of the total budget.[40] The gap widened for parishes between local giving and reliance on diocesan money, and the diocesan staff soon grew from two to twenty-four persons.[41]

Meanwhile, Bates discontinued listing church membership statistics in the diocesan annual report, a feature of such reports since Tuttle's time. Bates said the church's numbers did not determine its true worth. In fact, the numbers were flat. Such information, required of all dioceses for compiling national statistics, was available in the national church's *Episcopal Church Annual.* Utah's figures reveal only a modest increase in active member numbers—4,061 communicants in 1990 and 4,626 in 1995—despite the substantially increased availability of funds.[42]

In 1995, the last complete year of Bates's episcopate, diocesan records showed the bishop's total compensation had risen from $48,000 in 1986 to over $750,000. The bishop's basic 1995 salary of $450,690 came from two sources, $110,162 from the diocese, and $340,528 from the Corporation of the Bishop.[43] Additional benefits that year included $317,899 in various retirement plans, including a $50,000 retirement bonus and $50,000 for club memberships.[44] "I recognize my pension is large—Thank God," Bates wrote in 1999, shortly before his death.[45]

The Election of a New Bishop, June 20, 1986

Bates originally came to Utah as a nominee because of his leadership of two sizable western parishes and his service to the national church, which included chairing the Standing Committee on the Church in Small Communities, 1979–1985. The Church of the Redeemer, Pendleton, Oregon, where he served from 1970 to 1984, was a sizable church in eastern Oregon, a parish split into Capulet and Montague factions, as a former member described it. One prominent family would not kneel at the communion rail when another did. Bates patiently worked with both sides. "George was an archdiplomat, managing to keep it all in balance," Julie Fabre Stewart, a parishioner there, recalled later.[46] The future bishop was part of a Wednesday afternoon golf foursome, including her father, which was followed by cards and whiskey in the clubhouse. Toward the end of his time in Oregon, he confronted a growing dependence on alcohol, and underwent two cancer surgeries. Parishioners rallied to their priest. "He really lived that [Alcoholics Anonymous] program and the Senior Warden helped him," Stewart remembered. "As in many small towns there was a lot of secretiveness. George walked his walk openly and he brought that out in others." Later Stewart, then a comparative literature major at Radcliffe College, was seriously injured, and Bates visited her weekly during her recovery. He recommended theological works for her to read. "We would talk. I have very fond memories of how George became my spiritual director. He spent time with people in the kind of traumatic events every family goes through, divorces, deaths, and sickness. He was always there."[47] Stewart then attended seminary, was ordained to the deaconate, and was engaged in a productive ministry to the elderly in Salt Lake City. Dirk Rinehardt Pidock, a clergy colleague for eight years in a team ministry with Bates in

Pendleton, called him "an imposing figure, tall and authoritative in manner, and formal. He tried to be casual, but couldn't be."[48]

Next, Bates exercised a wide-ranging pastoral ministry at St. Mark's-on-the-Mesa in Albuquerque, New Mexico, an expanding church in a college community. He spent only two years there, 1984–1986, before the Utah election. Bates was popular in Albuquerque, and when he was elected bishop, forty church members made the trip to Salt Lake City for his consecration.

The future bishop was born on August 11, 1933, and grew up in Binghamton, New York. His father, a midwestern Baptist before becoming an Episcopalian, was a physician who took early medical retirement because of a heart condition. Bates attended Deerfield Academy, but left it during his father's illness, and returned to Binghamton to finish high school. He graduated from Dartmouth College in 1955 as a sociology and English major, and in 1958 completed work at the Episcopal Theological School in Cambridge, Massachusetts. On June 9, 1956, while at seminary, Bates married Mary Sue Onstott from Short Hills, New Jersey. She was "a committed Christian, a choir member of long standing and an active communicant," he said, who joined her husband in several Leadership Skills Institutes, Cursillos, and Marriage Encounters.[49] Pidcock said, "Sue was a loyal partner and a rock in his life, compensating for him many times. He clearly was the dominant one in this relationship and in almost every relationship."[50] The young cleric studied clinical pastoral education at the Massachusetts General Hospital, where his supervisor was Chaplain William P. Spofford, bishop of Eastern Oregon from 1962 to 1979. Later Bates studied at the Menninger Clinic.[51] Ordained a deacon in 1958 and a priest in 1959, from 1958 to 1970 he served parishes in Ithaca and Syracuse, New York, and became a consultant on church conflict, the vacancy process, and parish life evaluation to the Diocese of Idaho from 1962 to 1973.[52]

The Bateses had two children, Richard Howard Bates, born on September 22, 1960, and Katherine Bates Schey, born on July 6, 1962, and later five grandchildren. A son, Curtis Edmonds, had died in 1965 after living only two months. Memories of the death stayed with the couple, allowing them to empathize with others experiencing the grief of a child dying young.

Bates had contacted Spofford about job possibilities in his diocese, and arrived in Oregon at age thirty-seven. He began to dress and act the part of a Westerner. He listed himself as an outdoorsman, a former National Rifle Association member who enjoyed bird hunting, fishing, golf, and the popular western fiction of Louis L'Amour.[53] Almost all his correspondence was signed with a smiley face inside the initial G in "George." As his health declined in later years, the signature and features grew increasingly shaky. In eastern Oregon, the future bishop served as chair of the diocesan Department of Communication, was a member of Coalition 14, and its secretary from 1971 to 1974. Interest in the national church was a constant in his life, and Bates served as a deputy to several General Conventions between 1967 and 1982.[54] He was a board member of Recovery Ministries, the National Episcopal Coalition on Alcohol and Drugs (NECAD), and was its "Person of the Year" award recipient.[55]

On December 1, 1985, the profile for Utah's new diocesan bishop was released following a survey of parishes.[56] The state's population was now 1,461,000, and Utah was the fifth fastest-growing state in the nation, with a birth rate double that of the rest of the United States. The diocese had twenty congregations, eighteen seminary-trained clergy, six Canon 8 priests, and five local deacons. The total number of church households was 2,486; the total number of communicants, 4,172. St. Mark's Hospital was mentioned in a passing paragraph of the profile, with no suggestion that its sale would soon become the central issue in the diocese's life.

The profile of the bishop Utah desired was a standard job description. Desirable traits were being a spiritual leader, pastor/counselor of the clergy, teacher, liturgical leader, theologian, preacher and administrator.[57] The laity wanted a leader to help the diocese grow numerically; many expressed frustration at their isolation, distance from the diocese, meager financial resources, and limited program possibilities. The clergy wanted "a warm, effective person who is appropriately present with and available to the clergy of the diocese . . . who will share significant time with clergy families . . . who is supportive in dealing with clergy in conflict situations . . . who honestly confronts destructive behavior and provides guidance." No mention was made of local, national, or international public policy issues, and by now the new Prayer Book and hymnal, and women priests, were accepted in church life. These were contentious subjects elsewhere, but not issues in Utah, where many Episcopalians had come from out of state or had left the less-progressive LDS Church.

An initial list of over a hundred candidates was reduced to nine, from which the Nominating Committee, headed by Albert J. Colton, a cathedral clergy member and leading local attorney, selected four finalists. In addition to Bates, the others were Charles Ellsworth Bennison, Jr., rector of St. Mark's Church, Upland, California, and later bishop of Pennsylvania; Donald Wylie Seaton, rector of St. Paul's, Oakland, California, and Francis L. Winder, rector of Church of the Good Shepherd, Ogden, a longtime Utah priest. It was difficult to learn much about the candidates from their responses to the written questions. Most answers were cautious; for example, Bates wrote, "As a diocese, how we treat each other, respecting divergent opinions, is often more important—in the long run—than positions taken and works accomplished. Pastoral care, the good news of God's incredible love, and the search for appropriate moral posture are held together in our Lord Jesus Christ." In relations with clergy, he desired an atmosphere of "collegiality, honesty, good fun, loyalty and the kind of spirituality that allows the team and each individual to live into ministry, with hope, enthusiasm and integrity."[58] It was difficult to disagree with such a response, but difficult to make much of it, either.

Meeting at St. Mark's Cathedral on June 20, 1986, 168 lay and clerical delegates to the special Diocesan Convention elected Bates as their bishop on the third ballot. He received 75 of the 126 lay and 21 of the 40 clerical votes.[59] Earlier that month, he had lost the episcopal election in Delaware. He told a reporter he had been considered in nine other dioceses previously, but declined to run. "This time it seemed appropriate."[60]

Bates was ordained as diocesan bishop on October 25, 1986, and on the following day was seated in the bishop's chair at St. Mark's Cathedral. The Most Rev. Edmond Lee Browning, presiding bishop of the Episcopal Church, served as chief consecrator, assisted by six other bishops. The service was held in the Grand Ballroom of the Hotel Utah, scene of many civic functions, and more spacious than the Episcopal cathedral. The Roman Catholic cathedral was not available; relations were strained since Bates's predecessor had received the Roman Catholic cathedral's former rector, Jerald Merrill, into the Episcopal priesthood. The bishop's old friend and mentor, Rustin R. Kimsey, bishop of Eastern Oregon, was the preacher, and Bates celebrated the Eucharist.[61] His previous parish gave the bishop's ring, his pectoral cross was from Church of the Redeemer, Pendleton, Oregon, and the Standing Committee of the Diocese of Utah contributed a cope and miter.[62] "Many, many family and friends arrived from all over the country. . . . It was a wonderful time of reunion, filled with laughter and tears of joy. . . . Utah was affirmed over and over again," the Bateses wrote friends in their Christmas letter.[63]

As a denominational leader, Bates rarely spoke out on public issues; consequently, the Episcopal Church was not a visible presence in most of Utah's public policy debates of the mid-1980s to 1990s, unless the cathedral dean took a stand on an issue. In a press conference shortly after his election, Bates said eradicating racism and sexism would be priorities of his administration. On racism Bates said: "Because if we can do this to men and women and blacks and whites we can do it to Russians and Chinese and everybody else. That's how you start world wars. It makes no sense at all. . . . We're a tiny minority, white people are. It's just an accident of skin and sun and nature."[64] He opposed sexism as well. "The idea that women have a role in life which somehow theologically makes them different from men, I just don't find any truth in that. Sure they have a role in life. Women can get pregnant and men can't. So what else is new?" On abortion, the bishop said this was a woman's decision to be made in consultation with others beyond her family. "I think the thing that disturbs me most about the abortion issue is that historically in the church this decision has been made by men. They're not the ones having the abortions. They're not the ones carrying the child."[65]

These comments were in response to media questions. Bates did not anticipate commenting on the moral implications of political issues as bishop of Utah—how could one person speak for the whole church, he asked? Issues like nuclear disarmament and national defense "were concerns church members must each address personally," he said in drawing a distinction between personal and official views. He clearly did not place himself in Utah's line of outspoken bishops: Spalding, Jones, and Charles. "I've already told the Episcopalian people here 'I'm not speaking for you unless you voted on it. . . . But I will also speak out for myself,'" which rarely happened.[66] In another press interview, the reporter observed, "if visitors came expecting to get an earful they probably left disappointed. Bates . . . is saying as little as he can. He says he'd rather listen." "I am faced with decisions that affect me," Bates concluded. "I can't make decisions for anybody else. That would be immoral."[67]

When Presiding Bishop Browning issued an October 1990 declaration on the Persian Gulf crisis, Bates wrote to congratulate him but said he could never make a similar statement. "I . . . can say this to you personally, but would not put this in writing to the Diocese of Utah, nor for that matter, anybody else. It is so clear it would be redundant. And for those to whom it is not clear, such a statement would only be inflammatory and not convincing. Therefore, I congratulate you thrice on your pastoral stance. You do good work, my friend."[68] But at some point Bates did speak about the Gulf War, and in the January 1991 *Diocesan Dialogue* he wrote, "I cannot and will not defend the posture of this government as we prepare, for whatever reason, to engage in, or perhaps even initiate, a war in the Middle East in response to the invasion of Kuwait."[69]

Still, the bishop was no theological conservative. Most of his positions would place him in the center-to-liberal wing of the Episcopal Church of the 1980s and 1990s. "He had a radical sense of grace. An individual was saved by grace and that was all there was to it," recalled Bradley S. Wirth, Canon to the Ordinary during much of Bates's tenure, adding, "He brought a sense of the Protestant tradition with him."[70] His sermons place him in the camp of most church progressives of the 1980s. When Charles announced he was gay, Bates publicly supported his colleague, with whom he maintained a cordial relationship. Likewise, he issued a pastoral letter on AIDS, and endorsed the action of Episcopal Bishop Walter Righter in ordaining a gay man living in a committed relationship.[71]

He was for women's ordination, and supported the 1989 decision of St. Paul's, a large Salt Lake City parish, to call as rector Caryl A. Marsh, an Englishwoman and graduate of San Jose State College and the Church Divinity School of the Pacific. The locally trained versus seminary educated clergy issue was also alive when Bates came to the diocese, triggered by Charles's ordination of many local clergy. Bates's solution was to ordain aspirants in the pipeline, and support those already ordained, but to otherwise limit the program and recruit seminary-trained clergy for future openings.[72] His main concerns were about training and continuing education for the local clergy. "We still have twenty-nine persons in process, only five of whom are in seminary. Unavoidably, there is some division among the seminary trained and non-seminary trained clergy. . . . While Bishop Charles was very careful to 'contract' specific ministries for specific purposes, we are, of course, finding some difficulty with overlap."[73]

Largely through the efforts of archdeacon Francis L. Winder, a Utah Council of Churches was in place. Bates had little contact with the LDS leadership. He hoped for more cooperation with the Roman Catholic Church, although neither he nor that church's leadership could move beyond the cautious positions both denominations held in the late 1980s. Notwithstanding, Bates maintained a cordial relationship with his Roman Catholic counterpart, William K. Weigand, who prayerfully kept contact with Bates throughout his illnesses, at one point writing, "I greatly admire your faith and peace in the face of all this. I am edified by, and in full agreement with, your decision not to resign but to continue to serve as bishop of Utah. Your ministry could end up being more powerful and effective than before."[74]

In 1991–1992, Bates gave the Roman Catholic Cathedral of the Madeleine restoration fund $37,500.[75] He raised the possibility of jointly issued public pastoral letters from the bishops of the two denominations, but a brake was put on future cooperation when, on August 6, 1989, he received into the Episcopal Church a highly visible Salt Lake City Roman Catholic priest, W. Ivan Cendese, a now-married former monk. Cendese had been principal of two major high schools, including the Roman Catholic Church's flagship Judge Memorial High School, but had been laicized by the church. He had been active in the Episcopal Church for six years, including a term as senior warden of St. Mark's Cathedral.[76]

The bishop was at his best as a pastor. Clergy said he was responsive when asked, but otherwise kept his distance from many of them and the laity.

Sometimes parishes became locked in controversy with their priest. Letters and phone calls flew in all directions. Contracts and agreements were reviewed in disputes, and the bishop's name was invoked in support of one or both sides. "George was very directive and faithful and large numbers of people sought out his counsel. As counselor, he attracted large numbers of emotionally needy people," Pidcock recalled. "In a pastoral crisis he came through."[77]

In 1994, Grace Church, St. George, a small congregation in an expanding southern Utah retirement community, was enveloped in such a controversy. Both sides appealed to the bishop; the confrontation was between a newly arrived, young and inexperienced priest and an entrenched "Pillar of the Church" senior warden, a civil engineer who lacked human interaction skills. Who worked for whom? Each Monday morning the senior warden gave the priest a list of assignments for that week. The power conflict extended into every aspect of the small community's life. Saying he supported the priest at Grace Church, Bates wrote a parishioner: "The fact that we cannot solve the problem to their satisfaction, or anyone else's satisfaction, is a major frustration for all of us. It is also what I believe the journey of life is all about. It is not about feeling good or having ones needs met. It is about working with God in the midst of an imperfect world filled with imperfect situations and people."[78]

The bishop made several visits to St. George, and actively engaged the parish in open discussion. He said it was inappropriate for the Vestry to meet without the Vicar being present. "In group life work we call this 'sewer work' in its most extreme form," he said. "Normally the sewer workers are those that say little during a meeting—then go home and get on the telephone. I know clergy who have operated that way; I know laity who have operated that way. It is . . . never helpful to the Church at large."[79] Eventually the priest left for another diocese, but the issue had been exposed to the light of day and faced openly by the congregation.

The bishop maintained an extensive pastoral correspondence, much of it short and to-the-point letters compassionately responding to individual needs. Bates once telegraphed a grieving mother, "Barbara—having lost a son much, much younger than Andy, we cannot even imagine the horror you are going through. But, we can taste it. And it is awful. Love, Sue and George."[80] At the loss of another child he wrote the parents: "While his pain and suffering is over, and I know that lightens the weight in your heart on the one hand, your loss is now final and more complete. I pray with you, I cry with you, I suffer with you."[81] Bates intuitively read a person's moods and emotions, and could respond thoughtfully to them. In 1993, the bishop wrote a priest whom he saw at a large church gathering, but with whom he was unable to speak. "How hard it must have been for you to see me [at the celebration]. . . . Non-verbally I could tell you were not doing well, but until your good letter I did not know with certainty of your divorce in June of this year. Lonely and hard times. Yet, I know the relationship was also difficult. I am sure that God's grace will continue to offer healing and hope."[82]

On January 21, 1995, Bates gave the wedding homily for Patti and Jeff Sells; the latter was a clergy colleague who designed the bishop's pectoral cross. Bates, nearly voiceless now, said: "Marriage is not about perfection. Marriage is about miracles. Marriage is not just about feeling good. Marriage is about commitment. Marriage in not about the highs and the lows. Marriage is about living into wholeness. Marriage is not just about walking with Jesus. Marriage is about walking with Jesus individually and sharing the story together. Marriage is not about saving each other. Marriage is about blessing each other. . . . Not a fifty-fifty proposition—but a relationship of total giving. Marriage is not about staying young with each other or growing old with each other. Marriage is about being with each other. Marriage is not about perfection. Marriage is about miracles. Expect miracles. I love you both. God bless you."[83]

The liturgical season with which Bates most identified was Lent; his writings about it were compelling, perhaps informed by the early loss of his son and his own severe medical problems. In 1994, decrying the plain-vanilla texture of Utah life, he said, "Lent offers us an opportunity to reassess who we are and where we are on our journey."[84] "The crucible of life is what Jesus faced. The crucible of life is what he voluntarily—though not without pain—entered with an integrity unknown to others. His offering was blessed as your offering is blessed."[85]

A major event for the bishop was spending Maundy Thursday mornings with the clergy. In 1989, he sent each a copy of the book *Addiction and Grace* by the psychiatrist–spiritual leader Gerald May. Bates said, "Please do not believe that it deals with substance abuse alone. It deals with all the things that all of us do that are, in fact, addictions."[86]

"For years I honestly thought and prayed that many things I sought would happen," he said in his 1994 Maundy Thursday meditation. "I was asking, begging, crying for God to help, but I did not know I had to let go. I wasn't raised that way. I wasn't educated that way." He concluded: "Finally, I came to understand that I was not bad, was not weak, but rather had a primary, awesome, escalating disease. I was alcoholic. Cutting to the marrow, I finally found AA and the twelve-step program. The success I have celebrated, one day at a time, is because of turning the behavior over to God and not taking it back."[87]

Addiction keeps a person's love for his neighbor incomplete and creates rival gods, he said in a 1990 clergy meditation. On a carefully enunciated personal note, he remarked, "given my health and age, I am sometimes attached to worry." He worried about his wife and family, and his responsibility for them both financially and emotionally. "This time-consuming concern and—even without dwelling too much on it—is sin. Sue and the children and their children are God's concern. Yet, I am attached to those concerns. From time to time I am addicted to those concerns."[88]

Articles he had recently read, or speakers heard at conferences, provided the central ideas for many of Bates's key sermons or addresses. For example, each section of the bishop's twenty-one-page 1989 diocesan convention address began with a lengthy quote from prominent figures—the church historian John Booty; Bishop Furman C. Strough of the Presiding Bishop's Fund for World Relief; local law professor Edwin B. Firmage; a General Convention Call to Evangelism; a Diocese of Eastern Oregon paper on the role of the bishop; and, finally, from Archbishop Desmond Tutu.[89]

As a liturgical celebrant, his style has been described as "flat" or "country and western." Bates did not try to dominate the service; he had no standard way of conducting ceremonies, and no demonstrable musical preferences.[90] "I have no interest in baptisms," he wrote a local rector, "though at an Easter Vigil baptism would make sense. I do have an enormous conviction regarding Confirmations and Receptions. I do believe the clergy in Utah who do not present young people for Confirmation misunderstand totally the culture in which we live. We need more rites of passage, not less."[91] "He was not a gifted preacher," a longtime clerical colleague and friend recalled; Bates relied on "long manuscript sermons with little human interest. His liturgical leadership was uninspired."[92]

Although the image the bishop sometimes projected was that of the blunt Westerner, to others he appeared aloof, presiding over the small diocese's conventions in floor-length purple cassock and matching colored zucchetto (skullcap). Following his installation, the new bishop purchased a collection of copes, miters, and other church garments. One package arrived at the cathedral, when his office was still there, and a visitor recalled seeing the tall bishop trying on the ceremonial headdress before a long restroom mirror. Then he turned and, exiting through a much lower door, knocked it off.

Albert J. Colton, Jack C. Potter, W. Lee Shaw

The bishop was not the only leading clergy presence in the Utah diocese. The ministries of Francis L. Winder as archdeacon and Lincoln Ure as St. Mark's Hospital Chaplain have been mentioned earlier. No less important was the work of Albert J. Colton, a lawyer and priest, Jack. C. Potter, dean of

St. Mark's Cathedral, and W. Lee Shaw, who instituted a significant ministry to ex-Mormons and the gay community.

A lawyer with a leading Salt Lake City firm and canon chancellor of the Diocese of Utah, Albert J. Colton was a major presence in the Utah ecclesiastical landscape until his death of cancer in 1988, at age sixty-three. Born in 1925 in Buffalo, New York, Colton was a Rhodes Scholar after leaving Dartmouth College, where he was class valedictorian. After graduating from Yale Law School, he was a highly successful, aggressive young attorney until abruptly changing careers and attending seminary in 1960. Of that experience he wrote: "The story might be different for the newly married couple just out of college, but most of us had gone through the Bohemian joys of orange crates for furniture many years before, and didn't relish returning to it. Not only was there the grayness of marginal economic life, and the physical drain on wives who had to find employment and still care for the family, but the ridiculous cases of seminarians working fifty or sixty hours a week and thereby only able to give their seminary work an occasional glance."[93]

Following graduation from the Church Divinity School of the Pacific, in 1962 Colton became vice dean and canon chancellor at Grace Cathedral, San Francisco, to Bishop James A. Pike, also a formidable attorney with strongly held opinions. Colton served four years as rector of St. Francis's Episcopal Church, San Francisco, before returning to Utah. Eventually he became director and president of the law firm of Fabian & Clendenin, and a member of St. Mark's Cathedral staff. As canon chancellor of the diocese, he and his firm prepared the initial legal work for the sale of St. Mark's Hospital. As a delegate to the national church's convention, he was remembered mainly for his successful effort to retain the Birthday prayer—"Watch over thy child, O Lord, as his/her days increase"—which was slated for removal from the 1979 *Book of Common Prayer*.[94]

Possessed of a confident manner and booming voice, for many years Colton celebrated the Wednesday morning Eucharist at the cathedral, open, he said, "to anyone who wishes to share the Spartan pleasure of meaningful activity at 7:00 A.M."[95] He is remembered especially for a letter he sent to St. Mark's parish members shortly after learning he had inoperable lung cancer that led to his death on November 7, 1988:

> I do have 'a sure and certain hope' that I will be accepted by a loving hand. I do not believe in the Greek separation of body and soul. . . . I believe with the Jew that we creatures are a totality. . . . And when this totality dies, it dies in its totality. It is only by the grace of Almighty God that this is given meaning again. . . . We will have an individual identity.

> We will again live in relationships. The sharing of the Beatific Vision would include relationships with others cleansed by this Presence from those elements which so often separate us now. . . . I have avoided talk of judgment, hell, etc. This is because I believe from my life as a Christian, in the way it is expressed in the Anglican Communion, that judgment is certain, but that hell is self-imposed. I have been given the means of grace and the hope of glory.[96]

From 1990 to 2002, Jack C. Potter was the cathedral's dean, bringing to the position experience in interracial and intercultural ministries, an arresting liturgical presence, and strong pastoral skills. Potter had participated in inner-city work in Providence, Rhode Island, and social–racial ministries in Cincinnati, Ohio, in the 1960s. He was rector of two Indiana parishes in the 1970s, and of the thousand-member Grace Church parish in Tucson, Arizona, 1982–1989, before coming to Utah. Potter and his wife, Patty, had been long-time friends of Dean William Maxwell and his wife, Sue, and Maxwell asked if he could put Potter's name on the list of candidates.[97]

More than 10 percent of Salt Lake City was Hispanic, and the new dean launched an active Hispanic ministry at the cathedral and hired a young priest from the Episcopal church in Mexico, Pablo Ramos, to build a Hispanic congregation. Eventually, the cathedral's social services ministry joined with the diocese's full-time Jubilee Center, offering compassionate assistance to people on society's margins. Potter continued the cathedral's tradition of being an open forum on controversial issues. The cathedral was well known for its musical programs, but to Bach's motets Potter added a Winter Solstice jazz series, and opened its doors to other contemporary musicians and visual artists. From his work with the Anglican Council of North America, he brought Caribbean and Latin American music to the cathedral, plus a variety of other liturgical expressions.

Possibly 60 percent of the cathedral congregation were ex-LDS or from LDS families. It was not the cathedral's policy in Potter's time to proselytize, but to be a welcoming place. Often the ex-Mormons stayed two or three years at St. Mark's, were exposed to Anglican liturgy and beliefs, then moved on to suburban churches nearer their homes. Potter was remembered for his statement on "What is St. Mark's Cathedral?"

> If you are passing by and feel intimidated or angry because of religion, please know that there is immunity granted when you enter St. Mark's Cathedral. Immunity from the ravages of religion and misuse of Divine

> revelation. We live in a time of religious zealots, abortion clinic bombings, and TV evangelists attempting to take power in our land. How do you find persuasiveness rather than coercion and will-to-dominate in religion? An answer is St. Mark's Cathedral. Here operates an unconditional surrender to the freedom of God to speak to whomever in whatever language is understandable to you. Immunity from religious control is granted to you upon entry. St. Mark's offers sanctuary and promises this glorious freedom of God as the climate to explore the healthiest living that religion affords.[98]

W. Lee Shaw, whom Bates ordained, in addition to an active parish ministry in several churches, launched a ministry to those leaving, or who had left, the Church of Jesus Christ of Latter-day Saints, as well as to gays and lesbians. Shaw said, "I do not consider myself to be a 'gay' priest. Rather, I am a priest and pastor who is gay, among other things in my life, and I am trying to live out my baptismal covenant and ordination vows as I serve in the Episcopal Church."[99]

Born in Helena, Montana, on May 20, 1948, Shaw was the son of an Air Force officer who was stationed in Finland. As a youth he was raised in the LDS Church and, at age nineteen, returned to Finland to serve an LDS mission. A 1972 University of Utah graduate, he married Christine Barlow that year in a temple ceremony. Their son, Matthew, was born in 1974. After a period of questioning, in 1982 Shaw requested excommunication from the LDS Church. He said: "The more I read about the history and theology of the LDS Church, the more uncomfortable I became in this very fallible institution claiming to have all the truth. I also could not imagine that 2,000 years of Christian history amounted to nothing until Joseph Smith. And I had a very hard time accepting the fact that only one church in all the world would have absolute truth and authority." His marriage ended during this period of questioning.

Next Shaw explored several Christian churches, settling on St. Mark's Cathedral, where he was baptized and confirmed on May 22, 1983. He subsequently held several lay positions at the cathedral, and wrote a pamphlet, "A Thoughtful and Rational Alternative—The Episcopal Church in Utah." Shaw attended the Episcopal Divinity School of the Pacific, Berkeley, California, from 1989 to 1992, where he wrote the Forward Movement publication, "When Mormons Enquire." Ordained a priest by Bishop Bates on December 5, 1992, he subsequently served at St. Michael's, Brigham City; St. James's, Midvale; and St. Stephen's, Valley City. St. Michael's church members remember Shaw starting the church's first youth group, and being an active presence in the community. Once when the regular driver was a no show, the newly arrived priest was asked by a funeral director to drive the firm's limousine to a burial service. "I don't know the way to the cemetery," Shaw replied. "Just follow the hearse," the owner said. The service took place in a snowstorm, and at the wake the funeral parlor director showed up to make a contribution to the vicar's discretionary fund.

While at the cathedral, Shaw helped found the Society of St. Chad, a discussion and support group for persons leaving the LDS Church. He also started a branch of Integrity, a support and advocacy group for Utah gays and lesbians. Shaw has testified before legislative committees on hate crime legislation, and initiated the first Episcopal presence at a Salt Lake City Gay Pride event.

The Corporate Executive

At his friend's funeral, Bishop Rustin R. Kimsey spoke of Bates's fondness for being considered a senior executive, and once the hospital was sold, the bishop set about installing the trappings of corporate office, including a new large car each year, spacious offices with custom furnishings, club memberships, floor level VIP basketball seats, and hospitality rooms at national conventions where he entertained in vicereagal style. But despite it all, he lacked the executive skills to accompany the image; the overriding vision and day-to-day management abilities eluded him. He was often hesitant and indecisive in making decisions, not open in financial matters, and awkward as a communicator. Bates's administrative reflections are strewn with airline-flight-magazine management concepts, words like "new paradigms," "postures," and "multi-phasic programs" that unraveled with the telling. Although the staff was large, divisions of responsibilities were never clear and competency levels varied. "As a recovering alcoholic George loved rescuing people," Maxwell recalled, "and that is why the diocesan staff became so huge. We had the biggest staff of any diocese in the country. They were all nice people, some of them folks that just needed a job."[100] Bates had a quick temper and could be harsh with colleagues in the office or church settings, but always apologized, "sometimes within the hour, always by the next day," a close associate recalled.[101] And there was no trace of lingering vindictiveness or double-dealing.

Charles had worked hard to build up the diocese's lay leadership; Bates gave it only lip service. There was no question who ran the diocese. Maxwell remembered: "When he was first elected somebody said to him, 'What kind of trouble are we going to have with you?' George drew himself up to his full height and said, 'Arrogance.'"[102] "He was an imperious windbag," a prominent Salt Lake City attorney and church school board member recalled. "He was incredibly arrogant. He loved to hear himself talk and drop names about how worldly he was, and how conversant he was with rich and famous people."[103] "George's passion was administration and finance and functioning in the councils of the Church, the higher the better," Pidcock, who worked eight years with Bates, noted."[104] Bates functioned well in the church's corridors of power, Alan F. Blanchard, head of the Church Pension Fund, recalled, admiring his bluntness in settings often filled with sanctimonious prelates. "I liked George, he was attractive, appealing, engaging," Blanchard stated.[105]

In 1991, Bates completed an employee evaluation form, answering the question, how successful was he in fulfilling his goals as bishop? Medical problems hindered his mobility, and visitations and out-of-office activities were substantially curtailed. "My personal goal of bonding with new clergy has been met with those that could travel to Salt Lake to meet with me," but building effective relationships with other clergy remained incomplete.[106]

Anne Campbell, when a staff chaplain–social worker at St. Mark's Hospital, recalled Bates as "a very large man and when he had his voice it was a strong voice. He wanted to be central to everything. He thought large and the staff shot upward. George was monarchical from my point of view. As a pastor, he could share his AA experience, but not his personal spirituality. He was very authoritarian, very grand. He liked to have a lot of people working under him, but never gave them any power. He played favorites. The money was freely flowing. It didn't feel very good to be part of an institution where that was happening."[107]

Lincoln Ure, a respected senior priest and hospital chaplain, recalled his encounters with Bishop Bates. "I ran a parish based nursing program and when one of the employees left, Bates cut the funding in half. I protested and he sent me two front row tickets for a Jazz game. I didn't feel good about that so I sent them back. I learned later from a diocesan staff member he said how immature I was. Later Bates told me I did not have to worry about my daughter's college tuition, but I did not take any money from him. That sort of thing was going on all the time. Many people fed themselves at the trough."[108]

"George would have been considered a B grade executive," a long-time diocesan treasurer recalled. "He was a secretive man. Once he had sold the hospital, knowledge of it didn't go any further than he wished it to go. He liked to operate so that not too many knew what was going on." Yet, "He was a fun person. I liked George very much. He didn't drink at all because he had had drinking problems in his past. He traveled a lot and the way he did it was not to buy a helicopter but to buy the very most expensive large cars he could."[109] Kathryn Miller, who worked for the diocese for nineteen years, remembered Bates as "a very complicated man, tough, controversial, but a great pastor."[110] Bishop William P. Spofford, who knew Bates for over three decades, said "George was an enigma."[111]

Bates wanted to purchase a ranch in a canyon at the town's edge as the bishop's residence, but settled instead on a large house in the Avenues district of Salt Lake City, where the couple lived, joined by their two children and their families for part of their time in Utah.[112] Bates, whose only planned trip to England was cancelled for medical reasons, called it "Bishopstead," after an English bishop's residence, and ordered an accompanying "Bishopstead" letterhead in Gothic type. Visitation itineraries announced "Depart Bishopstead at 8:30 A.M." when the episcopal party, with Perpetual Deacon Richard Frank at the wheel, emerged in a top-of-the-line-black Lincoln town car and a backup van filled with staff members to visit one of the diocese's twenty-some parishes.

The Investment Committee met at resorts like the Broadmoor in Colorado, or in Scottsdale, Arizona, where discussion time soon gave way to golf. And the whole management team flew to New York for conversations with bankers and investment counselors. Bates said that Alan F. Blanchard, head of the Church Pension Fund, supported him in believing that as CEO of a multimillion-dollar corporation, he deserved a senior corporate executive's salary and perks. "That is really not accurate," Blanchard said, adding he never knew what the bishop's salary was, nor did he discuss setting its level.[113] Bates was an excellent golfer until his health declined, and played with a twenty-six handicap.[114] He was also an avid Jazz basketball fan.[115] The bishop wrote to two leading Jazz players whom he encountered on an airplane: "You are not only superb athletes, you are exemplary representatives from Utah. I thank God for that, and want you to know that 'win, lose or draw,' I am always behind you and the team."[116]

Each year the bishop held a New Year's Day open house, which diocesan clergy and their families were expected to attend. "Sue and I will provide food and refreshment. Just bring yourselves! Some of us like to watch the games on New Year's Day, and we are making provision for that."[117] His 1998 party invitation contained a Christmas check of $250 or $500 for each clergy and staff member, a holiday custom he continued. The bishop also gave each clergy attending the annual diocesan convention $250 for the purchase of vestments.[118] Favored staff employees were given supplemental contracts and scholarship money for themselves and/or their children, and his own son and daughter were added to the church payroll as staff numbers expanded.

"It was difficult when he put his daughter in a staff position here and nobody knew what she did," a lay official of the period recalled. "His son was supported for a while by the Corporation of the Bishop. Those were real trouble spots."[119] The 1994 directory listed a diocesan staff of twenty-four persons for twenty-one congregations, plus sixty-three clergy (local and seminary-trained), three educational institutions, a hospital chaplaincy, and an Urban Indian Support Center.[120] The days of the small, struggling church, shaping its identity in an alien culture, were gone.

Bates saw the need for a diocesan Vision Statement by 1990, to accompany the diocese's new wealth. Despite the corporate image he projected following the hospital's sale, there never was a definition of where the church was headed. The diocese "began to build and fly a new wonderful and clumsy blimp," Bates observed. "For almost three years, once airborne, we have continued to build as we fly it. We have watched it closely, scrutinized it; and now it is in need of a tune up and repairs."[121] Bradley S. Wirth, commenting on the vision statement exercise, wrote: "I don't think we are in bad shape. I think that with several pots of coffee, and in the bad ol' days, many cigars, David, Pete and you, George, can hammer out a mission statement that would fit the bill." His comments were triggered by a Bates proposal to add four additional positions to the diocesan staff.[122] Wirth said the diocese should have a statement of future goals in place before any new persons were hired. The new draft statement was presented to and passed at the 1991 convention. Over the next five years, church members were called to witness boldly in their communities, establish new congregations, and love and serve their neighbors through compassionate outreach, prophetic advocacy, and inclusive congregational life.[123] Few would question the statement, but few hearts would be quickened by it either. Church bodies are given to laboriously crafting declarations and then ignoring them; this was the fate of the Operational Mission of the Episcopal Diocese of Utah.

Bates bought choice land and contracted an Atlanta church architect, unfamiliar with the extremes of heat and cold in Utah, to build two new churches, one in the growing snow capital, Park City, the second in the hot climate of St. George. The bishop hired his son as supervisor of both projects. Climate-related problems, such as a slate roof that had to be replaced after a Park City winter, and other architectural flaws required expensive reworking of both projects. The decision to build came from the bishop, as did the land purchases and the building designs. Friction thus resulted between the two local congregations and the diocese, and also among various bodies responsible for the work but not consulted about it.[124]. Ronald S. Winchell was hired as regional missioner to southwestern Utah in 1988, charged with building up the small congregations in Cedar City and at St. George.[125] Grace Church, St. George, began its later klife in the warm-weather southern Utah retirement community in 1981, when about thirty persons responded to a newspaper ad, placed by a few families, inviting Episcopalians to meet on a Sunday afternoon in a Roman Catholic church. Lay readers from Cedar City came regularly to support the St. Gorge community, and in 1983 John Yoder, a priest from nearby Las Vegas, Nevada, came twice a month and held services, continuing to do so for three years. Telemarketing campaigns in 1990 and 1991 were attempted, and the congregation, now about one hundred persons, moved to the local Lions Club, then in 1992 to the Senior Citizens Center for regular Sunday morning services. Later that year, the diocese purchased five acres of land at 1072 East 900 South in the St. George suburbs, and a church was built in 1993. By then, Sunday attendance during the winter months averaged ninety-five persons.[126]

Now that the diocese had money, Bishop Bates also revived work with Native Americans. By the 1980s, both the Whiterocks and Randlett missions were in a decrepit state, lacking clergy, congregations, and facilities. The Whiterocks Indian School had been closed in 1952, which had resulted in a sharp drop in church attendance. Still, the church stayed open for the next twenty years, largely through the work of lay leaders such as Harriet Taveaport, Henry Wopsock, Irene Gardner, and her sister Geneva Chimburas, who sometimes held services in their homes for the Whiterocks congregation. Nancy Pawwinnee and her three sisters, Mary, Ruth, and Clarice, also worked faithfully to keep an Episcopal presence alive at Randlett. At the 1987 convention, delegates from Whiterocks described the difficulty of keeping birds out of the church building, and placed a birdcage where delegates could contribute to the cost of wire to cover its windows. Bates gave money to refurbish the historic church of St. Elizabeth, and on an adjacent site to build a modern parish hall and community center. St. Elizabeth's was rededicated on January 28, 1989. Quentin F. Kolb, a Native American priest who spent ten years with the Church Indian Ministries and in various other clerical capacities, recalled that the procession began in twenty-nine degree below zero weather. As it passed from parish hall to church, members saw birds with feet frozen to the telephone wires.[127] The church in Randlett was also restored. Although the Navajoland Area Mission to the south was no longer part of the Diocese of Utah, Bates provided money to reduce its debt. The bishop also actively supported Kolb, who founded a successful storefront ministry in downtown Salt Lake City, recognizing that by the 1980s more Native Americans lived in cities than on reservations. "Bates did a lot for Native American ministries," Kolb reflected. "He does not always get the credit he deserves."[128]

In addition to the extensive renovations at Whiterocks and Randlett, St. Paul's, Vernal, was refitted for a physically handicapped rector. All Saints' and St. James's, two suburban Salt Lake City parishes, were encouraged to complete their new buildings to accommodate growing congregations.[129]

To improve communication within the diocese, Bates held the first of several Bishop's Weekends in 1988. These were family times for golf, relaxation, camaraderie, a chance to hear a major speaker on church life, and meet informally with the bishop in a Park City resort hotel. An estimated 500 persons attended in 1988, and the diocese paid the $40,000 cost, while participants contributed $6,000 to the Presiding Bishop's Fund for World Relief.[130]

Although Rowland Hall–St. Mark's School had only a nominal tie with the Episcopal Diocese by the 1990s, it was still influenced by its historic roots, and continued to expand its course and extra-curricular offerings. In 1992, construction was completed for the Larimer Center for the Performing Arts, named for Tony Larimer, a beloved teacher and community arts leader for over twenty-five years. A state-of-the-art gymnasium was part of the building program, and in 1994 the school opened the doors of a new middle school campus at 970 East 800 South. Within a few years, the school had once again outgrown its facilities. On May 4, 1999 Rowland Hall–St. Mark's purchased a nine acre site on Guardman's Way near the University of Utah to build a new beginning and lower school.[131]

Retirement and Death

In October 1994, Bates, then sixty-one, announced his forthcoming medical retirement. "My body is no longer up to what you deserve and have earned by your constant support, prayers, and collaboration," he told Utah Episcopalians. Doctors urged him to limit the use of his voice, not easy for someone in a church leadership position, and move to a more humid climate.[132] The bishop said, "cancer of the larynx, radical irradiation, further biopsies, hyperbaric treatments, and two total hip replacements" were nowhere on the horizon when he accepted the Utah episcopacy eight years earlier. But in the summer of 1994, "I noticed further considerable change in energy and resiliency, along with a shortened and painful window of voice usage."[133] The early announcement would allow the diocese to elect a successor, and for Bates to complete visitations and take a medical sabbatical from September to December 1995. A special convention was scheduled on December 3 to elect a bishop coadjutor. The bishop said he would stay in office through June 1996. "I do not want to disappoint your expectations. Rather, I would like to be able to finish more of what we have started together. . . . God may be calling me to remain in office and if that is God's will, I believe you and I can work this out together."[134]

Bates's later life was a study in contrasts. His faith was unwavering, his abilities as a pastor could be exemplary, and his support of the disadvantaged was real. But he was also autocratic and secretive. And if he gave readily of diocesan money to parishes and clergy in need, he rewarded himself far more generously than his peers in salary and retirement benefits.

His medical retirement was effective on June 29, 1996, and Bates died March 30, 1999, in Medford, Oregon, at a recently-built, spacious family home. At his April 6 funeral at St. Mark's Episcopal Church there, his old friend Bishop Kimsey, preacher at his consecration, delivered the eulogy. Drawing on Bates's struggle with addiction, Kimsey said the Alcoholics Anonymous "program freed him from the prison of dependency and offered him a freedom of choice and obedience which I find remarkable, even awesome." Kimsey drew contrasting pictures of Bates–the-executive, who presided over the sale of St. Mark's Hospital, and Bates–the-constant-pastor. "The side of George which loved the board rooms and intrigue of difficult organizational and financial arenas was in clover," he reflected. "But it was equally true George was one of the finest pastors I have ever known. I have the image of his managerial prowess . . . but I also have the image of a large man kneeling beside the bed of an elderly, dying woman, holding her hand and anointing her forehead with oil. His influence as one who efficiently dealt with corporate matters should not overshadow the compassion he so ably offered to us all."[135]

10

Building the "Goodly Fellowship"

The Summing Up

So ends the story, as of 1996, a story of an adventure that began in the summer of 1867 when a dust–covered, pistol-packing eastern bishop arrived by stagecoach in the frontier town of Salt Lake City. The Utah Territory was still under federal occupation; it would not become a state until 1896. Relations with the Latter-day Saints were prickly for decades, but Daniel S. Tuttle, Utah's first resident Protestant missionary, carved out his own mission strategy, a spiritual and educational presence, alternative to the Latter-day Saints. An indefatigable pastor, traveler, and fundraiser, he built schools, churches, a hospital, and a cathedral before moving on to Missouri in 1886. Tuttle is among the giants of nineteenth-century American religious history.

No less imposing a figure was Franklin Spencer Spalding, bishop from 1904 until his tragic death in 1914. Spalding was a national and international voice for Christian Socialism, who also built churches and expanded the missionary district's ministry in his time. His successor, Paul Jones, formerly of St. John's House, Logan, and later archdeacon of the missionary district, lasted only three-and-a-half years as bishop. In an encounter that invites comparison with a Greek tragedy, a hostile local Council of Advice and a timid House of Bishops forced the idealistic Jones to resign in a clash between Christian pacifism and patriotic fervor. Then came the long episcopate of Arthur W. Moulton, 1920–1946. During the Depression years, the church was in a survival mode, but Moulton still expanded activity in several isolated communities and supported Native American work, begun by the Church in the 1890s on the Ute reservations, and was a voice for international cooperation in one of America's most isolationist states.

The brief episcopate of Stephen Cutter Clark, missionary bishop from 1946 to his death in 1950, show Clark as a careful planner who laid the foundations for the church's postwar expansion in the growing Salt Lake

City region. Richard S. Watson, lawyer, actor, and bishop, then worked tirelessly from 1951 to 1971 to expand the impoverished missionary district in membership. He caught the rising curve of the postwar population expansion, and many of the most active parishes of later times were built or started on a shoestring in Watson's time.

Next came two contrasting episcopates, one open, one closed; one communal, one corporate; one poor, one wealthy. Otis Charles, 1971–1986, was a creative figure, long involved in liturgical renewal and church reform movements. It was the 1970s, and the newly independent diocese sped into the modern era while never looking back. With the sale of St. Mark's Hospital on December 31, 1987 by Bishop George E. Bates, the face of the Utah Diocese changed. Money flowed—the hospital sold for possibly $100 million—but the former closeness of clergy, laity, and bishop was replaced by increasing detachment and competition for funds. When Bates took medical retirement in June 1996, Carolyn Tanner Irish, a Utah native, became the tenth bishop of Utah and third bishop of the independent diocese.

What are the main conclusions about the history of the Episcopal Church in Utah? The Episcopal Church represented a number of firsts: the first permanent non-LDS religious presence in Utah, beginning in May 1867; the first non-LDS private schools in Utah, also in 1867; the first non-Mormon church building in Utah, Good Samaritan, Corrine, in June 1869; the first non-LDS church building in Salt Lake City, St. Mark's Cathedral, whose cornerstone was laid on July 30, 1870; and the first modern hospital between Denver and San Francisco, in 1872. It was also among the first American dioceses to make widespread use of the ministries of locally ordained clergy in the 1970s. But "firsts" are not ends in themselves, only road markers pointing the direction of history's trails.

As for the Episcopal Church in Utah:

—Its numbers were always small, slightly over five hundred communicants in 1886, and slightly over five thousand a century later. In a state of nearly 85,000 square miles, its twenty-plus churches and chapels always maintained their distinctive character—small, enthusiastic islands in the shadow of the Latter-day Saints culture surrounding them.

—Episcopal Church attitudes toward Native Americans mirrored their times. Bishop Leonard began church efforts to "elevate the Red Man" in 1895. Milton J. Hersey actively introduced modern educational and farming methods to the Utes, and simultaneously contributed to the destruction of traditional Ute culture through suppression of the Sun Dance, a unifying force for many Utes. Meanwhile, a small but loyal cadre of Native American

Episcopalians emerged, and kept the reservation churches functioning. Some missionaries, like Buckaroo Joe Hogben at St. Elizabeth's and H. Baxter Liebler at St. Christopher's, were remembered for their support of indigenous culture and life.

—In most parishes women were, then as now, the main fundraisers, teachers, cooks, altar guild members, musicians, and visitors to the sick and grieving. Only gradually were they admitted to governing councils and ordination. For example: Bishop Paul Jones's proposal to make women convocation delegates was rejected in 1915; it was not until 1934, during the height of the Depression, that two women of means were elected to St. Mark's Cathedral vestry. Yet, from earliest times, women missionaries were active in Utah. Sara Napper worked as a teacher and church worker from 1892 until 1927, when she retired at age eighty-two. No less effective were several women reservation workers, in the early twentieth century among the Utes, and among the Navajo in the 1940s and 1950s.

—Its basic relationship with the dominant culture was one of wary tolerance, and sometimes-vocal conflict on both sides in the early years; and little contact in the later years. Tuttle, Spalding, and Jones publicly challenged Mormon beliefs. Tuttle declined to welcome Latter-day Saints to communion, and Watson would not accept Mormon baptism, but Episcopalians generally coexisted with their more numerous neighbors and increasingly welcomed avenues of cooperative action.

—Despite the tragic conflict between Bishop Paul Jones and the missionary district's Council of Advice in 1917 over pacifism and World War I, the Missionary District and later Diocese of Utah was free of religious factionalism and the quarrels that made newspaper headlines elsewhere. Nationally, Utah belongs in the progressive wing of the Episcopal Church. Key changes, like welcoming minorities and women to the ministry, and gays and lesbians to the priesthood, as well as the various Prayer Book and hymnal revisions, were accomplished with relative ease. Despite their geographic isolation, Utah Episcopalians have always been a lively community, willing to try new ideas, sometimes reflecting trends in the wider church, and sometimes affecting the larger church's life, as in its contributions to the new service for the Burial of the Dead and the Reconciliation of a Penitent in the 1979 *Book of Common Prayer*.

—It was decidedly a mission church in its formative years, 1867 to 1920, and then again briefly in the post-World War II period, in the 1950s and 1960s. Largely within those two eras, the Episcopal Church in Utah established nearly a hundred preaching stations, teaching stations, house churches, missions, or parishes. Many of them were short-lived in places like Roosevelt, Green River, Dutch John, or Magna, but others took root.

Amazingly, almost half such communities were founded in the church's early years, (the 1870s to 1920), when its human and material resources were scarcest.

—When "Missionary" went out of the missionary district's name in 1971, founding new churches ceased to be a priority for the new diocese. No new churches were started under Charles or Bates, although Charles encouraged an already established Mission in Southwestern Utah, primarily a congregation gathering in Cedar City that also worked with Episcopal families in St. George to establish a mission. Bates built or refurbished several church buildings, but started no new mission churches.

—Church numbers did not grow in proportion to the state's population. If Episcopalians represented one-half of one percent of the population in Charles's time, they were closer to one-fourth of one percent at century's end. Church membership numbers had increased slightly, but the state's population more than doubled in the same period.

—The Church was poor and struggling for most of its history, and did not have a strong base of affluent members or financial resources until the sale of St. Mark's Hospital in late 1987. Clergy salaries were at most $1,000 in Leonard's time, and total clergy compensation was $9,700 a century later under Charles. This meant turnover was high, keeping out of debt was a problem for some clergy, and many of the most able clergy took jobs elsewhere.

—The sudden availability of possibly $100 million to the bishop in 1988 was a watershed event, resulting in a before and after diocese. Money-related issues became a leverage point in clergy–episcopal relations. Among parishes, a "let the Diocese do it" attitude grew in communities that formerly worked hard to raise money locally. Congregational giving, generally representing less than ten percent of parish budgets, remained flat or declined, for example, totaling $285,000 in 1988; $228,277 in 1991.

—Clergy pay, once among the nation's lowest, became among the nation's highest. Average Utah full-time annual clergy compensation was $64,596 in 2002, placing the diocese in the top decile nationally at a time when average national full-time clergy compensation was $56,930.[1]

—Many of Utah's bishops were outspoken. Tuttle articulated his needs for the missionary district, and laid bare the flaws of Mormonism as he saw them. Spalding wrote at length on the Social Gospel and Christian Socialism. Jones was both an articulate Socialist and a pacifist. Moulton was an early supporter of the United Nations. Charles led church opposition to MX missile deployment in Utah, and supported gay rights. Parenthetically, the environment as a religious issue, so evident a concern in a state like Utah, was not addressed by the Episcopal Church until the late twentieth century.

Wesley Frensdorff, dean of St. Mark's Cathedral in the 1960s, reflected his Utah experiences when he called for a church where "each congregation is in mission and each Christian, gifted for ministry; a crew on a freighter, not passengers on a luxury liner. Peacemakers and healers abhorring violence in all forms, as concerned with societal healing as with individual healing; with justice as with freedom, prophetically confronting the root causes of social, political, and economic ills."[2]

For isolated parishes of the Utah Episcopal Church, where a congregation of thirty-five persons represented a good turnout on most Sundays, the tension between biblical demands and local realities was reflected in the activities of its members. They visited or prayed for the sick, buried the dead, and comforted those who mourned. As a community, the church welcomed children into its midst, and provided a place where they could feel important as students, singers, and acolytes. It welcomed newcomers who might arrive with questions, having recently moved to Utah, or those leaving "the dominant religion."

A place for joyful celebrations during festive and solemn seasons, its choirs sang their best anthems and favorite hymns. The church drew Christians to the liturgical year, from Advent through Pentecost, connecting them to the wider church through time and eternity. When a St. Paul's, Salt Lake City, vestry report noted after a 1918 service, "the choir never in its career did better work," it echoed a widespread aspiration of other parishes. The Episcopal churches were a gathering place for community groups and Bible study, and for potlucks and fellowship meals to reduce the cultural and geographical isolation. The "miles of fund-raising spaghetti and gallons of spaghetti sauce" that the Church of the Resurrection, Bountiful, prepared, as did twenty-some other parishes, strengthened bonds of intergenerational fellowship, and the modest but constant sums of money raised built churches, sent children to camp, or helped the needy at home and abroad.

The church was a place to speak out freely on social and political issues such as war, gun control, immigration, capital punishment, civil rights, and the place of women in society and/or the place of persons of same-sex orientation in the wider life of the community. Finally, it was a prayerful setting where members realized the sad cost of divisions, and the joy of a purposeful community gathering to happily proclaim the news of the "goodly fellowship" in Christ.

> The Church must become Christian, and, therefore, missionary in its real essence. It must realize it can only know the Doctrine by doing the work. The Church's history, its form of government, its liturgical services offer constant temptation to waste time and thought and dissipate energy. Just

as truly as the individual must forget himself in the cause to which he is devoted, if he is to advance the interests of that cause, so the Church must forget herself, her boastings about her Catholic heritage, her efforts to perfect her liturgical forms, her fussing over already too complicated national, Provincial, and Diocesan organization and make it her one and only duty to keep her members to be like Jesus Christ, who lived and died to save men from sin and all the misery which sin creates. She must realize that the only reason there is a Church is that collective action is more efficient than individual action. We in Utah are a feeble folk and we have little or no influence over the Church at large—but we can do our duty in the little sphere of service to which Christ has called us.[3]

—Bishop Franklin Spencer Spalding, convention address, 1914

Notes

Abbreviations

The following archival abbreviations are employed in this study:

Accn Bx Fd/Bk (Accession, Box, Folder/Box), Series 426 (later 486), designates the Episcopal Church Archives, housed in the J. Willard Marriott Library, Special Collections, University of Utah, Salt Lake City, Utah. When Professor Harold Dalgliesh was Diocesan Historiographer he arranged for the scattered and uncatalogued diocesan records to be collected and catalogued professionally in the Special Collections Library, University of Utah. He kept a file, mostly duplicates of what he regarded as significant documents, which I have noted as the "Dalgliesh Collection" within the larger archive.

MSS 11 (Caine Manuscript Collection 11), Utah State University Library, Special Collections & Archives, Logan, Utah. Most of the papers, tapes, and films of H. Baxter Liebler are contained in this collection.

D. A. (Diocesan Archives). Uncatalogued papers of several episcopates were housed in the diocesan Tuttle Center and later transferred to the Episcopal Church Archives at the University of Utah. Copeland Johnson, a seminarian, assisted in the move by sorting out and cataloguing many of the papers.

MSS B, the cataloging system used by the Utah State Historical Society Archives, Salt Lake City.

RG (Records Group) for various entries in the Archives of the Episcopal Church, USA, Austin, Texas.

Introduction

1. In this text the words "priest," "minister," and "clergy" are used interchangeably.

2. Hymn 680, *Prayer Book and Hymnal* (New York: Church Hymnal Corporation, 1986).

Chapter 1

1. Daniel Sylvester Tuttle, *Missionary to the Mountain West: Reminiscences of Episcopal Bishop Daniel S. Tuttle, 1866–1886*, forword by Brigham D. Madsen (reprint, Salt Lake City: University of Utah Press, 1987), p. 15. Originally published as *Reminiscences of a Missionary Bishop* (New York: T. Whittaker, 1906). Although referred to in the text by the shortened title *Reminiscences*, the page references are to the 1987 reprint.
2. Ibid., pp. 17–18.
3. Ibid., p. 3.
4. Charles F. Rehkopf, "The Episcopate of Bishop Tuttle," in *The Bulletin–Missouri Historical Society* 18, no. 3 (1962): 207.
5. Tuttle, *Missionary*, p. 24.
6. Ibid., p. 42.
7. "The Consecration of Bishop Tuttle," *The Spirit of Missions*, June 1867, p. 413.
8. Tuttle, *Missionary*, pp. 267–268.
9. Ibid., p. 65.
10. Ibid., p. 67.
11. Ibid., p. 85.
12. Ibid., p. 89.
13. Ibid., p. 90.
14. Ibid., p. 107.
15. "Eleventh Annual Report of the Missionary Bishop of Montana, Idaho, and Utah," 1877, p. 3. The annual reports covering Bishop Tuttle's time in Utah, 1867–1886 were published annually, through 1878, as part of the *Proceedings of the Board of Missions of the Protestant Episcopal Church in the United States of America*. Subsequently, they were published with other annual reports by the Board of Managers of the Domestic and Foreign Missionary Society of the Protestant Episcopal Church of the U.S.A. Most if not all of Tuttle's annual reports were also published separately. Copies of the twenty reports, including a final report, were retained and microfilmed, without publication data, in the Archives of the Diocese of Missouri and sent to the author by Sue Rehkopf, archivist.
16. Tuttle, *Missionary*, Madsen introduction, p. 2.
17. "Another Letter from Bishop Tuttle," *The Spirit of Missions*, October 1867, p. 69.
18. Ibid., p. 69.

19. "Report of the Bishop of Montana, Idaho, and Utah," 1868 (microfilm copy without publication data, Archives of the Episcopal Diocese of Missouri), p. 115.
20. *Journal of the Second Annual Convocation of the Missionary District of Utah and Idaho*, 1884, p. 14.
21. Tuttle, *Missionary*, p. 102.
22. Bishop [Daniel S.] Tuttle, " How Our Church Came to Montana, Idaho, and Utah," *The Spirit of Missions*, September 17, 1917, p. 636.
23. Tuttle, *Missionary*, pp. 245–246.
24. Ibid., p. 313.
25. Ibid., pp.103–104.
26. Ibid., p. 108.
27. Ibid., p. 6.
28. "Dear Christian Brethren," Salt Lake City, October 8, 1867, Dalgliesh Collection, Tuttle, Bishop 1867–1886, D. A.
29. "Report of the Bishop of Montana, Idaho, and Utah," 1869 (microfilm copy without publication data, Archives of the Episcopal Diocese of Missouri), p. 264.
30. "Seventeenth Annual Report of the Missionary Bishop of Utah and Idaho," 1883 (microfilm copy without publication data, Archives of the Episcopal Diocese of Missouri), p. 3.
31. Jotham Goodell, *A Winter With the Mormons*, ed. David L. Bigler (Salt Lake City: Tanner Trust Fund, University of Utah, 2001).
32. Tuttle, *Missionary*, p. 60.
33. Ibid., p. 371.
34. Ibid., p. 113.
35. Howard R. Lamar, *The Far Southwest, 1846–1912: A Territorial History*, rev. ed. (Albuquerque: University of New Mexico Press, 2000), pp. 295–300.
36. Tuttle, *Missionary*, p. 114.
37. Ibid.
38. Ibid.
39. Ibid., p. 331.
40. "The Twentieth Annual Report of the Bishop of Utah and Idaho," 1886 (microfilm copy without publication data, Archives of the Episcopal Diocese of Missouri), p. 50.
41. Quoted in Robert Joseph Dwyer, *The Gentile Comes to Utah* (Salt Lake City: Western Epics, 1971), p. 153.
42. Tuttle, *Missionary*, pp. 354–355.
43. "Report of Bishop Tuttle," 1870 (microfilm copy without publication data, Archives of the Episcopal Diocese of Missouri), p. 69.

44. Ibid., p. 70.
45. "What the Church is Doing for the Mormons in Salt Lake City," *The Spirit of Missions,* May 1873, p. 343.
46. "Tenth Annual Report of the Missionary Bishop of Montana, Idaho, and Utah," 1876 (microfilm copy without publication data, Archives of the Episcopal Diocese of Missouri), p. 2.
47. "Nineteenth Annual Report of the Missionary Bishop of Utah and Idaho," 1885 (microfilm copy without publication data, Archives of the Episcopal Diocese of Missouri), p. 575.
48. Daniel S. Tuttle, "Mormons," in *A Religious Encyclopedia,* ed. Philip Schaff, Samuel M. Jackson, and D. S. Schaff (New York: Funk and Wagnalls, 1891), p. 1580.
49. "Report of the Bishop of Montana, Idaho, and Utah," 1868, p. 112.
50. Quoted in Dwyer, *Gentile* (Utah), p. 153.
51. Tuttle, *Missionary,* p.343.
52. Ibid., p. 308.
53. "Twelfth Annual Report of the Missionary Bishop of Montana, Idaho, and Utah," 1878 (microfilm copy without publication data, Archives of the Episcopal Diocese of Missouri), p. 2.
54. Tuttle, *Missionary,* p. 361.
55. Lamar, *Far Southwest,* p. 335.
56. "Eighth Annual Report of the Missionary Bishop of Montana, Idaho, and Utah," 1874 (microfilm copy without publication data, Archives of the Episcopal Diocese of Missouri), p. 119.
57. Tuttle, *Missionary,* pp. 370–71.
58. Ibid., p. 372.
59. Mary R. Clark, "Rowland Hall–St. Mark's School: Alternative Education for More Than a Century," *Utah Historical Quarterly* 48, no. 3 (1980): 272–275.
60. "Report of Bishop Tuttle," 1870, p. 65.
61. "Eleventh Annual Report," 1877, p. 3.
62. "Nineteenth Annual Report," 1885, p. 575.
63. "Report of Bishop Tuttle," 1870, p. 69.
64. Tuttle, *Missionary,* p. 374.
65. "The History of Rowland Hall," *Crimson Rambler* (1927 yearbook), p. 77.
66. Tuttle, "How Our Church," p. 637 (see n. 22).
67. "Letter from Bishop Tuttle," *The Spirit of Missions,* July 1871, pp. 305–306.
68. Tuttle, *Missionary,* p. 391.
69. Ibid., p. 388.
70. Ibid.
71. "Letter from Bishop Tuttle," *The Spirit of Missions,* July 1874, pp. 397–398.

72. Tuttle, *Missionary*, p. 381.
73. *Cathedral Church of St. Mark, Salt Lake City, Utah, Walking Tour*, (pamphlet, [2000?]), p. 7.
74. Tuttle, *Missionary*, p. 385.
75. Ibid.
76. Ibid., p. 383.
77. Ibid.
78. Ibid., p. 384.
79. Ibid.
80. Ibid., p. 387.
81. Ibid., p. 393.
82. W. Dee Halverson and David M. Walden, *St. Mark's Hospital, 1872–1997: A 125-Year Legacy of Quality Health Care in Utah* (Salt Lake City: Heritage Associates,1998), pp. 19–21.
83. "Bishop Tuttle's Report, " *The Spirit of Missions*, September 1875, p. 678.
84. Halverson and Walden, *St. Mark's Hospital*, p. 26.
85. Lydia Luceila Webster was born on April 22, 1846, and was educated at schools in Warsaw, New York, and entered the State Normal School in Albany at age sixteen, graduating in 1863, the youngest person in her class. For the next six years she taught mathematics and vocal music at a Carlisle, Pennsylvania, boarding school for young women, declining the position of Vice-Principal of the Mary Institute in 1870 to marry James Lee Gillogly. Gillogly was born on December 23, 1854, in Lancaster, Erie County, New York, and graduated first in his class at St. Stephen's College, Annandale, New York in 1867. Three years later he graduated from the Berkeley Divinity School, Middletown, Connecticut. See Thelma Ellis, *Church of the Good Shepherd, Ogden, Utah: A Short History*, (pamphlet, Ogden, 1992), and L. Lucelia Webster Gillogly, "Early Missionary Life in Ogden, Utah," Alameda, California, January 1900, Accn 426 Bx 57 Fd 9.
86. Ibid.
87. Ibid.
88. Ibid.
89. Ibid.
90. Ibid.
91. Daniel S. Tuttle to Lydia Lucelia Webster Gillogly, March 7, 1881, Thelma S. Ellis Collection, D. A.
92. A. J. Simmonds, *The Gentile Comes to Cache Valley* (Logan: Utah State University Press, 1976), p. 9.
93. Ibid., p. 26.
94. Quoted in Brigham D. Madsen, *Corinne, The Gentile Capital of Utah* (Salt Lake City: Utah State Historical Society, 1980), p. 203.
95. Ibid., p. 204.

96. Ibid., p. 205.
97. Ibid.
98. *Salt Lake Tribune*, May 4, 1880.
99. *Salt Lake Tribune*, October 31, 1880.
100. Tuttle, *Missionary*, p. 350.
101. Ibid.
102. *Journal of the Third Annual Convocation of the Missionary District of Utah and Idaho*, 1885, p. 17.
103. "Thirteenth Annual Report of the Bishop of Montana, Idaho, and Utah," 1879 (microfilm copy without publication data, Archives of the Episcopal Diocese of Missouri), p.2.
104. "Sixteenth Annual Report of the Missionary Bishop of Utah and Idaho," 1882 (microfilm copy without publication data, Archives of the Episcopal Diocese of Missouri), p. 2.
105. *Journal of the Fourth Annual Convocation of the Missionary District of Utah and Idaho*, 1886.
106. Mary S. Donovan, "Women Missionaries in Utah," *Anglican and Episcopal History* 66, no. 2 (1997): 159.
107. Tuttle, *Missionary*, p. 272. See also "In Memoriam," *The Spirit of Missions*, January 1873, pp. 79–80. A stained glass window in St. Mark's Cathedral commemorates the life of Emily Pearsall. The Bavarian firm, Franz Mayer of Munich, made at least one of the cathedral's early windows (1900), most likely this one. Mayer made windows for the Cathedral of the Madeleine in Salt Lake City in 1906, and St. Peter's Church (Vatican) in Rome.
108. Daniel S. Tuttle, "In Memorium," *Spirit of Missions*, January 1873, pp. 79–80.
109. Tuttle, *Missionary*, p. 249.
110. Mary Sudman Donovan, *A Different Call: Women's Ministries in the Episcopal Church, 1850–1920* (Wilton, CT: Morehouse-Barlow, 1986), p. 127.
111. Tuttle, *Missionary*, p. 467.
112. Tuttle was bishop of Missouri from 1886 to 1923 and presiding bishop, through seniority, from 1903 to 1923.
113. "Twentieth Annual Report," 1886, pp. 1–5.
114. *Daily Evening News*, Salt Lake City, August 26, 1886, p. 2.

Chapter 2

1. Dwyer, *Gentile* (Utah), p. 155; Frederick Quinn, "Abiel Leonard, the Bishop as Builder," *Utah Historical Quarterly*, 72, no. 3 (2004):239–52.
2. Abiel Leonard papers, Western Historical Manuscript Collection–Columbia. http://www. umsystem.edu/whmc/invent/1013.html. (These are Bishop Leonard's father's papers.)

3. *Salt Lake Utah Herald*, December 6, 1903.
4. Abiel Leonard to W. S. Leake, San Francisco, July 6, 1900, p. 131, Accn 426 Bx 11 Fd 1.
5. Quoted in James W. Beless, Jr., "The Episcopal Church in Utah: Seven Bishops and One Hundred Years," *Utah Historical Quarterly* 36, no. 1 (1968): 82.
6. "Western Missionary Work," *The Spirit of Missions*, March 1897, p. 123.
7. "Missionary District of Salt Lake, Abiel Leonard, Bishop" (typed report, n.d. [filed in March 1901]), pp. 371–383, Accn 426 Bx 11 Fd 1.
8. *The Missionary District of Salt Lake, Journal of Convocation*, 1901, p. 24.
9. Abiel Leonard to Rabbi [Louis G.] Reynolds, May 29, 1903, *Nevada and Utah Official Correspondence, June 1898–November 1903*, p. 50, Accn 426 Bx 10.
10. Abiel Leonard to C. H. Schultz, Cleveland, Ohio, February 21, 1901, pp. 325–326, Accn. 426 Bx 11 Fd 1.
11. Lamar, *Far Southwest*, p. 353.
12. Beless, "Episcopal Church," p. 83.
13. Kathleen Irving, "St. Paul's Celebrates Centennial," August 8, 2001, http://www.vernal.com/aug8/so.stpaulschurch.html.
14. *Journal of Convocation*, 1901, p. 24.
15. Beless, "Episcopal Church," p. 83.
16. Abiel Leonard to the Bishop of Pennsylvania, October 6, 1900, p. 276, Accn 426 Bx 10.
17. *Journal of Convocation*, 1901, p. 28.
18. Ibid., p. 13.
19. Abiel Leonard to George H. Cornell, Geneva, New York, July 6, 1900, p. 130, Accn 426 Bx 11 Fd 1.
20. Abiel Leonard to O. E. Ostenson, August 21, 1903, *Nevada and Utah Official Correspondence, June 1898–November 1903*, p. 135, Accn 426 Bx 10.
21. Abiel Leonard to Johnson, January 28, 1902, *Bishop Leonard Copy Book, 1902–1903*, pp. 94–95, Accn 426 Bx 11.
22. [Abiel] Leonard to Hare, August 17, 1903, *Nevada and Utah Official Correspondence, June 1898–November 1903*, p. 129, Accn 426 Bx 10.
23. Abiel Leonard to unidentified diocesan clergy, August 26, 1903, *Nevada and Utah Official Correspondence, June 1898–November 1903*, p. 143, Accn 426 Bx 10.
24. Abiel Leonard to Grout, January 24, 1902, p. 76, *Bishop Leonard Copy Book, 1902–1903*, Accn 426 Bx 11.
25. George C. Hunting to Franklin Spencer Spalding, January 30, 1906, p. 2, D. A.
26. Abiel Leonard to the Bishop of Pennsylvania, October 6, 1900, p. 276, Accn 426 Bx 11.

27. *Journal of Convocation*, 1901, p. 15.
28. Abiel Leonard, regarding the Bishop's house, Salt Lake City, September 22, 1899, Accn 426 Bx 8 Fd 6.
29. Abiel Leonard to John Love, Eureka, Utah, June 4, 1903, *Nevada and Utah Official Correspondence, June 1898–November 1903*, p. 9, Accn 426 Bx 10 Fd 2.
30. Abiel Leonard to G. W. Garth, New York City, December 17, 1901, p. 9, Accn 426 Bx 11.
31. "Articles of Incorporation of The Corporation of the Episcopal Church in Utah, No. 2248," filed by Abiel Leonard with David Dunbar, County Clerk, Salt Lake County, June 29, 1898, D. A.
32. *Journal of Convocation*, 1901, p. 16.
33. Abiel Leonard to F. F. Johnson, Redlands, California, January 28, 1902, pp. 94–95, Accn 426 Bx 11 Fd 2.
34. Abiel Leonard to L. H. Morehouse, Milwaukee, Wisconsin, March 22, 1899, D. A.
35. Susan Lyman, "A Look at Utah's First Hospital," *Deseret News*, n.d. [probably 1978].
36. Halverson and Walden, *St. Mark's Hospital*, pp. 38–40, 50–51.
37. Clark, "Rowland Hall", pp. 281–285 (see chapt. 1, n. 59).
38. James W. Beless, Jr., "The Missionary District of Utah," centennial issue, *The Utah Churchman*, October 1967, D. A.
39. *Journal of Convocation*, 1901, pp. 24–26.
40. A. J. Simmonds, "Strength Out of Zion: A History of St. John's Episcopal Church and the Anglican Presence in Cache Valley," (unpublished manuscript, St. John's Foundation, Logan, Utah, 1985), p. 18, D. A.
41. David Rich Lewis, *Neither Wolf nor Dog: American Indians, Environment, and Agrarian Change* (New York: Oxford University Press, 1994), p. 27.
42. Joseph G. Jorgenson, *The Sun Dance Religion: Power to the Powerless* (Chicago: University of Chicago Press, 1972), pp. 37–38.
43. Lewis, *Neither Wolf nor Dog*, p. 42.
44. "Eleventh Annual," 1877, p. 1.
45. Quoted in Beless, "Episcopal Church," pp. 84–85.
46. Lewis, *Neither Wolf nor Dog*, p. 20.
47. Ibid., p. 49.
48. Jorgenson, *Sun Dance*, p. 50.
49. Ibid., p. 55.
50. F. S. Spalding, "Doing Things Out West," *The Spirit of Missions*, December 1912, pp. 881–883.
51. Abiel Leonard, "A Statement," 1894, Accn 426 Bx 11 Fd 1.
52. Jorgenson, *Sun Dance*, p. 56.
53. Spalding, "Doing Things Out West," p. 882.

54. Abiel Leonard to Henry Y. Satterlee, Salt Lake City, November 8, 1901, Accn 426 Bx 11 Fd 1.
55. Abiel Leonard to Lucy N. Carter, Whiterocks, March 25, 1899, D. A.
56. Abiel Leonard to Bishop Hare, Salt Lake City, March 25, 1899, D. A.
57. [Abiel] Leonard to Major H. P. Myton, Whiterocks, June 27, 1901, pp. 473–474, Accn 426 Bx 11 Fd 1.
58. Abiel Leonard to John F. Weston, July 5, 1901, Accn 426 Bx 11 Fd 1.
59. Grant M. Ford, "An Indian Christmas," *The Spirit of Missions*, May 1907, pp. 368–370.
60. Donovan, "Women Missionaries," pp. 165–170.
61. Lucy Nelson Carter, "What Happens to Some Indian Babies," *The Spirit of Missions*, March 1903, pp. 183–184.
62. Lucy Nelson Carter, "The Story of the Whiterocks Mission," *The Spirit of Missions*, November 1903, pp. 834–835.
63. Ibid.
64. Carter, "Indian Babies," March 1903, pp. 183–184.
65. Katherine Murray's reports are contained in a file under her name in the Archives of the Episcopal Church, Austin, Texas. The report forms from the national church contained a notation, "The Treasurer will await this report at the close of the quarter before sending stipend."
66. Katherine Murray, "With Miss Carter at Whiterocks," *The Spirit of Missions*, September 1903, pp. 673–674.
67. Donovan, "Women Missionaries," 1997, p. 169.
68. Rosa M. Camfield, "Happenings at Whiterocks," *The Spirit of Missions*, July 1907, pp. 140–141.
69. *Salt Lake City Utah Herald*, December 6, 1903.
70. Beless, "Episcopal Church," p. 86.
71. Ibid., pp. 82–86.
72. *Salt Lake City Tribune*, December 3, 1903.
73. *Salt Lake City Utah Inter-Mountain Catholic*, December 5, 1903.

Chapter 3

1. John S. McCormick and John R. Sillito, "Socialists in Power: The Eureka, Utah, Experience, 1907–1925," *Weber Studies* 6 (Spring 1989):1–2. http://weberstudies.weber.edu/archive/archive%20A%20%20Vol.%201-10.3/Vol.%206.1/6.1McCormickSilito.htm; John R. Sillito, "'Prove All Things, Hold Fast That Which Is Good,' Franklin Spencer Spalding: A Christian Socialist Dissenter from Capitalist Values, *Weber Studies* 1 (Spring 1984). http://weberstudies.weber.edu/archive/archive%20A%20%20Vol.%201-10.3/Vol.%201/Sillito.htm.

2. John Howard Melish, *Franklin Spencer Spalding, Man and Bishop* (New York: Macmillan, 1917), p. 46.
3. Ibid., pp. 80–81. See also Chris Bolieu, "Bishop Spalding and the Grand Teton," n.d., p. 9, copy in the author's possession.
4. Ibid., p. 84.
5. Ibid., pp. 236– 237.
6. John R. Sillito, "'A Spiritual and Moral Socialism': Franklin Spencer Spalding and Christian Socialism, 1901–1914," in *Socialism and Christianity in Early 20th Century America*, ed. Jacob H. Dorn (Westport, CT: Greenwood Press, 1998), p. 114.
7. Melish, *Spalding*, p. 85.
8. Ibid., p. 115.
9. Ibid., pp. 254–255.
10. Ibid., p. 249.
11. Irwin Tucker, "Impressions of Bishop Spalding," *The Christian Socialist* [Chicago] no. 18 (November 1914): 3.
12. Quoted in Sillito, "Spiritual and Moral Socialism," p. 117.
13. Melish, *Spalding*, p. 243.
14. Ibid., p. 250.
15. Ibid., p. 244.
16. Ibid., p. 223.
17. Ibid., p. 231.
18. Ibid., p. 232.
19. Ibid., p. 231.
20. Ibid., pp. 232–233.
21. "In Memoriam," edition devoted to Franklin Spencer Spalding, *The Utah Survey*, 2 no. 1 (1914):20–21; *The Christian Socialist* [Chicago] no. 18 (1914): 2.
22. Henry Knox Sherrill, *Among Friends* (Boston: Little, Brown, an Atlantic Monthly Press Book, 1962), p. 41.
23. Melish, *Spalding*, pp. 233–234.
24. Ibid., p. 234.
25. Ibid., p. 127
26. Ibid., p. 286.
27. "Bishop's Annual Address," *Journal of Convocation, Missionary District of Utah*, 1908, p. 21.
28. "Bishop's Annual Address," *Journal of Convocation, Missionary District of Utah*, 1911, p. 29.
29. Franklin S. Spalding, "Some Utah Children a Bishop Knows," *The Spirit of Missions*, February 1909, pp. 114–116.
30. Ibid., p. 118.

31. M. J. Hersey, "The Easter Feast Displacing the Bear Dance," *The Spirit of Missions*, August 1912, p. 596.
32. Lewis, *Neither Wolf nor Dog*, p. 32 (see chapt. 2, n. 41).
33. Hersey, "Easter Feast," p. 596.
34. Ibid., p. 596.
35. Ibid.
36. Jorgenson, *The Sun Dance Religion.*
37. Ibid., p. 25.
38. Ibid., p. 211.
39. Lewis, *Neither Wolf nor Dog*, p. 62.
40. John R. Sillito and Timothy S. Hearn, "A Question of Conscience: The Resignation of Bishop Paul Jones," *Utah Historical Quarterly* 50, no. 3 (1982): 112.
41. Melish, *Spalding*, p. 262.
42. Ibid., pp. 129–130.
43. Ibid., p. 219.
44. Ibid., p. 123.
45. Ibid., p. 124.
46. Ibid., p. 221.
47. *The Christian Socialist* [Chicago] no. 18 (November 1914), p. 8.
48. Sherrill, *Among Friends*, p. 42.
49. David H. Streets, "St. Mary's Episcopal Church," in *Protestant and Catholic Churches of Provo: A Study of the Non-LDS Christian Congregations*, ed. David M. Walden, with the assistance of Charles G. Hidenshield and David H. Streets (Provo, UT: Center for Family and Community History, Brigham Young University, 1986), pp. 71–72; Melish, *Spalding*, p. 125.
50. Melish, *Spalding*, p. 215.
51. Ibid.
52. Ibid., p. 219.
53. "First Annual Address of the Bishop of Salt Lake," May 2, 1905, unpublished draft, pp. 13–14, Accn 426 Bx 1 Fd 6.
54. "Bishop's Annual Address," *Journal of Convocation, Missionary District of Utah*, 1909, pp. 19–20.
55. *Journal of the Convocation, Missionary District of Utah*, 1910, p. 50.
56. "Payroll of Utah Missionaries 1912", Dalgliesh Collection, 1912–1914 Spalding, D. A.
57. Melish, *Spalding*, p. 146.
58. *Journal of Convocation*, 1911, p. 25.
59. F. S. Spalding to Arthur S. Lloyd, New York City, January 11, 1911, RG 52-73-8.

60. "Bishop's Annual Address," *Journal of Convocation, Missionary District of Utah*, 1914, pp. 27–28.
61. James B. Eddie to Franklin Spencer Spalding, December 14, 1905, D. A. A bound transcript of the trial and appeals process and lengthy correspondence on the matter are contained in the Diocesan Archives, Salt Lake City.
62. G. F. Putnam to Franklin Spencer Spalding, December 14, 1905, D. A.
63. G. F. Putnam to Franklin Spencer Spalding, January 29, 1906, D. A.
64. George C. Hunting to Franklin Spencer Spalding, January 30, 1906, p. 1, D. A.
65. Franklin Spencer Spalding to George Y. Wallace, February 1, 1906, D. A.
66. *Utah State Journal* [Ogden], March 7, 1906.
67. *Deseret Evening News*, May 16, 1906. Sexual issues were only hinted at in the paper in 1906. *The Inter-Mountain Republican* explained why in an editorial called "Excusable Silences": "There is a pretty sharp line between offenses of law and offenses of decency. Forbidden acts which offend not only the moral law, but the very fundamentals of the code of man are unclean. . . . No fever for publishing all the news should ever be regarded as warrant for fouling the minds of the young."
68. Percival Watson Woods to John C. Johnes, January 25, 1907, D. A.
69. Unidentified Salt Lake City newspaper clipping, January 8, 1908, D. A.
70. *The Inter-Mountain Republican*, January 9, 1908.
71. "In the Court of Review of the Protestant Episcopal Church in the United States of America for the Sixth Judicial Department as Provided by the Canons for the Government of the Said Protestant Episcopal Church adopted in General Conventions 1789–1904 as Printed for the Convention of 1905," p. 3, n.d., D. A.
72. Ibid., pp. 7–8.
73. Daniel S. Tuttle to Franklin Spencer Spalding, January 16, 1908, D. A.
74. Franklin Spencer Spalding to "Dear Brother" [James B. Eddie], January 24, 1908, D. A.
75. James B. Eddie to Franklin Spencer Spalding, January 27, 1908, D. A.
76. Melish, *Spalding*, p. 163. See also Franklin Spencer Spalding, *Joseph Smith, Jr., as Translator* (Salt Lake City: Arrow Press, 1912; repr. New York: Presiding Bishop and Council, Department of Missions, 1922). Page references are to the reprint by the Episcopal Church; John Sillito and Martha Bradley, "Franklin Spencer Spalding, an Episcopal Observer of Mormonism," *Historical Magazine of the Protestant Episcopal Church* 54 (December 1985): 339–349.
77. Melish, *Spalding*, p. 172.

78. Ibid, pp. 172–173.
79. Susan Young Gates, letters to the editor, *Deseret Evening News*, n.d. Included in a folder of Spalding's newspaper clippings, mostly from that publication between June 1913 and January 1914, Episcopal Church Archives, Salt Lake City, Utah.
80. "Bishop's Annual Address," *Journal of Convocation, Missionary District of Utah*, 1913, p. 22.
81. "Bishop's Annual Address," *Journal of Convocation, Missionary District of Utah*, 1907, p. 19–20.
82. "Bishop's Annual Address," *Journal of Convocation, Missionary District of Utah*, 1909, p. 14.
83. Sara Napper funeral notice, *Salt Lake Tribune*, May 5, 1931.
84. George C. Thomas to Sara Napper, Salt Lake City, September 4, 1908, in F. S. Spalding file, Archives of the Episcopal Church, Austin, Texas.
85. Only a handful of Sara Napper's reports remain, from 1902 to 1904. They are contained in the Archives of the Episcopal Church, Austin, Texas, in a file under her name.
86. Sara Napper, "St. Peter's Mission, Salt Lake," *The Spirit of Missions*, July 1905, pp. 562–563; Sara Napper, "A Land of Promise," *The Spirit of Missions*, October 1920, p. 660.
87. Napper, "A Land of Promise", pp. 659–661.
88. Quoted in Donovan, "Women Missionaries," p. 163.
89. *Journal of Convocation*, 1909, p. 14.
90. *Journal of Convocation*, 1910, p. 18.
91. Ibid.
92. Mary Latimer James, M. D., "A Medical Missionary in Utah," *The Spirit of Missions*, May 1910, p. 342.
93. Mary Latimer James, M. D., "Some of My Ute Patients," *The Spirit of Missions*, September 1910, pp. 743–745.
94. *Journal of Convocation*, 1914, p. 24 (see n. 64).
95. F. S. Spalding, "Making New Friends in Utah," *The Spirit of Missions*, October 1912, p. 762.
96. Ibid., p. 765.
97. Ibid., p. 767.
98. *Journal of Convocation*, 1909, pp. 17–18. See also Franklin Spencer Spalding, "Christian Unity," *The Atlantic Monthly*, (vol. 111) 1913, pp. 640–649.
99. Melish, *Spalding*, p. 35.
100. Ibid., p. 119.
101. Ibid., pp. 246–47.
102. Ibid., pp. 286–87.
103. Melish, *Spalding*, pp. 287–288.

104. Ibid., p. 289.
105. Ibid., pp. 149–150.
106. T. S. Pengdergrass to Franklin Spencer Spalding, December 10, 1907, St. Mark's Hospital, D. A.
107. "A Memorial for a Valiant Leader," *The Spirit of Missions*, July 1907, pp. 551–554.
108. Melish, *Spalding*, p. 150.
109. Ibid., p. 151.
110. Ibid., p. 153.
111. *Journal of Convocation*, 1909, pp. 22–23 plus Appendix.
112. *Journal of Convocation*, 1911, p. 26.
113. *Journal of Convocation*, 1909, p. 11.
114. Spalding–Jefferd correspondence, Accn 426 Bx 14 Fd 14. Underlinings are in the original; I have made minor modifications of spellings and abbreviations.
115. F. S. Spalding to J. W. Wood, copy of letter, September 26, 1912, Accn 426 Bx 14 Fd 1.
116. Melish, *Spalding*, pp. 262–263.
117. Ibid., p. 292.
118. *The Evening Tribune*, Salt Lake City, September 26, 1914.
119. Melish, *Spalding*, p. 293.
120. *The Salt Lake Tribune*, September 29, 1914.

Chapter 4

1. One Tuttle-Jones photo is contained in the Utah State Historical Society Collection, no 726.53—Episcopal Church—Utah Convocation (1917) p. 1.
2. *The Episcopal Church News, Missionary District of Utah*, January 28, 1917, p. 2.
3. Jones Day Book, p. 55, Dalgliesh Collection, 1914–1915 Bishop Jones, D. A.
4. Paul Jones, "On the Road to Utah," *The Spirit of Missions*, April 1911, pp. 305–306.
5. Ibid., p. 306.
6. Paul Jones, letter to the editor, *The Spirit of Missions*, August 1917, p. 559.
7. Ibid.
8. "St. Paul's, Vernal, Utah," *Exalt*, November–December 1977, p. 3.
9. Quoted in Sillito and Hearn, "A Question of Conscience," p. 210.
10. John Howard Melish, *Paul Jones, Minister of Reconciliation* (New York: Fellowship of Reconciliation, 1942), p. 2.
11. Ibid., p. 23.
12. Simmonds, "Strength Out of Zion," pp. 34–35.

13. A near complete set of *The Portal* is contained in the Utah State University Special Collections and Archives, Logan.
14. "Local Minister Named Utah Episcopal Bishop," 1914, newspaper clipping in Accn 426 Bx 15 Fd 2.
15. Melish, *Paul Jones*, p. 22.
16. Paul Jones, *Points of Contact: A Consideration for Dissatisfied Latter-day Saints* (Salt Lake City, Utah: Arrow Press, 1801), p. 12.
17. "Local Minister Named Utah Episcopal Bishop".
18. Melish, *Paul Jones*, pp. 24–25.
19. Ibid., p. 25.
20. Sillito and Hearn, "Question of Conscience," p. 219.
21. Quoted in Sillito and Hearn, "Question of Conscience," p. 210.
22. Melish, *Paul Jones*, p. 10
23. Sillito and Hearn, p. 219.
24. Thompson also gave the large grillwork screen (1924) that divides the sanctuary from the chancel in the cathedral as a memorial.
25. "Bishop's Annual Address," *Journal of Convocation, Missionary District of Utah*, 1917, p. 25.
26. *Journal of the Proceedings of the Eighth Annual Convocation of the Protestant Episcopal Church in the Missionary District of Utah,* 1915, Appendix 12.
27. *Journal of Convocation*, 1917, pp. 65–66.
28. Ibid., p. 31.
29. "Agreement Between Bishop and Cathedral Organization, Joint Act, January 18, 1917," Dalgliesh Collection, 1917, D. A.
30. "Bishop's Annual Address," *Journal of Convocation*, 1915, pp. 24–28.
31. Ibid., p. 25.
32. Archdeacon Reese, "When the Church Comes to Some Utah 'Cities,'" *The Spirit of Missions*, May 1917, p. 326.
33. Ibid.
34. Ibid.
35. Maxwell W. Rice, "After a Vacation," *The Spirit of Missions*, November 1917, p. 747.
36. Ibid.
37. Ibid., p. 752.
38. Maxwell W. Rice, "Christmas on the Overland Trail," *The Spirit of Missions*, December 1918, p. 801.
39. Ibid., p. 803.
40. *Journal of Convocation*, 1917, p. 24.
41. Paul Jones, "A Hillside Funeral," *The Spirit of Missions*, March 1915, pp. 168–169.

42. "Three Bishops—and a Dean—at the 'Four Corners,'" *The Spirit of Missions*, October 1915, pp. 691–692.
43. Omer C. Stewart, *Peyote Religion, a History* (Norman: University of Oklahoma Press, 1982) pp. 197–199.
44. *Journal of Convocation*, 1917, p. 27.
45. Grant M. Ford, "An Indian Christmas," *The Spirit of Missions*, May 1907, pp. 355–370.
46. Ibid., p. 369.
47. Ibid.
48. Floyd A. O'Neil, oral interview, Salt Lake City, June 14, 2002.
49. "Report of Indian Work," *Journal of Convocation*, 1917, p. 44.
50. Floyd O'Neil, oral interview, Salt Lake City, June 14, 2002.
51. Dean L. May, *Utah: A People's History* (Salt Lake City: University of Utah Press, 1987), p. 172.
52. Quoted in Sillito and Hearn, "Question of Conscience," p. 214.
53. Ibid, p. 222.
54. "Votes Cast for State Officers and on Constitutional Amendments," and "Nominations for State Officers of Socialist Party," (photocopied documents, n.d. [1916]). I am grateful to Prof. John Sillito for providing copies of these documents.
55. Sillito and Hearn, "Question of Conscience," p. 219.
56. May, p. 172.
57. Prayer composed by John Walcott Thompson, MSS B 672, Bx 1 Fd 2.
58. Daniel S. Tuttle, "Letter from the Presiding Bishop," *The Spirit of Missions*, August 1917, pp. 529–530.
59. Douglas Warren, "Chapter III. The Case of Bishop Paul Jones," in "Freedom of Speech and Political Dissent in the Episcopal Church, 1914–1918" (PhD dissertation, Graduate Theological Union, Berkeley, California, 1979), pp. 172–173. Reproduced copy in Episcopal Diocese Archives, Salt Lake City, Utah.
60. Ibid., p. 178.
61. Elizabeth Twelves Miller, e-mail to the author, March 17, 2004. Miller was Twelves's daughter. She wrote, "Because of the outcome of that conflict my father left Utah in 1919 feeling that he could no longer work there with such opposition in the Utah district. He moved to a more congenial climate in Connecticut."
62. *The Salt Lake Tribune*, July 31, 1917.
63. *Journal of Convocation*, 1917, pp. 29–31.
64. Arthur B. Lloyd to J. Walcott Thompson, Salt Lake City, September 28, 1917, Accn 426 Bx 15 Fd 5.

65. Ibid.
66. *The Salt Lake Tribune*, October 3, 1917.
67. Ibid.
68. William W. Fleetwood to Paul Jones, Salt Lake City, October 4, 1917, Accn 426 Bx 15 Fd 5.
69. Paul Jones to "Dear Friend," October 8, 1917, Accn 426 Bx 15 Fd 5.
70. George M. Marshall to Paul Jones, Salt Lake City, n.d, Accn 426 Bx 15 Fd 5.
71. George M. Marshall to Daniel S. Tuttle, St. Louis, October 5, 1919, Accn 426 Bx 15 Fd 5.
72. George M. Marshall to William Lawrence, Chicago, October 19, 1917, Accn 426 Bx 15 Fd 5.
73. Ibid.
74. Edwin T. Lewis to Council of Advice, Logan, Utah, October 29, 1917, Accn 426 Bx 15 Fd 5.
75. J. Wesley Twelves to William F. Bulkley, October 17, 1917, Accn. 426 Bx 15 Fd 5.
76. Warren, "Case," pp. 213–214.
77. "Report of the Commission in re Case of Bishop Jones of Utah," December 12, 1917, Accn 426 Bx 15 Fd 5. Also Warren, "Case," pp. 259–260.
78. Ibid.
79. Ibid., p. 258.
80. "Report of the Commission," p. 2.
81. Ibid.
82. Ibid.
83. "Bishop Asked to Resign Has Not Changed His Views," *St. Louis Post Dispatch*, December 13, 1917.
84. Paul Jones to Daniel S. Tuttle, December 20, 1917, *The Living Church*, p. 341, Accn 426 Bx 15 Fd 5.
85. Paul Jones to George M. Marshall, December 20, 1917, Accn 426 Bx 15 Fd 5.
86. *Journal of Convocation*, 1917, p. 26.
87. Ibid.
88. "Minutes of the Meeting of the Council of Advice of the Missionary District of Utah," Salt Lake City, Utah, March 29, 1918, Accn 426 Bx 15 Fd 5.
89. Warren, "Case," p. 293.
90. "Report of the Commission," p. 2.
91. Warren, "Case," p. 296.
92. William B. Spofford to the author, September 8, 2002.
93. Melish, *Paul Jones*, p. 56.
94. "Resolution 1991-A120, Consider Eighteen Proposed Commemorations for the Church Calendar, General Congregation," *Journal of the General Convention of the Episcopal Church*, 1992, p. 825. See also Michelle J.

Kinnucan, "The Christian Witness of Bishop Paul Jones," *The Record* [Detriot], October 2002, http://www.the-record.org/0210/jones.html

Chapter 5

1. Jane Moulton Stahl (Moulton's granddaughter), oral interview, Boston, October 7, 2002.
2. James W. Beless, Jr., "Episcopal Church," p. 92.
3. Lucile May Francke, "Biography: The Rt. Rev. Arthur Wheelock Moulton, S. T. D.," Lucile May Francke Papers, 1892–1952, pp. 1–3, MSS B 11 Fd 5. Ms. Francke included her personal astrological charts in the archival collection as well.
4. Jane Moulton Stahl, e-mail to the author, June 21, 2002.
5. Ibid.
6. John P. Moulton, "Biographical Sketch of Arthur W. Moulton," (typescript, 1991), copy provided by Jane Moulton Stahl, in the author's possession.
7. Betty Dalgliesh, oral interview, Salt Lake City, April 12, 2002.
8. Thelma S. Ellis, oral interview, Ogden, Utah, June 24, 2002.
9. *Deseret News*, May 12, 1928.
10. *Salt Lake Tribune*, November 8, 1926.
11. David O McKay diary excerpt, September 8, 1951, D. A.
12. Arthur W. Moulton to Lewis B. Franklin, New York City, August 24, 1934, RG 55-3-47.
13. Arthur W. Moulton to Carroll M. Davis, New York City, February 28, 1928, D. A.
14. Arthur W. Moulton to Carroll M. Davis, New York City, April 24, 1929, RG 55-3-52.
15. Lewis B. Franklin, Treasurer, to the National Council, February 6, 1933, RG 55-3-52.
16. Arthur W. Moulton to Lewis B. Franklin, New York City, August 24, 1935, RG 553.
17. Clark, "Rowland Hall," pp. 286–289.
18. Obert C. Tanner, *One Man's Journey in Search of Freedom* (Salt Lake City: Humanities Center, University of Utah, 1994), pp. 190–191.
19. *Proceedings of the Sixteenth Annual Convocation of the Missionary District of Utah*, (Salt Lake City, 1923), p. 28.
20. *Proceedings of the Thirtieth Convocation of the Missionary District of Utah*, (Salt Lake City, 1937), p. 36.
21. *Proceedings of the Sixteenth Convocation*, 1923, p. 28.
22. Rev. F. B. Bartlett's survey, 1928, p. 3, Accn 426 Bx 34 Fd 1.
23. Ibid., p. 2.

24. Ibid., p. 7.
25. Ibid., p. 2.
26. Ibid., p. 8.
27. Ibid., p. 9.
28. Ibid., p. 3.
29. Ibid., p. 11.
30. Ibid., p. 10.
31. Ibid., p. 16.
32. *Proceedings of the Thirteenth Annual Convocation of the Missionary District of Utah*, (Salt Lake City, 1920), p. 38; *Proceedings of the Twenty-Fourth Annual Convocation of the Missionary District of Utah*, (Salt Lake City, 1931), p. 67.
33. Arthur W. Moulton to Carroll M. Davis, New York City, February 27, 1929, Dalgliesh Collection 1925–1929, D. A.
34. Thomas G. Alexander, "From War to Depression," in *Utah's History*, ed. Richard D. Poll, with the assistance of Thomas G. Alexander, Eugene E. Campbell, and David E. Miller (Logan: Utah State University Press, 1989), pp. 463–466.
35. Quoted in May, *People's History*, p. 177.
36. Arthur W. Moulton to Howard Chandler Robbins, New York City, February 26, 1934, Howard Chandler Robbins Collection of Bishops' Papers, General Theological Seminary Library, New York City.
37. Arthur W. Moulton to Howard Chandler Robbins, December 4, 1929, Howard Chandler Robbins Collection of Bishops' Papers, General Theological Seminary Library, New York City.
38. Arthur W. Moulton to Howard Chandler Robbins, n.d. [1932?], Howard Chandler Robbins Collection of Bishops' Papers, General Theological Seminary Library, New York City.
39. Recipe for St. Michael's pudding or Episcopal Church pudding, Thelma Ellis Collection, D. A.
40. *Proceedings of the Eighteenth Annual Convocation of the Missionary District of Utah* (Salt Lake City, 1925), p. 17.
41. Moulton, "Sketch of Arthur W. Moulton."
42. *Proceedings of the Twenty-Seventh Convocation of the Missionary District of Utah* (Salt Lake City, 1934), p. 27.
43. Thelma S. Ellis to the author, November 3, 2003.
44. Thelma S. Ellis, oral interview, Ogden, Utah, June 23, 2002.
45. *Proceedings of the Thirtieth Annual Convocation*, p. 13.
46. *Proceedings of the Twenty-Fifth Convocation of the Missionary District of Utah* (Salt Lake City, 1932), p. 46.

47. *Proceedings of the Twenty-Ninth Annual Convocation of the Missionary District of Utah* (Salt Lake City, 1936), p.35; *Proceedings of the Eighteenth Annual Convocation*, p. 50.
48. *Proceedings of the Thirty-First Annual Convocation of the Missionary District of Utah* (Salt Lake City, 1938), p. 33.
49. *Proceedings of the Eighteenth Annual Convocation*, pp. 33–41.
50. *Proceedings of the Twenty-Ninth Annual Convocation*, p. 30.
51. John Dixon Stewart, oral interview, Salt Lake City, June 12, 2002.
52. Alwin E. Butcher to Franklin D. Roosevelt, Washington, D. C., October 9, 1935. http://newdeal.feri.org/clergy/cl019.htm.
53. *The Utah Trust: The Episcopal Church Paper in Utah*, November 1920, p. 10, Accn 426 Bx 34 Fd 4.
54. Bartlett's survey, p. 5.
55. May, *People's History*, p. 175.
56. Ibid., pp. 489–490.
57. Ibid., pp. 31–32.
58. *Proceedings of the Tenth Annual Convocation of the Missionary District of Utah* (Salt Lake City, 1920), pp. 28–29.
59. *Proceedings of the Twenty-Fourth Convocation*, pp. 17–18.
60. Halverson and Walden, *St. Mark's Hospital*, pp. 77–95.
61. "Flames Ravage Historic St. Mark's Cathedral Causing Heavy Damage; Rebuilding Plan to be Considered," *Salt Lake Telegram*, March 31, 1935. The cathedral was given two Tiffany Studio stained glass windows in 1916, one in 1929 (the Thompson "Resurrection" window) and on in 1936 ("Christ on the Road to Emmaus," in memory of Bishop Spalding). Following the 1935 fire when the Resurrection window was badly damaged St Mark's records note that "May Dascher took (the) glass to Tiffany in a suitcase" to New York for repairs.
62. *Proceedings of the Eighteenth Annual Convocation*, p. 27.
63. Ibid., p. 28.
64. "Nonprofit Corporations," *Revised Statutes of Utah 1933*, Chapter 6, 1–15.
65. Tuttle, *Missionary*, p. 391.
66. "Joint Act", signed by Paul Jones, Bishop of Utah, January 18, 1917, ratified by the Vestry, January 10, 1917, D. A.; "Articles of Incorporation of St. Mark's Episcopal Cathedral Parish, Inc.," August 30, 1985, D. A.
67. "St. Mark's Cathedral Parish, Annual Report of the Parish Treasurer for the Year 1937," Dalgliesh Collection 1935–1939, D. A.
68. "You are Invited to Attend," Dalgliesh Collection 1935–1939, D. A.
69. *Salt Lake Tribune*, November 27, 1927.
70. *Salt Lake Tribune*, November 26, 1927.

71. Ibid.
72. May, *People's History*, p. 185.
73. Ibid., pp. 498–500.
74. Ibid., p. 183.
75. John E. Christensen, "The Impact of World War II," in *Utah's History*, pp. 504–5.
76. During the war, over 62,000 Utah soldiers served at home, abroad, or in other states, and more than 3600 died. See Christensen, "Impact," p. 508.
77. Owanah Anderson, *Jamestown Commitment: The Episcopal Church and the American Indian* (Cincinnati, OH: Forward Movement Publications, 1988), p. 107.
78. Quoted in Anderson, p. 106.
79. Arthur W. Moulton, "Bishop's Day in the Basin," *The Spirit of Missions*, January 1923, p. 10.
80. *The Utah Trust: The Episcopal Paper in Utah*, January 1921, p. 7, Accn 426 Bx 34 Fd 4.
81. Rosa Camfield, "Letters from U. T. O. Missionaries," *The Spirit of Missions*, July 1922, pp. 468–471.
82. Bartlett's survey, p. 24.
83. Ibid.
84. Ibid.
85. Walter Preston Cable to Arthur W. Moulton, "Annual Report of Activity, St. John's Church, Logan, Utah, January 28, 1944," MSS 77 Bx 4 Fd 2.
86. Walter Preston Cable to Arthur W. Moulton, Salt Lake City, April 3, 1943, MSS 77 Bx 4 Fd 1.
87. "Observations and Impressions in the Pacific North-West," sent by Mr. Merrix, 1947, RG 553.
88. *Proceedings of the Thirty-Ninth Annual Convocation of the Missionary District of Utah* (Salt Lake City, 1946), p. 40.
89. *Proceedings of the Fortieth Convocation of the Missionary District of Utah* (Salt Lake City, 1947), p. 24.
90. *New York Times*, April 7, 1951.
91. *Salt Lake Tribune*, April 7, 1951.
92. "Appendix to Hearings before the U. S. Congress, House Committee on Un-American Activities," in *Communist Political Subversion* (Washington, DC: U. S. Government Printing Office, 1957), vol. 2, Exhibit 159A, pp. 7152-7153.
93. Ibid.
94. *Reports of the Subversive Activities Control Board* (Washington, DC: U. S. Government Printing Office, 1966), vol. 2, p. 394.

95. Ibid.
96. *Salt Lake Tribune*, April 7, 1951.
97. Moulton's FBI file was obtained by his granddaughter, Jane Moulton Stahl, who shared it with the author.
98. James W. Beless, Jr., oral interview, Salt Lake City, June 20, 2002.
99. Jane Moulton Stahl, oral interview, Boston, October 3, 2002.
100. John W. Sherman, *A Communist Front at Mid-Century: The American Committee for Protection of Foreign Born, 1933–1959* (Westport, CT: Praeger, 2001), pp. 142–150.

Chapter 6

1. "Consecration of Bishop Clark," *The Living Church*, December 15, 1946, p. 6.
2. Ellis interview, June 23, 2002.
3. "Afterthoughts B," Clark report on 1946 visit to St. Christopher's, p. 6, Accn 426 Bx 57 Fd 22.
4. "Utah Looks to the Future," Accn 426 Bx 17 Fd 3. Erroneously attributed to Watson.
5. Ibid., p. 8.
6. Stephen C. Clark, "A Suggested Ten Year Program for the Missionary District of Utah, 1949 to 1959," D. A.
7. Mrs. F. H. Moreland, "The Early History of All Saints"(two page typescript, n.d.), D. A.
8. James W. Beless, Jr. to the author, September 3, 2002.
9. Moreland, "Early History."
10. Clark, "Ten Year Program," p. 6.
11. Ibid., p. 5.
12. Ibid., p. 4.
13. Stephen C. Clark to George A. Wieland, April 27, 1949, RG 553.
14. Clark, "Ten Year Program," p. 12.
15. Ibid., p. 14.
16. Ibid., p. 11.
17. Clark, "Ten Year Program," p. 17.
18. Ibid., pp. 15–17.
19. Ibid., p. 18.
20. Ibid., p. 19.
21. Ibid., p. 20.
22. Clark to Wieland, April 27, 1949.
23. Ibid., p. 22.

24. Ibid., p. 23.
25. Penciled caption on the back of a photograph of Hogben and posse, Utah State Historical Society photo collection, C-136, Bx 1, Fd 12, #7.
26. Clark, "Ten Year Program," p. 25.
27. Ibid., p. 3.
28. *Proceedings of the Fortieth Convocation*, 1947, p. 28.
29. *The Episcopal Churchman of Utah*, May 1947.
30. "Canons of the Missionary District of Utah of The Protestant Episcopal Church in the United States of America (1949)," D. A.
31. Clark, "Ten Year Program," p. 8.
32. Ibid.
33. Ibid., p. 9.
34. William Fisher Lewis, "The Bishop's Convocation Address, 1951," (typescript, April 1, 1951), D. A., p. 6.
35. Anderson, *Jamestown Commitment*, p. 90 (see chapt. 5, n. 79).
36. Marjorie S. May, *The Highly Adaptable Gospel: A Journey through the Life of H. Baxter Liebler* (Chicago: dv polymedia, 2003), p. 90.
37. William J. Hannifin, oral interview, Tooele, Utah, June 12, 2002.
38. Wayne L. Pontious, oral interview, Erie, Kansas, March 29, 2002.
39. H. Baxter Liebler to James W. Post, February 20, 1945, Accn 426 Bx 31 Fd 7.
40. Joan E. Liebler, oral interview, Moab, Utah, April 2, 2002. Over forty boxes of H. Baxter Liebler's papers are in MSS 11. Also useful in the study of Liebler is a film by April Chabries Haws, *A River in the Desert* (Provo, UT: Brigham Young University, 2000).
41. Hannifin interview, June 12, 2002; May, *Gospel*, pp. 126–128.
42. H. Baxter Liebler, "The Social and Cultural Patterns of the Navajo Indians," *Utah Historical Quarterly* 30, no. 4 (Fall 1962): 321.
43. H. Baxter Liebler, *A Voice in the Desert*, 5th printing (Bluff, UT: St. Christopher's Mission, 1954).
44. Robert S. McPherson, "'He Stood for Us Strongly': Father H. Baxter Liebler's Mission to the Navajo," *American Indian Culture and Research Journal* 23, no. 2 (1999): 117.
45. May, *Gospel*, pp. 45–49.
46. Ibid., p. 115.
47. Quoted in H. Baxter Liebler, *Boil My Heart for Me* (New York: Exposition Press, 1969), p. 173.
48. McPherson, "He Stood for Us," p. 119.
49. Ibid., p. 118.
50. Pontious interview, March 29, 2002.
51. H. Baxter Liebler, "Saint Christopher's Mission to the Navajo, Bluff, Utah, Tenth Anniversary," 1953, pp. 2–3, MSS 11.

52. Joan Liebler, oral interview, Moab, Utah, April 1, 2002. The Navajo spoke of her as "She-who-cries-a-lot." The manuscripts Liebler left include a Roman Catholic priest's translation into Navajo of "St. Patrick's Breastplate," but Liebler never used it, despite the similarities of its content to the Blessing Way.
53. This copy of the After-Mass Prayer, St. Christopher's Mission to the Navajo, Bluff, Utah, was given to the author on March 20, 2002, by Marjorie S. May, who worked among the Navajo and wrote a master's thesis on Father Liebler at the Salt Lake Theological Faculty. I have adapted the English translation to fit the cadences of modern English usage. The original is contained in May, *Gospel*, p. 155.
54. Liebler, "Social and Cultural Patterns," p. 321.
55. Hannifin interview, June 12, 2002.
56. H. Baxter Liebler, "Christian Concepts and Navaho Words," *Utah Humanities Review* 2, no. 2 (1948), p. 174.
57. McPherson, "He Stood for Us," p. 122.
58. Liebler, *Boil My Heart*, p. 30.
59. Ibid., p. 114.
60. Ibid., pp. 55–56.
61. McPherson, "He Stood for Us," p. 125.
62. H. Baxter Liebler, *Autumn 1962 Newsletter*, St. Christopher's Mission to the Navajo, Bluff, Utah, p. 5.

Chapter 7

1. "*Murder in the Cathedral* by T. S. Eliot," St. Margaret's Chapel, Rowland Hall School, February 19, 20, 22, 1959," Accn 426 Bx 17 Fd 15.
2. Richard S. Watson to Anne Pannell, Sweet Briar, Virginia, August 10, 1967, Accn 426 Bx 5 Fd 4.
3. Richard S. Watson to Paul B. Baughman, Logan, Utah, December 14, 1956, D. A.
4. Watson to Pannell, August 10, 1967.
5. Richard S. Watson to Bishop of Olympia, Seattle, March 6, 1951, Accn 426 Bx 17 Fd 1.
6. Letter to Bishop Bayne [unknown author], January 14, 1951, Accn 426 Bx 17 Fd 1.
7. Watson Consecration program, May 1, 1951, Accn 426 Bx 17 Fd 2.
8. "Parishes, January 1952 for 1951," Accn 426 Bx 18 Fd 14.
9. Richard S. Watson to George, Good Friday, 1952, p. 2, D. A.
10. Richard S. Watson to William Shattuck, Mason City, Iowa, October 26, 1964, Accn 426 Bx 17 Fd 3.

11. Frances B. Affleck to Richard S. Watson, Salt Lake City, January 14, 1959, D. A.
12. [Richard S.] Watson to unnamed recipient, Good Friday 1952, Accn 426 Bx 12 Fd 13.
13. Ibid., p. 5.
14. James W. Beless, Jr. to the author, September 2, 2002.
15. "1955 Convocation Address," pp. 2–4, Accn 426 Bx 18 Fd 20.
16. Richard S. Watson to Willliam A. Wright, New York City, April 29, 1957, Accn 426 Bx 17 Fd 7; "Work Begins on Additions to St. Mark's Cathedral," undated press release, D. A.
17. Centennial Organ dedicatory concert, September 17, 1967, D. A.
18. "Parishes, 1959," Accn 426 Bx 18 Fd 15.
19. Richard S. Watson to Victor Lallier, Dallas, October 20, 1960, Accn 426, Bx 17, Fd 16.
20. Tony Larimer, oral interview, Salt Lake City, June 20, 2002.
21. J. A. Frazer Crocker, Jr. was interviewing with Watson for a position at St. Mary's, Provo. "I went over to a hotel in Manhattan, a crummy second- or third-class hotel with a room on an air shaft. He told me how poor Utah was and how much room there was for work there. I tried to call him next day at the hotel, but they said he had checked out. He told me he would be in New York another four or five days. I called the office and they said, 'Oh, he's at the Waldorf Astoria.' He also had a pair of shoes with a hole in the sole. I never saw him with crummy shoes again." J. A. Frazer Crocker, Jr., oral interview, Eugene, Oregon, September 20, 2002.
22. Beless interview, Salt Lake City, June 20, 2002.
23. Betty Dagliesh, oral interview, Salt Lake City, March 8, 2002; also Crocker interview, September 20, 2002.
24. "1955 Convocation Address," p. 5.
25. Richard S. Watson to William S. Lea, Denver, February 10, 1958, Accn 426 Bx 17 Fd 14.
26. Godfrey W. J. Hartzel to Richard S. Watson, Salt Lake City, n.d., Accn 426 Bx 17 Fd 10.
27. Richard S. Watson to A. W. Noel Porter, Sacramento, January 3, 1957, Accn 426 Bx 17 Fd 11.
28. Francis L. Winder, oral interview, Salt Lake City, June 17, 2002.
29. *Pacific Churchman*, March 1958, p. 2.
30. Winder interview, June 17, 2002.
31. Watson to Shattuck, October 26, 1964.
32. Richard S. Watson "To All the Clergy," May 27, 1965, Accn 426 Bx 17 Fd 6.
33. "Bishop's Guidelines for Use of the Experimental Liturgy," December 1967, Accn 426 Bx 17 Fd 24.

34. "Bishop's Convocation Address," St. Mark's Cathedral, October 13, 1967, p. 5, Accn 426 Bx 18 Fd 21.
35. "Summary of Clergy Conference," n.d. [possibly late 1950s, early 1960s], MS 11 Bx 7 Fd 2.
36. Ibid., p 1.
37. Ibid., p. 4.
38. Ibid., p. 6.
39. Richard S. Watson to Thomas R. Miller, Lubbock, Texas, April 8, 1958, Accn 426 Bx 17 Fd 14.
40. "Bishop's Address to Convocation, 1956," pp. 7–8, Accn 426 Bx 18 Fd 20.
41. Ibid., pp. 10–11.
42. "The Missionary District of Utah, Minutes of the Clergy Conference," September 11, 1962, Accn 426 Bx 17 Fd 5.
43. Richard S. Watson to J. Duane Squires, New London, New Hampshire, July 8, 1957, Accn 426 Bx 17 Fd 13.
44. "Convocation Address," October 11, 1959, p. 6, Accn 426 Bx 18 Fd 20.
45. Hannifin interview, June 12, 2002.
46. Richard S. Watson to George H. Quarterman, Amarillo, Texas, January 27, 1958, Accn 426 Bx 19 Fd 2.
47. Ibid., p. 2.
48. Barbara Losse, oral interview, Salt Lake City, October 30, 2002.
49. Larimer interview, June 20, 2002.
50. Halverson and Walden, *St. Mark's Hospital*, pp. 112–113, 250.
51. Richard S. Watson to Kenneth G. Nelson, July 17, 1959, p. 1, Accn 426 Bx 5 Fd 4.
52. Ibid., pp. 2–3.
53. "Brother Juniper's Tales of Navajoland," Hat Rock Retreat Center, 1970, p. 8, D. A.
54. Beless interview, June 20, 2002.
55. Richard S. Watson to Wilson Hunter, May 8, 1967, New York City, D. A.
56. Captain William A. Roberts, Church Army, 1965–1967 typed reports, D. A.
57. Watson to Quarterman, January 27, 1958.
58. Richard S. Watson to Edward Hamilton West, Jacksonville, Florida, December 8, 1960, Accn 426 Bx 17 Fd 16.
59. Richard S. Watson to Henry L. Louttit, Winter Park, Florida, October 5, 1966, Accn 426 Bx 18 Fd 10.
60. Richard S. Watson to clergy, February 14, 1967, Accn 426 Bx 17 Fd 9.
61. Richard S. Watson to Matthew Costigan, New York City, March 25, 1969, p. 1, Accn 426 Bx 17 Fd 9.
62. "Bishop's Address," St. Mark's Cathedral, October 13, 1967, p. 4, Accn 426 Bx 18 Fd 21.

63. "Bishop's Address to Convocation," October 25, 1969, p. 9, Accn 426 Bx 18 Fd 21.
64. Ibid., p. 10.
65. Matthew Gilmour, oral interview, Salt Lake City, June 12, 2002.
66. "Bishop's Address to Convocation," p. 15.
67. Watson to Costigan, March 25, 1969, p. 1.
68. "Utah's 1970 Journal," [November 13–14], Exhibit A, Accn 426 Bx 4 Fd 2.
69. Beless to author, Salt Lake City, Utah, July 9, 2002.
70. Richard S. Watson to Matthew Costigan, New York City, March 2, 1971, Accn 426 Bx 17 Fd 9.
71. Richard S. Watson to Girault M. Jones, New Orleans, November 6, 1958, Accn 426 Bx 17 Fd 14.
72. Richard S. Watson to J. J. Slaughter, Dallas, April 16, 1958, Accn 426 Bx 17 Fd 14.
73. Richard S. Watson to Mrs. Bob Rusack, Santa Monica, California, December 29, 1960, Accn 426 Bx 17 Fd 16.
74. Richard S. Watson to Arthur Lichtenberger, New York City, November 1, 1961, Accn 426 Bx 17 Fd 17.
75. Richard S. Watson to John E. Hines, New York City, January 22, 1971, Accn 426 Bx 17 Fd 23.
76. Beless to author, September 3, 2002.
77. "Bishop Watson Resigns Episcopal Post in Utah," *Salt Lake Tribune*, January 19, 1971.
78. Watson to Costigan, March 25, 1969.
79. Francis L. Winder, oral interview, Salt Lake City, December 17, 2003. Hogben also published a book of poems, *Sainte Chapelle and Other Poems* (Jericho, New York: Exposition Press, 1970). One entry:

    That was springs ago in Paris, when the chestnuts were ablaze,
    And the intervening autumns have bestowed September haze . . .
    But the memory beats inside me like that old Franciscan bell,
    And tomorrow, God be willing, I'll return to Saint Chapelle! (p. 14)

80. Beless interview, July 9, 2002; "Episcopal Ceremony Dedicates New Church," *Salt Lake Tribune*, January 24, 1955; "All Saints to Institute Rector," *Salt Lake Tribune*, January 10, 1959.
81. Virginia Cochrane, oral interview, Price, Utah, February 6, 2004.
82. Centennial issue, *The Utah Churchman*, October 1967, p. 4.
83. Sanford E. Hampton to Frances Wilson, Salt Lake City, July 23, 1974, Accn 426 Bx 26 Fd 8.
84. Streets, "St. Mary's," pp. 77–78.

85. Nelson Abbott, oral interview, Provo, Utah, November 8, 2002.
86. "St. Peter's, June 29, 1958–1997," (mimeographed article drawn from diary of Phyllis Larson, 1997), copy in the author's possession.
87. Charles R. Voris, *The History of St. Michael's Episcopal Church, Brigham City, Utah*, (pamphlet Brigham City, 1993), p. 5.
88. Ibid., p. 9.
89. One priest allegedly remarked of the buffalo, "I wonder how fast they had to run to get that far into the room."
90. "Draft of April 9, 1968," St. Mark's Cathedral, D. A.
91. "Shared Ministry to be Celebrated," *Davis County Clipper*, August 24, 1993, sec. C6.
92. Hall Blankenship, "Talk Delivered to Final Joint Service at BCC," August 29, 1993, (photocopied manuscript) copy in the author's possession.
93. Paula Patterson, oral interview, Salt Lake City, December 5, 2003. Mrs. Patterson also shared notes on the history of St. James, which she uses for a talk with parish newcomers.
94. Debbie Matticks, "St. James Episcopal Church, History, 1963–1986" (photocopied manuscript, Salt Lake City, 1987), copy in the author's possession.
95. "Rectors of St. James," (parish publication, probably 2003), copy in the author's possession.
96. "Parish Profile, St. James Episcopal Church, Salt Lake City, Utah," (pamphlet, 1998), p. 2, copy in the author's possession.
97. Dorothy Alley and Stanley Daniels, oral interviews, West Valley City, Utah, November 17, 2002.
98. "St. Barnabas Episcopal Mission," Tooele, Utah, December 12, 1967, (photocopied article), copy in the author's possession.
99. "Frank Bowman to be New Episcopalian Minister," *Tooele Transcript*, June {day?}, 1974.
100. "Mission Members Renovate Military Chapel to Church," *Tooele Transcript*, February 16, 1968.
101. John W. Traver to Paul J. Taylor, Stockton, California, December 16, 1967.
102. John W. Traver to L. V. De Haney, Brooklyn, New York, October 14, 1973.
103. "St. Barnabas Episcopal Mission."
104. Alan C. Tull oral interview, Salt Lake City, November 15, 2002.
105. "ECW [Episcopal Church Women] Minutes 1951–1952," MSS 77 Bx 6 Fd 1.
106. Richard S. Watson to Paul J. Habliston, Logan, Utah, April 14, 1971, MSS 77 Bx 4 Fd 15.
107. Fred S. Finch, "History of St. David's Episcopal Church, Page, Arizona," N.D. N.P. (probably Page, Arizona, 1962.) Copy in author's possession.
108. Stephen Keplinger to Frederick Quinn, email, August 5, 2004.

Chapter 8

1. Otis Charles, oral interview, San Francisco, May 1, 2002.
2. Otis Charles to Norman Pittenger, Cambridge, England, January 27, 1976, Accn 426 Bx 5 Fd 13.
3. Dalgliesh interview, April 12, 2002.
4. Anne Campbell, oral interview, Seattle, July 7, 2002.
5. Charles interview, May 1, 2002.
6. Ibid.
7. Ibid.
8. "Episcopal Priest Choice for Bishop," *Salt Lake Tribune*, May 16, 1971.
9. Otis Charles to Richard S. Watson, Salt Lake City, Utah, May 27, 1971, Accn 426 Bx 57 Fd 4.
10. James W. Beless, Jr. to Otis Charles, Salt Lake City, June 4, 1971, Accn 426 Bx 5 Fd 3; Charles interview, May 1, 2002.
11. Dr. Matthew Price, Director of Analytical Research, Church Pension Fund, telephone communication with the author, November 17, 2003.
12. Patricia R. McCoy, "Colorful Rites Consecrate Utah's Episcopal Bishop," *Salt Lake Tribune*, September 13, 1971.
13. Minutes of meeting of Consecration Committee, July 15, 1971, Accn 426 Bx 5 Fd 3.
14. Ibid. p. 2. Charles constantly added to his own colorful liturgical wardrobe, aided by Margaret Rowsell, a skilled seamstress and cathedral Altar Guild member.
15. "The Clergy of Utah," Accn 426 Bx 19 Fd 3.
16. Dorothy W. Gordon, oral interview, Salt Lake City, November 7, 2002.
17. Charles interview, May 1, 2002.
18. Ibid.
19. Otis Charles, "Address to Convention," October 8, 1971, p. 1, D. A.
20. Ibid.
21. Ibid.
22. "Coalition 14," Accn 426 Bx 5 Fd 21.
23. Ibid., p. 3.
24. "The Convocation of the Diocese of Utah, Title I, Canon 23, Sections 1 and 2, Convention 1976," MSS 77 Bx 16 Fd 8.
25. "Bishop's Annual Address to Convention," 1973, p. 1, Accn 426 Bx 19 Fd 15.
26. Charles interview, May 1, 2002.
27. "Address to Convention," 1971, p. 5.
28. Meeting notes, Accn 426 Bx 48 Fd 4.

29. Winder interview, June 17, 2002.
30. "Job Description for the Position of Dean, St. Mark's Cathedral," rough draft, December 1973, p. 2, D. A.
31. Otis Charles, oral interview, Minneapolis, August 5, 2003.
32. "Bishop's AnnualAddress," 1973, p. 6.
33. Letter from Otis Charles, American Airlines Flight No. 315, The Feast of St. Mary the Virgin, August 15, 1974, p. 2, Accn 426 Bx 5 Fd 12.
34. Campbell interview, July 7, 2002.
35. Ibid.
36. Francis L. Winder, "The Ogden Covenant: Reflections on an Ecumenical Venture," (unpublished manuscript, Salt Lake City, n.d.), copy in the author's possession.
37. "Convention Address, 1976," MSS 77 Bx 16 Fd 8.
38. Charles interview, May 1, 2002.
39. Otis Charles, pre-involvement questionnaire, Accn 426 Bx 48 Fd 11.
40. "The Bishop of Utah," Accn 426 Bx 48 Fd 4.
41. Sonja B. Wycoff, "St. Jude's: the Story of a Church," *The Episcopalian/ Diocesan Dialogue*, September 1988.
42. *The Utah Churchman*, Vol. 8 No. 4, October 1966, p. 3.
43. "Bishop's Annual Address," 1973.
44. "Description of Ministry, Qualifications and Training of Canon III.8 Priests and Deacons for the Diocese of Utah," May 3, 1978, Accn 426 Bx 48 Fd 8.
45. Ibid., p. 2.
46. Elizabeth Dalaba, oral interview, Clearfield, Utah, May 5, 2002.
47. Dalgliesh interviews, March 8 and April 12, 2002.
48. Dovie M. Hutchinson, oral interview, Salt Lake City, June 13, 2002.
49. Mrs. Ralph J. Anslow to Otis Charles, Provo, Utah, November 27, 1972, Accn 426 Bx 48 Fd 4. The small clergyless St. Andrew's United Episcopal congregation met at St. John's Lutheran Church, Salt Lake City. It was visited by Archbishop C. Dale Dorne in February 1982. See "Episcopal Archbishop Dorne Visits Utah," *The Salt Lake Tribune*, February 20, 1982.
50. "Lights: Easter Vigil," Accn 426 Bx 48 Fd 13.
51. Charles interview , May 1, 2002.
52. Otis Charles to Richard Trelease, Albuquerque, November 13, 1974, Accn 426 Bx 48 Fd 3.
53. Quoted in Alan C. Tull, "On Mormon Baptisms: A Report from Hippo," (unpublished manuscript, n.d.), p. 2, copy in the author's possession.
54. Francis L. Winder, "A Position Paper on the 'Validity' of L. D. S. Baptism," (unpublished manuscript, n.d.), copy in the author's possession.

55. Wesley Frensdorff, "The Dream," in *Reshaping Ministry: Essays in Memory of Wesley Frensdorff*, ed. Josephine Borgeson and Lynne Wilson (Arvada, CO: Jethro Publications, 1990). http://members.shaw.ca/athomas125/vision.htm.
56. Capital punishment ballot, (St. Mark's Cathedral) January 23, 1977, D. A.
57. Robert M. Anderson, oral interview, Monarch Beach, Ca., December 20, 2003.
58. "Utah Clerics React to Execution," *Salt Lake Tribune*, January 18, 1977.
59. William F. Maxwell, oral interview, Port Townsend, Washington, September 16, 2002.
60. Ibid.
61. Bradley S. Wirth, oral interview, Bigfork, Montana, November 8, 2002.
62. Kristen Rogers, "Utah's Missile-Guided Economy," *Beehive History 28* (2002): 18.
63. Edwin B. Firmage, "MX: A Personal Essay," *Beehive History 28* (2002): 26.
64. Charles interview, May 1, 2002.
65. Otis Charles, nuclear testing statement, January 26, 1982, Accn 426 Bx 47 Fd 6.
66. "J. A. Frazer Crocker, Jr.", May 8, 1982, Accn 426 Bx 48 Fd 14.
67. "Christians Urged to Oppose 'Immoral' MX System," *Salt Lake Tribune*, April 13, 1980.
68. "A Commemoration and Celebration of Saints and Martyrs of Our Time," Cathedral Church of St. Mark, Salt Lake City, Utah, October 13, 1978, Accn 426 Bx 5 Fd 21.
69. Otis Charles to President [Gerald] Ford, Washington, D. C., September 3, 1974; Otis Charles to Congressman Wayne Owens, Washington, D. C., September 11, 1974; Otis Charles to President Ford, Washington, D. C., September 11, 1974, all in Accn 426 Bx 5 Fd 12.
70. Charles interview, May 1, 2002.
71. "Navajo Mission Nears Reality," Accn 426 Bx 5 Fd 16.
72. Nancy Pawwinnee, oral interview, Randlett, Utah, November 5, 2002.
73. Clifford Duncan, oral interview, Whiterocks, Utah, October 28, 2002.
74. Charles, interview, May 1, 2002.
75. "Episcopalians Plan High-Rise Housing," *Salt Lake Tribune*, March 17, 1979.
76. Lisa M. Jones, oral interview, Salt Lake City, October 29, 2002.
77. The old hospital site became the temporary home for various medical research companies. Also, the abandoned hospital building proper became the subject of several Salt Lake City ghost stories. Halverson and Walden, *St. Mark's Hospital*, pp. 150–152.
78. "RHMS in Historical Perspective" (typescript, September 25, 2003), provided by Julie A. Barrett and Susan Koles, in the author's possession.

79. Charles interview, May 1, 2002; Peggy Fletcher Stack, "Episcopal Bishop Goes Public, Admits He's Gay," *Salt Lake Tribune*, October 9, 1993.
80. Elvira Charles, oral interview, Salt Lake City, Utah, May 3, 2004.
81. "Bishop Explains Move to Sanction Colleague Who Wed Gay Partner," San Jose/Valley, *Mercury News*, May 10, 2004. Swing added, "I have lived through many of his idiosyncrasies and special insights. Otis is a charming and gifted pilgrim. Now the time has come for him to be retired completely from the Diocese of California."

Chapter 9

1. Winder interview, June 17, 2002 (see chapt. 7, n. 28).
2. George E. Bates, progress report, August 23, 1988, D. A.
3. George E. Bates to William K. Wiegand, Salt Lake City, November 18, 1988, D. A.
4. "Medical Update—Carcinoma of the Larynx," George E. Bates memorandum to Diocese, October 12, 1988, D. A.
5. When they heard of his medical condition, the First Presidency of the Church of Jesus Christ of Latter-day Saints wrote Bates, sending "heartfelt prayers for a timely and complete recovery." The First Presidency recalled that Spencer W. Kimball, one of the members of the Council of the Twelve Apostles, who loved singing, had vocal chord surgery and soon "his raspy speaking voice became almost a hallmark. During his tenure as President of the Church from 1973 to 1985, the membership delighted to hear his words and reverenced his faith and determination." The First Presidency to George E. Bates, Salt Lake City, June 28, 1988, D. A.
6. George E. Bates to Kenneth Kaisch, Fullerton, California, February 8, 1994, D. A.; George E. Bates to Dr. Lonnie Paulos, Salt Lake City, January 23, 1992, D. A.
7. Maxwell interview, September 16, 2002; Charles, interview, June 17, 2002.
8. James S. Eckels, oral interview, Salt Lake City, September 11, 2002; Stephen F. Hutchinson, oral interview, Salt Lake City, September 21, 2002.
9. Ed Freiss, "Mid-November Sale of St. Mark's Set," *Enterprise* [Salt Lake City], October 5, 1987.
10. Ed Bean, "A Lighter Load for Hospital Corp's Frist," *Wall Street Journal*, November 17, 1987.
11. Episcopal Diocese of Utah, press release, August 28, 1987, D. A.
12. Ibid.
13. Memorandum to hospital employees, September 2, 1987, D. A.
14. Anne Campbell, oral interview, Seattle, July 8, 2002.

15. Lincoln Ure, oral interview, Salt Lake City, December 24, 2003.
16. "HCA Acquires St. Mark's Hospital in Salt Lake City," diocesan press release, December 30, 1997, D. A.
17. George E. Bates to Edmond L. Browning, New York City, December 3, 1992, D. A.
18. "Liquidating Trust, Balance Sheet, All Departments," July 31, 1991, D. A.
19. George E. Bates to Delbert C. Glover, Boston, November 22, 1998, D. A.
20. Maxwell interview, September 16, 2002.
21. Losse, October 30, 2002.
22. Sheila R. McCann, *Salt Lake Tribune*, December 21, 1996.
23. W. Lee Shaw, "Episcopal Church Makes Major Grant to Help the Homeless," (press release, March 25, 1988).
24. "Episcopal Diocese Gives $1 Million in Grants to Community Groups," *Deseret News*, January 1, 1989.
25. Wirth interview, November 8, 2002.
26. The largest grant recipients included Citizens Against Physical and Sexual Abuse, a Logan-based program for the children of battered women; the Indian Alcoholism Counseling and Recovery House Program; Catholic Community Services; the Easter Seal Society of Utah; United Way of the Great Salt Lake Area; the Utah Girl Scouts Council; the Indian Walk-in Center; and St. Paul's Episcopal Church, which received $40,000 for a housing project for persons with AIDS.
27. George E. Bates, certification of corporate seal, December 1, 1987, D. A. The initial trust was created by Bishop Charles to hold $30,000 he had saved. Charles wanted the flexibility to move quickly and buy land if he needed to without the slow-moving process of seeking Standing Committee authorization. Information from Otis Charles, oral interview, Minneapolis, August 7, 2002.
28. The provision for a corporate sole appears first in the *Utah Code* (1901) and remains in subsequent versions, including the *Revised Statutes of Utah*, Title 16, Chapter 7-1-14 (1933 and 1953).
29. When the 1995 profile for Bates's successor was prepared by a diocesan committee, some of the challenges facing the diocese, it said, were to "embrace and balance the range of emotional responses to the rapid change in Diocesan finances, such as joy, anger, gratitude, confusion and anxiety" and "discern the appropriate degree of disclosure of financial matters involving the Diocese and the Corporation of the Bishop." See *Profile for a Bishop Coadjutor*, Episcopal Diocese of Utah, 1995, p. 10, D. A.
30. George E. Bates, "Utah Diocesan Convention Address," May 19, 1989, p. 4, D. A.
31. Ibid.
32. Ibid., pp. 4–5.

33. Ibid. The Bishop concluded the financial section of his 1989 address, "We know that the assets I have described along, with your tithe, will address some of these needs and opportunities. On your part, I plead with you to be patient and gentle." (p. 5)
34. George E. Bates memorandum, Salt Lake City, December 27, 1991, D. A.
35. "January 1992: Bishop's Column," *Diocesan Dialogue*, D. A.
36. Ibid.
37. Hutchinson interview, September 21, 2002.
38. Investment Committee meeting, J. P. Morgan Investment Management, Inc., November 17, 1994. There Robert Gordon said, "Through the year 1995 income needs would be $7.4 million out of an approximately $96 million portfolio." Other places where the seven million figure appear include "total availability in 1992 for distribution should be seven million" in "Meeting of the Investment Subcommittee," Broadmoor, Colorado, August 8–11, 1991, p. 3, D. A. Also, in an untitled Investment Subcommitte minute, it is noted, "For the next ten years we can expect $7,000,000 in income per year" (probably 1991, p. 4). But a lower cap of 5 percent was later set in an untitled document beginning "We have a lot of expenditures," n.d. All documents in D. A.
39. "Episcopal Diocese of Utah—1990 Budget," *Journal of the Eighty-Fifth Convention of the Episcopal Church in Utah*, May 18–20 1990, p. 1, D. A.
40. *Journal of the Eighty-Seventh Convention of the Episcopal Church in Utah*, 1992.
41. "Episcopal Diocese of Utah—1990 Budget," p. 2.
42. The following are representative figures from the *Episcopal Church Annual* (Wilton, CT: Morehouse-Barlow) for the years 1990 to 1996. The first figure is the total number of baptized members for that year, the second is confirmed communicant members, a more accurate reflection of active church membership numbers. In seven years the church gained an increase of 552 new communicant members:

    1990 baptized 4,819–communicant 4,061,
    1991 baptized 5,030–communicant 4,138,
    1992 baptized 5,223–communicant 4,202,
    1993 baptized 6,235–communicant 4,488,
    1994 baptized 5,471–communicant 4,615,
    1995 baptized 5,529–communicant 4,526,
    1996 baptized 5,776 –communicant 4,613.

43. Esther R. Frank to Sheela Patel, Church Pension Fund, New York City, February 28, 1996, D. A. The combined compensation for January 1–June 30 1996, the date of Bates's retirement, was $301,112.

44. "The Bishop's General Fund No. 1, Operating Statement, Twelve Month's Budget vs. Twelve Months Actual Ending December 31, 1995," pp. 1–2, D. A.
45. George E. Bates to Stephen Hutchinson, February 15, 1999, D. A. Church Pension Fund statistics on bishops's compensation were not systematically kept until the early twenty-first century. A 1998 total compensation estimate for bishops was: low $50,000, median $60,000, and high $80,000 or above. More exact figures are available for 2002: low $80,000, median $105,000, and high $120,000 and above. Information from Dr. Matthew Price, Director of Analytical Research, Church Pension Fund, telephone communication with the author, November 17, 2003.
46. Julie Fabre Stewart, oral interviews, Salt Lake City, June 12 and September 13, 2002.
47. Ibid.
48. Dirk Rinehardt Pidcock, e-mail to the author, April 23, 2004.
49. "Diocese of Utah, George and Sue Bates," *New Faces in New Places,* House of Bishops Meeting, San Antonio, Texas, September 19–25, 1986, D. A.
50. Pidcock e-mail, April 23, 2004.
51. William B. Spofford, interview, The Dalles, Oregon, April 20, 2004.
52. "Rt. Rev. George E. Bates, Personnel Profile & Update Form, Utah, June 1, 1987," D. A.
53. "Diocese of Utah, George and Sue Bates."
54. "June Sees Spate of Episcopal Elections," Diocesan Press Service/Episcopal Church Center, DPS 86142, D. A.
55. "The Rt. Rev. George E. Bates, Ninth Bishop of the Diocese of Utah," n.d., D. A.
56. "The Episcopal Diocese of Utah: A Profile," December 1, 1985, D. A.
57. Ibid., p. 16.
58. "The Episcopal Church in Utah, Nominating Committee Report," 1986, pp. 9–10, D. A.
59. "Ninth Episcopal Bishop of Utah is Elected During Convention," *Deseret News,* June 21, 1986.
60. John DeVilbiss, "New Bishop Prefers to be Listener," *Ogden Standard-Examiner,* November 1, 1986, Church News, p. 6.
61. W. Lee Shaw, "Ninth Episcopal Bishop of Utah to be Ordained in Special Service," press release, October 15, 1986, D. A.
62. "The Order of Service for the Ordination and Consecration of George Edmonds Bates as a Bishop in the Church and Ninth Bishop of Utah," October 25, 1986, D. A.
63. Sue & George [Bates], Christmas, 1986, D. A.
64. John De Vilbiss, "New Bishop Prefers to be Listener," *Ogden Standard Examiner,* Church News, November 1, 1986, p. 6.
65. Ibid. p. 7.

66. "Episcopal Bishop Plans to Speak Out on Issues," *Deseret News,* June 23, 1986.
67. DeVilbiss, "New Bishop," p. 1.
68. George E. Bates to Edmond L. Browning, October 16, 1990, D. A.
69. George Bates, "On the Persian Gulf Crisis," *Diocesan Dialogue,* January 1991, p.2.
70. Wirth interview, November 8, 2002.
71. George E. Bates, sermon, June 29, 1996, p. 3, D. A.
72. "Draft Document on Development of Local Ministry–Revised 9/30/92," D. A.
73. George E. Bates to Leopoldo J. Alard, Houston, Texas, December 10, 1986, D. A.
74. William K. Weigand to George E. Bates, Salt Lake City, November 10, 1988, D. A.
75. George E. Bates to William Weigand, Salt Lake City, July 2, 1991, D. A.
76. George E. Bates to William K. Weigand, Salt Lake City, August 8, 1989.
77. Pidcock e-mail, April 23, 2004.
78. George E. Bates to Janis S. Smith, St. George, Utah, August 1, 1994, D. A.
79. George E. Bates to Alfred Painter, St. George, Utah, September 14, 1994, D. A.
80. Sue and George [Bates] to Barbara and Tim, n.d., D. A.
81. George E. Bates to Mr. and Mrs. James Linford, St. George, Utah, September 6, 1994, DA.
82. George E. Bates to Anne Campbell, Seattle, July 15, 1993, D. A.
83. "Homily, Patti and Jeff," January 21, 1996, D. A.
84. George E. Bates, "Lent," *Diocesan Dialogue,* January 26, 1994.
85. Ibid.
86. George E. Bates to all clergy, March 6, 1989, D. A.
87. George E. Bates, "Meditation II: Maundy Thursday," March 31, 1994, p. 4, D. A.
88. George E. Bates, "Maundy Thursday 1990, First Meditation, Bishop to Clergy," extrapolating from Gerald G. May, *Addiction and Grace* (San Francisco: Harper and Row, 1988).
89. George E. Bates, "Utah Diocesan Convention Address," May 19, 1989, D. A.
90. Dalgliesh interview, March 8, 2002.
91. George E. Bates to Peter J. Van Hook, Salt Lake City, April 14, 1992, D. A.
92. Pidcock e-mail, April 23, 2004.
93. Albert J. Coulton, "Pilgrimage with Detours," in *Essays in Ministry,* ed. Walter D. Wagoner, C. Shelby Rooks, and Robert P. Montgomery (Princeton, NJ: Fund for Theological Education, 1967).
94. *A Grace Observed: Sermons by the Reverend Canon Albert J. Colton,* ed. Bradley S. Wirth (Salt Lake City: All Saints Trust, 1994), p. xii.
95. Ibid., p. 550.

96. Ibid., pp. 549–550.
97. Jack C. Potter, oral interview, Salt Lake City, June 21, 2002.
98. The statement in its entirety is reproduced frequently on St. Mark's Cathedral Sunday bulletins.
99. W. Lee Shaw, e-mail to the author, October 30, 2003.
100. Maxwell interview, September 16, 2002.
101. Francis L. Winder, oral interview, Salt Lake City, July 17, 2002.
102. Maxwell interview, September 16, 2002.
103. Alan Sullivan, oral interview, Salt Lake City, November 13, 2002.
104. Pidcock e-mail to the author, April 23, 2004.
105. Alan F. Blanchard, oral interview, New York City, April 27, 2004.
106. George E. Bates, personal evaluation, fall 1991, D. A.
107. Campbell interview, July 8, 2002.
108. Ure interview, December 24, 2003.
109. Eckels interview, September 11, 2002.
110. Kathryn Miller, oral interview, Salt Lake City, February 6, 2004.
111. Spofford, interview, April 20, 2004.
112. Ralph and Mildred Bradley to Corporation of the Bishop, deed of sale, October 4, 1988, DA.; Eckels interview, September 11, 2002.
113. Blanchard interview, April 27, 2004.
114. Bishop William E. Swing of California, an avid golfer and sometime golfing partner with Bates, said, "George was an excellent athlete. He had a fine swing and shots until his health declined." William E. Swing, oral interview, Province VIII Bishop's Meeting, Taipei, Taiwan, Republic of China, January 13, 2004.
115. Julie Quayle to Nola Wayman, memorandum, Salt Lake City, March 13, 1989, D. A.
116. George E. Bates to John Stockton, Salt Lake City, February 13, 1989, D. A.
117. George E. Bates to clergy and spouses, November 20, 1986, D. A.
118. George E. Bates to the clergy of the Diocese of Utah, December 12, 1988, D. A.
119. Hutchinson interview, September 21, 2002.
120. "January 1994 Directory," Episcopal Diocese of Utah, D. A.
121. "Meeting of the Investment Subcommittee," Broadmoor, Colorado Springs, August 9–11, 1991, D. A.
122. "Response to the Bishop's Memo Regarding Three Staff Positions," to Bishop [Bates] and Kathy Miller, October 16, 1990, D. A.
123. *Journal of the Eighty-Sixth Convention of the Episcopal Church in Utah*, May 31–June 2, 1991, p. 38.
124. Eckels interview, September 11, 2002; Judy Hanley, oral interview, Park City, Utah, April 7, 2004.

125. "Episcopal Church Appoints Missionary Priest to Southwest Utah," diocesan press release, September 20, 1988, D. A.
126. Melva Smith, "A History of Grace Church 1981 through January 1996,"(unpublished manuscript, St. George, Utah, n.d.), copy in the author's possession.
127. Quentin F. Kolb, oral interview, Salt Lake City, June 14, 2002.
128. Ibid.
129. Bradley S. Wirth, oral interview, Bigfork, Montana, November 9, 2002.
130. "Funds for Bishop's Weekend," RMG and ERF memorandum, March 6, 1989, D. A.
131. "RHSM in Historical Perspective."
132. R. Kim Davis and T. H. Craine to George E. Bates, Salt Lake City, October 10, 1994, D. A.
133. [George E.] Bates to "Dear and Blessed Family of Utah," October 17, 1994, with a letter to Bates from Doctors R. Kim Davis and T. H. Craine, October 10, 1994, D. A.
134. "Bishop of Episcopal Diocese to Retire for Medical Reasons," *Deseret News*, November 19, 1994.
135. Rustin R. Kimsey, Bishop of Eastern Oregon, "A Homily for George E. Bates," April 6, 1999, D. A.

Chapter 10

1. Utah, at $64,596, was ahead of New York, but behind Connecticut (at $65,450) and the District of Columbia (at $76,102), all of which had higher costs of living. See Dr. Matthew Price, *The 2002 Church Compensation Report*, (New York: Church Pension Fund, June 2003), p. 13.
2. Frensdorff, "The Dream."
3. *Journal of Convocation*, 1914, pp. 27–28.

Bibliography

Books

Anderson, Owanah. *Four Hundred Years: Anglican/Episcopal Mission Among American Indians.* Cincinnati, OH: Forward Movement Publications, 1997.

———. *Jamestown Commitment: The Episcopal Church and the American Indian.* Cincinnati, OH: Forward Movement Publications, 1988.

Bigler, David L. *Forgotten Kingdom: The Mormon Theocracy in the American West, 1847–1896.* Logan: Utah State University Press, 1998.

Conetah, Fred A. *A History of the Northern Ute People.* Edited by Kathryn L. MacKay and Floyd A. O'Neil. Salt Lake City: University of Utah Printing Services, 1982.

Cuch, Forrest S., ed. *History of Utah's American Indians.* Salt Lake City: Utah Division of Indian Affairs / Utah State Division of History, 2000.

D'Azevedo, Warren L., ed. *Great Basin.* Vol. 11, *Handbook of North American Indians,* ed. William Sturtevant. Washington, DC: Smithsonian Institution Press, 1986.

Donovan, Mary Sudman. *A Different Call: Women's Ministries in the Episcopal Church, 1850–1920.* Wilton, CT: Morehouse-Barlow, 1986.

Dwyer, Robert Joseph. *The Gentile Comes to Utah: A Study in Religious and Social Conflict (1862–1890).* Salt Lake City: Western Epics, 2001.

Furness, Norman E. *The Mormon Conflict, 1850–1859.* New York: Greenwood Press, 1977.

Goodell, Jotham. *A Winter with the Mormons.* Edited by David L. Bigler. Salt Lake City: Tanner Trust Fund, University of Utah, 2001.

Halverson, W. Dee and David M. Walden. *St. Mark's Hospital, 1872–1997: A 125-Year Legacy of Quality Health Care in Utah.* Salt Lake City: Heritage Associates, 1998.

Hogben, Joseph Forster. *Sainte Chapelle and Other Poems.* Jericho, NY: Exposition Press, 1970.

Jones, Paul. *Points of Contact: A Consideration for Dissatisfied Latter-day Saints.* Salt Lake City: Arrow Press, 1801.

Jorgensen, Joseph G. *The Sun Dance Religion: Power for the Powerless.* Chicago: University of Chicago Press, 1972.

Lamar, Howard R., ed. *New Encyclopedia of the American West.* New Haven, CT: Yale University Press, 1998.

Lamar, Howard R. *The Far Southwest, 1846–1912: A Territorial History*, rev. ed. Albuquerque: University of New Mexico Press, 2000.

Lewis, David Rich. *Neither Wolf nor Dog: American Indians, Environment, and Agrarian Change.* New York: Oxford University Press, 1994.

Liebler, H. Baxter. *A Voice in the Desert*, 5th printing. Bluff, UT: St. Christopher's Mission, 1954.

———. *Boil My Heart for Me.* New York: Exposition Press, 1969.

Madsen, Brigham D. *Corinne, The Gentile Capital of Utah.* Salt Lake City: Utah State Historical Society, 1980.

May, Dean L. *Utah: A People's History.* Salt Lake City: University of Utah Press, a Bonneville Book, 1987.

May, Gerald G. *Addiction and Grace.* San Francisco: Harper and Row, 1988.

May, Marjorie S. *The Highly Adaptable Gospel: A Journey through the Life of H. Baxter Liebler.* Chicago: dv polymedia, 2003.

McCormick, John S. and John R. Sillito, eds. *A World We Thought We Knew: Readings in Utah History.* Salt Lake City: University of Utah Press, 1995.

Melish, John Howard. *Franklin Spencer Spalding, Man and Bishop.* New York: Macmillan, 1917.

———. *Paul Jones, Minister of Reconciliation.* New York: Fellowship of Reconciliation, 1942.

Milner, Clyde A., II, and Floyd A. O'Neil, eds. *Churchmen and the Western Indians, 1920–1920.* Norman: University of Oklahoma Press, 1985.

Notarianni, Philip F. *Faith, Hope, & Prosperity: The Tintic Mining District.* Eureka, UT: Tintic Historical Society, 1982.

Poll, Richard D., ed. *Utah's History.* With the assistance of Thomas G. Alexander, Eugene E. Campbell, and David E. Miller. Logan: Utah State University Press, 1989.

Powell, Alan Kent, ed. *Utah History Encyclopedia.* Salt Lake City: University of Utah Press, 1994.

Prayer Book and Hymnal. New York: Church Hymnal Corporation, 1986.

Report of the Subversive Activities Board. Vol. 2. Washington, DC: U. S. Government Printing Office, 1966.

Representatives of the Religious Denominations, comps. *World's Fair Ecclesiastical History of Utah.* Salt Lake City: George Q. Cannon and Sons, 1893.

Ricks, Joel E., ed. *The History of a Valley.* With the assistance of Everett L. Cooley. Logan, UT: Cache Valley Centennial Commission, 1956.

Rockwell, Wilson. *The Utes, a Forgotten People.* Denver: Sage Books, 1956.

Sherman, John W. *A Communist Front at Mid-Century: The American Committee for Protection of the Foreign Born, 1939–1959.* Westport, CT: Praeger, 2001.

Sherrill, Henry Knox. *Among Friends.* Boston: Little, Brown, an Atlantic Monthly Press Book, 1962.

Simmonds, A. J. *The Gentile Comes to Cache Valley: A Study of the Logan Apostasies of 1874 and the Establishment of the Non-Mormon Churches in Cache Valley, 1873–1913.* Logan: Utah State University Press, 1976.

Spalding, Franklin Spencer. *Joseph Smith, Jr., As a Translator.* New York: Presiding Bishop and Council, Department of Missions, 1922. First published 1912 by Arrow Press, Salt Lake City.

Stewart, Omer C. *Peyote Religion.* Norman: University of Oklahoma Press, 1982.

Tanner, Obert C. *One Man's Journey in Search of Freedom.* Salt Lake City: Humanities Center, University of Utah, 1994.

Tuttle, David Sylvester. *Missionary to the Mountain West: Reminiscences of Episcopal Bishop Daniel S. Tuttle, 1866–1886.* Forward by Brigham D. Madsen. Salt Lake City: University of Utah Press, 1987. Originally published as *Reminiscencs of a Missionary Bishop.* New York: T. Whittaker, 1906.

U. S. Congress. House. Committee on Un-American Activities. "Appendix to Hearing," *Communist Political Subversion.* Vol. 2. Washington, DC: U. S. Government Printing Office, 1957.

Utley, Robert M. *Frontier Regulars: The United States Army and the Indians, 1866–1891.* Lincoln: University of Nebraska Press, 1973.

Wirth, Bradley S., ed. *A Grace Observed: Sermons by the Reverend Canon Albert J. Colton.* Salt Lake City: All Saints Trust, 1994.

Articles and Book Chapters

Alexander, Thomas G. "From War to Depression," in *Utah's History,* ed. Richard D. Poll, with the assistance of Thomas G. Alexander, Eugene E. Campbell, and David E. Miller. Logan: Utah State University Press, 1989, pp. 463–466.

Beless, James W., Jr. "Daniel S. Tuttle, Missionary Bishop of Utah." *Utah Historical Quarterly* 27, no. 4 (1959): 357–378.

———. "The Missionary District of Utah," centennial issue, *The Utah Churchman,* October 1967.

———. "The Episcopal Church in Utah: Seven Bishops and One Hundred Years." *Utah Historical Quarterly* 36, no. 1 (1968): 77–96.

Christensen, John E. "The Impact of World War II," in *Utah's History,* ed. Richard D. Poll, with the assistance of Thomas G. Alexander, Eugene E. Campbell, and David E. Miller. Logan: Utah State University Press, 1989.

Clark, Mary R. "Rowland Hall–St. Mark's School: Alternative Education for More than a Century." *Utah Historical Quarterly* 48, no. 3 (1980): 271–292.

Donovan, Mary S. "Women Missionaries in Utah." *Anglican and Episcopal History* 66, no. 2 (1997): 154–174.

Firmage, Edwin B. "MX: A Personal Essay." *Beehive History* 28 (2002): 25–31.

Frensdorff, Wesley. "The Dream," in *Reshaping Ministry: Essays in Memory of Wesley Frensdorff*, ed. Josephine Borgeson and Lynne Wilson. Arvada, CO: Jethro Publications, 1990.

Jones, Paul. "The Philosophy of a Madman." *The Christian Century* [Chicago], September 13, 1923: 1164–1166.

———. "What War Did to My Mind." *The Christian Century* [Chicago], March 8, 1928: 310–312.

Keller, Roger R. "Episcopalian Bishop Franklin S. Spalding and the Mormons." *Utah Historical Quarterly* 69, no. 3 (2001): 232–247.

Liebler, H. Baxter. "Christian Concepts and Navaho Words." *Utah Humanities Review* 2, no. 2 (1948): 169–175.

———. "The Social and Cultural Patterns of the Navajo Indians." *Utah Historical Quarterly* 30, no. 4 (1962): 298–325.

Lyon, T. Edgar and Glen M. Leonard. "The Churches in the Territory." In *Utah's History*, edited by Richard D. Poll, with the assistance of Thomas G. Alexander, Eugene E. Campbell, and David E. Miller, 317–325. Logan: Utah State University Press, 1989.

McCormick, John S. and John R. Sillito. "Socialists in Power: The Eureka, Utah, Experience, 1907–1925." *Weber Studies* 6, no. 1 (Spring 1989). http://weberstudies.weber.edu/archive/archive%20A%20%20Vol.%201-10.3/Vol.%206.1/6.1McCormickSilito.htm.

McPherson, Robert S. "'He Stood for Us Strongly': Father H. Baxter Liebler's Mission to the Navajo." *American Indian Culture and Research Journal* 23, no. 2 (1999): 109–196.

O'Neil, Floyd A. "An Anguished Odyssey: The Flight of the Utes, 1906–1908." *Utah Historical Quarterly*, 36 no. 4 (1968): 315–322.

———. "The Reluctant Suzerainty: The Uintah and Ouray Reservation." *Utah Historical Quarterly*, 39 no. 2 (1971): 130–144.

Quinn, Frederick. "Abiel Leonard, the Bishop as Builder," *Utah Historical Quarterly*, 72, no. 3 (2004):239–253.

Rehkopf, Charles F. "The Episcopate of Bishop Tuttle." *The Bulletin–Missouri Historical Society* 18, no. 3 (1962): 207–231.

Rogers, Kristen. "Utah's Missile-Guided Economy," *Beehive History* 28 (2002): 17–19.

Sillito, John R. "'Prove All Things, Hold Fast That Which Is Good,' Franklin Spencer Spalding: A Christian Socialist Dissenter from Capitalist Values." *Weber Studies* 1 (Spring 1984). http://weberstudies.weber.edu/archive/archive%20A%20%20Vol.%201-10.3/Vol.%201/Sillito.htm.

———. "'A Spiritual and Moral Socialism': Franklin Spencer Spalding and Christian Socialism, 1901–1914." In *Socialism and Christianity in Early 20th*

Century America, edited by Jacob H. Dorn, 111–136. Westport, CT: Greenwood Press, 1998.

——— and Martha Bradley. "Franklin Spencer Spalding: An Episcopal Observer of Mormonism." *Historical Magazine of the Protestant Episcopal Church* 54, (December 1985): 339–350.

——— and Timothy S. Hearn. "A Question of Conscience: The Resignation of Bishop Paul Jones." *Utah Historical Quarterly* 50, no. 3 (1982): 209– 225.

——— and John S. McCormick. "'Our Political Faith is Socialism, Our Religious Faith is the Latter-day Saints': Socialist Mormons and their Millennial Vision in the Early Twentieth Century." In *Expectations for the Millennium, American Socialist Visions of the Future*, ed. Peter H. Buckingham, 111–130. Westport, CT: Greenwood Press, 2002.

Streets, David H. "St. Mary's Episcopal Church." In *Protestant and Catholic Churches of Provo: A Study in Non-LDS Christian Congregations*, ed. David M. Walden, with the assistance of Charles G. Hidenshield and David H. Streets, 70–80. Provo: Brigham Young Center for Family and Community History, 1986.

Tuttle, Daniel S. "Mormons." In *A Religious Encyclopedia*. Vol. 3, edited by Philip Schaff, Samuel M. Jackson, and D. S. Schaff, 1575–1581. New York: Funk and Wagnalls, 1891.

Pamphlets

Campbell, Anne. *Being a Christian Woman in the 1980s*. Mormon Theological Symposium, August 1981.

Cathedral Church of St. Mark, Salt Lake City, Utah, Walking Tour, 2000.

Dixon, John Stewart. *A History of St. Mark's Cathedral Parish, 1867–1967*. Salt Lake City, 1967.

Ellis, Thelma. *Church of the Good Shepherd, Ogden, Utah: A Short History*. Ogden, 1992.

Jones, Paul. *Points of Contact: A Consideration for Dissatisfied Latter-day Saints*. Salt Lake City, 1801.

Spalding, Franklin Spencer. *The Call of the West*. Service Series No. 7. New York: Church Mission House, n.d.

Thornley, John D. "Introductory Essay." In *History and Bibliography of Religion in Utah: Utah Historical Records Survey*. Inventory of Church Archives of Utah, Salt Lake City, June 1940. A Works Project Administration (WPA) project.

Voris, Charles R. *The History of St. Michael's Episcopal Church, Brigham City, Utah*, (pamphlet Brigham City, 1993), p. 5.

Unpublished Manuscripts

Brown, Marilyn Hersey. "A Missionary's Journey: The Life and Times of the Reverend Milton J. Hersey." Typescript, 2001.

Gillogly, L. Lucelia Webster. "Early Mission Life in Ogden, Utah." Typescript, Alameda, CA, January 1900.

Eskell, Joan, interviewed by Daniel B. Kelly, June 24, 1972. "St. Christopher's Mission and Hat Rock Retreat, O. H. 1173." Southeastern Utah Project, Utah State Historical Society and California State University–Fullerton Oral History Program, 1987.

Finch, Fred S. "History of St. David's Church, Page, Arizona," n.p., n.d. (probably Page, Arizona, 1962.)

Sillito, John. "'Mainstays of the Liturgical Life': Episcopal Women in Late 19th and Early 20th Century Utah." Paper, Utah State Historical Society Annual Meeting, Salt Lake City, August 17, 2002.

Simmonds, A. J. "Strength Out of Zion: A History of St. John's Episcopal Church and the Anglican Presence in Cache Valley." Typescript, St. John's Foundation, Logan, Utah, 1985.

Tull, Alan C. "On Mormon Baptisms: A Report from Hippo." Typescript, n.d.

Warren, Douglas G. "The Case of Bishop Paul Jones. Chapter 3 in "Freedom of Speech and Political Dissent in the Episcopal Church, 1914–1918." PhD diss, Graduate Theological Union, Berkeley, CA, 1979."

Winder, Francis L. "The Ogden Covenant: Reflections on an Ecumenical Venture." Typescript, Salt Lake City, n.d.

———. "A Position Paper on the 'Validity' of LDS Baptism." Typescript, 1972.

Videotapes, Films, Sound Recordings

Chabries [Haws], April. *A River in the Desert.* Provo, UT: Brigham Young University, 2000; 27 minutes. Filmstrip on the life and work of H. Baxter Liebler, Episcopal priest, at St. Christopher's Navajo Mission.

Rice, Maxwell W. "Rev. Maxwell W. Rice's Utah Stories, 1908–1918." Recorded in a Northampton, Massachusetts nursing home when Rice was nearly 100 years old. Compact discs 1 and 2, provided by Theodore Rice, grandson, and Cheri Winter, Resource Center Specialist, Episcopal Diocese of Utah.

Archival Sources

Caine Manuscript Collection 11, Revered H. Baxter Liebler Papers. Special Collections and Archives, Utah State University, Logan, Utah. Contains over

41 boxes of material dating from 1943 to the 1960s, including correspondence, bulletins, newsletters, silent movies, and reel-to-reel tape recordings.

Church of Jesus Christ of Latter-day Saints Church Library, Salt Lake City. Collection of nineteenth century anti-LDS literature by eastern Protestant groups. The Archives show a few entries for the Episcopal Church.

Episcopal Church Archives, on the campus of the Episcopal Divinity School of the Southwest, Austin, Texas. Contains extensive files of quarterly reports by early missionaries to Utah, including many women district workers and missionaries to the Utes, and correspondence from Missionary Bishops Tuttle, Leonard, Spalding, Jones, Moulton, and Clark.

Episcopal Diocese of Utah Records. Manuscripts Division, J. Willard Marriott Library, University of Utah, Salt Lake City. Includes 57 boxes of documents, including bishops's correspondence, parish reports, photographs, newspaper clippings, and record books, beginning in 1867. Several boxes of records from earlier times through the episcopacy of Bishop Bates were being catalogued for transfer to the university at the time this book was being written. Such documents are listed as Diocesan Archives (D. A.) until they receive permanent classification in the University of Utah Special Collections.

General Theological Seminary Library, New York City. Contains complete runs of several church publications, including *Spirit of Missions* and *Forth*, and a collection of Tuttle and Spalding letters.

Pierpont Morgan Library, New York City. Contains a collection of Episcopal Bishops's letters, including some by Tuttle, Leonard, and Moulton.

Sterling Memorial Library and Beinecke Rare Book and Manuscript Library, Yale University. Contain a vast collection of materials on the American West, including a complete set of the Missionary Diocese of Utah Annual Convocation Reports.

Utah State Historical Society, Salt Lake City. Has an extensive collection of holdings about the Episcopal Church, including archival manuscripts, newspaper clippings, publications, and photographs.

Index